IN *VERY SPECIAL AGENTS*
THE LINES ARE DRAWN. . . .
AND YOU STAND ON
BOTH SIDES OF THE LAW

Special Agent Alex D'Atri. On assignment to the Organized Crime and Racketeering Strike Force in New York, he outfitted himself with silk suits, a diamond pinkie ring, and a gleaming limo, passing himself off as a Mafia mobster. A year of wining and dining with gangsters on the Upper East Side and in Little Italy produced enough evidence to arrest twenty-five racketeers.

Charles Voyde Harrelson. The father of actor Woody Harrelson achieved notoriety of his own . . . as a contract killer in Texas. In 1978 he used a high-powered rifle to kill John H. Wood—the first federal judge to be assassinated in a hundred years. It took two years to catch him, but it was a tip to an ATF agent that ultimately led to Harrelson's arrest and a sentence of three life terms.

Special Agent Ariel Rios. He was raised in the housing projects of the Bronx and grew to despise the criminals who preyed on the innocent. He was a man of unquestioned integrity and courage, who would not back away from any assignment . . . including the drug-buy operation in South Florida that ended with him at the wrong end of a .357 Magnum.

David Koresh. Driven by a Messiah complex, he assumed power over his Branch Davidian followers after a shoot-out with his predecessor. Calling his Waco headquarters "Ranch Apocalypse," he set out to ensure that his prophecy of doom—at the hands of the government—was fulfilled. Amassing a cache of contraband weapons, he ultimately incited the fiery and tragic raid that shocked the country and rocked numerous law enforcement agencies . . . including ATF.

VERY SPECIAL AGENTS

THE INSIDE STORY OF AMERICA'S MOST CONTROVERSIAL LAW ENFORCEMENT AGENCY— THE BUREAU OF ALCOHOL, TOBACCO & FIREARMS

James Moore, ATF (Ret.)

[signature: James Moore]

POCKET BOOKS
New York   London   Toronto   Sydney   Tokyo   Singapore

An *Original* Publication of POCKET BOOKS

POCKET BOOKS, a division of Simon & Schuster Inc.
1230 Avenue of the Americas, New York, NY 10020

ISBN: 0-671-57035-8

First Pocket Books printing March 1997

10 9 8 7 6 5 4 3 2 1

POCKET and colophon are registered trademarks of
Simon & Schuster Inc.

Cover photo by Les Stone/Sygma
Insert photos are courtesy of ATF unless otherwise noted

Printed in the U.S.A.

For all the federal agents
who gave their lives
in the service of their country

Acknowledgments

This book, in its present form, would not have been possible without the generous assistance of Senator Williams S. Cohen, who "encouraged" the FBI to release certain documents legally accessible but withheld until the senator intervened; former ATF assistant director Phil McGuire, who authorized agents to cooperate with certain phases of the story; the special agents who gave of their time and shared their memories, sometimes beyond the scope of what was officially authorized—all have requested anonymity, and their request shall be honored; Mr. Bob Pritchett of ATF's Disclosure Branch, who assembled numerous documents and labored over uncounted files to ensure that no innocent person's identity would be revealed; the friends who helped by reading the manuscript and offering innumerable editorial improvements: Ann Brahms, Kathy Fritz, Cheryl Doyle Lewallyn, Karen Trella Mather (with the "helicopter vision"), Marilyn Nulman, Kate Cone Theberge, and Susan Winslow; Tris Coburn, my editor at Pocket Books, whose professionalism gave this book its final polish; my own "very special [literary] agent," Jane Dystel, who recognized the value of this work and guided my first steps; and finally but foremost in every sense of the word, the *very* special agents of ATF who have, over the past 134 years, made this story.

Contents

Appendices

CONTENTS

Introduction

This is the biography of a federal agency: the U.S. Treasury Department's Bureau of Alcohol, Tobacco and Firearms. During its long history it's been reorganized and renamed numerous times. [See Appendix G for chronology.] To avoid confusion and reinforce a sense of its continuity, I'll refer to it simply as "ATF" throughout this book.

Just as we get to know people—by hearing their history, by seeing how they act or react in different situations, by noting their friends and their enemies—I'm hoping the reader will come to know ATF. Every individual we meet has his or her own unique combination of qualities and shortcomings; ATF's variety is illustrated by the agents and executives you'll meet in this book.

The cases recounted here weren't selected because they're ATF's greatest; they were chosen to illustrate the characteristics of this little-known bureau.

Sixty-five years ago, the Untouchables fought Al Capone. Thirty years ago, these Treasury agents were still chasing moonshiners. For the past quarter century, ATF has aimed federal firearms and explosives laws at society's most vicious outlaws. Offical reports issued by the U.S. courts and the Federal Bureau of Prisons reveal a variety of interesting facts: ATF's conviction rate exceeds the federal average;

and, with less than three percent of the government's law enforcement officers, the weapons law enforced by this bureau account for nearly six percent of the federal prison population. The "quality" of these criminals is suggested by the fact that, once convicted, they are more likely than the average federal defendant to receive a sentence of imprisonment and, once jailed, they're less likely to win parole.

This small federal agency has lost more agents to criminal gunfire than have all the other government investigative bureaus *combined.* But violent gun crimes drop when ATF agents are most active—and rise again when the agents' efforts decrease. Conclusion: The agents have an impact, when they're allowed to.

Which makes one wonder: Who'd hold them back?

The history of this bureau is crammed with conflict and controversy. Aside from the battles with bad guys, there's been friction between agents and their revenue-oriented chiefs, antagonism between ATF agents and the FBI, and outright hostility initiated by the well-oiled gun lobby and its lackeys in Congress.

This book isn't politically correct. It's not polite. It's written with faith that the truth is worth knowing. And telling.

As for why *I* am writing this book, perhaps it's because I offer a unique combination of perspective and objectivity.

My objectivity derives from the fact that I never climbed to the executive level. Frankly, I lack the talents required for management. So I have no axe to grind, no bureaucratic record to defend. I was a good agent, I loved working the street, and I should probably have resisted the higher salary (and increased pension) that came with promotions to paper-pygmy positions. But I can't complain. My career ended happily at my post of preference as agent in charge for Maine and New Hampshire.

My perspective is based on the crucial years of my service and the positions I held. When I joined ATF at Newark, New Jersey, in 1960, it was an arm of the IRS with one job: to catch the Mafia bootleggers whose Prohibition-style distilleries each cheated Uncle Sam of $20,000 a day in revenue. Twenty-five years of evolution saw our shift to enforcing gun laws, our re-birth as a separate bureau, and the challenge of solving the cases most lawmen wrote off as impossible: bombings and arsons. On the street, I met the enemy at ground level. As part of the Organized Crime and Racketeering Strike Force, I grappled with the mob and witnessed the inner workings of other agencies. Two years at INTERPOL let me observe law enforcement around the globe.

At bureau headquarters, I probed management across the country via field inspections; I found disturbing facts in the secret files of our Office of Internal Affairs; I watched the hierarchy's crisis reaction during a brief stint with Public Affairs; and last, but certainly not least, I observed how the strengths, weaknesses and personal philosophies of three very different directors affected America's war against weapon-wielding outlaws.

Many readers will not like this book. Members of the firearms fraternity will be displeased. Too bad. It's their selfish dedication to preserving the *convenience* of their hobby through lies that's responsible for thousands of needless crimes against innocent citizens. I'm less comfortable with my disclosures about certain bureau leaders because I really believe they were doing the best they could, but the country paid a high price for their deficiencies. And I regret the realization that many FBI agents will be offended because I've rarely known a G-man I didn't like. But the peculiar practices promoted by their bureau have had a profound impact on ATF. They are a part of this story.

Bottom line: no apologies.

1

It Was in the Bleak December

Far I hear the bugle blow
To call me where I would not go
And the guns begin the song . . .

Stand and do the best, my lad
Stand and fight and see your slain,
And take the bullet in your brain.
—A. E. Housman,
"A Shropshire Lad" (1896)

"I don't feel like going to work tomorrow."

"Why don't you take the day off?" Elsie asked him.

He said he couldn't.

Exhausted mentally and physically, he'd sunk onto the bed in his Miami hotel room and phoned his home in Connecticut because he hadn't seen Elsie and the kids for a month, and it was still three weeks till they'd visit his parents for Christmas, and he'd had a grueling day. He needed to hear his wife's voice.

Homicide would affect 21,012 American families in 1982. Miami, with a score of 190, became the year's Murder City.

Had the twenty-eight-year-old man in that hotel room taken his wife's suggestion, the tally might have stopped at 189. But he didn't. He died.

The president and vice president tried to comfort Elsie and the children. They named a building after the loving husband and gentle father, a huge structure on Pennsylvania Avenue between the White House and the Capitol.

It was a nice gesture. The best they could do.
But he was still dead.

The afternoon of December 1 was cool and sunny. Thirty-year-old Jose Dearmas was offering silencer-equipped pistols to a pair of New York mobsters. Guns were common currency in South Florida, an area plagued by the vicious dregs of Fidel Castro's prisons and psycho wards. These were the *Marielitos*—thousands of men bearing physical and mental scars inflicted by years of sadistic torture. Here in Florida, they trafficked in drugs and violence. One ferocious firefight saw daytime crowds at a shopping mall raked by machine-gun fire. "Home-invaders" posed as police to enter homes and strip terrorized families of their money, their dignity and, not infrequently, their lives.

Dearmas led a brutal gang. Two of his henchmen were out on bail on charges of shooting a policeman who'd happened to jog by while they consummated a drug sale. But sly and streetwise as he was, Dearmas never guessed that the lackeys he'd sent for the weapons were being tailed by a government airplane. Nor did he imagine that the "gangsters" he chatted with—slender Ariel Rios, with his manicured brown beard, and husky Alex D'Atri, with a confidence born of many such business transactions—were special agents of ATF, the U.S. Treasury Department's Bureau of Alcohol, Tobacco and Firearms. Their current assignment to the vice president's Miami Task Force charged them with suppressing the violence that attended the wholesale narcotics business.

When the errand boys returned, undercover man Rios tested one of the guns by firing it into the 2½-inch-thick Greater Miami yellow pages. The pistol functioned as quietly and smoothly as the agents, who promptly made their arrests. Dearmas and his sidekicks were held on half-million-dollar bonds. Agents and police raided the house where Dearmas's henchmen had picked up the weapons. They found dozens of pistols and silencers, hundreds of stolen credit cards, and police radios, badges and ID cards. This was the den of the dreaded home-invaders.

Rios and D'Atri were already enroute to their next job.

They met another trio of Castro castoffs—Machin and Company—at a convenience store on SW 312th Street. After a brief conversation, the Marielitos departed to arrange a cocaine delivery. While the agents waited outside the convenience store, they were approached by a man wearing an expensive suit, white shirt, red silk tie and white Panama hat. A Cuban named Eduardo Portal, he represented a third gang.

Agent D'Atri cataloged the new suspect's description: thirty-five, five-foot-seven, 170 pounds, black hair and brown eyes.

Portal spoke to Ariel in Spanish. "Hello, my friend. Are you in the market for product?"

Rios nodded. *"Sí."*

"Mañana." Portal gave him a phone number and reverted to English so that both New Yorkers would understand. "Call at noon. We'll sell you a kilo of coke, but I'll tell you something." His eyes narrowed and his tone turned menacing. "You guys better not be *federales."*

Rios frowned. *"Federales?* Are you kidding?"

"I spent seventeen years in a Cuban prison," Portal said. "My friend, he spent nineteen years. We ain't afraid of dying, but we ain't going back to prison."

D'Atri answered easily, "Just make sure the stuff is good and we'll all be happy."

"Tomorrow," Portal said. "Call at noon." Then he was gone.

Special Agent Ariel Rios lived his boyhood in a dreary succession of squalid Bronx housing projects where the only prosperous neighbors were pimps and drug peddlers. Young Ariel ignored them and the wealth they flaunted until the day thieves pillaged his family's small apartment. That's when he began to despise the festering crime that victimized helpless innocents.

As a teenager, Ariel liked children, animals and gardening. And he loved Elsie Morales. All through their high-school years, they worked together at the supermarket. She was a cashier, he bagged groceries. Neither of them would ever be content to merely escape the poverty of their world. Elsie aspired to become a nurse, Ariel aimed for a police career. They worked to attain their goals—Ariel graduated from the John Jay College of Criminal Justice—and they married.

Starting as a guard with the New York City Department of Corrections, he worked his way up to the Internal Affairs Unit, where he investigated homicides, prison escapes, and the more serious assault cases. In 1978 he applied to become a special agent with the U.S. Treasury Department.

Friends, neighbors, teachers and former employers offered investigators a unanimous assessment of the slender candidate with the soft brown eyes: Ariel Rios was a man of unquestioned integrity . . . and courage! A fellow guard remarked, "He's small [Ariel stood five-seven] but he's always in there giving you a hand when the going gets rough." Treasury accepted him and assigned him to ATF's Hartford District. He was twenty-four.

Machin returned to the Miami convenience store. "We'll go to the Kendall Lakes Shopping Center," he told the undercover agents. "A man in a black Toyota will have four kilos. You ready?"

D'Atri said, "Let's go."

Alexander D'Atri was thirty-eight, a muscular supervisor with a strong, square face, jet-black hair, neatly trimmed beard and a pronounced Brooklyn accent. He'd perfected his mobster pose in the Big Apple, playing Boss to a "gang" of agents that infiltrated organized crime to bag an enviable assortment of Mafiosi. He had a wife and eight children. To D'Atri, with thirteen years on the job, Rios was "the kid." It was still two days before the younger agent's fourth anniversary with ATF.

Rios took ATF's oath of office on December 3, 1978:

I do solemnly swear that I will support and defend the Constitution of the United States against all enemies, foreign and domestic; that I will bear true faith and allegiance to the same; that I take this obligation freely, without any mental reservation or purpose of evasion; and that I will faithfully discharge the duties

of the office on which I am about to enter. So help me
God.

His formal education at the Federal Law Enforcement
Training Center in Georgia started with "Ethics and Conduct" and went on for fifteen weeks: from "The Constitution and Civil Rights" to "Conspiracy and Criminalistics";
from "Psychology and Physical Combat" to "Pursuit Driving" on a cleverly constructed mile-and-a-half roadway of
varying surfaces and curbed streets; from "Street Gangs and
Organized Crime" to forty more specialized subjects designed to prepare new agents for their careers. The center's
1,500-acre campus, once a naval base, included a residential
community where students practiced surveillance, practical
investigations and raids.

Bomb exercises were conducted outdoors under the wide
Georgia sky. ATF's scientists examine the clues collected
by agents to determine what explosives were used, but
accounts by eyewitnesses facilitate immediate inquiries.
That's why every agent must recognize the signs of various
explosive materials when they respond to the scene of a real
bombing.

Trainees sat in bleachers, watching the first blast.

"White smoke," one of Rios's classmates said aloud.

"Commercial dynamite," another called out.

"Right," the instructor told them. "Now watch this."

It was gasoline. The next one erupted with orange flame
and black smoke. Thundering reports rocked the stillness as
students observed and absorbed the telltale signatures of
TNT, plastic explosives and half a dozen others. For a
finale, the station wagon parked at the edge of the field was
blown up. Its roof peeled back. Its hood ripped free, sailing
forward and upward. One tire rose lazily, almost straight
up, paused in midair, then plummeted back to earth and
bounced into the trees.

"That one's yours," the instructor announced. "Examine
the scene. I'll want to know what explosive was used, how it
was detonated and"—he chuckled—"who did it."

Back in the classroom, instructors emphasized teamwork.
"Everyone helps everyone else. This isn't some office job

where working together just increases efficiency. Out on the street it might make the difference between life and death."

Any prima-donna tendencies were ruthlessly erased. "Sometimes you'll have to be a one-man army, but there's no such thing as a one-man team. Use the Bureau's resources. Work with your partner. Work with the police. If you don't, you're not a pro and you'll never make it in ATF."

The marksmanship course designed by another ATF agent, National Pistol Champion Gary Peach, went beyond hitting the elusive, moving pop-up silhouettes. Treasury's policy—when to shoot and when to hold your fire—was drilled into each student with real-life examples. ATF man Phil Orsini was right when he fired six bullets into the excon who had opened fire on DEA agent Mike Vowell in Arkansas. ATF agents William Alfree and William Petraitis were correct to hold their fire when Anthony LaRocca snatched $10,000 and tried to flee through a crowded Pittsburgh shopping mall. The Treasury men pointed their car at LaRocca, braved the hail of bullets that shattered their windshield and, after they'd closed the distance, alighted with guns drawn and shielded by the open doors of their auto. The furious LaRocca surrendered.

Distance was also a factor when a pair of gun traffickers pointed pistols at undercover agent Pete Tsipis behind a restaurant in Kent, Ohio, and announced, "We're going to waste you." Tsipis backed away slowly until he'd put forty feet between himself and the gunmen. He could shoot accurately at that distance; they probably couldn't. Then he drew his own revolver. "ATF! If anybody gets wasted here, it'll be you."

"No, no," said the taller assailant, dropping to his knees. "We don't want no violence here." Both men surrendered.

The instructor repeated the Treasury policy: "You shoot *only* to save a life—yours or someone else's. Once that test is met, and only then, you *always* shoot to kill."

Every new class has at least one student who questions the necessity of shooting to kill. This time it was Rios. And, as always, the instructor distributed glossy photographs. "These are agents murdered by criminals." It's sobering to have the names from ATF's Honor Roll assume real faces.

"There are times when it's beyond your control, but you can't gamble that the man aiming a gun at you won't shoot, and hitting him in the arm or leg won't keep him from pulling his trigger. *Letting* him kill you signs a death warrant for his future victims."

The Big Case—a practical investigation from the first clue through a mock trial—took up Rios's final week. Monday began like every other day at the center. By 7:00 A.M. each trainee had completed either the mile run or the obstacle course. They'd showered, donned their dress clothes, eaten breakfast and taken their places in the classroom. Divided into teams, they were assigned a case—a crime to investigate. Instructors played the roles of witnesses, policemen, informers and suspects. Virtually every move, every word spoken, was recorded on videotape for later critique. If the students did everything right, Thursday would see them raiding the lair of the "criminals."

While trainees readied their equipment for that raid, the chief instructor addressed his staff. "We're looking for reactions. Does he or she make cool, deliberate decisions, or do they avoid the stressful situation altogether? Any unnecessary roughness in making arrests? Any unnecessary risks or exposure? When they get in a tight spot, they have to think before they shoot but not for too long. We can resurrect the dead ones here, but out on the street . . ."

Raiders and "suspects" loaded their weapons with blanks. It's noisier than the fancy laser-light guns some agencies use to train their investigators, but realism generates the stress the agents will encounter in actual raids.

With cameras rolling inside the hideout and out on the street, cars cruised through the typical suburban neighborhood dropping agents, who closed in around a ranch-style house occupied by suspects "known to be dangerous." One driver parked across the street, stepped out with a bullhorn.

"Federal officers with a search warrant! We're ATF. Come out or we'll have to come in and get you."

No response from the house.

Two trainees closed in on either side. Others covered the rear. The team leader and three more approached the front door.

Two trainees forced the rear screen door and were driven

7

back by gunfire from within. From somewhere outside, a rifle cracked two quick shots. Trainees on one side went down. Another keyed his walkie-talkie. "Where the hell'd that come from?"

One of Rios's classmates—an attractive young woman described by former employers, teachers and neighbors during ATF's preemployment investigation as "very intelligent and genteel; a real lady"—reacted to the palpable stress of realism and her two fallen friends. "He's up the fuckin' tree!"

Minutes later she helped colleagues subdue the sniper and resumed her normal demeanor. Today, close acquaintances might know that the petite agent will cry over the body of a child at a bombing scene, but they'd never guess she'd utter such language, or shoot so straight, or have the courage to snatch a gun from an excon's hand.

Rios and another agent smashed through the rear door. One suspect was "killed." Another, forced to surrender, was rushed outside, made to lie on his belly and handcuffed. More gunfire, and a third suspect was captured in a barricaded bedroom.

What seemed an eternity to the trainees was clocked at sixteen minutes.

After the basic course, Rios's training continued: "Advanced Conspiracy Course"; "Advanced Bombing Investigation"; "Arson for Profit." The most secret was "Advanced Undercover"—the weeks-long ordeal of ATF classes and practical exercises that experienced investigators from other federal, state and local agencies competed most heavily to attend. ATF's own graduates joined the Bureau's elite Tactical Squad, where they were given elaborate and thoroughly documented undercover identities complete with birth and school records, legitimate and illegitimate employment histories, official police records and living "references"—from street-corner bookies to INTERPOL. All agents performed the everyday undercover work that has earned ATF its reputation in this field, but the administrative backup for a Tac Squad member might involve up to thirty surveillants, technical personnel and contact agents. They're the *crème de la crème*.

* * *

Early in his career, Rios demonstrated an uncanny ability to impersonate the outlaws he'd worked among in New York's prisons. This skill was combined with a talent for improvisation to spell success in the art of undercover work. When the orders arrived assigning him to the Miami Task Force, he'd just finished working with Connecticut State Police detective Nick Berone to nail outlaw biker Dan Bifeld, branded by lawmen the state's most dangerous criminal. Berone said later, "Ariel was the most likable guy I ever worked with."

Competence and likability notwithstanding, Rios received a—Reduction in Force—RIF Notice in July of 1982. It's the process of firing government employees when circumstances dictate an agency's downsizing. These RIF Notices, given to all agents with less than five years' service, were prompted by congressional threats to reduce ATF's ranks—threats spawned by a campaign of lies and half-truths prompted by leaders of the National Rifle Association, an organization that sees gun laws as inconveniencing its members' pursuit of their hobbies.

It wasn't an original idea. The NRA, with numerous members in prison for peddling guns to criminals and making illegal weapons—not to mention burglary, robbery, rape, pornography and homicide—had merely copied the creed of the criminal lawyer: "If the evidence is against you, dispute the law. If that doesn't work, attack the cops."

Some agents, opting to beat the RIF, fled to the Secret Service, the FBI and other agencies with openings. Ariel Rios stayed with ATF and put every ounce of mind and heart into his work. "If I do a good job, maybe it'll make a difference."

It wouldn't have. RIF procedures are locked in the cement of bureaucratic regulation. As it turned out, Congress changed its mind. The RIF never happened.

Miami was a temporary assignment. Elsie and their two children remained at home—a raised ranch on a quiet hillside in a small Connecticut town.

At Miami's Kendall Lakes Shopping Mall, a man named Sierra waited in the black Toyota. Under the watchful eyes of Machin and two other confederates, Rios examined the coke and gave the signal. Surrounding agents closed in.

Machin pulled a gun.

Rios deflected the weapon and gripped the Cuban's gun hand. During the violent struggle, Machin made several savage attempts to jerk his hand loose, but Rios, who'd subdued tougher men as a prison guard, wrenched the revolver free. Machin, Sierra, and the others were handcuffed. The agents confiscated guns, four kilos of cocaine and $82,000 in cash. Their prisoners were charged with drug trafficking, assaulting a federal agent and using a firearm in a federal crime; each was held on $1 million bail.

A good day's work. Two cases wrapped; another set for tomorrow.

That night in his hotel room, Rios contemplated the hazards of his job, aware that ATF had lost more agents to criminal gunfire than have all the other federal bureaus combined. He relived that drug dealer's lightning move with the gun.

He telephoned Elsie in Connecticut. "I don't feel like going to work tomorrow." She suggested he take a day off, but he told her, "I can't. We've got something big lined up."

They talked about their vacation, still three weeks away: Christmas in Bayamon, Puerto Rico, the town to which his parents had retired, a quiet village where children played beside a narrow, winding road and cool breezes wafted across a clear lake. Bayamon was a refuge from a career amidst the chaos.

The next day at noon, Ariel Rios telephoned Portal. The trafficker told him, "The powder's ready. Meet me in the parking lot behind El Palacio de las Fritas. It's a restaurant on SW 8th Street."

Alex D'Atri and Ariel Rios stepped out of their dark blue Cadillac wearing three-piece suits—the underworld executive image—and sauntered over to the black Granada, where Portal waited with Victorio Concepcion.

A nine-man surveillance team was already in place.

Rios translated Concepcion's words: "Okay, one of you guys stay here and I'll take the other guy to see the stuff."

D'Atri shook his head. "No way. We stay together."

Concepcion shrugged. "Follow us."

D'Atri told Rios to ask where they were headed so the surveillance agents could take up a position.

Rios turned back to Concepcion. *"¿Donde vamos?"*

Concepcion replied, "The Hurricane Motel. Flagler Street."

"Bueno." Rios and D'Atri followed in their Cadillac to the shabby, pink-stucco motel and went inside with Concepcion. Portal stood in the courtyard.

Surveillance cars were positioned around the block. A green truck, disguised as a utility vehicle, cruised in from the other end of the street and parked across from the Hurricane. Inside that van, an agent with binoculars noticed that Portal's jacket bulged on one side.

In the motel office, Concepcion introduced the undercover men to Oscar Hernandez, owner of the Hurricane. A few minutes later, Jose Lopez drove up in a yellow Buick, nodded to Portal and entered the office. Then Mario Simon arrived in a black Cutlass and joined them. They talked for twenty minutes. The merchants of death had to be sure they were dealing with genuine mobsters.

Satisfied by the agents' performance, Concepcion said, "Three kilos. Forty-nine thousand each. Come back in an hour."

The agents met their contact-agent in a supermarket parking lot two miles away. D'Atri reported, "Hernandez is directly involved. The others are just bodyguards."

The odds weren't good: two agents versus two traffickers and three bodyguards. A radio call brought reinforcements. Now the surveillance team numbered fifteen agents from ATF, the U.S. Customs Service and the Drug Enforcement Administration.

A watcher at the Hurricane reported: "A man in a black Grand Prix just delivered a paper bag." His name was Alvarez.

Rios and D'Atri returned. Concepcion met them out front. "You"—he pointed to Rios—"wait here. Your friend can go in."

"No." The agent was firm. "He needs me to translate."

They entered the office. Mario Simon stood in the corner. Rios sat on a sofa patterned with bright flowers. Alex huddled around the table with Concepcion, Hernandez and

11

Alvarez. The atmosphere was friendly—D'Atri could tell by the suspects' eyes, the expressions on their faces. When they reached a final agreement on price, Simon went to his car and returned with a silver Pinch Bottle gift box. It was filled with coke.

D'Atri tested the white powder. "Okay, it's good stuff. The money's out in the car." He nodded to the younger agent. For a moment he detected a trace of tension, but it eased when Rios brought inside the package containing $55,000 from the trunk of the blue Cadillac.

The surveillance team poised for action. Forty-five seconds from the time Rios went inside, they'd crash the door.

As Rios entered, he left the door ajar. Simon leaned over and slammed it shut. Rios shrugged and tossed the bundle to his partner, then resumed his seat on the couch printed with all those cheerful red and yellow flowers.

D'Atri counted out the cash slowly and deliberately to hold the suspects' attention, but Alvarez got up, went to the door and locked it. D'Atri looked at them, from one to the other. The sight of the cash had changed their expressions. A feeling of dread came over the agent. Something was about to happen. He stood up, thinking, *Oh, shit.*

Raiders converged at the entrance, but a practiced kick failed to budge the locked metal door.

The next nine seconds were a kaleidoscope of gunfire and splattered blood. D'Atri heard Rios shout "No!"

The room rocked with the thunder of a .357 Magnum.

Within that first second, D'Atri's eyes flashed from the smoking revolver held by the skinny, balding Mario Simon, to Rios with his hand on his abdomen, blood spurting between his fingers. D'Atri drew his revolver. The three at the table were frozen. D'Atri fired quickly and hit Simon. They scuffled. Alvarez snatched the Magnum from Simon's hand and shot Rios again. The slug entered just below the young agent's eye.

Alvarez stood in front of D'Atri, who pulled his trigger. *Click.* Out of ammo. Alvarez looked him straight in the eye and began firing. D'Atri felt pain in his chest, then a burning sensation. The impact threw him back against the wall. *Do something,* he thought. *Hit the sonofabitch with your gun.*

Explosion. Orange flame. A second bullet plowed into

D'Atri's chest. Lifted him into the air. A third hit his shoulder. He was falling. Watching Alvarez. Expecting a bullet in the brain. The Magnum thundered. The slug struck his head. Alvarez's revolver clicked. Empty. D'Atri blacked out.

The ninth second: A shotgun blast opened the door. Agents burst in. To their right, D'Atri lay sprawled with gushing wounds. To their left lay Rios, his blood ebbing onto the couch. All the bright yellow flowers were stained crimson.

Mario Simon, critically wounded by D'Atri, crouched in the center of the room amidst pistols, fluttering hundred-dollar bills and kilos of almost pure cocaine.

Alvarez ran into a rear room, pursued by an agent. The killer reached for a shotgun, but the agent shot him. Alvarez tried again. The agent shot him again. Alvarez would live.

Alex D'Atri came to. Had to keep from falling asleep. No pain, but he couldn't get up. Knew he was losing blood. Saw it coming out of his chest. Felt it soaking his back. Tasted it in his mouth. The temperature that day was ninety-eight degrees, but he felt cold. His nerves tingled. The pain kept him from falling unconscious. Agent Switzer leaned over him.

D'Atri asked, "How do I look?" He saw the answer in his friend's face. "Get me a priest."

Switzer blurted, "I'll hear your confession." But Alex D'Atri had passed out.

Awakened by the pain and the screaming of the siren that echoed inside the ambulance, D'Atri would realize later that waking up kept him fighting, kept him alive. As they wheeled him into the emergency room, all sorts of thoughts ran through his mind. *An hour ago I was a big federal agent. Now I'm lying on a table like a piece of meat and they're stripping my clothes off. Why Ariel? Why me?*

Miraculously, after five hours of surgery, Alex D'Atri survived his grievous wounds. He would return to work.

Rios died just hours shy of beginning his fourth year as an agent.

By the time ATF's Miami Task Force reached that six-month point, they'd taken 803 guns away from 180 criminal defendants; forty-seven were already convicted and twenty of them sentenced to prison terms totalling more than a century. The average would have been higher, but some judges didn't understand why Miami was Murder City. Luis Figueredo was a Marielito whose long record of arrests over the two short years he'd been in the States included carrying concealed weapons, attempted rape and murder. Convicted now of lying about his felony conviction to buy 169 pistols, his punishment was 109 days in jail.

In Bayamon, Puerto Rico, a silver crucifix was mounted above a flag-draped, chestnut coffin. The Rios family and twenty-six of Rios's co-workers filed by to pay their last respects. Agents looked at the haunted Elsie, the infant son, the pretty daughter for whom Christmas would be barren. They gazed at the stoic father and the stunned mother. Some agents wept. Some visualized their own loved ones standing there. It could happen to any of them. So quickly.

They buried their friend wearing his best black suit in the sweet, fresh earth of Jayuya—the mountain village where Rios had once told his father he could rest forever.

Citizens of Miami contributed $23,000 to the Ariel Rios Memorial Fund. President Ronald Reagan brought the Rios and D'Atri families to the White House. The secretary of the Treasury presented medals to Elsie Rios and Alexander D'Atri. Vice President George Bush's moving tribute concluded, "It is a debt we can never repay."

Alvarez and Simon got life; the others got thirty years.

D'Atri said, "It's fair, I guess, but Ariel's still dead."

Today he tells young agents, "It can happen any time, any day. It doesn't matter how careful you are or how good you are. It's just reality. It's the job."

Seven months later in Miami, Special Agent Eddie Benitez said goodbye to his mother and his disabled sister—he was their sole support—and went to work dressed for an undercover assignment. He seemed happy. He was twenty-seven. He'd been an agent for three years. He loved his job because he hated violence, and he was planning to become engaged.

In a parking lot just a few miles from the spot where Rios died, Eddie Benitez leaned in the window of a car driven by an exconvict named Ruoco who'd already sold him a bomb and eight silencers. For no apparent reason, Ruoco suddenly raised a pistol from the front seat and shot Benitez between the eyes.

Backup agents captured the killer. Ruoco got life plus seventy-five years. The 177th name was added to the list of ATF men who died in the line of duty. There were sympathetic words from the White House.

Eddie's girlfriend, his mother and his three sisters still grieve, still miss him.

Federal agencies tend to memorialize the personification of their values and traditions—the foundation of their strength. FBI headquarters in the J. Edgar Hoover Building.

Nothing better illustrates the difference between these two bureaus than the event that took place on February 5, 1985. The block-long edifice at 1200 Pennsylvania Avenue that houses ATF Headquarters was officially renamed the Ariel Rios Federal Building.

2

Three Detectives

To insure the adoration of a theorem for any length
of time, faith is not enough, a police force is
needed as well.

—Albert Camus

The first ATF agents were hired because they were needed to
sustain the United States of America as a nation. Their
traditions—independence, courage and dedication to the
country's best interests—are rooted in our earliest history
and personified by a rebel turned patriot named Gallatin.

Our founding fathers thought they could run the country
they'd created on monies raised by customs import duties.[1]
That pleasant little delusion lasted for all of fifteen years. In
1791, faced with a $21 million Revolutionary War debt,
Congress imposed a tax on spirits and snuff. That's when
they learned that Americans didn't like taxation *with*
representation any more than they'd liked it King George's
way.

Three years of violent resistance climaxed with a fire-
brand named Albert Gallatin leading seven thousand Penn-
sylvanians in a mass protest. When the governor refused to
summon his militia, President Washington raised 15,000
troops from other states. In one bold move, our first chief
executive achieved a peaceable end to the Whiskey Rebel-
lion and firmly established the federal government's authority over the states.

The liquor tax was abolished in 1802 and levied again ten
years later to pay for the War of 1812. This time the
proposal was advanced by Thomas Jefferson's secretary of
the Treasury: Albert Gallatin.

16

Today, Gallatin's profile adorns the bronze medallion awarded for honorable service to retiring Treasury agents.

Tax evasion wasn't much of a problem until the convulsive year that Lincoln wrote "Four score and seven years ago . . ." That same year, General William Tecumseh Sherman wrote his brother, "Though full of corruption and base materials, our country is a majestic one, full of natural wealth and good people."

The "corruption" included gangs of whiskey distillers evading the revenue tariffs desperately needed to finance the Civil War. Paying no tax, gangs sold their product so cheaply that legitimate manufacturers were forced into bankruptcy.

On March 3, 1863, the day Abraham Lincoln signed a bill making Idaho a territory, Congress authorized the hiring of "three detectives" to investigate the whiskey gangs. Not a very bold step, but this was a time when Washington, D.C.'s own police department was only two years old, its six-man detective force less than a year old, and militiamen still herded crooks down Pennsylvania Avenue with placards labeling them "thief" or "pickpocket." Then, too, there were other problems. Aside from the war, the troubled nation contended with Quantrill's Raiders—a gang that included Jesse James and Cole Younger.

Those first three ATF men uncovered proof that revenue officers had conspired with certain distillers to bribe high government officials and congressmen, but it would take more that a trio of agents to solve the nation's fiscal deficit. By 1871, tax collections were down $9 million. Internal Revenue Commissioner E. A. Rollins recruited a few more detectives, "men of the highest caliber," he'd record later.

One multistate conspiracy cost Uncle Sam somewhere between $200,000 and a billion dollars; the crooks' records didn't permit a closer estimate.

By 1875 the agents had smashed the whiskey rings.

In the aftermath of the Civil War, one problem remained: Southern "blockaders"—men who ran the blockade of lawmen to sell their untaxed product. The Yankee government wasn't popular in Dixie, and local revenue officials were ineffective. Agent Jacob Wagner tried "an experiment": a well-armed twelve-man posse that avoided towns where local folks could see them and tip the enemy. Camping in the woods and moving quietly across the countryside, they raided twenty-five stills a month.

Other revenue officers traveled through small towns posing as fur traders, peddlers, or hunters to pick up information.[2]

In 1876 President Grant appointed Green B. Raum as his commissioner of Internal Revenue. A large, balding man with a neatly trimmed beard, Raum was a former Union general wounded at Missionary Ridge, a former congressman, the past president of an Illinois railroad, and a staunch Republican who once asserted that he "wouldn't hire a Democrat." He even went so far as to fire Agent W. H. Chapman for refusing to assist a congressional candidate the agent considered corrupt. Chapman appealed to President Grant; his dismissal was reversed.

Most historians use the term "revenuers" to include the deputy collectors and federal marshals who carried out the bulk of day-to-day enforcement. Some were corrupt; many were brutal. A few marshals conspired with venal court officers to arrest innocent men so they could collect court fees. And the deputy collectors, according to a report filed by an agent named Olney, were "generally the roughest sort of illerate men . . . unnecessarily severe . . . men of no polish or brains and . . . the most arrant of cowards."

In 1876 the agent force was an elite cadre numbering less than twenty, but it was Commissioner Raum, despite his political priorities, who would institutionalize the values he found in the "men of the highest caliber" recruited by his predecessor.

"The important thing," Raum wrote, "in enforcing any law where seizures and arrests are made is to perform the duty in such a manner as not to offend well-meaning citizens. . . . Observe the law yourself in seeking to make others observe it. Appoint to office as subordinates men of intelligence, honesty, fidelity, experience and sobriety so that the laws can be enforced not only with vigor, but with moderation and discretion."

Moderation wasn't always possible. Moonshiners in the

Cumberland Mountains of Tennessee at the time were led by Morgan Campbell, the educated, eighteen-year-old son of a Presbyterian minister. Campbell was arrested, according to a report by S. D. Mather of the U.S. Circuit Court, after Agent James M. Davis and twenty-five lawmen had won a blazing two-day gun battle against a hundred Campbell men. Convicted, and having mistaken Agent Davis's chivalrous behavior after the gun battle for a sign of the government's gullibility, Campbell wrote to Raum on November 9, 1878, presenting himself as an unoffending citizen, unjustly harassed. He asked for clemency.

Raum posted his gentlemanly reply nine days later:

> To me, it is a matter of extreme regret that it is necessary, in the enforcement of the laws of the United States, that officers should go around ready to defend their lives against assault and to meet force with force. In this free country of ours, every citizen should have such a love of the Government and its laws as to cheerfully give obedience to their provisions, and not to be found engaged in defrauding its revenues, or forcibly resisting, with firearms, the officers engaged in the enforcement of the laws. . . . I am not advised of any reason that would warrant a pardon in your case.

The "monarch of the moonshiners," impressed by the revenue officials' combination of courtesy and idealism, served his prison term and upon his release went to work for the man who had arrested him, Agent James Davis. One assignment took them on an arduous hundred-mile horseback ride south of Atlanta against "Moonshine King" Bill Berong. They captured two of Berong's sons and treated them as honorable opponents—a surprise to men steeped in stories of revenuer crudity. The sons surrendered their still. Before departing, Davis and Campbell convicted the King himself and converted him into an ally.

In 1879, following a series of raids against a St. Louis whiskey ring and scores of arrests among venal Internal

Revenue employees, Congress raised the number of agents to thirty-five. Still not a formidable force, but enlarging an investigative agency wasn't undertaken lightly in the days when London's now-famous Scotland Yard was only a year old.

The new recruits—lawyers, accountants, exsoldiers, former teachers and shop clerks hungry for adventure—brought the law to men who wanted none. Under Raum's rules their performance won respect—even in Georgia. Agent W. H. Chapman reported that "the best people" there were becoming friendly, and the *Atlanta Constitution,* formerly sympathetic to blockaders, began encouraging the public to cooperate with agents.

In 1882, the year Jesse James was killed, Agent James Davis was ambushed while escorting a prisoner to court; his corpse was found with twenty bullet holes and a crushed skull. Green Raum resigned as commissioner, but his agents' successes had increased revenue collections so much that by 1888—the year Jack the Ripper was baffling Scotland Yard—the U.S. Treasury reported a surplus.

Congress rewarded the agents' efficency with a move to slash the force from thirty-five to five. The new commissioner, Walter Evans, stated that the agents were "absolutely essential where enforcement of the law is so hazardous that local officers shrink from it."

Congress relented, and only fifteen agents were laid off.

The replacement rate must have been substantial during those first nineteen years. Incomplete records report twenty-nine agents killed and sixty-three wounded.

Blockaders suffered more than a hundred casualties.

Author David Maurer would write:[3]

In the late nineteenth and early twentieth centuries, these men were truly a heroic breed . . . for open warfare existed between them and the moonshiners. . . . Kentuckians, isolated in the backwoods, attained . . . a high reputation for personal combat with fists, Bowie knives, or firearms. Federal agents, therefore, had to be strong men capable of meeting moonshiners on their own grounds and highly dedicated to the work in which they specialized. Like federal marshals of the Old West, they were often sustained by a love of combat and almost unlimited reserves of controlled violence.

Legends created by agents like James Davis and traditions institutionalized by Green Raum remained with the force for another forty years, but as Maurer notes:

> During Prohibition . . . a new and different type of federal officer entered the picture. Replacing the strong, level-headed, courageous frontier lawman represented by the federal revenue agents came a horde of undisciplined, untrained, unprincipled men known as Prohibition Agents.

The Constitutional amendment outlawing the production or sale of alcoholic beverages culminated a long, tireless battle waged by well-meaning optimists.

At midnight on January 16, 1920, churchbells ushered in the Prohibition era while William Jennings Bryan—revered orator and three-time candidate for president—assured the prominent citizens gathered in the First Congregational Church of Washington, D.C., that the purveyors of demon rum were a thing of the past. "They are dead that sought the child's life," Bryan promised. "They are dead!"

For dead men they seemed pretty lively. While Bryan soothed upright Washingtonians, six armed and masked bandits gagged a watchman in Chicago's railroad yard and looted two freight cars of $100,000 in whiskey reserved for medicinal use.

Undaunted, the Women's Christian Temperance Union sang the praises of Prohibition. "An enemy, the equal of Prussianism in frightfulness has been overthrown."

And at dawn, world-renowned evangelist Billy Sunday cracked his stentorian voice across 10,000 shining faces in Norfolk, Virginia. "Goodbye John [Barleycorn], goodbye. You were God's worst enemy. You were Hell's best friend. I hate you with a perfect hatred. I love to hate you!" Each phrase punctuated by wild cheering, he shouted, "The reign

21

of terror is over. The slums will soon be a memory. We will turn our prisons into factories and our jails into storehouses and corncribs. Men will walk upright now. Women will smile and children will laugh. Hell will be forever rent."

Instead, the embryo of organized crime was fertilized.

If Prohibitionists were jubilant and others hopeful, lawmen were reluctant. Bureaucrats, notoriously acquisitive when opportunities for expansion arise, retreated. Treasury noted that the Volstead Act provided no revenues and called its enforcement a Justice Department responsibility. The attorney general pointed to Treasury's existing force of agents and declined with uncharacteristic humility.

The Justice Department won and Treasury got the job.

IRS commissioner John Kramer displayed the supreme confidence of a tax collector who knows nothing about law enforcement—an understandable ignorance that endured through his successors into recent administrations. "This law will be obeyed in cities large and small, and in villages, and where it is not obeyed it will be enforced." His agents would ensure that "ardent spirits are not manufactured nor sold nor given away, nor hauled in anything on the surface of the earth, or under the earth of in the air."[4]

Mr. Kramer had probably learned his arithmetic but he must have dozed through his geography lessons. The United States boasted three and a half million square miles of farms and forests, not to mention thousands of cities with warehouses and factories where anyone could hide a still. Our Atlantic and Pacific seaboards offer 88,653 miles of shoreline and coves where boats could land. Our barely guarded border with Canada, where liquor was still legal, stretched nearly four thousand miles.

To detect and apprehend violators, Congress expanded the force of agents to 1,550 and paid them a respectable forty-five dollars a week—more than twice the salary of a Philadelphia policeman, who also had to buy his own gun and uniform. But appointments were exempted from civil service requirements. Political patronage crammed the agent corps with illiterates, incompetents, misfits and outright criminals. Those who entered as honest men saw bootleggers delivering to the White House, and, as the decade ended, opportunities for easy wealth lay everywhere amidst the gritty despair of the Great Depression.

Even if every agent had been a paragon of virtue, courage and intellect, effective enforcement would have been impossible. New York City's 15,000 licensed saloons burgeoned into 32,000 speakeasies. Booze was manufactured in elaborate distilleries and massive breweries, cooked in mountain hollows and tenement bathtubs. Convictions were plea-bargained down to probation, a fine or a short stay in jail, because if all the 50,000 liquor law violators arrested in New York during 1926 had demanded a jury trial, the backlog would have occupied federal judges for twelve years. And the following year's workload would have tied them up until 1950.

High revenue officials were authorized to issue permits to purchase "medicinal" alcohol from government warehouses for 62¢ a gallon. Bootleggers paid them $8.00 a gallon and cut the straight alky three times, increasing its value to $24.00. Thus a single boxcar load, purchased "legitimately" for $3,720, was worth $144,000 on the black market—a sum equal to the Prohibition commissioner's salary for eighteen years. Or an agent's salary for sixty years. Its value in 1996 dollars: $1.3 million, just for that one boxcar.[5]

Prohibition agents arrested their Pennsylvania state director and four aides for peddling 215 permits covering 500,000 gallons—worth $12 million. They arrested administrators in Chicago and Ohio. They nailed acting commissioner Millard West for conspiring with Congressman John Langley to divert 4,000 gallons of bonded whiskey. Langley went to prison.

Corruption was rife among lower-level employees as well. Aside from the 257 agents prosecuted for outright larceny, 1,587 bureau employees were fired for false statements on their applications, concealing criminal records, extortion, bribery, phony expense accounts, collusion, conspiracy, illegal disposal of liquor, embezzlement, failure to report violations, theft, warehouse robbery, intoxication, immorality, assault, gambling, revealing confidential information, insubordination, contempt of court, perjury, subornation of perjury, political activity, writing bad checks, failure to file tax returns and misuse of firearms.

Many of these crimes were uncovered by agents of the IRS Intelligence Division—men selected under the civil service rules that also protected them from political pressure. IRS unit chief Elmer Irey reported how one Prohibition agent went bad after he'd had a good case dismissed by a judge "with a few words of apology to the grinning bootlegger and quite a few words of castigation for the 'snooping' agent."

Two days later, Irey says, the agent "was parked outside a garage, from which he momentarily expected a truck to emerge. The truck was loaded with good whiskey and was therefore worth $40,000. . . . The garage doors opened and a pleasant-faced man came out. He walked up to the agent and said, 'If you will turn your back for sixty seconds I'll give you $10,000.'

"The agent's ears were still crimson from the dressing down he'd gotten forty-eight hours before. He turned his back. A truck motor coughed and started, a car rolled out of the garage, and the pleasant-faced man said to the agent, 'Your sixty seconds are up. Thank you.' Then he handed over ten crisp thousand-dollar bills and sauntered away."[6]

In 1927 Congress brought the Prohibition bureau into the civil service system. Over the next two years, investigators of the Civil Service Commission conducted more than 3,000 inquiries. Forty percent of the Prohibition people they checked—current employees and newly recruited candidates—had records that proved them unfit for federal service.

An agent's pay depended upon length of service, starting at $2,300 a year and climbing ultimately to $2,800 before taxes and the 3.5 percent retirement deductions were subtracted. He worked the normal government work week of six, seven-hour days, and overtime could be required beyond those forty-two hours. "However," the Field Office Manual stated, "no compensation will be given for such overtime work unless otherwise specifically authorized."

While traveling, regulations allowed 30¢ a day for maids

and bellboys and 60¢ each day for tips to waiters. Receipts were required for expenditures exceeding one dollar, but paragraph 515 made an exception for pay telephones:[7]

> Should a slot machine be used whereby no receipt could be taken, an explanation should be made on the Standard Form 1034 to that effect, giving the nature of the message.

Just as today, the ponderous bureaucracy thrived on paperwork. On June 19, 1927, a new order told agents:[8]

> Your attention is invited to the requirement of the Bureau relative to procuring permission from Washington before having repairs made on government-owned automobiles in excess of $10.00. Due to the delay incidental to procuring this authority, the limitation has been raised to $50.00.

The terminology hasn't changed much, either.

Racketeers "rented" U.S. Coast Guard vessels and hired their crews to unload liquor cargoes. When Chicago police chief Charles Fitzmorris admitted that sixty percent of his officers were in the bootleg business, state's attorney Robert Crowe demanded forty detectives to work under his personal direction. Within weeks, his handpicked squad was known as Ali Baba's Forty Thieves. New York's Mayor LaGuardia stated that Prohibition enforcement would require a quarter million policemen, with another 250,000 to watch the first army. T-man Frank J. Wilson (who would later become chief of the U.S. Secret Service) was present when the prosecution of a Philadelphia alcohol case was quashed by two special representatives sent by the attorney general of the United States. FBI director J. Edgar Hoover proclaimed his own bureau "a haven for hacks and deadbeats."[9]

It's not surprising that many agents failed; what's amazing is that so many perserved. Obtaining evidence required an agent to conceal his activities from gangsters, neighbors who might tip the bootleggers, anyone owing a debt to a politician, dishonest cops patroling the area around the distillery, even from his own colleagues who might be on the mob's payroll.

Nevertheless, the second year of Prohibition saw 5 million gallons of beer and liquor seized and 77,000 bootleggers arrested.

And seven agents murdered.

North of Chicago, Special Agent Clarence Pickering found a mining shed packed with 3,400 cases of bourbon whiskey labeled "Explosives." Twelve agents were concealed around the shack when four old army trucks—with puncture-proof tires, cabs reinforced with heavy steel and drivers armed with Springfield rifles—rolled out carrying 1,000 cases of liquor. An agent used a megaphone to call for their surrender, but in vain.

Agent Pickering answered their fire with a burst from his Thompson submachine gun. "I rushed [the first truck] with two of my grenades," he wrote later. "The first pineapple killed the gun guard and broke the driver's arm and blinded him as well."[10]

But violence wasn't *de rigueur*. Agents Isreal Einstein and Moe Smith posed as anyone and everybody—from baseball players to streetcar conductors—to buy booze in New York speakeasies. By 1925, having closed 3,000 juice joints, they'd become darlings of the press. But Izzy and Moe (as their public fondly called them) crossed a line with a raid on the Assembly—a Fulton Street watering hole catering to lawyers and politicians. Izzy got in by calling himself "Judge Einstein." The legal community wasn't amused, and both men were dismissed from the Prohibition Bureau.[11]

Former Seattle police lieutenant Roy Olmstead was a nonviolent bootlegger. His ships wore paths through the open seas from British Columbia to Puget Sound while his trucks—disguised as the vehicles of cheese and cotton merchants—rumbled through the city's streets. Olmstead's initial investment of $10,000 (eleven partners contributed an additional $1,000 each) founded a business whose daily sales, averaging 200 cases, yielded $176,000 in a bad month. Olmstead's share was half the profits. He employed a regiment of truck drivers, loaders, salesmen, collectors, clerks, lawyers and accountants, and he used them shrewdly to insulate himself from incriminating acts.[12]

Special Agent William Whitney employed a wiretap. Transcripts of the conspirators' conversations filled 775 typewritten pages. One call came from a bootlegger named Green:

GREEN:	"Hello there. How are you, you old jail-bird?"
OLMSTEAD:	"Hello there. They came pretty close to getting you, didn't they?"
GREEN:	"No. Any time I can't get away from that damn fool Whitney, I want someone to shoot me."

It's not recorded whether Agent Whitney had a sense of humor, but his roundup of Olmstead and ninety accomplices became famous as the Whispering Wires Case. Wiretaps weren't illegal under federal law, but Olmstead's attorneys assured him that the federal courts would never accept such evidence. One of those lawyers snapped his fountain pen in half when the Supreme Court validated the technique as a legitimate source of evidence. It would be ten years before Congress outlawed wiretapping with enactment of the Federal Communications Act.

It was still legal when Special Agent Eliot Ness and his famed squad—dubbed the Untouchables because they couldn't be bribed—used wiretaps against Al Capone. Some of the hoodlums' conversations enabled agents to intercept liquor loads smuggled in from Canada; others led to dozens of the Capone empire's distilleries and breweries.[13]

Having failed at bribery, the gangsters tried threats and murder, but nothing stopped Ness's squad. While agents of the IRS Intelligence Division (today the Criminal Investigation Division) sought witnesses to prove Capone guilty of tax evasion, the Untouchables' raids eroded Chicago's liquor supply and dammed the river of cash that purchased immunity. The tap on mob treasurer Jake Guzik's phone yielded proof of the squad's effectiveness:

"Hello, Jake?"

"Yeah."

"This is Turk."

"Uh huh."

"I ain't gettin' all the beer I can use."

"Nobody is."

Another call signaled the crumbling of police protection:

"Lieutenant Sands is in again. What's he get?"

"Nothin'."

"Whattya mean, nothin'?"

"Listen, Hymie. Tell the boys they'll have to take a pass this month."

"They ain't gonna like it."

"Too bad, but we just ain't makin' any dough. And if we ain't got it, we can't pay it."

With the foundation corroded, the structure collapsed. Police protection evaporated. Witnesses talked. IRS agents established Capone's income, proved he hadn't paid his taxes and sent the "Big Fella" to Alcatraz for eleven years. By the time he came out, syphillis had eaten his brain. His crime career was ended.

All during the long battle against the powerful Capone empire, Eliot Ness never spoke to his enemy face to face. Special Agent Robert Bridges was more direct. Assigned to investigate Cleveland's notorious Mayfield Road Gang, he was offended by the hoodlums' lack of respect. He drove to the Brotherhood Club, a storefront where the Milano brothers—local Mafia chieftains—held court. The door was locked.

"Come out," Bridges shouted. "Come out or I'll drive through the window."

Frank Milano opened the door. "What's going on?"

Bridges showed his credentials. "When I come around here on official business, I conduct myself like a gentleman. I'm not going to stand for anyone throwing rocks or shooting guns at my car. Understand?"

Milano's eyes widened. He nodded.

"I'll hold you responsible, personally."

Milano gave him a phone number. "If anyone bothers you, call me."

"I'm not going to be paid off and I'm not going to be intimidated."

"Yeah. Okay."[14]

George Remus, a personable German immigrant and Cincinnati lawyer, became the Bootleg King of the Midwest by bribing cops, local agents and the attorney general of the United States. The New Year's Eve party at Remus's ten-acre Price Hill estate featured professional swimmers and divers performing a water ballet while an orchestra played for a hundred guests seated around the $100,000 marble-columned pool. At dawn, gentlemen received a party favor of diamond cufflinks; each of the ladies was presented with a brand new automobile.

When a special squad of agents raided Remus's plants, the attorney general admitted he couldn't help, but Remus remained calm. Even as his private railroad car sped him toward Atlanta to serve his two-year sentence, he schemed to buy his way out. He sent his wife to corrupt Franklin Dodge, the agent who had brought about his downfall.

Instead, Mrs. Remus stripped the bootlegger of his wealth, divorced him and married the agent.

Remus did his two years, murdered the wife who'd betrayed him, convinced a court he was crazy and served a few months in an asylum.[15]

Gunfire became the trademark of Prohibition. Nearly 800 hoodlums were slaughtered in Chicago's gang wars—largely because, once Johnny Torrio had corrupted the administration of Mayor "Big Bill" Thompson, Al Capone augmented Thompson's political machine with the Thompson machine gun.

Dozens of agents died in car crashes while in hot pursuit; one was pushed from the running board of a speeding auto; one was scalded to death in a boiling mash vat; one was asphyxiated by mash fumes while raiding a still. Eighty-five were slain by criminal gunfire during the Prohibition years. The official toll of agents killed in the line of duty totaled

126. Another 255 were assaulted, a hundred wounded by gunfire and 274 suffered other injuries. Add to the debit line seven policemen killed and six wounded while assisting agents.[16]

The bad guys—men with the option of drawing first and shooting first—fared only slightly worse: 135 killed and two wounded by agents; seven more were killed by policemen working with the agents.

The price of Prohibition wasn't limited to corruption and murder. The fabric of American society was stained and rent, and organized crime gained a foothold it would never relinquish. "The Noble Experiment" lasted for thirteen years and ten months. Its repeal brought tavern prices down anywhere from 30 to 50 percent.

A bit of contemporaneous doggerel captured the flavor of the time:

> Prohibition is an awful flop.
>   We like it.
> It can't stop what it's meant to stop.
>   We like it.
> It's filled our land with vice and crime.
> It don't prohibit worth a dime.
> Nevertheless, we're for it.

Former Congressman Andrew Volstead, author of the National Prohibition Act, died at the age of eighty-seven on January 20, 1947. Al Capone outlived him by five days; he was forty-eight.

America didn't win the Prohibition war, but the nation did discover limits to the power of simply passing a law.

ATF survived, despite corrupt politicians.

Organized crime flourished because of them.

3

Gentlemen
Don't Boast

Anyone can be heroic from time to time, but a
gentleman is something you have to be all the
time.

—Luigi Pirandello

Torrio was the brain that made the rackets Big Business. As
the Chicago Crime Commission's Virgil Peterson wrote,
"By 1924, John Torrio had reached the height of his power.
Politicians vied with one another for his support. Rival
gangsters feared him."

During Prohibition, he had taken over Chicago's domi-
nant mob, eliminated rival gangs, organized the nationwide
combine of Mafia chieftains and—shortly after an attempt
on his life, and just before leaving town to serve a short term
for bootlegging—he bequeathed his Chicago empire to Al
Capone. Supposedly retired after Prohibition, he remained
in fact a voting member of the national Mafia Commission.[1]

On May 25, 1935, ATF's New York chief received a
memo from his Washington headquarters: "This office has
information to the effect that John Torrio . . . is now finan-
cially interested in the [liquor] importing firm of Prendergast and Davies Co., Ltd., New York City."

Post-Prohibition Treasury regulations required liquor
wholesalers to disclose the names of everyone holding a
substantial interest in their business. Although Prendergast
and Davies was apparently respectable as the largest firm of
its kind, doing millions of dollars in business every month,
special agents William Dunn and Lewis West paid a visit to
the company's plush Manhattan offices.

General Manager Sam Borden snorted, "Johnny Torrio?

Involved with P and D? Ridiculous!" The company's financial reports made no mention of the racketeer, so agents Dunn and West left to do more research. They learned that a man named William Slockblower had bought into the firm just after Prohibition had ended. A quick check of Slockblower whetted the agents' curiosity. They pulled Torrio's picture from the file and returned to Prendergast and Davies.

Sam Borden seemed impatient. "What now?"

Dunn glanced into an adjoining room and pointed to a man wearing striped trousers with a cutaway coat. "Who's he?"

"Why, that's Mr. McCarthy. He's in and out a lot."

The man resembled the Torrio photo, but Dunn proceeded methodically. "We'd like to speak with Mr. Slockblower."

How unfortunate. Just that morning, Borden said, Mr. Slockblower had left for an extended vacation in Canada.

"Mr. Slockblower's a partner and a member of your board of directors, right?"

"Yes, of course."

"We noticed that he's carried on your books as a warehouse superintendent earning $150 a week. Isn't that an unusual position for a partner in the firm?"

Borden squirmed. "You'd have to see Mr. Slock—"

"Before investing in P and D, he was a railroad clerk earning $125 a week. Where'd he get the money to invest—"

"Say, now, you'll really have to talk with Mr. Slockblower about all that."

The agents took another look at "Mr. McCarthy" on their way out, and West agreed with Dunn. The man looked like Torrio.

No one answered their knock at Slockblower's White Plains apartment, but a neighbor told the agents, "He's not going on any trip. I just talked to his wife and she's upstairs cooking pork chops for supper."

"Tell me, who owns this apartment building?"

"A Mr. Torrio. Mr. John Torrio."

Back in Manhattan, a perspiring Sam Borden agreed to

have Slockblower available for an interview the "day after tomorrow."

Two days later, Slockblower greeted the agents with a twitchy smile and introduced his companion, "Mr. McCarthy."

Agent Dunn asked, "Are you connected with the company?"

Slockblower's companion shook his head. "No."

"Well then, sir, since this matter involves the confidential affairs of Prendergast and Davies, I'll have to ask you to wait outside."

"No, sir! I will not permit you to question my brother-in-law without my being present."

"Oh? Did you marry Mr. Slockblower's sister?"

"No. He married my sister."

Mrs. Slockblower's maiden name was Torrio.

That afternoon, Torrio vanished.

The agents learned that he'd applied for a passport using a post office box in White Plains. Dunn put a slip in Torrio's box, notifying him to appear at the counter and sign for a registered letter. Then he and West took up positions behind the bank of post office boxes and waited.

The next day, the box was opened. A hand withdrew the slip. Agent West ran to the back of the post office for the car while Dunn slipped into the lobby, saw one man there and tailed him down the street. By the time West had brought the car around and parked in front, Dunn was nowhere in sight, but a woman was coming down the front steps of the post office. She climbed into a limousine, and a minute later, "Mr. McCarthy" stepped from the limo and entered the post office. West followed him.

The man went to the clerk's window. "Excuse me, I understand you have a letter for me. My name's John Torrio."

The clerk left the window.

Torrio waited for his letter.

West stood behind him, waiting for Dunn.

Finally, looking puzzled, Torrio turned away.

West touched his arm. "Mr. Torrio?"

"Yes." He smiled anxiously, apparently without recognizing the agent from their meeting at Prendergast & Davies. "Do you have my letter?"

"Please come this way." West ushered the elegantly attired racketeer through a door and offered him one of the chairs the agents had been using.

Torrio sat, then stood up. "I'll have to go tell my wife."

"That'll have to wait," Agent West told him.

Torrio tried to leave.

The slender twenty-six-year-old former schoolteacher with only two years on the job showed his credentials and arrested the nation's number-one godfather in typical Treasury fashion—without fanfare, flashbulbs or firearms. Torrio spent the night in jail.

At the arraignment the next day in New York City's federal courthouse, bail was set at $100,000. Torrio's wife opened her purse and counted out the full sum in thousand-dollar bills.

Torrio got off on the hidden-ownership charge. Although the regulations required liquor wholesalers to identify all owners, the wording of the government application form was ambiguous. The IRS—with its mantra that "we're tax collectors, not policemen"—wouldn't get around to correcting that little oversight for nearly fifty years. Torrio also beat a charge of smuggling untaxed liquor when two of the government's witnesses vanished—permanently.

Success came when two Treasury agencies joined forces. Evidence obtained in an ATF raid was added to facts acquired by the IRS Intelligence Division. The combination was enough to put Torrio away for two and a half years.[2]

Treasury agents got results when government agencies cooperated with one another as ATF and IRS men had in the Torrio case, but teamwork was a "sometimes" thing.

Two years earlier, when Prohibition was repealed and the alcohol tax reinstated, the job of enforcement was returned to the Internal Revenue Service's ATF unit. Franklin Roosevelt's secretary of the Treasury, Henry Morgenthau Jr., a prosperous apple grower who'd studied at Cornell—fought Congress to staff ATF without regard for politics. He retained just 700 men from the Prohibition Bureau: "lawyers, accountants and men of similar experience," he wrote in his diary, "on the basis of competence." He reversed the IRS bureaucrats' practice of sending agents to "the Allegheny Mountains . . . going out after 5- and 10-gallon stills [to build paper statistics while ignoring] people with a suite of rooms at the Waldorf."[3]

Agents racked up 24,000 felony convictions over the next two years, but it didn't do much good. Bootlegging thrived. It was so profitable that mobster Moe Davis erected a $250,000 plant in Zanesville, Ohio, and employed twelve still hands to work around the clock. His daily cost to produce 5,000 gallons of 190-proof alcohol was $2,500; his profit came to $47,500—nearly half a million in 1993 dollars—every day until agents finally cracked the plant's security and raided it.[4]

A year later, agents raided a $200,000 distillery in Elizabeth, New Jersey. The raw materials to supply this and the Zanesville operation came from Moluska—a corporation owned by crime lords Meyer Lansky, Joe Adonis, "Bugsy" Siegel and Frank Costello, but these bosses were never charged. Their involvement in Moluska was known only to IRS Intelligence—a separate Treasury unit with a separate file system.

Treasury's crime data was scattered among its six law enforcement agencies: ATF, Customs, IRS Intelligence, the Secret Service (and still part of Treasury at that time), the Coast Guard and the Bureau of Narcotics.

ATF, Customs and today's IRS Criminal Investigation Division were, and are, sections within revenue agencies; IRS and Customs agents serve under career tax collectors.

Morgenthau, an organizational genius whose Victory bond drive would raise more that $200 billion during World War II, saw waste and inefficiency as downright stupid. The dispersal of crime intelligence and the funding of six separate executive and administrative hierarchies in Washington (plus six field offices in every city across the country—each with its own agent in charge, receptionist, clerical pool and vehicle fleet—all six working independently of one another) was absurd.

Criminals were more pragmatic, more flexible, more mobile. Shifting from one racket to another, they'd escape the agents who knew their habits to challenge investigators who'd never heard of them. They slipped from bootlegging to counterfeiting or smuggling (and always tax evasion) faster than Morgenthau's men could close a petered-out investigation and ship it to dead storage. And so, "to eliminate duplication and improve the effectiveness of Treasury's investigative agencies" Morgenthau suggested implementing a recent recommendation by the prestigious Wickersham Commission by merging all his agents into a single unit. Efficient crimefighting at less cost to the taxpayer.

Morgenthau expected complaints from agency executives who would be demoted by the merger, but these whiners were joined by men with murkier motives: the attorney general and FBI director J. Edgar Hoover. Together, these men—bureaucrats to whom keeping a high position or crushing a rival agency was more important than crushing crime—demonstrated the strength of unity. Their confederation, not unlike the team Morgenthau would have aimed at the underworld, mustered enough political support to defeat the plan.[5]

After Prohibition, Congress passed a law adding five to ten years to the sentence of anyone caught at a still where firearms were present. Mobsters weren't stupid. They'd seldom won those shootouts anyway. From that day forth, guns were rarely found around a Mafia distillery.

Down South, things were . . . well, they were different.

Author Andrew Tully describes the early post-Prohibition years as "a throwback to the early days of the West when law officers and posses went after gunslinging rustlers and other desperadoes. They seldom got their man without a fight."[6]

And some battles went beyond gunfire—to the courts.

Treasury taught its agents, "Don't worry about what happens after you've finished your investigation. Do your job, and the prosecutors and the courts will do theirs."

The inevitable exception occurred in 1940, when the Supreme Court impugned ATF's honor with an accusation that agents had violated the law to convict three killers.

It all began on the hot afternoon of Wednesday, July 31. Agents in Chattanooga, Tennessee, were tipped that the

McNabb gang—a clan of mountaineers living about twelve miles outside the city—would be selling a load of moonshine whiskey that night. Informers met the McNabbs and accompanied them to the family cemetery where the booze was hidden.

Agents followed quietly, and just as the cans were being carried to the car, they closed in. "All right, boys, federal officers!"

The McNabbs scurried into the darkness.

A shot rang out.

Special Agent Samuel Leeper fell to the ground, dead. A second blast sent eight shotgun pellets plowing into Special Agent Frank Renick's face, neck, arm and chest. A search of the area proved futile. Renick was rushed to a hospital, while other agents brought the sad news to Leeper's widow.

A few hours later, agents stormed the McNabb home and arrested four brothers, all in their twenties. Supervisor Howard B. Taylor spent all day Thursday studying the case. That evening, the prisoners were brought from the jail for interrogation. The *Miranda* decision lay in the distant future, but Taylor followed Treasury policy with each suspect.

"I'm investigating the murder of Agent Leeper. You don't have to say anything and no one will try to force you to talk, but any statement you make can be used against you."

The men were interrogated until one o'clock in the morning.

On Friday morning, the questioning resumed, one brother at a time. Later that day, a fifth McNabb, twenty-year-old Benjamin, surrendered himself at the office. Confronted with his brothers' statements, he admitted firing the shot that killed Agent Leeper. Benjamin was convicted, along with the brothers who'd confessed to being present.

The Supreme Court reversed the convictions. Delivering the decision, Justice Felix Frankfurter wrote:

> The circumstances [of the confessions] reveal a plain disregard of the duty enjoined by Congress upon federal law officers. Freeman and Raymond McNabb were arrested in the middle of the night at their home.

Instead of being brought before a United States commissioner or a judicial officer, as the law requires, in order to determine the sufficiency for their detention, they were put in a barren cell and kept there for fourteen hours. . . . Benjamin's confession was secured by detaining him unlawfully and questioning him continuously for five or six hours. . . . The record leaves no room for doubt that the questioning took place . . . before any order of commitment had been made.

As law professor Fred E. Inbau of Northwestern University writes, "The Court conceded that since the [McNabbs] had not been threatened, abused or otherwise coerced, there was no problem of constitutional law." The convictions were overturned, Inbau says, because the agents' so-called failure to bring the prisoners before a judicial officer without unreasonable delay was a "flagrant disregard of federal laws."

"A rather amazing feature of this case," Inbau continues, "is the fact that the defendants actually *had* been arraigned promptly." The prosecutors simply hadn't mentioned this routine formality in the trial record.

The agents had violated nothing. Since there was no merit to the McNabbs' other claims, the Justices had no valid reason to reverse the convictions.

"Moreover," Inbau continues, "the fact of the actual arraignment was even called to the Court's attention in the government's petition for a rehearing, but to no avail."

The Justices were content. They had achieved their goal: to warn America's lawmen that failure to comply with all laws would invalidate a criminal's conviction.

Some agents resented the unwarranted insult and the Justices' refusal to apologize. Others saw the irony. The Supreme Court of the United States had succumbed to the same sin they condemned so blithely when committed by policemen: They'd bent the facts to suit their purposes.

The three McNabbs were tried and convicted again. Each served a ten-year sentence for voluntary manslaughter.[7]

Ten years? Agents left the courtroom remembering the sad faces of Sam Leeper's family members when they'd placed his body on a train for the final journey home.

The Supreme Court has never acknowledged its mistake.

Violence wasn't uncommon but, generally speaking, the players in "the game"—agents and bootleggers—recognized their roles and understood their adversary's position.

In *Moonshine: Its History and Folklore,* author Esther Kellner characterizes ATF agents as having "many qualities that did not originate in their enforcement training. They are men of impressive physique, with quick and resourceful minds, fertile imaginations, fast reflexes and innate honesty and decency; they are at all times gentlemen."

A flattering portrait, if not always accurate. In reality, physical prowess and intelligence varied. But the latter attributes—honesty, decency and gentlemanly behavior— were required by Treasury and reinforced through training and tradition. These traits forged an attitude of mutual respect between agents and outlaws, illustrated by the relationship between Special Agent Homer Powell and bootlegger Ralph Wickersham.

The story began with a raid and Wickersham's capture after a footrace through the forest. Agent Powell knew the man—he'd arrested him before—so he told Wickersham, "Catch your breath and come on back to the still when you're rested."

Wickersham agreed, but he didn't show. The next morning, he shambled into the ATF office.

"Ralph," Powell snapped, "why did you do that?"

"I'm sorry, Homer. I apologize."

"I can't stand that. I do you a favor, I expect you to appreciate it."

"Well, I *do* appreciate it, Homer. I didn't mean to run off. I know it was wrong and I apologize 'cause you treated me all right."

Wickersham served his year and a day behind bars and

came out swearing vengeance against "everyone involved in sending me up." The word was flashed to Powell.

It was evening when the agent found Wickersham coming out of a small cinderblock beer joint at the edge of a woods. Wickersham greeted him like an old pal, but Powell mentioned what he'd heard and asked, "Do we have something to settle?"

The 240-pound bootlegger with the 22-inch biceps looked down at the slender agent. "No."

"I'm not wearing my gun, Ralph. It's just you and me and the trees."

"Homer, as far as I'm concerned, you treated me right and done your job. You caught me, told the court the truth, and you did it like a gentleman. I haven't got anything against you at all. Come on in and have a beer with me."

After their second drink, Powell got up to leave. He'd reached the door when Wickersham called, "Hey, Homer. If I was to buy you some new clothes, would you wear 'em?"

The agent hesitated. "Well, I don't know, Ralph. What did you have in mind?"

"If I was to buy you a red shirt and a pair of red pants and a bright red cap, would you wear 'em?"

The room exploded with loud guffaws and peals of laughter. Everyone in the county knew Powell's preference for camouflage clothing when he prowled the woods.

The agent smiled. "I appreciate the offer, Ralph. You buy it and I'll wear it. To court."

Powell would arrest Wickersham again, but it was always professional, never personal. Treasury tradition. The years went by, but bootlegger and agent always exchanged friendly greetings when they passed on the street.[8]

When William B. Henderson played baseball in college, comparisons with famed pitcher Christy "Big Six" Mathewson gave him a nickname he'd carry through life. In 1941 the young 6'2" lawyer joined ATF. The 5,400 arrests Big Six Henderson made during his twenty-seven-year career would create a new legend in Kentucky folklore. Boys playing Moonshiner and Revenuer were heard to say, "You be Uncle Zeke and I'll be Big Six."

Little girls jumping rope recited:

> My mother told me
> To watch the still
> In case Big Six
> Comes over the hill.

Henderson epitomized ATF's tradition of treating everyone, colleagues and criminals alike, with respect. When a man he'd arrested five times bought a car, he asked Henderson to teach him to drive. Big Six complied. When the agent's government car (G-car, in agent parlance) became mired on a muddy road, the nearest resident—a man he'd arrested six times—brought a tractor, pulled the car free and refused payment. "Thank you just the same, Big Six, but I wouldn't think of charging an old friend." When a young three-time loser was paroled, Henderson took him home, gave him supper and put him up for the night. Next day, he drove the man a hundred miles to a city, recommended him to an elderly lady who rented clean rooms and took him to the job he'd arranged before the youthful offender's release—working in a licensed distillery.

In his free time, Henderson officiated at basketball games for the University of Kentucky and Western University. Sports writers pronounced him "as trusted as Big Ben." The agent scouted athletes for local colleges, and two of his discoveries—basketball star Cliff Hagan and football hero Paul Hornung—honored their friend by wearing a big 6 on their uniforms.

Henderson had hundreds of adventures—he'd arrested many murderers, even a mailman delivering white lightning along his appointed rounds—but his favorite story recounted the night be disguised himself in frayed overalls, splashed himself with moonshine and walked into a small store suspected of selling corn liquor. "Say, mister," he drawled, "I'm pretty thirsty. Where can I get a drink around here?"

"Well," the grocer replied, "if you don't know, Big Six, who does?"

In 1976, after he'd retired from ATF, Henderson won a presidential appointment as United States marshal for

Kentucky. Letters of congratulation poured in from the White House, the Federal Bar Association, lawmen, newsmen and several prisons where Big Six's admirers still resided.

Big Six Henderson died at the age of eighty-three.[9]

Not all ATF agents died in bed. A congressional study undertaken in 1948 to support special retirement benefits for federal crimefighters reported the following grim statistics:[10]

Fatalities in the Line of Duty
(as of 2/19/48)

ATF (during Prohibition).	126
(from 1934 through 2/48).	26
Bureau of Narcotics.	8
FBI (until 1934).	10
(from 1934 through 2/48).	6
U.S. Customs Service.	24
U.S. Secret Service.	8

Those who find fascination in numerical coincidence will be intrigued to learn that Special Agent William J. Jackson was recorded as ATF's 138th fatality; he was thirty-eight years of age, and he was shot with a .38 caliber revolver during a car-to-car gun battle on 3/8/38.[11]

ATF's longest hunt for the killer of an agent began on September 24, 1929. Agents had smashed through heavy barricades and barbed-wire entanglements to raid an elaborate operation near San Antonio, Texas, that had cost the bootleggers $20,000 to build, and they were heading back to town with their prisoners when they came upon a truckload of cabbages blocking the highway. As the agents stepped from their car, ambushers fired from the roadside underbrush. Bootleg leader Lynn Stephens rushed up to the government car, rammed his gun through the window and shot Agent Charles Stevens to death. ATF's twenty-year search for Stephens took them from Mexico to Miami to New York and back to Texas. On October 1, 1949, with the net drawing tight, the killer surrendered. He'd been thirty-one when he'd murdered Agent Stevens. Two decades on the run had shrunk the husky 240-pounder to 170 pounds. He walked with a stoop. He suffered from ulcers. If he served the full term imposed for killing Agent Stevens, he'd be eighty-nine when they let him out.[12]

Gunfire wasn't the only killer. The men who brought white lightening from backwoods stills to their markets in the cities drove cars built for speed. Most of them preferred the 1940 Ford coupe—its factory-built flathead 100-horsepower engine improved by expert mechanics with a Mercury camshaft, Edelbrook finned aluminum cylinder heads and an intake manifold that accommodated three Stromberg "97" carburetors. They would port and relieve the valves and cannibalize a Lincoln, adapting the transmission system and installing its V-12 distributor to allow dizzying acceleration in second gear. Every car was customized with matched and balanced components. Springs borrowed from a Model-T Ford were mounted crosswise beneath the rear axle to stabilize the car and keep it high after it had taken on its load. More than a hundred gallons of corn whiskey, centered behind the driver, improved the car's road-hugging ability.[13]

Many a night saw the powerful cars hurtling down narrow, twisting moonless roads, rumrunner and G-car side by side smashing fenders, sending sparks through Stygian nights as they jockeyed for the lead. A typical ridgerunner technique was the high-speed U-turn on a short, straight stretch of highway. Unlike movie stuntmen, who perform the trick in brief, carefully choreographed camera takes, drivers making this maneuver at sixty miles an hour on dark, narrow, bumpy roads needed raw courage and split-second timing. The difference between a breathtaking escape and sudden death depended on the driver's ability to spin his steering wheel in a full circle while exerting precise and simultaneous pressure on accelerator, handbrake, clutch and gearshift.

Agents matched the move or lost the chase. Or crashed.

Some luggers installed smoke bombs: burning rags soaked with creosote and crankcase oil, spewing black smoke that clung to a pursuer's windshield. Others used a tank with a cable release to spread oil across the highway—a gimmick they'd use on a curve so the agent's car would crash. The first six years after the repeal of Prohibition saw seven ATF men killed during these high-speed chases, but these "unfair" tactics went out of fashion when Congress provided stiff penalties for anyone possessing a car equipped with such devices.[14]

Another technique was the sudden, midchase stop on a gravel road. When the G-car halted behind him, the transporter would ram his accelerator to the floor. Spinning wheels spewed stones that extinguished the agents' headlights, while the liquor-lugger raced into the night to lose himself in clouds of dust. This was an accepted practice, and one driver used it constantly until the night he miscalculated. Swerving from the highway onto a favorite gravel lane, he lost control and skidded into a ditch. Then he breached etiquette by shooting at the agents. By the time his pursuers got a chance for a clear shot, he'd run out of ammo and fled into the woods.

A few days later, his lawyer visited ATF to complain. "It's what you're doing to my client."

"I don't know what you're talking about," a supervisor told him.

"No? Well, he tells me a couple of your agents drove over to the creek where he was washing his car yesterday."

"Yes?"

"And, well, they weren't bumble bees he heard whizzing past his head. Are you people trying to kill him?"

"That's ridiculous, counselor. Our men always hit what they're aiming at."[15]

By the mid 1950s, the moonshine problem had grown out of hand. Some bootleggers were building mobile distilleries on trucks and house trailers. Others constructed modern plants in mineshafts and warehouses, barges and dairy barns, even under a backyard swimming pool.

Lazy bootleggers sealed the joints of their stills with lead solder or used old auto radiators for condensers—little time savers that laced their product with poisonous lead salts. Cities were plagued by epidemics of sickened consumers—

44

some went blind and some died—but that didn't bother the moonshiners. They had a slogan: "This liquor's made to sell, not to drink."

One bootleg ring erected a string of distilleries across fifteen counties in three states and hired vicious hoodlums who conscripted hundreds of independent moonshiners into a superefficient organization. Local lawmen were corrupted. Suspected informers were murdered by car bomb and machine gun, gangland style.

The Licensed Beverage Industry organization estimated that corn whiskey accounted for fully 20 percent of the booze consumed nationwide. While legitimate distillers made anywhere from $1.60 to $4.00 a gallon, depending on the brand of liquor, bootleggers were producing a gallon of white lightning for $1.00 and wholesaling it for $8.00. None of this 700-percent profit was wasted on licenses, purity standards, taxes or employee fringe benefits. The liquor lobby pressed the government for stronger enforcement.[16]

In 1957 Treasury hired sixty-three new agents, bringing ATF's strength to 975. The southeastern states were saturated with manpower, and a concentrated effort was launched with all the precision and discipline of a military campaign. Squads of agents swept across the countryside arresting moonshiners and smashing their stills. Roving patrols intercepted loads headed into the cities. Raiding parties hit the Dixie syndicate's drops, fronts and major customers. Special squads focused on high-level racketeers. Prisoners turned informer and bosses went to prisons.

But there have never been enough federal agents to round up all the criminals in the country. The key to ATF's victory was the same strategy Eliot Ness had used against Al Capone: cut the racketeers' profits to halt payoffs. Diminished graft motivates corrupt state and local officials to resume law enforcement. When that happens, the syndicate is washed up.[17]

The late fifties also brought a resurgence of Prohibition-style bootlegging to the northeast. Mafia-built column distilleries sprouted two and three stories high. Each one gushed a thousand gallons a day of 180-proof alcohol. The mobs set up rectifying plants to cut, color and flavor their product. Bottles were labeled with phony Canadian brand names to pass as foreign whiskey, "smuggled in"—a ploy to avoid the necessity of forging federal tax stamps.

Bootlegging carried a five-year prison term; counterfeiting the tax stamp could get a guy fifteen years.

Reading, Pennsylvania, had the busiest red-light district on the eastern seaboard, the biggest dice game east of the Mississippi, and an alcohol plant turning out 4,800 gallons a day—the largest illegal still set up since Prohibition. The small city was so thoroughly corrupted from the mayor on down that on June 7, 1958, ATF agents were compelled to take over its police headquarters and "manage" its radio and telephone communications before they launched their raid.[18]

Two months later, agents raiding a distillery in Long Island, New York, finally nailed syndicate mastermind John Levigno. The bad news was that during its thirty-month run, Levigno's still had already cheated Uncle Sam out of $4.6 million in alcohol taxes. A year later, even before Levigno was brought to trial on that charge, ATF smashed a $50,000 distillery he'd built into three silo-like concrete coal hoppers that stood, of all places, on city-owned land in Brooklyn. Levigno's newest investment was a total loss. This operation was smashed before it shipped a single pint.[19]

ATF made a practice of monitoring sources of raw materials—sugar shipments and five-gallon cans left trails that often led to plants—so mobsters resorted to more devious tactics. That's why agents raiding a huge distillery in Endicott, New York, were so intrigued by a slip of paper found in the pocket of the operation's strawboss, Pasquale Turrigiano. It was a receipt for a payment on Turrigiano's bank loan—a payment made by the owner of the local Canada Dry bottling plant.

Soda bottlers use tons of sugar—enough to disguise diversions to illegal ventures. They also have the money to finance $40,000 operations like Turrigiano's. And this particular bottler, Joseph Barbara, had an interesting history: Born in Sicily, he'd been arrested twice for murders in Pennsylvania. Both cases were shelved for lack of evidence.

In 1946 Barbara had been arrested by ATF and convicted for illegally acquiring 300,000 pounds of sugar.

Once they'd noted the connection between Turrigiano and the soda bottler, agents checked Barbara's activities from time to time. And as usual, they took the local police into their confidence. One such officer was Sergeant Edgar Crosswell of the New York State Police.

It was a cool, cloudy November day in 1957 when Crosswell noticed the bottler's son reserving rooms at a local motel "for a convention." The sergeant cruised past Barbara's sprawling estate, and when he observed Turrigiano's car parked there beside several out-of-town vehicles, he telephoned Special Agent Arthur Rustin of ATF's Binghamton office.

"We'll be right there," Rustin told him. Half an hour later, he and Special Agent Kenneth Brown parked their G-car near the soda bottler's home and joined Crosswell in his black sedan to discuss the possibilities. The sergeant reported that a dozen guests had checked into the reserved motel rooms, but none had signed the register. A limousine was ferrying more men from the airport to the Appalachian estate.

At this point on that peaceful autumn day, these unfolding developments were nothing more than somewhat curious incidents involving a suspected Mafia don who also operated several legitimate businesses. Like so many little mysteries agents encountered in their daily routine, this one might turn out to be nothing at all. Some prominent lawmen even asserted that there was no Mafia. 'Twas a fairy tale, they said—a myth, an ancient figment of the fiction writer's imagination. But Treasury agents had been battling organized crime for too long, and Sergeant Crosswell's doubts evaporated when look-ups came in on some of the license plates: Big John Ormento, with three convictions for trafficking in narcotics; and Vito Genovese—the man identified by Treasury as the Boss of all Bosses.

"That does it," Crosswell said. "Let's go get them."

"For what?" Agent Rustin asked. "We've no evidence of any crime." Then he smiled. "But we could take a closer look."

Crosswell drove to the entrance of Joseph Barbara's estate and stopped. "Want to go in?"

Agent Brown, relatively quiet until now, mused, "It's true we've no evidence of any crime, but we do know there are some scary guys up there. I wonder if Mr. Barbara knows what kind of men have come to his convention."

Rustin nodded. "The poor man might be in danger. The least we can do is make sure he's all right."

"It's our *duty,*" Crosswell said, grinning. He radioed for assistance and placed troopers at strategic locations surrounding the fifty-three-acre property. Then he put his cruiser in gear and proceeded slowly up the long driveway.

Inside the mansion, Vito Genovese addressed the largest Mafia assembly ever known to law enforcement, telling the underworld executives gathered from across the country why he'd ordered the assassination of their former chief executioner, Albert Anastasia. The man had cheapened *Cosa Nostra* by selling memberships, Genovese said, and honor must be preserved.

While the Boss of Bosses redistributed Anastasia's rackets and territories, Crosswell's plain black police car circled in the wide parking lot behind Barbara's nine-car garage.

The garage screened the asphalt lot from Barbara's summer house and the barbecue pit where lesser hoods were enjoying a cookout. The three officers scanned the dozens of Lincolns, Chrysler Imperials and Cadillacs nestled fender to fender, and the state policeman remarked, "Nice cars for soda salesmen."

The investigators were busily copying license numbers when one of the minor hoodlums from the barbecue strolled around the corner of the garage and recognized the character of that plain sedan. Shock registered on his face and he froze for a moment before scurrying back to his fellow soldiers.

"Cops!" he shouted.

A runner was dispatched to alert the underworld generals.

Agent Rustin closed his notebook. "Any ideas?"

"Without a warrant," Brown said, "we've no authority to hang around."

"*We* have authority," the state trooper said, "on the

highway." Crosswell eased his cruiser back down the drive-way and parked across the exit. Agent Brown positioned his G-car so that approaching autos would have to negotiate a narrow gap.

The advantage of hindsight makes it obvious that Rustin, Brown and Crosswell were lifting a rock that concealed America's secret crime confederation. At the time, however, all they knew for sure was the risk they were taking. This was more than a mere confrontation with a horde of hoodlums. No crime was apparent, and the men inside Barbara's house had political connections. Politicians are unpredictable, and the IRS (of which ATF was still a part) loved telling people, "We're not policemen, we're tax collectors." If the Monday morning quarterbacks decided that the three lawmen had exceeded their authority, complaints would rain down from Albany and Washington.

But Rustin, Brown and Crosswell knew something else: They couldn't walk away without learning more.

Barbara's guests panicked. Some scrambled through fields and forests where troopers waited to greet them. Others hustled into long cars and hurried toward the highway.

It was a bit late for the ATF men to consider the IRS reaction.

The first limousine to reach the improvised roadblock was a Cadillac occupied by Boss of all Bosses Genovese. He and his companions alighted and produced identification.

"What were you men doing at Mr. Barbara's, Mr. Geno-vese?"

"We heard the poor man was sick. We just stopped in to visit him." And the softspoken racketeer added, "But then, I don't have to answer your questions, do I?"

"That's quite true."

"Thank you," Genovese said, accepting the return of his driver's license, "very much."

The roundup of fleeing racketeers netted sixty-three of the most notorious criminals in the country. Rustin and Brown sent out a call for reinforcements. Agents from ATF and Treasury's Bureau of Narcotics came in from New York and New Jersey to assist in the interrogations.

The racketeers were questioned at the nearby state police

barracks, and before long, newsmen were swarming into upstate New York. The agents, following normal Treasury procedure, stepped into the shadows. Sergeant Crosswell was doing a fine job of making announcements and granting interviews.

The event generated banner headlines for weeks, books and feature stories for years, but a decade would pass before ATF's role was publicly revealed, because Treasury's traditions include the canon: Gentlemen don't boast.[20]

A few years after he'd taken the "First Godfather" John Torrio into custody, Agent West would make another quiet arrest: Carlo Gambino, owner of an alky shipment. Gambino was destined one day to become the Mafia's Boss of all Bosses.

West got his share of gunfire in 1940 when a pair of Florida bootleggers opened fire and left him with four bullet wounds. One of the assailants died en route to the hospital. The other went to prison.

Lewis West retired to Mississippi with his wife in 1964. By 1991—an artist eighty years old and looking rather distinguished in black-rimmed glasses and a short white beard—his sculptures were on display in galleries and museums throughout the South.

Torrio was seventy-five when he suffered a heart attack in a Brooklyn barber shop and died on March 16, 1957.

Exactly two months later (and twenty years younger), Eliot Ness passed away in Coudersport, Pennsylvania. That autumn, publication of Oscar Fraley's *The Untouchables* would give him a fame in death he'd never known in life.

4

End of a
Hundred-Year War

Another such victory, [and] we are undone.
—attributed to Pyrrhus, by Bacon

John F. Kennedy was designing his New Frontier when I
joined ATF at Newark, in 1960. Scientists at Cape Canave-
ral were reaching for the moon. New Jersey gangsters—like
throwbacks to bygone days—were bootlegging. They
erected massive column distilleries, each one spewing a
thousand gallons a day of 180-proof alcohol. We found
them in factory buildings, in huge pits excavated beneath
the gutted shells of innocent-looking houses, even in the
bellies of barges anchored at city waterfronts. Each one was
costing Uncle Sam $140,000 a week in unpaid alcohol taxes.
The mob built plants to color and flavor the raw alcohol and
plaster the product with phony foreign labels so they could
say they'd smuggled it into the country. They couldn't sell it
as "Made in the USA" unless they sealed each bottle with a
federal tax stamp. They paid no tax—that was the whole
point of their racket—and counterfeiting a stamp could get
a guy fifteen years in prison. Bootlegging carried a mere five
years. Mobsters aren't stupid.

They sold their product through mob-owned taverns and
catering companies and anyone else they could intimidate
into buying the stuff.

ATF was still part of the IRS. Our mission was to protect
the revenue.

You'd never find a still by tailing the men who worked
there. From the day it began producing, the small-time
hoods who performed the labor lived on the premises. We

51

didn't bother following the bigshot financiers of organized crime; they never went near the stills.

The police were no help. No gangster invested tens of thousands of dollars in such an elaborate operation until he'd corrupted the local constabulary—cops who'd tip their Mafia masters the moment "the feds" came nosing around. Most police officers were honest, but—with no way of knowing who'd been bought—we dared not trust any of them. Citizens who stumbled on the secret were bribed or frightened into silence.

We weren't allowed to tap phones and our budget for informers was minuscule, so ATF watched sales of the raw materials required by a bootlegging enterprise—primarily vast quantities of sugar and five-gallon cans. Each district assigned an agent to leaf through thousands of invoices every week, looking for suspicious purchases. Officially, he was designated the Raw Materials Coordinator.

We called him the Sugar Dick.

No one realized it at the time, but the government's century-long war against bootleggers was nearly ended. The good guys had won.

Our "reward" made us wish we hadn't been so smart.

Growing up in a small town, graduating from the University of Maine, spending two years with the army in Korea and working as an insurance investigator for a few years, I was twenty-five and I'd never even seen a gangster. Then one day—new to ATF—I found myself in a Jersey City diner, seated just a few stools from two bonafide Mafiosi.

"Please, God, let my hand stop shaking." Every time I raised my cup, coffee sloshed into the saucer. My partner had sent me in because, as a new agent, I wouldn't be recognized, regardless of which bad guys showed up to join the meeting. I couldn't hear their conversation. I dared not look toward them.

Undoubtedly, their meeting concerned a transaction occurring down the street: the purchase of a truckload of sugar. We'd been tipped by a suspicious wholesaler. Special Agent Tom O'Connell posed as one of the laborers on the wholesaler's loading dock. The rest of us were scattered, in cars and on foot, throughout the commercial district.

When the suspect arrived, O'Connell used a special crayon to mark each hundred-pound sack loaded onto the man's green Ford boxtruck. Wherever the load turned up later, we'd be able to tie *these* suspects to *that* conspiracy. The driver strolled down the street to the diner, where he was seen shaking hands with an olive-complected man in an expensive brown suit. That's when my partner sent me in. "See what you can find out," he told me.

Up until then, I'd looked forward to each day's work. We took our government cars home at night because we were always on call, and we'd drive direct from home to the next day's assignment. We rarely went to the office. We seldom had to interview honest citizens, because they didn't know anything that would interest us, so we didn't have to dress up in suits and ties. We wore sport shirts and khakis, with a windbreaker to conceal our shoulder holsters. We weren't out to impress anyone with our natty appearance; we were out to be invisible. We drove old cars and classy cars, family sedans and flashy convertibles—most of them confiscated from our clientele for having been used to transport contraband liquor—so we could tail suspects, or pose as crooks to hang out with real criminals, or meet informers who wouldn't be caught dead speaking to a suit-and-tie investigator-type. Unless they wanted to be caught dead.

Mr. Brown Suit drove away from the diner in a shiny black Chrysler. An agent got his license number. The truck driver walked around the corner, met a man in a short-sleeved shirt and handed him an envelope. Mr. Shortsleeves went to the now-loaded truck. It had Pennsylvania license plates when it pulled in; now it bore South Carolina tags.

Five ATF cars followed the truck south on the Jersey Turnpike and handed it off via radio to cars from our Philadelphia office. They passed the surveillance to Baltimore agents, who followed it to Virginia and a big still that had been running for months.[1]

FBI chief J. Edgar Hoover was still telling the country there was no such thing as organized crime operating across state lines. Perhaps he was ill-informed.

On a rainy morning in Philadelphia, agents watched a truckload of five-gallon cans leave a wholesaler's loading dock and cross the bridge into Camden, New Jersey. The truck was accompanied by two tail cars driven by alert mobsters, their eyes peeled for signs of surveillance. When the cavalcade entered the Jersey Turnpike northbound, the agents pulled off. If the tail-car crew became suspicious, they'd signal the truck driver. He'd park his load and walk away. No one would ever return to that vehicle. Nothing about it would lead us to the bootleggers.[2]

So the agents pulled off. Better to let them go than risk getting burned.

This investigation had begun with a letter reporting "suspicious men" buying large quantities of five-gallon cans. The note named the wholesaler, but it didn't say who was buying the cans, or how many, or when they'd make their next pickup. It was unsigned.

The tipster had to be someone with knowledge of the transactions; someone who knew the purchases were irregular; someone who knew whom to tell. Agents identified all of the wholesaler's employees without alerting anyone that a probe was underway. Samples of each employee's penmanship were collected from banks, utility companies, rental leases. None matched the anonymous letter.

Specimens of handwriting by everyone in each employee's immediate family were obtained. A clerk's daughter had written the letter. The clerk was startled by the agents' visit, and frightened. Assured that her identity would remain secret, she pointed to one of the photos she was shown—of a known bootlegger—and she promised to alert the agents when the next delivery was scheduled.

She did, and the first load of cans was picked up; then agents discontinued the tail when they'd determined the direction the suspects drove from Philedelphia.

The next pickup occurred two weeks later. We had every road leading north through New Jersey covered—none of our cars closer than eighty miles to Philadelphia. By the time the suspects reached the agents posted on the Turnpike, the mob's tail cars had satisfied themselves there was no surveillance and dropped off. Special Agent Jerry Kolb, driving a dusty tan pickup, alternated with Special Agent Andy Shumack in an elderly Cadillac to keep the truckload of five-gallon cans in sight until it parked behind a row of garages on Slater Street in Paterson.

Two of us perched among bushes on a ledge in Garrett Park overlooking the garages. Two men showed up in a different truck; my partner recognized them from past cases and radioed the G-cars parked on nearby streets. They tailed the new truck to a factory complex on the other side of town. At midnight, agents Bob Rose and Tom O'Connell prowled the factory rooftops and detected the distinctive yeasty odor of fermenting mash. That odor, the cans purchased under a phony name and the presence of known bootleggers were enough for a search warrant.

When the suspects' truck arrived the next morning, its driver used a walkie-talkie to radio inside and make sure all was well. The overhead door began to lift.

Six of us leaped from a delivery van parked fifty feet away. Two agents ahead of me grabbed the driver and his helper. Adrenaline banished the tremors I'd experienced sitting close to those gangsters in the Jersey City diner a few weeks earlier. I slipped past the truck, ran inside—past huge bags of insulation stacked high to screen the interior from passersby—and spotted a man I'd tailed my first day on the job, Frank Siematowski. He stood beside the gleaming copper column and asked me, "What have you got?" Having received the radio message from the truck driver, he must have thought I was one of them.

"I've got you, Frank." I showed him the gold badge.

My first arrest.

The racketeer who owned the still had never been there. There were no fingerprints to link him to the crime, no signed check, no documents. The only person he'd even talked to about the operation was his strawboss—the man he'd hired to set up the distillery and run it. We'd caught him, but strawbosses didn't blab unless they were contemplating suicide. Even if one did testify, his unsupported word would be worthless.

So the bigshot went free, having already made a tidy profit. Raids were a routine business expense. For $30,000, he'd soon have another still going.

* * *

We couldn't make any real headway smashing stills after they'd already cheated Uncle Sam out of $600,000 a month in alcohol revenues—$2 million in 1994 dollars. Considering the money to be made and an endless pool of brawny laborers—willing to work and smart enough to keep their mouths shut—bootlegging would continue until we eliminated the profits. The only way to do that was to hit the distillery before it produced enough booze to cover the costs of building it.

There were only eight Mafia men in New Jersey with the knowledge and experience to have a column still constructed, recruit the workers, arrange the clandestine acquisition of raw materials and make the contacts for distribution. These were the strawbosses—the key men to whom Mafia chiefs entrusted their investments.

An agent devised the Major Violator Program. Each strawboss became the sole assignment of a senior special agent. Instead of hunting ratholes, we'd watch the rats.

On a winter night in 1961, Special Agent Jerry Kolb parked his G-car on a sloping street of single-family homes in Nutley, New Jersey. At the foot of that street, a road. Just beyond that road, a narrow river. Across that river, in Lyndhurst, a brightly lite diner.

Kolb was a tall man in his early thirties with dark-rimmed glasses and brown curly hair clipped short. Prim, precise and highly intelligent, Kolb rarely went home until he'd put his Major Violator to bed.

Beside Kolb sat a rookie with just seven months on the job. That was me.

No one near the diner could see our G-car in the darkness of that narrow street across the river, but the need to remain inconspicuous was absolute. And so, although it was January and the temperature well below freezing, we couldn't run the engine to use the car's heater. Exhaust fumes would attract eyes to the G-car; a nervous neighbor, noticing strangers near his home, might call the police. We'd have to identify ourselves. The patrolman would advise the dispatcher who'd sent him to check out the "suspicious persons in a parked car," and rumors would get around. Sometimes to the wrong people.

Among ATF agents, risking discovery for mere comfort was a sign of personal weakness, so Kolb and I kept our gloves on and our mackinaws buttoned tight. Our breath plumed in the frigid air. From time to time, I'd scrape the rime from the inside of the windshield.

We were watching Angelo "Slim" DiOrio—an old, experienced strawboss with a string of stills stretching back to Prohibition days. He was Jerry Kolb's Major Violator.

Within weeks of receiving the assignment, Kolb knew DiOrio's friends, male and female. He knew DiOrio's haunts and his uncomplicated habits: mornings playing cards with hoodlum cronies at the Fifth Ward Democratic Club in Newark; lunch at the Arlington Diner in suburban Lyndhurst, where he nibbled and chatted with friends. Dinner there, too, unless he visited his twenty-six-year-old girlfriend's apartment. Kolb noticed that the aging hoodlum's dalliances were brief, and apparently tiring.

Sometimes Kolb lunched at the Arlington, just a few feet from his subject, but the conversational snippets he overheard were invariably useless. Kolb collected license numbers—anyone who spoke with DiOrio—and spent some days checking their owners' backgrounds. Prosaic work until DiOrio's routine changed, as it had twice before.

The first time was the previous June. Kolb asked for help. We'd tailed DiOrio to a huge still under construction in a four-story chickenhouse in southern Jersey. After every dollar of the financier's investment had been sunk into the plant, equipment and vehicles, Kolb led the raid. DiOrio and his crew went free on bail to await trial.

Then in September, Kolb had spotted DiOrio meeting three men in a pea-green Mercury. It was registered to a fictitious address. Teams tailed the Merc to a dairy farm eighty miles north of Newark. An eighty-foot pit, excavated inside a Dutch barn, made room for a towering copper column. We watched from the woods. When the smokestack puffed, we hit. DiOrio recognized some of us this time. After the initial excitement, postraid etiquette was observed: Prisoners maintained a stoic silence; agents stifled our satisfaction. Treasury had taught us it's rude to gloat.

DiOrio faced a dilemma. He owed his boss a debt for two financial catastrophes. Free on bail, he was obliged—if the

Mafia chief so desired—to erase this blot on his profession-al reputation. One success would convert disaster into riches.

Now, while Kolb and I shivered and stamped our feet in the G-car across the river, DiOrio enjoyed a late roast beef dinner and hot coffee in the cozy diner. I wiped my scarf across the windshield just in time to see a squat, swarthy man emerge from a Pontiac parked beside the diner. He went inside and sat down with DiOrio. Kolb raised his binoculars, but he couldn't read the Pontiac's license num-ber. We drove across the bridge, two blocks south of where we'd been parked, made a pass, glimpsed DiOrio's compan-ion through the window. I jotted the Pontiac's tag number and asked, "Want me to go in?"

"No need," Kolb drove on. "It's Jimmy the Weasel."

James "The Weasel" Roselli was a veteran still foreman. The car he drove was registered to a vacant lot. We switched our surveillance to him.

Six nights later, in Jersey City, shortly after midnight, the Weasel supervised four men struggling to unload five canvas-covered cylinders from a large truck. As they trun-dled the last section across the dock and into the eight-story loft building, its shroud slipped. Dim light glinted on penny-bright copper. The two agents on a nearby rooftop packed their equipment and departed quietly.

At four o'clock the next morning, twenty-five of us assembled in the squadroom of ATF's fifth-floor suite across from MacArthur Park in Newark. Some stood in clusters, sipping coffee. A few used the lull to catch up on paperwork. When the raid leader rapped for attention, all eyes focused on a table-sized replica of the Jersey City loft building.

Forty minutes later, we climbed into the rear of an old box truck. The doors swung shut. The rumbling ride began. Two agents had gone ahead to notify Jersey City police—we wouldn't embarrass the honest cops by making it obvious they'd been kept in the dark. After the raid, precinct captains and detectives would give interviews and pose for news photographers. Treasury had taught us to avoid re-porters. We took pride in working quietly.

Some of us squatted on the floor of the swaying truck. Others braced themselves against its walls. A few exchanged jokes. I felt the same nausea I'd experienced as stagefright when I'd performed in high-school plays. Half an hour later, we heard our driver radio the G-cars. The truck stopped, backed up, halted with a jolt. The latch clicked. The doors swung wide. We surged across the loading dock. Startled workers from the legitimate warehouse occupying lower floors whirled, froze, stood agape. G-cars and marked police cruisers ringed the building.

Four agents commandeered the freight elevator. Some of us rushed up the concrete stairs to the fifth floor. I was hacking at the padlocked metal fire door with my ax when Andy Shumack shouldered me aside and snipped the hasp with his bolt cutters. We swarmed inside.

The gleaming copper column, thirty inches in diameter, reached up through holes hacked in the concrete floors of the sixth and seventh stories. Walls were lined with stacks of shiny five-gallon cans and hundred-pound sugar sacks; 20,000 gallons of mash bubbled in immense wooden vats.

DiOrio and his cohorts were found in the basement, trying to rejuvenate an ailing oil furnace. DiOrio shook his head and held his wrists forward for the handcuffs. "Somebody's been talking, right? Somebody's tipping you guys off."

Agent Kolb smiled. "You have the right to remain silent."

They always thought there'd been a tip-off.

Two days later, just minutes after midnight, a long black Cadillac entered New York's Holland Tunnel to emerge in Jersey City. It rolled into the deserted lot beside the loft building that had housed DiOrio's last plant. Its headlights went out. Three men stepped onto the gravel; one wore a blindfold. The driver removed the black cloth and they mounted the creaking wooden steps to the loading platform. The tall man in the dark topcoat and snapbrim fedora rapped three times on the corrugated metal door of the freight elevator.

From inside, a muffled, "Who's that?"

"Open up," the tall man commanded. "It's me."

The door lifted, its rusty chain rasping over its pulleys. A man in workclothes smiled nervously. "Everything'll be all right pretty soon, Boss."

No one spoke as the elevator creaked up to the fifth floor. A man on a ladder was tightening bolts on the second section of the copper column. "Have it going in a couple hours, tops," he said.

The tall man grunted.

The man who'd been blindfolded gazed about—at the ten-foot stacks of cans, at the tons of sugar. He climbed a ladder, peered into one of the mash vats. "Real nice," he drawled. "Just about ready to run." He was the top lieutenant to a Florida syndicate boss, in New York to finalize a pact with Manhattan gangsters. Satisfied, he'd take a New Yorker back home for an insider's look at the Miami setup. He hadn't objected when these men blindfolded him. He appreciated good security, and this tour of the Big Apple distillery was a pleasant surprise.

He'd have been even more surprised had he known he was not in upstate New York, where the tall man had said he was taking him. And surprise would have given way to astonishment, had he even suspected that he was the only crook in the building.

Everyone else—the snarling boss, the stolid bodyguard, the roughclad still workers—all of them were agents. A month later, after the Florida boss had opened his complete operation to the "big city racketeer," the Miami gang felt even more dejected than DiOrio. Warrants and handcuffs were poor pay for the southerners' generous hospitality.[3]

Little things like that can shake a man's faith in his government.

We knew we should thank Slim DiOrio for providing a realistic setting for our little undercover play, but expressing gratitude might seem like rubbing it in.

And people think being a gentleman is easy.

Special Agent John W. "Bill" Kern traced some cardboard cartons we'd seized at a column distillery—boxes used to ship five-gallon cans of 180-proof alky—to a wholesaler on New York's lower East Side. The wholesaler chose the photo of a man we'd caught in the raid. "That's the guy that made the deal."

The wholesaler recounted how the man had questioned

him about the cartons' weight capacity, delivery and cost. "The other guy didn't say a word."

Kern, a tall and powerfully built lawyer who'd once wrestled giant prizefighter Primo Carnera "for the fun of it," asked the man, "Other guy? What other guy?"

"Beats me," said the wholesaler, waving his hand over the photos on his counter. "He isn't here."

Kern brought another set from his briefcase. "Try these."

The man turned them over slowly and stopped at the mugshot of Freddy Salerno. "He's older than in this picture, but that's him."

Kern suppressed his excitement. "You're sure?"

Salerno was a mob chieftain who'd begun his rise to power as an enforcer. Intelligence credited him with thirteen assassinations on behalf of the Organization. IRS Commissioner Sheldon Cohen described Salerno as "ruthless and notorious . . . with a long record including crimes of violence dating back to 1931 . . . head of a strongly entrenched interstate illicit alcohol manufacturing and distribution syndicate with large scale operations on the East Coast."

"Sure I'm sure," the wholesaler replied to Kern. "I'm positive."

"Tell me exactly what he did."

"He didn't do anything. Just stood over there by the door while this other guy did all the talking."

"Nothing at all?"

"Never said a word. Just, after this first guy got all the poop from me about the cartons"—the wholesaler tapped the first photo he'd identified—"he went over and told it to this other guy." He planted a finger on the second picture.

"Yes, and . . ."

"And nothing. He told everything I said to the other guy and asked if it was okay."

"Go on."

"And the other guy nodded. That's all. I guess that don't mean much, huh?"

But it did. Under federal law, anyone acting to further a crime is guilty of conspiracy. Salerno drew the max—five years' imprisonment. For nodding his head. He came out a broken man, his power gone, his rackets parceled out to other mobsters.

Within six months, ATF's Major Violator Program sent ninety-seven big-time crooks to prisons across the country.

Special Agent Bill Kern became the leading expert on the U.S. conspiracy statute, conducted seminars for agents, and co-authored (with another ATF agent) the book that Treasury and the Justice Department adopted as the standard training material. Chief Justice Warren Burger termed the text "the best I've ever seen on the topic of conspiracy" and ordered twenty copies for his colleagues on the Supreme Court. When Kern retired from ATF, he accepted invitations from several top-rated law schools to instruct embryo attorneys in the complexities of that law.

Agents did a creditable job because we liked the work and we enjoyed taking on an adversary—the Mafia—that the best-known bureau was afraid to challenge. Unfortunately, we were less enthusiastic about the men who'd floated to the top in our revenue-oriented agency.

In 1962 field managers complained of difficulty in recruiting suitable candidates for agent positions. Treasury's personnel specialists found something more: ATF's quit rate—agents leaving for reasons other than retirement—was 4 percent: well below the government average, but the Secret Service's quit rate was only 2 percent; for Customs agents, a mere 1 percent. The reason? According to the department's report, ATF executives had saved money by bastardizing the normal progression of pay-grade increases, stalling ATF agents at lower levels than their peers in other agencies.

Treasury suggested that ATF managers get in line with the others.

Instead, many managers—mostly in the South, where liquor cases were abundant and uncomplicated—alleviated their manpower shortages by hiring men who'd never be capable of solving anything more complex than a simple catch-'em-and-charge-'em still case. They even signed these men on as agents before completing their background checks. One such routine investigation revealed that a new agent, already on the job with ATF, had played footsie with bootleggers while employed as a state liquor agent. Fired by

Treasury, he was later arrested for bootlegging. And still later, he was convicted in the brutal murder of three policemen.[4]

Two years passed before ATF chiefs eliminated that substandard salary level.

In 1963 illicit liquor defendants peaked at 5,500 nationwide. "Protecting the revenue" was still ATF's first priority, but the Mafia was getting out of the bootleg business. Our surveillance stints became so boring that we'd while away the dreary hours playing chess. With a magnetic board on the front seat between us, I'd watch our suspect's car while my partner moved; he'd watch while I decided on my move. When the suspect drove away, we'd lay the board on the rear seat and take up the tail.

The Major Violator Program took its toll, and rising sugar prices cut into the bootleggers' profits. By 1979 bootleg defendants had plummeted to a paltry seventy-five. Smart crooks shifted to other rackets, but we couldn't pursue the gangsters we knew so well because narcotics, counterfeiting, smuggling, illegal gambling and the ever-popular tax evasion were the business of other Treasury units.

Some people say that small, highly specialized agencies are best. It's odd, but those who praise Treasury's separate-specialized-agency setup never recommend the same "improvement" for the FBI. We *could* subdivide the G-men into five or six small specialty bureaus: one mini-FBI for interstate thefts, another for bank robberies, another to handle kidnapping, a fourth for counterespionage, and round it off with a catchall bureau to take care of people who misuse the Smoky Bear symbol or drive a stolen car across a state line. They'd have five administrative hierarchies, five different filing systems, five bands of radio frequencies, five vehicle fleets. They'd open five separate offices in cities across the country, each with its own agent-in-charge, receptionist, secretaries, support staffs and agent cadre. If one of these mini-FBIs needed help, they wouldn't enlist their colleagues in those other, separate mini-FBIs. They'd pay for air fares and hotels to bring agents from distant offices of their own little outfit.

If that seems idiotic and inefficient, why is it so good for Treasury?

And so, since we'd suppressed bootlegging in northern New Jersey and we had no other function, we received our reward for a job well done: seventeen of ATF-Newark's twenty-five man force were transferred out.

The Secret Service happened to be recruiting new agents to handle an upsurge in counterfeiting and increased protection duties in the wake of the Kennedy assassination; the Bureau of Narcotics (at that time a Treasury agency) was hiring more agents to combat the burgeoning drug trade there. The men they'd test, interview, investigate, select and hire for their Newark offices would have identical qualifications to those of us who were moved from Newark with our families and household goods at a cost equaling twenty agents' annual salaries. While these rookies were given the same training we'd already completed, we were starting fresh in cities where we knew none of the underworld characters, nothing of the local geography. I was sent to Omaha.

Shakespeare wrote that "nothing can seem foul to those that win."

Shakespeare never worked for the Treasury Department.

5

New Battlefields

A lie that is half a truth is ever the blackest of lies.
—Alfred, Lord Tennyson

With the conquest of bootlegging everywhere except in the
Deep South, there was no reason for ATF's existence
elsewhere. The only work its agents could do—the only
other laws under its jurisdiction—were two firearms laws
enacted decades earlier as reactions to the Capone and
Dillinger era of the 1930s.

One of these statutes, the National Firearms Act (NFA),
required that machine guns, sawed-off shotguns and
silencers—the so-called gangster guns—be registered. Registration was free; making or selling one of these weapons
incurred a $200.00 tax. Honest citizens complied and kept
their weapons. Criminals, who invariably defied the law,
could be jailed without waiting for them to use the firearm
on innocent victims. Throughout the thirty years since the
NFA was passed, few such firearms showed up in crimes of
violence.

The NFA was a revenue law because, while the Constitution reserves ordinary police authority to the states, Congress retained the power to tax. The legislature enacted the
other statute—the Federal Firearms Act (FFA)—under the
government's right to regulate interstate commerce.

Originally proposed by President Franklin Roosevelt's
attorney general, the FFA might have been effective, but the
National Rifle Association launched what they termed a
"campaign to save the sportsmen's guns" and offered a bill
of their own.[1]

Ever courageous, Congress enacted the gun club's version.

The statute required gun dealers to be licensed, but only if they did business across state lines. ATF couldn't touch the traffic in stolen firearms unless agents proved the business operated interstate. Licensed dealers had to keep sales records, but they weren't required to verify a customer's identity and it wasn't illegal for buyers to use phony names. The dealer's license only cost a dollar a year, but few crooks wasted their time applying for one because wholesalers could ship tons of guns via the United Parcel Service without verifying that a customer used his true name or really had a license. Extremist paramilitary groups like the Minutemen bought bazookas by mail for $24.95, mortars for $19.95 and antitank cannons at $400.00 each. It was quite legal.

Lee Harvey Oswald got the guns he used to murder Dallas police officer Tippitt and assassinate President John F. Kennedy via mail order, under a fictitious name. None of these acts constituted a crime until he pulled the triggers.

Convicted felons could have all the guns they wanted, as long as they didn't get caught taking one across a state line.

The NRA called this "a workable law . . . all the law [the attorney general] needs."[2]

NRA member Al Nussbaum demonstrated the law's workability.

Nussbaum's story began in 1962, when Customs and ATF agents caught Thomas Wilcoxin taking a Finnish antitank gun across the Florida state line. It would have been legal if Wilcoxin hadn't been a convicted felon. He said the weapon was destined for a licensed gun dealer named Karl Kessler at 182 Parade Street in Buffalo, New York.

The Parade Street premises were vacant when ATF men arrived. No gun shop, just a few abandoned hand grenades (perfectly legal in 1962) and shipping labels addressed to Charles Gorman and Glenn Davis. Davis's apartment was empty. Neighbor's descriptions matched that of Wilcoxin's son, Bob. He was an excon too.

The other name on those shipping labels—Gorman— had been used to order a new barrel for a Thompson machine gun by mail. That wasn't illegal either, unless and until the barrel was used to reactivate a DEWAT, deactivated war trophy. Next, the agents learned that "Gorman" and "Kessler" were both aliases for Al Nussbaum.

Nussbaum loved guns. Arrested at eighteen for stealing one, he was caught five years later taking an unregistered machine gun across a state line. He served three years and came out in 1960. His parole officer described him as a model citizen, working hard to succeed in the business world. "He's even taking correspondence courses."

The agents obtained a list of the subjects Nussbaum was studying: criminology, chemistry, physics, firearms, locks, safes and explosives. They decided to visit him.

"Pretty busy right now," Nussbaum said, smiling. "Can you come around tomorrow?"

The agents had no choice. There was no law against having hand grenades, and felons could buy all the guns they liked under phony names unless ATF proved they'd received them across a state line. The agents were sure Nussbaum had used the Kessler alias, but they couldn't act until *after* they proved that he'd signed that name to the license application.

"Okay," said one agent with a shrug, "see you tomorrow."

Nussbaum fled that night.

New York City police recovered a machine gun near the scene of a bank robbery where a guard was killed. It had a new barrel. The FBI tracked down buyers of a thousand such barrels in twenty-four states. When they came to the Buffalo hotel where "Kessler's" barrel was shipped, the desk clerk mentioned that ATF had asked about the same man.

The Treasury agents gave G-men the names, photos and fingerprints of the suspects Nussbaum and Bob Wilcoxin. Armed with these, the FBI established that over the past year, starting shortly after Nussbaum's release from prison on the old machine gun charge, he and Wilcoxin had heisted a quarter of a million dollars from eight banks and shot a New York City policeman. A third gang member had murdered that bank guard. The G-men found a farm where Nussbaum had stashed pistols, rifles, even mortars—an arsenal the FBI called "unequaled in the annals of crime." Nussbaum and Wilcoxin remained on the FBI's top-ten fugitive list for nearly a year—until Nussbaum phoned his wife and asked her to meet him. She turned him in.

Wilcoxin made the mistake of choosing to hide in a quiet residential neighborhood, across the street from the home of an FBI agent.[3]

Some states passed their own laws to limit criminal access to guns. For the most part, they were hollow. Outlaws circumvented these statutes by simply hopping across a state line. By 1965, 87 percent of the firearms used in Massachusetts crimes (including six of the seven used to murder police officers) had been bought beyond the jurisdiction of that state's authorities. Police files bulged with records of mobsters and murderers who'd armed themselves in Maine, Vermont and New Hampshire—states where 70 percent of all the guns sold by licensed gunshops were bought by Massachusetts residents.[4]

Nebraska, where I'd been transferred, ranked seventh in the percentage of murders by firearm. Federal laws were inadequate, but that didn't matter much. ATF was still an arm of the IRS, and they didn't want us doing anything that didn't produce revenue.

Three of us were stationed in Omaha. We could have helped the Secret Service probe threats to the president or track down counterfeiters. Or assisted Treasury's lone Bureau of Narcotics agent—his assigned territory reached all the way into Minnesota. Instead, the IRS had us making sure that taverns purchased the $54.00 federal liquor dealer's tax stamp. When I tracked the trio that had robbed Zink's Bar with a sawed-off shotgun and turned them over to police (the penalty for armed robbery was greater than for the weapons offense) IRS chiefs groaned because we didn't even get a conviction statistic.[6]

Nebraska didn't want any new gun law. Their state legislature even enshrined an old NRA canard into an official resolution:[7]

Whereas no nation in modern times has fallen to tyranny without first imposing upon itself a strict system of firearms controls and registration: Now,

68

therefore, let it be *Resolved by the Members of the Nebraska Legislature in the 75th session assembled.* That this body, (1) is opposed to Federal legislation which interferes with the rights of our law-abiding citizens under the second amendment to the U.S. Constitution. . . .

That authoritative ring of history snags on some awkward facts. The Nazis never required their citizens to register guns. The Soviet Union didn't prohibit Russians from having firearms. In Communist China, citizen access to firearms was evident from articles in the NRA's own publications: Red Chinese marksmen consistently beat the NRA-trained U.S. competitors in every significant shooting event.[8]

Connecticut senator Tom Dodd tried to make a gun law that would let ATF attack violent crime. He was opposed vociferously by Michigan congressman John Dingell.

Dingell was on the NRA's Board of Directors.[9]

The NRA mailed frightening exaggerations of Dodd's proposed law to its members again and again, even after Dodd had contacted NRA leaders to correct these "errors." When Dodd asked NRA executive vice president Franklin Orth about these repeated falsehoods, Orth insisted piously, "There is no attempt at deliberate misrepresentation."

Hilliard Comstock, past president of the NRA and current chairman of its legislative committee, was claiming that the American Legion and the Boy Scouts of America opposed Dodd's bill. Dodd asked him, "Were the Boy Scouts against the bill?"

Under oath now, Comstock replied, "Not opposing the bill, but people high in the Council of the Boy Scouts."

"Who are they?"

"Well, I forget the name of the man."[11]

While the NRA men weaseled before the Senate subcommittee, *Charade,* a film starring Cary Grant as a U.S. Treasury agent in Paris, was playing in Washington theaters. In one scene, costar Audrey Hepburn asks him, "Why do people lie?"

69

"Generally," he replies, "it's because they want something and the truth won't get it for them."

The NRA's lies worked. The 89th Congress went home without passing a gun law.

In Omaha, some teens were threatened with a sawed-off shotgun in the parking lot outside the Polish Hall. I identified the assailant as a recently paroled excon named Ron Kirby, tracked him down and took the gun away from him. But my case was put on hold because a man named Haynes, charged with the same offense in Texas, was appealing his case to the Supreme Court. Eventually, the high court held that requiring a person to register a "gangster gun" violated his Fifth Amendment privilege by causing him to admit a previous offense—i.e., having made or received that weapon without ATF permission.

The National Firearms Act was dead.

So the Kirby case was dropped. He served a few months on a local conviction for pointing a pistol at two city detectives. Released from jail, he took two friends and a revolver to the home of a man named Batson who'd dated Kirby's girlfriend while Kirby languished in a cell. He dragged Batson to the basement, forced him to kneel between the washer and dryer, and he blew the man's brains out.[12]

The state of Nebraska gave Kirby a life sentence. Batson's family was *so* pleased.

On April 7, 1967, NRA president Harold Glassen expressed his fear that Senator Dodd's persistent efforts would get some sort of gun law through Congress. Addressing his followers with a rare candor, Glassen revealed his true fears. "Let us be sure that when [it] is passed," he warned, "it is not something that carries the seeds of destruction of the National Rifle Association."[13]

NRA members buried Congress in frenzied echoes of Glassen's fears.

The body count of victims murdered by firearm climbed 37 percent that year.[14]

* * *

Violent crimes are easy to commit, hard to prove. Throughout the 1960s, less than 5 percent of all robberies brought prison terms. Police have their highest success rate with the ultimate crime and yet, even up through the 1990s, about one in five murders resulted in a homicide conviction.[15] But we still have gun lovers resisting legislation that lets officers disarm outlaws before innocents are robbed or killed. Harking back to an Old West they've only seen in cowboy movies—an era that never really existed quite the way Hollywood would have us believe—they yearn wistfully for frontier justice, Texas style.

The case that introduced me to Texas-style justice began on the breezy afternoon of June 3, 1968, after ATF had granted my request for a transfer to Kansas City, Missouri. Ronald Closterman, a Kansas City police sergeant, received an informant's tip that a man at the Alton Hotel had a condom filled with hashish and a sawed-off shotgun in the trunk of a red Cadillac convertible with Texas license plates. The Alton Hotel catered to working-class transients with a smattering of local denizens—whores, drunks and druggies. Closterman sent detectives Bill Linhart and Donald Grasher to investigate.

The red 1967 Cadillac with Texas tags was parked at the Alton, as advertised. When a man matching the informant's description of the suspect drove it away, the detectives halted him and asked him to open his trunk. No drugs now, but the double-barreled shotgun, its barrels cut to fourteen inches, its stock fashioned into a short pistol grip. The detectives took man and gun to headquarters and notified ATF.

Special Agent Jack Smith made the IRS happy by seizing the Caddy convertible. I talked to the detectives and went through the suspect's billfold: laminated Texas driver's license, registration for the Cadillac, Social Security card, credit cards and a folded-up certified photocopy of a birth certificate—all in the name of Charles S. Stoughtenborough. Business cards pegged him as a salesman for Slendertron exercise machines.

"Stoughtenborough" didn't seem like the handle a crook would choose for an alias, but how many men carried photocopies of their birth certificate in their wallets? How many men in their midthirties owned a Social Security card that looked freshly printed—one with big red numerals? Duplicates replacing lost cards came with the number typed in.

Stepping into the room marked "Interrogation," I saw a tall blond man with clear blue eyes seated calmly on a straight-backed wooden chair at the plain oak table. He was well built, clean cut, with the sleeves of his expensive-looking gold-knit sweater shoved halfway up his forearms. If anything, he looked collegiate.

Bright sunlight streamed through the steel-mesh screened window onto his hands, resting comfortably on the table that was scarred by cigarette burns. I sat across from him and showed him my credentials. "I'm here about the shotgun." I recited his *Miranda* warnings.

He understood, he said, and he didn't care to call a lawyer. "Okay, so I had the gun. A man has a right to defend himself."

"What's your name?"

"Stoughtenborough. Charles Stoughtenborough." He looked candid, honest, respectable.

I just stared at him.

A minute of silence seems very long when it ticks by, second by second, and you know that the conversation isn't over. You know there are more questions, still unasked. His placid manner deteriorated into a fidget. He picked at one of his well-gnawed fingernails. When another endless minute had ticked by, I asked, "What's your name?"

"They've got my papers. Check 'em out."

"You can get five years for that sawed-off shotgun, and your pretty car now belongs to Uncle Sam."

"My car? You're taking my car?"

"Sawed-off shotguns are contraband—illegal to possess, just like narcotics or counterfeit money. Any vehicle, vessel or aircraft used to transport contraband is forfeited to the government. What's your name?"

He rubbed his thumb across the black line of a cigarette burn at the edge of the table. "Okay, I'm Charles Harrelson."

"What do you do?"

"I collect debts for gamblers."

"How many arrests?"

"You'll find out when you pull the record."

"Suspense annoys me. How many arrests?"

"One. For armed robbery. In California. That's all."

"Convicted?"

He nodded.

"Tell me about the gun."

He smiled and shook his head.

Released on $2,500 bail, he had one question before walking out. "How can I get my car back?"

"File a claim and cost bond, but it won't do you any good unless you're innocent."

A toll receipt we found in the Cadillac showed he had left the Oklahoma Turnpike at an interchange that had no exit until it entered Missouri. Being a convicted felon, if he'd brought that firearm across the state line he could get five years. If it was sawed off before he brought it over, he could get another five. We couldn't charge mere possession, since the Supreme Court's *Haynes* decision had nullified that crime, calling the registration requirement a violation of a criminal's Fifth Amendment rights, but "making" a gangster gun was still unlawful. If he'd cut the barrels himself, the total could come to fifteen years.

ATF Los Angeles checked his prior conviction. Harrelson and an accomplice had robbed an eighty-four-year-old doctor at gunpoint.

The shotgun was traced to Crawford Booth, owner of Backstage, Inc., a private club in Houston. He admitted buying it and lending it to Harrelson, but when Special Agent Lawrence Whatley showed Booth a photo of the weapon we'd seized, the club owner shook his head. "Oh, no. The gun I loaned Chuck was real long." But the serial number was the same.

Agent Whatley's report lay on my desk when I looked up to see Harrelson standing in front of me. He smiled and sat down. "How are you doing?"

"So-so. How've you been?"

"Not too bad."

"You know," I told him, "you don't have to talk to me."

"Yeah, I know."

"We've talked to Mr. Booth in Houston. He says the gun wasn't cut down when he gave it to you."

"Nah. I cut it off. Look, I'm wondering if there isn't some way I can get my car back."

"File a claim and cost bond—hey, didn't I tell you this already? We file a civil action against the car. If it wasn't used to transport—"

"Yeah, yeah," he said, looking disappointed. "You told me."

The next morning, assistant U.S. attorney William Kitchen told me Harrelson's lawyer had been in. "He's not disputing the charges, but he wants to get the car."

"Dammit, Bill, this is weird. The guy admits the crime and all he wants is that car."

"Probably needs it to pay his lawyer. That's why the lawyer's here—the car's his fee."

Agent Whatley called again from Houston. "The Texas Rangers think Harrelson's a contract killer." Two days before Harrelson had departed from Houston, a carpet company executive named Alan Berg had vanished. Rumor had it he owed money to gamblers.

Special Agent Duane Nichols and I searched the Cadillac again, this time looking for clues smaller than guns or drugs. The carpeting in its trunk had been replaced with a scrap of rug. The cardboard wall lining the trunk compartment was pierced by two holes to accommodate hooks that held it in place. The back side on one hole marked the beginning of a brownish dried trickle.

Blood.

Later, I'd learn that on July 6—a month after Harrelson's release on bail from our charges in Kansas City—he'd flown from Houston to McAllen, Texas, with a curly-haired excon named Jerry Watkins. They rented a car. Watkins drove. They explored the roads south of town until they came to an abandoned shack. Harrelson looked the area over, and they returned to McAllen for a late lunch at a motel dining room.

Harrelson telephoned the home of Sam Degalia, a grain and cotton broker.

When Degalia hung up, he walked out to his pool and

informed his wife and kids that he "had to see a man in McAllen about a grain deal."

He met Harrelson at a motel restaurant. They had a cup of coffee and departed. Watkins drove, with Harrelson beside him in front and Degalia alone in the back seat. Degalia and Harrelson talked grain deals until Watkins entered the road to the abandoned shack. That's when Harrelson pointed a gun at the astonished broker.

"My god!" Degalia shouted. "What's the matter?"

Harrelson snapped, "Get on the floor."

Degalia tried to obey, but he was 6'2" and 210 pounds. He couldn't get his shoulders below the seat level. Harrelson told Watkins, "Move the seat forward." He did. Degalia scrunched down, his face against the floor. Still pointing the gun, Harrelson used his free hand to bring a short length of rope from his pocket and slip a loop around the helpless broker's wrists. "Now Sam," he said as he jerked the knot tight, "don't do anything foolish."

Degalia kept asking, "What's wrong?"

Harrelson said, "I'll have to teach you to keep your nose out of other people's business." In truth, he'd been hired by Degalia's partner to kill him. The motive: sole ownership of their business and a $25,000 insurance policy. Harrelson's fee was $2,000—about a third of what he'd need to replace his year-old red Cadillac convertible.

Watkins parked the car. Harrelson helped Degalia out of the back seat. Gripping his gun in one hand and holding the end of the rope binding Degalia's wrists in his other hand, he walked his captive through the high weeds toward the shack.

Watkins, still in the car, was lighting a cigarette when he heard the first shot. He dropped the cigarette. He was picking it up when he heard the second shot.

Forty-five minutes later, Harrelson and Watkins were flying back to Houston. A pretty stewardess would remember the tall blond killer. "He made a pass at me and tried to kiss me on the cheek two or three times."

On October 16, Harrelson pleaded guilty to ATF's gun charge. The judge gave him three years.

A month later, carpet executive Alan Berg's decomposed

corpse was found in a thick clump of cedars along a beach in Brazoria County, Texas. A Ranger and a deputy sheriff flew to Kansas City. We gave them the wallboard with the bloodstain from Harrelson's red Caddy. Harrelson was charged, tried and acquitted of the Berg murder.

The three years he served for the sawed-off shotgun was extracted from a busy career. Convicted of the Degalia murder, Harrelson got fifteen years and served five.

Pete Scamardo, convicted of hiring Harrelson to commit the murder, was sentenced to seven years *probation*.[16]

So much for justice, Texas style.

Gun murders rose another 16 percent in 1968.[17] Convictions under our outdated gun laws totaled 222 that year. Senator Dodd was still trying for a better statute.

The NRA sent 900,000 bulletins warning members of the "complete abolition of civilian ownership of arms" and urged a write-in campaign against controls.[18] NRA President Glassen stated publicly, "We have yet to spend a single dollar on lobbying. We don't tell anyone to write to his congressman."[19]

On a sunny winter day in December, an exconvict named Edward Conrad Butler bought a .45 pistol at a gun show in Overland Park, Kansas. When he drove across the state line into Missouri, I stopped his car and arrested him.[20] This was the last time an agent would have to wait for a felon to take his gun across a state line, because it was Sunday, December 15, 1968.

At midnight, Senator Dodd's new Gun Control Act of 1968 went into effect.

The senator hadn't won his battle simply because thousands of criminals used guns to prey on the innocent, or merely because millions of Americans had favored tough gun laws for more than thirty years. Dodd won because, within a brief span of weeks, one psychotic shot presidential candidate George Wallace, another assassinated Robert F. Kennedy, and a third man murdered Martin Luther King.

The NRA could make congressmen ignore the preceding decade's 50,887 gun murders but these three attacks, two against politicians, electrified nerves the gun lovers couldn't touch.

Charles Voyde Harrelson served three years for his sawed-off shotgun and five years for the contract murder in Texas. He could have spent those years learning a new trade. Instead, on a sunny May morning in 1978, he used a high-powered rifle to kill John H. Wood—the first federal judge to be assassinated in a hundred years.

The FBI's $4.8-million investigation suggested that Harrelson had been hired for the hit by Jimmy Chagra, a convicted druglord due to be sentenced by Judge Wood. Gunshop records required under the Gun Control Act showed that, just days before the crime, Harrelson's wife had purchased a rifle exactly like the one ballistics experts tagged as the murder weapon. But the FBI couldn't make an arrest because witnesses who could have cinched the case saw certain disadvantages to testifying against a man who murdered for mere money. They wouldn't talk as long as Harrelson roamed free.

The G-men persisted with seventy agents, court-authorized bugs and wiretaps, jailhouse snitches and—as a tribute to their determination—214,000 investigative entries into their computer. Seven months passed.

It was February 1, 1980, when ATF Special Agent Mike Taylor got a tip that Harrelson was in Houston to hijack a high-stakes poker game—in town and armed. Agent Taylor combed Harrelson's hangouts, found him and enlisted the aid of two city detectives to keep the killer under surveillance. They tailed him to an apartment in the city's southwest section. After an interminable fifteen hours of discreet observations with no action, Taylor decided, "We'll make ourselves obvious."

He drove his G-car to a spot within sight of the suspect's windows.

Five men bailed out of the apartment. Four scattered throughout the neighborhood. Harrelson dumped five guns into his sleek new black Lincoln, screeched out of the driveway and barreled down the street.

Agent Taylor blocked him with his G-car.

Harrelson dove to the floor and came up holding a Colt Diamondback .357 magnum revolver. A police cruiser pulled up beside Agent Taylor. Another skidded to a halt behind the Lincoln. Harrelson scowled through his windshield, gun in hand, contemplating the 12-gauge shotgun Taylor aimed at his face. He surrendered.

Aside from the weapons, the officers found a pair of loaded dice and some cocaine in the Lincoln. The court gave Harrelson forty years for the drugs, twenty for the guns. Now, with the hitman safely salted away, witnesses talked to the FBI. Harrelson ended up with three life sentences tacked onto his sixty-year sentence. Chagra, who'd hired him to murder Judge Wood, went up for thirty years.

In 1995 Harrelson found a special way to celebrate the Fourth of July. The following blurb appeared in *Newsweek:*

> SURRENDERED: Convicted killer Charles Harrelson, 56, during an alleged escape attempt, in Atlanta, July 4. Authorities say Harrelson, father of actor Woody Harrelson, and two bank robbers approached a prison wall with a makeshift ladder. They gave up when a guard fired a warning shot.

The man who liked to shoot unarmed victims wasn't ready to find out what it felt like.[21]

In the years to come, ATF's enforcement of the Gun Control Act proved its worth. Whenever the agents' efforts increased, violent crime dropped across the United States; when agents were slowed by mismanagement or budget cuts, violent crime soared.[22]

6

New Ammunition for the Government Gun

> No passion so robs the mind of all its powers of
> acting and reasoning as fear.
>
> —Edmund Burke

The early and mid-1990s saw many Americans terrified by
the bombings of New York City's World Trade Center and
an Oklahoma City federal building, and a tragic shootout at
Waco, Texas—violence instigated by ultra right-wingers,
armed to the teeth, frightened by and eager to attack a
government they call oppressive.

The violence had escalated, but the phenomenon wasn't
really new.

Thirty years earlier, in 1961, Robert "Bolivar" DePugh
founded the Minutemen. He organized its secret members,
he said, because "even within months, our nation could be
conquered and enslaved by the Communists."

He was born in Independence, Missouri. Schoolmates
knew him as a loner, called him "Bolivar," and avoided
him. Thirty-eight when he created the Minutemen, he had a
wife, six children and a small but profitable veterinary drug
firm in rural Norborne. For $100, he'd become a lifetime
member of the NRA. For one dollar under the old gun law,
he'd become a licensed dealer in firearms. He told a
reporter that he'd read Hitler's *Mein Kampf* "two or three
times," Karl Marx's *Das Kapital,* and *The Collected Works
of Lenin* "for academic purposes."

A *Newsweek* cover story on the far right gave him passing
mention: ". . . on the fringe of lunacy, the gun-toting Minutemen arming against a Russian invasion."

For five dollars, any "patriot" could get a newsletter and a

79

secret number. One could buy Minutemen mail-order courses: "How to Make Silencers," "Constructing Booby Traps" and "How to Make a Machine Gun"—all protected under the First Amendment. A course titled "Counterintelligence" told how to detect spies, infiltrators and government agents. He exhorted members, "Acquire weapons, train yourself in their use." His early rhetoric focused on repelling an imminent Soviet invasion.[1]

Headquartered in a storefront at 613 East Alton Street in Independence, DePugh hired high school girls to sort his mail. Cash filled bushel baskets—cash because "the Reds in our government can learn your secret identity by tracing checks."

They were farmers and factory workers, cab drivers and shopkeepers, Nazis and Klansmen, fundamentalist backslappers and dedicated gun lovers with more than a few exconvicts. Their newsletter, *On Target,* "exposed" grocers selling Polish hams, bookstores with "Red" books on their shelves. Teachers, librarians and local politicians who criticized them were branded Communists. Every president from Roosevelt to Kennedy was a "tool of the Communist conspiracy." The *O* in *On Target's* masthead was split by the crosshairs of a telescopic gunsight. Beneath it, this caveat: "We guarantee that all lawsuits filed against this newsletter will be settled out of court."

DePugh was widely ignored, even when he wrote, "We are morally justified in resorting to violence to discourage Communists and fellow travelers."

Then in March 1963, *On Target* called twenty congressmen "Judases" for voting to discontinue funding for the House Committee on Un-American Activities—a Red-baiting successor to Senator Joseph McCarthy's discredited witch-hunters. Above the twenty names were the words "In Memoriam." And above that, a bold threat:

TRAITORS BEWARE

See the old man at the corner where you buy your paper? He may have a silencer-equipped pistol under his coat. That extra fountain pen in the pocket of the insurance salesman that calls on you might be a cyanide gas gun. What about your milkman? Arsenic works slow but sure. Your auto mechanic may stay up nights studying booby traps.

These patriots are not going to let you take their freedom away from them. They have learned the silent knife, the strangler's cord, the target rifle that hits sparrows at 200 yards. Only their leaders restrain them.

Traitors beware! Even now the crosshairs are on the backs of your necks.

Congress screamed.

"Traitors Beware" stickers appeared mysteriously in men's rooms, phone booths, on anonymous postcards to any person seen by any Minuteman as "an enemy."

ATF policy disregarded rhetoric until words turned into criminal acts but the Minutemen hadn't been ignored by law enforcement. The FBI had been investigating them as a "national security" matter since 1962.[2] Local police raiding its headquarters seized TNT, five cases of dynamite, hand grenades and a box of land mines. In 1962 none of these items offended federal law. DePugh was charged under state law for possession of bombs. Then a Missouri grand jury indicted him for kidnapping a twenty-one-year-old divorcée and a sixteen-year-old girl; both claimed he'd flourished a gun, held them captive and "told us our purpose [in the Minutemen] was to use sex as a weapon to blackmail Communists. . . . He wanted us to seduce men in the high government."

Presumably, DePugh contemplated training these young ladies to perform this patriotic duty.

But nothing done by police, sheriffs or the FBI brought a single conviction.

DePugh's lieutenant, Walter Peyson—midtwenties, slight build, slick black hair, coal-black eyes and an olive complexion suggesting a Middle Eastern heritage—despised blacks and Jews. He bragged of his service as a Marine without mentioning that he'd spent his enlistment playing the snare drum in a small ceremonial band. Peyson invited a Marine buddy—piccolo player Raithby Husted, twenty-three—to join the Minutemen.

Pink-cheeked Ray Husted, longing to be a detective, leaped at the chance to spy on Communists. Instead, he found himself painting the headquarters, mailing literature and digging holes to hide machine guns. It was boring. Minutemen lamentations about the FBI prompted Husted to write to J. Edgar Hoover, offering his services. George Arnett, the Kansas City agent in charge of the FBI's Minutemen case, met Husted and asked him to furnish a membership list.

Husted fed Arnett information for months, but that too, became tedious. He informed G-man Arnett that he'd joined the Air Force. "I leave in a couple days."

Arnett rushed to first assistant U.S. attorney Calvin K. Hamilton with one of the tidbits Husted had offered weeks earlier. "He says he helped Peyson bury machine guns." Arnett and a colleague had inspected the alleged burial site and found nothing. "What do we do now?"

Hamilton said, "Take him to ATF."

ATF Special Agent John F. Smith drove Husted and the G-men to Carroll County, Missouri, invited Sheriff Johnson to join them, and proceeded to the cemetery in the town of Coloma. Husted pointed, and Smith unearthed four submachine guns packaged in grease. At an old farmhouse, Husted opened a closet door, lifted out the flooring and pointed again. A layer of earth concealed a plastic sheet spread across several planks. The planks covered a deep pit. The pit contained a .50-caliber machine gun and metal boxes filled with ammunition.

ATF Special Agent Judson Doyle was assigned to ramrod the investigation.

Doyle had the guns and he had Ray Husted's word that DePugh had ordered him and Peyson to bury the weapons, but no jury in the "Show Me State" of Missouri was about to convict a home-grown "anti-Communist" on the unsupported word of a piccolo player.

Doyle sent me undercover to find members who might become witnesses. I lived at Minutemen headquarters, performed menial tasks, answered the phones—"Of course our phone's not tapped," I'd say, truthfully. "But Mr. DePugh's not here right now, so tell me what's new and I'll pass it along to him when he comes in."

Alone there at night, I copied serial numbers from empty Smith & Wesson boxes stashed in a closet. Special Agent Ralph Chance traced them to an Iowa dealer who'd sold them to DePugh. He'd transported them interstate to Missouri while he was under that state indictment for kidnapping. That was an offense, even under the old gun law.

Special Agent Doyle had walked halfway across France, ducking Nazi patrols after his plane was shot down in World War II. As an agent, lanky and laconic, he wore scuffed shoes, wilted shirts, neckties advertising his last few meals and a suit jacket he often balled up and stuffed beneath the seat of his G-car. Supervisors shook their heads when the rumpled Doyle made oral reports from notes he'd scribbled on matchbook covers and supermarket receipts, but veteran federal prosecutor Cal Hamilton, who'd worked with hundreds of federal agents from all the bureaus, would tell the IRS commissioner that "Doyle's the best I've ever seen."

Doyle cackled his contempt for the G-men's assessment of the Minutemen. Sure, they thrived on secrecy; sure, they avoided the pitfalls that let lawmen catch ordinary criminals; sure, they were weird and well armed and dangerous. But a threat to the national security? Quietly, Doyle pursued his quest to thirty states. His humble, folksy manner won the confidence of those he interviewed. In the fall of 1966, his evidence yielded indictments against DePugh, Peyson and their California coordinator, Troy Haughton.

DePugh was furious when Haughton's record as a convicted sex offender came out, but he turned sullen when his own background was revealed. He'd always brushed off questions about his military service—"Top Secret," he'd say with a smile. Now prosecutor Hamilton petitioned the court for a psychiatric exam because DePugh's army discharge was based on a psychiatrist's diagnoses: "psychoneurosis . . . schizoid personality and incipient schizophrenia."

Nevertheless, DePugh was pronounced competent to stand trial.

Witness Al Somerford, former Minuteman #13022, had been assigned to teach fellow members how to make silencers and machine guns. Asked by DePugh's lawyer on cross-examination why he'd quit the organization, Somerford replied, "I got tired of training kooks and nuts to become assassins."

The lawyer objected.

Federal judge Elmo Hunter shook his head. "You asked him."

Peyson was sentenced to two years' imprisonment. Haughton drew three. DePugh was given four years on the machine gun conspiracy charge and another year for having transported those revolvers across a state line while under indictment for kidnapping.

All three men were released on bond, pending their appeals. Enroute home to California, Haughton was arrested for exposing himself to two girls. Soon afterward, Haughton disappeared, and no one has seen him since. The FBI would say he'd been murdered by DePugh and Peyson, but that was never proved.

The Supreme Court's decision in *Haynes vs. United States* trashed the National Firearms Act. Cases against DePugh and Peyson were sent back for retrial on one charge.

Both had vanished.

The FBI launched a nationwide hunt with wanted posters in every post office, a full-page spread in the bulletin mailed to police departments, and quiet offers to informers of a $10,000 reward. DePugh taunted them with newsletters sent from "Underground Headquarters."

In April 1967, NRA member Donald Telerman became an official "patriot"—Minuteman #103109. His wife, June, became member #103112.[3]

Donald was a slender man of average height with glasses and brown hair clipped in a crew cut. After two years in the navy, he studied at colleges in Illinois and Arkansas and opened a laundromat in his home town, in Michigan. His wife, June, was wholesome and attractive, a brown-eyed blonde with a fair complexion and a ready smile. Both believed that DePugh would defeat Communists and gun laws. Convinced that he'd been framed, they organized meetings and recruited members and raised money.

Donald was twenty-four, June nineteen.

In the spring, June had a baby. They named her Maryann.

Thousands of members paid cash for their delusion of Minutemen patriotism. The Telermans' education would cost more. Much more.

In July Donald received instructions from Underground Headquarters. A drive to Denver and several phone calls from public booths led to Albuquerque and a meeting with DePugh's aide and fellow fugitive, Walter Peyson. Donald was ordered to set up a print shop (at his own expense), where he printed bulletins informing followers that discipline was required, even of high-ranking coordinators. "There were . . . three cases in which we met with gross insubordination or proof of deliberate treason. In each of these cases, the coordinator was tried, found guilty and executed."

Donald wasn't worried. He was loyal. June and baby Maryann joined him. They were ordered to join Peyson in a rented house near Durango, Colorado, for ten days of training, target practice and lectures. The Communist takeover of the U.S. government was a *fait accompli*, proved by the FBI's persecution and ATF's prosecution of patriots. Minutemen would soon be given missions to assassinate pro-Communist officials. DePugh would designate the targets. When he produced his list, I was acquainted with three of those named: ATF supervisor Frank Belecky, FBI agent George Arnett, and me.[4]

Early on the fourth morning, DePugh knocked on the Tellermans' bedroom door. June, partly aroused from a deep slumber, called out that she and "Jerry" were here. DePugh concluded that Donald's real name was Jerry. He was an infiltrator! And so that evening, DePugh and Peyson took Donald into the forest. Peyson put a pistol to Donald's head and demanded, "Who's Jerry?" DePugh jerked the hapless Donald's trousers down so he couldn't run. They trussed him up, held a knife against his back and demanded desperately, all through the night, "Who's Jerry?"

Donald knew only one Jerry—an employee at his laundromat back in Michigan. By morning, DePugh seemed satisfied. Returned to the Minutemen house, Donald adopted what he considered "a forgiving Christian attitude" toward the incident.

On Labor Day, the five men and three women of Minutemen Underground Headquarters moved with baby Mary-ann to a new hideout at Pinos Altos, New Mexico—a plain, whitewashed five-room stucco bungalow on a rocky hillside overlooking a narrow highway and the shallow, winding Rio Grande. Four men, three women and baby Maryann slept in the main house. DePugh bunked in a smaller, adjoining building.

Dynamite was stored in the chicken coop.

The tiny house was gorged with desks and work tables, file cabinets and a shortwave radio. A bookcase was crammed with *My Silent War,* by Soviet spy Kim Philby; *The Craft of Intelligence,* by CIA chief Allen Dulles; *Guerrilla War* and other army manuals. *Haganah* shared a shelf with *Soviet Partisans in World War II, A Psychological Warfare Casebook* and Edward Hunter's *Brainwashing. I Saw Poland Betrayed* stood beside *Men Against America. How the FBI Gets Its Man* was sandwiched between *America's Concentration Camps* and former G-man Norman Ollestad's exposé, *Inside the FBI.*

The eight adults passed their time answering mail, drafting new bulletins, excavating a tunnel between the two houses and hiding more dynamite in caves on the hill above the bungalow. The forced confinement created tensions. Six-foot-four-inch Ed Hickey and the short, wiry Peyson were burying dynamite when Hickey complained that DePugh was sleeping with one of the women. Peyson cracked his pistol down on Hickey's head. The man's scalp bled profusely. Hickey packed his gear the next day, left a note and departed. DePugh told the others he'd gone to marry the girl he loved in Albuquerque. DePugh, Peyson, the Telermans, JoAnn, Janet and crusty old Ray Barnes would carry on the fight for freedom.

They were still fugitives in December 1968, when the Gun Control Act went into effect. Convicted felons were now prohibited from even possessing any firearm.

In Seattle, ATF agents arrested Minutemen network director and exconvict Arthur Eugene Williams with six loaded pistols in his car; New York police rounded up five Minutemen for plotting an armed raid on a pacifist camp; they'd get terms ranging from one to ten years. Illinois

Minutemen coordinator Richard Lauchli was paroled from a firearms conviction; two months later, ATF agents caught him with hand grenades (illegal under the new law) and machine guns; he went back to prison for twenty years. California ATF charged Minuteman Jack Leonard Karnes with manufacturing illegal firearms and possession by a felon (this "patriot's" prior conviction was for desertion in time of war).

Ray Barnes was a cantankerous coot with a gray-black beard, unkempt and crude. His cigarettes were costing Underground Headquarters two dollars a week, but he owned a jeep, several guns, and he converted .30-caliber carbines into machine guns. One day, after another of the incessant arguments over his repulsive conduct and his "expensive" smoking habit, Barnes went for a ride with DePugh and Peyson. He never came back.

Donald and June noticed that the cheap, possessive old man hadn't taken his jeep, his trailer, his guns or his clothes. They thought it odd, but they trusted DePugh implicitly. Trusted him, that is, until one Sunday when the group held its own religious service.

They couldn't join a real church without parrying ministers' questions: "Where were you baptized?" "Where did you last attend church?" So they came up with the idea of a do-it-yourself service. Forming a circle in the living room, each contributed a Christian thought. When DePugh's turn came, he stood up. "I'm an atheist. I don't believe in God."

That afternoon, June and Donald took a drive in the pickup they'd bought for the group, parked beside the river and looked at one another. Jane voiced a small Bronx cheer. They'd given nearly a year of their lives, thousands of hard-earned dollars, labor and loyalty—all to discover that the man they'd revered didn't share their belief in God. They'd go home, but rather than take the sudden, unannounced-departure method chosen by Ed Hickey, they informed DePugh of their decision.

DePugh talked them into staying, "until we find a new headquarters. If the FBI catches you, they'll torture you till you tell them about this place."

The Telermans agreed to stay for a little while, but every day or so, Donald or June would ask when DePugh intended to find a new hideout. Then, on a bright May morning while Donald was away with Peyson, burying more explosives, DePugh and the other two women explained to June the problems the Telerman desertion would create. Suddenly DePugh pointed a pistol at the young mother. "Make one false move, and I'll shoot you." JoAnn held a carbine. Janet took baby Maryann. They hustled June up to one of the caves in the hillside. DePugh ordered her to sit on the ground. She obeyed. He lifted her dress and handcuffed her with her wrists linked between her legs so she couldn't stand. He left a canteen of water, and told her a guard was posted outside and walked out.

That night, Janet brought her a comb and washcloth. "Sorry, I couldn't manage any food."

Later that night, DePugh entered the cave, removed the handcuffs, chained June's ankles and secured the chain with a padlock. She asked him something—later, she wouldn't be able to remember what it was—and he punched her in the mouth. Knocked her flat on the floor of the cave. Her lips bled.

"Save that sympathy shit for the girls," he snarled. And, ever fond of the worn cliché, he added, "I've got more sympathy for a snake in the grass." He whirled, kicked canteen, comb and washcloth out of the cave. Turning back toward the terrified nineteen-year-old blonde, he said, "I've got three alternatives: I can kill you; I can keep you prisoner; or I can let you go. I'm not going to let you go, so you give me a reason not to kill you." He stalked out.

An hour later, he returned to take her shoes and socks and to chain her ankles tighter. By morning, when he came for her answer, her feet were swollen. She offered a fourth alternative: She could resume her faithful service and work for the Cause.

He stood, hands on hips, glaring down at the pretty, brown-eyed blonde. "Is that all?" He told her that Ed Hickey had met with a fatal accident and that two others who'd abandoned him were also dead. He'd consider her offer to continue working for him.

Later in the day, one of the girls brought her a thin blanket, a bucket she could use to relieve herself, and baby Maryann. Still later, they brought her Maryann's potty chair and six diapers.

It was three o'clock that afternoon when Donald returned from burying the dynamite with Peyson. Breezing into the house with the air of a man who'd done a good two days' work, he said, "What's new and exciting?"

"Well," DePugh said, looking up from his chair at the chrome-and-plastic kitchen table, "June's gone."

Donald was stunned. Before he could react, he heard Peyson behind him. "Lay down on the floor." Donald turned. Peyson's silencer-equipped pistol was aimed at his chest. Peyson screamed, "Get down on the floor!"

Donald had started to obey when DePugh leaped from his chair, swearing and kicking him. He cuffed Donald's hands behind his back, chained his legs together and ordered Peyson, "Shoot him in the goddamned head if he says anything."

Donald lay on the floor for what seemed an eternity before they informed him that June and Maryann were alive, "at another camp. But if you do anything funny," DePugh said, reaching for another cliché, "you'll be shot, sure as the sun comes up." They dragged him to the next room and chained him to a hideaway bed.

DePugh trudged up to the cave and stared down at the helpless June. "The others want to shoot you and Donald. I'm the only one who voted not to kill you."

Donald spent the next few days chained to that bed with a five-gallon can to relieve himself, reading his Bible and *The Life of St. Paul.*

One of the girls brought food to the cave. June told her, "I've got no water to wash Maryann." Peyson brought water and a note from DePugh. "If you can't manage the baby, she'll be given to someone who can manage."

June kept the baby naked during the days and used one diaper per night. She had to stay awake to make sure Maryann didn't crawl away, as DePugh had assured her that the first head to pop out of the cave would be shot off.

DePugh came several times; he'd stand around as if

waiting for her to offer something more than secretarial services, then leave. Once he brought her a letter from Donald. Once he allowed her to write a note to him.

Donald's five-gallon toilet can wasn't emptied for nearly a week.

June lay chained, exhausted in that damp cave with her baby, the toilet bucket, the potty chair and occasional scraps of food for ten interminable days before Peyson came with his silenced pistol to bring mother and baby to the pumphouse. There she saw a box about the size of two coffins, one on top of the other, with a door for entering, and another through which they'd pass food and work materials. Both had padlocks. Inside at one end, a wooden seat and a typewriter. Maryann was laid in a crib nearby. Peyson said, "Get in." She obeyed. The baby began to cry.

The next day, crib and baby were taken into the main house, but they allowed her to have Maryann most afternoons. She typed lists for them, hundreds of names and addresses. When the gas man came to read the meter, JoAnn held a pistol on June until he'd gone.

June prayed a lot.

Donald's shoulder-wide box, reinforced with two-by-fours and metal strapping, stood in a bedroom. "If you ever try to escape," DePugh told him, "June and the baby will be shot."

One day the landlord came to the door. Peyson held a silenced pistol to Donald's head. "Say one word, and I'll let you have it. The landlord won't hear a sound and, well, I'd hate to have to kill the baby."

Over the ensuing weeks, husband and wife were permitted to exchange three heavily censored letters. Donald obeyed an order to write to relatives, assuring them that he and his family were fine. He typed excerpts from several volumes for a book DePugh planned to write. He clipped newspaper articles on socialism, disarmament and crime.

Over the six weeks she was held prisoner, June was permitted three baths. Each consisted of a half bucket of water. One day Peyson put a thermometer in her box. It registered ninety-eight degrees. The stench from her toilet bucket was overpowering. At first they fed her a sandwich and a bowl of sauerkraut or beans each day. Later it was cold cereal with the sandwich. Every day or so, someone brought her some ice cream or iced tea. During all of those weeks, she was allowed out of that box just once—when DePugh and Peyson came to check its "security."

They called her "Spook," for the hairy character in the *Wizard of Id* comic strip.

On the night of July 12, Donald waited until eleven o'clock for someone to bring him the baby. Then he dozed. When he awoke, it was morning. The baby hadn't been brought to him. He was out of food and nearly out of water. All he could hear was the drone of the air conditioner in the next room. He snaked one arm through the slit in the trapdoor, grasped a transistor radio lying on top of his box. He switched it on and caught the end of an announcer's sentence; ". . . DePugh and Walter Peyson, fugitives for seventeen months—were captured by the FBI near Truth or Consequences, New Mexico, yesterday afternoon."

Donald kicked his way out of the box and ran to the pumphouse. He cut the outside padlock with a hacksaw and used a hammer to smash the lock on June's box. He heard the baby cry, and a small voice: "Who is it?"

Until he spoke, June didn't recognize the sweaty man with the six-week beard who'd lost twenty pounds from his normally slender frame. They embraced and cried. Then they showered, donned fresh clothes and filled their pockets with handfulls of coins—cash they'd brought from the final emptying of the machines in their laundromat so long ago, the only money they'd had that DePugh hadn't used.

Still fearful of Minutemen, they ran across the road and followed the Rio Grande to Williamsburg, New Mexico. They bought a bus ticket home, but it was another month before they mustered the courage to confide in their minister. He suggested they contact the FBI.

DePugh wrote to his son while awaiting trial: "It would be hard for me to imagine adversity any greater than to be caged within this maximum-security penitentiary while everyone and everything I need is locked outside." This from a man in a cell with running water, a flush toilet and a bed; a cell where he could stand, and pace, and speak to fellow inmates; a prison where he was served three nutritious meals every day. This from the man who had locked a young couple in wooden boxes, hardly larger than caskets, under constant threats of death for six endless weeks.

The arsenal at Underground Headquarters—machine guns, silencer-equipped pistols and arrows tipped with bombs—earned Peyson eight and a half years in prison; DePugh received nine ten-year terms to run concurrently—meaning he'd serve all nine terms simultaneously. It was better than nothing.

Were it not for the new Gun Control Act, he'd have gone free.

No Minuteman is known to have ever inconvenienced a real Communist.

DePugh was paroled in 1973, after serving five years. He'd taken up art during his prison years. Home again, he used a nude model—a twelve-year-old girl.

Peyson served his term and returned to his native Chicago, where he lived in a small apartment with his wife and two children on $316-a-month G.I. Bill benefits and took college courses in economics and speech.

Special Agent Judson Doyle was eventually promoted to special agent in charge at Chicago but, like many street-agents, he detested paperwork. At his request, he was given a supervisor's slot at a small Illinois post. In 1975 he retired to the comfort of his hobby, antiques. He died in April 1991.

Five months after Doyle's death, DePugh was arrested by sheriff's deputies in Soldier, Iowa, for taking nude photos of girls as young as twelve. ATF Special Agent Cindy Grob proved his connection to guns uncovered by police in Missouri and charged him with new firearms offenses. A federal judge sent the sixty-eight-year-old DePugh back to prison for thirty months.[5]

Robert DePugh has faded from the scene, but the NRA's polemics nourish new terrorists in their war against the "oppression" of our government—men like David Koresh and the bombers who slaughtered innocents in Oklahoma City.

7

Attacking Terrorism

You never could devine his real thought
He was the mildest manner'd man
That ever scuttled ship, or cut a throat!
With such true breeding of a gentleman.
—George Gordon, Lord Byron

Back in the 1960s when we worked the Mob's illicit distilleries, we rarely crossed paths with a G-man. When Congress enacted GCA-68 (the Gun Control Act of 1968) and our investigations widened to embrace a broader spectrum of the underworld, we learned how the U.S. Marines would feel if they were suddenly and deliberately sabotaged by the U.S. Army.

The FBI has had a deep and lasting impact on ATF, and the effects were clearest and most destructive in terrorist cases.

The first instance occurred when the Black Panther Party waged war on society. They made "pig" a synonym for "policeman" in ghetto neighborhoods. They carried rifles into the gallery overlooking the California legislature—unloaded, but frightening nonetheless—to protest a proposed gun law. Within two years, the Panthers had established chapters in thirty cities.[1]

Some were real victims of injustice, some were sincere zealots, some were would-be reformers, but they were all angry and their anger blinded them to the outcasts and felons who became the Panthers' most active members. Some committed robberies; others extorted cash from local businessmen "for the cause." Some Panther leaders exacted tribute—a share of the loot.

Co-founder Bobby Seale told *Time* magazine how to kill policemen taking coffee breaks: "You walk up to him and shoot him down—*voom voom!*—with a 12-gauge shotgun." He called it "righteous power."

Fellow founder Huey Newton agreed: "Buckshot will drop the cops."

Dilettante liberals chuckled nervously. "It's mere rhetoric. Nothing more."

But the words became deeds: an armed attack on an Illinois police station; a bomb tossed into a San Francisco precinct house; patrolmen gunned down on the streets of Detroit and St. Paul; ambush slayings in San Jose, California, and New York City.

Their slogan: "Political power grows out of the barrel of a gun." FBI director J. Edgar Hoover branded them the number-one threat to American society.[2]

Panthers publicized the formation of a Kansas City chapter by posing with firearms and bandoleers of ammunition for news camermen. Chairman Pete O'Neal, an excon who'd served time for a stabbing, perched on the edge of a table with a shotgun.

GCA-68 prohibited felons from possessing guns, but ATF couldn't act without proving that the shotgun O'Neal held in the news photo met the legal definition—i.e., that it was capable of firing ammunition. An even greater problem was posed by the verbiage forbidding felons from "receiving, possessing or transporting [any firearm] in commerce."

In those early days of the new law, government lawyers felt that the words "in commerce" modified all three acts. An agent had to prove that an ex-convict had either received a gun in commerce or transported the gun in commerce (these were simple and straightforward), or that he'd possessed it "in commerce." Whatever that meant.

Pete O'Neal snatched headlines by invading a church during Sunday services and telling the pastor to "go to hell." And again, when he shoved into the police chief's office during a press conference, claiming to represent the Panther newspaper.

That newspaper gloated when three black bandits committing a robbery forced a policeman to kneel down and shot him through the head.

OFF DUTY PIG'S LAST ACT
OF TERROR

> The people of Kansas City are ecstatic today, following the execution of a pig. Three (3) heroic brothers had the pleasure of "offing a pig." . . . The brothers were in the process of getting back what was theirs.

ATF agents worked with detectives, using the excuse (to bureau headquarters) that the killers were "probably ex-cons who'd carried firearms at a business establishment catering to an interstate clientele." The theory of federal jurisdiction—useful to agents who wanted to help—was actually irrelevant. Everyone knew that the "heroic brothers," once caught, would be tried for murder in state court. They were convicted.

Headquarters wouldn't authorize an ATF investigation of Panther chairman O'Neal until Lieutenant James Hitchcock of the Kansas City, Missouri, Police Department's (KCMoPD's) Intelligence Unit relayed a tip that O'Neal had bought a gun across the river in Kansas.

That was easy to prove. The salesman at Sam's Loan picked O'Neal's photo from the pack I showed him. Their security guard fingered O'Neal as having threatened him before leaving the store with the shotgun he'd just purchased. And ATF's lab examined the Federal Firearms Transaction form (which GCA-68 now required gun buyers to sign) and certified the signature as O'Neal's. He'd falsified the form by using a phony name and lying about his felony conviction. But it was also unlawful—for anyone—to bring a firearm purchased out of state back into one's home state; and it was still illegal for ex-cons to transport a gun across a state line.

Proving these crimes presented a few problems.

The KCMoPD had confiscated a weapon of the same make and model from a Panther named Archie Weaver. Mr. Weaver informed me that he "don't converse with pigs." Unfortunately, this gun seized from him—like the one

O'Neal had bought—was a cheap model manufactured with no serial number. Were they the same weapon?

Then, too, before I could charge O'Neal with bringing that gun into his home state, I'd have to prove that he was, indeed, a resident of Missouri. The landlady at his apartment house on the Paseo in Kansas City, Missouri, gave me a sworn statement that O'Neal paid rent and lived in apartment nineteen. She also swore that she'd seen him bring a shotgun into the building, and she'd heard him brag about using it to "scare the black pig" security man at Sam's Loan.

The next morning an FBI Agent came to my office. "We'd prefer you don't use the landlady as a witness."

Puzzled, I asked, "Why not?"

"Well, she's our informant and we'd rather not have her exposed by testifying."

"Some informant," I snorted. "Did she tell you about seeing O'Neal bringing the shotgun into the apartment house, and hearing him admit he'd bought it in Kansas?"

"Certainly." The agent smiled. "She called us that day."

I was confused. "You mean you people knew back then that he'd bought a gun in Kansas and transported it interstate into Missouri?"

"Of course." The agent's grin brimmed with pride. "We keep pretty close tabs on these people."

"And you knew he was an ex-con?"

"Naturally. We knew everything about him."

"I don't get it. You knew he'd committed a crime, so why didn't you tell us?"

"Well," said the agent, turning somber, "that would have compromised our informant."

"What's the goddamned point in paying informers and building files if you won't use the information to put the jerk away?"

The G-man looked somewhat disconcerted by my outburst. "Well, we would . . . that is, we will arrest him if we find he's violated a law within our jurisdiction."

My first thought was that this agent was a nut. It would take me longer than it should have—more experiences like this, many more—to realize that this was the FBI's standard operating procedure.

"So, what do you say?" He regained his confident attitude

of good fellowship, as if his request were a mere formality. "Can I tell the landlady she won't have to testify?"

"We need her to prove the crime." I stood up. Our conversation was over.

But the G-man persisted. "You know, she can't really swear he's a Missouri resident." He smiled pleasantly again. "All she can say is he paid the rent, and she saw him going in and out. She can't say for sure he slept there." Still smiling, he walked out.

The next morning, the landlady came to my office. She said she would rather not testify. "All I can say is, he paid the rent and I saw him going in and out. I can't swear he slept there."

"That's all right," I told her soothingly. "We're just asking you to tell the truth."

"But . . . the FBI agent told me that I can't be his informer any more if I testify. He'll stop paying me."

"I really am sorry, but I'm afraid that's between you and the agent."

The G-man hadn't stopped at concealing evidence; he'd actually tried to sabotage our trial. My astonishment and disillusionment gave way to anger. As the years passed, I'd learn that it wasn't just the agent. It was the FBI.

One problem remained: to prove that O'Neal had possessed the same gun in Missouri that he'd bought in Kansas. I went to the KCMoPD evidence room, borrowed the gun taken from Archie Weaver and showed it to the salesman at Sam's Loan.

"Same one." He nodded. "See that long, jagged crack on the underside of the stock? I recognize that."

"How can you be so sure?"

"Listen, mister, I had that damned thing off the rack every time I thought I might have a customer I could push it off on. Saw it maybe fifty times. It's the same one."

Okay, so the shotgun O'Neal bought in Kansas had been possessed by Weaver in Missouri. But who brought it over there? His lawyer would challenge us to prove that the gun his landlady had seen was the same weapon. If I could show beyond a reasonable doubt that Pete O'Neal had held that very gun in Missouri, I'd be home free. I knew it had to be the same firearm. Hell, I thought, he'd even posed for news pictures with the damned thing when he'd launched the Kansas City chapter.

Of course!

ATF's lab enlarged a thumbtack-size circle of the *Kansas City Star*'s news photo to eight-by-ten inches and there it was: that distinctive jagged crack on the underside of the gunstock.

One of our new agents arranged a massive task force—like those garnering headlines for lawmen in other cities—to execute my arrest warrant. I told him, "Forget it, Don. I'd be embarrassed, taking an army to snatch one crummy dipshit off the street."

Special Agent Duane Nichols and I waited near the Panther house until O'Neal emerged with half a dozen cohorts. I pulled up to the curb, then we stepped out and showed our credentials. I informed Mr. O'Neal that he was under arrest for crimes under the Gun Control Act. While I braced him against the G-car and patted him down, he turned his face to his comrades and shouted, "Hey brothers, are you gonna let the Man do this?"

His "brothers" looked from me to the grim, stocky Agent Nichols and decided to "let the Man do this."[3]

The *Kansas City Star*'s front page headlined: "Federal Men Seize Panther." ATF was mentioned briefly on an inside page. Next morning, a G-man named Jay came to my office and asked, "Why didn't you tell us you were going to arrest O'Neal?"

Still smarting from their silence when they knew of O'Neal's crimes and still annoyed by the other G-man's attempt to neutralize the landlady as a witness, I asked Jay, "Why would we do that?"

"We get lots of calls when something like this hits the papers," Jay said. "You know, citizens congratulating us for doing a good job. And we like to have a little something ready to tell them about the case."

"Try telling them you had nothing to do with it!"

"Oh, we couldn't do that. People admire us. They expect us to—"

I walked away. It was the closest I could come to maintaining Treasury's requirement that we be gentlemen.

O'Neal was given four years. He went free on bail to appeal the case.

* * *

The FBI's superb public-relations operation convinced many that all federal agents were G-men. The media assisted—odd conduct for a profession whose practitioners prize their own bylines as credit for a job well done. Thousands of news stories attributed Treasury's achievements to the G-men. Some were ludicrous by contradiction:

FBI ARRESTS OMAHAN
IN ARMS CRACKDOWN

U.S. Treasury Department agents arrested a 25-year-old Omahan Wednesday.[4]

FBI AGENTS POSE AS MOB

A 20-year-old Boston man was held. . . . Albert Merola was arrested Monday by agents of the Bureau of Alcohol, Tobacco and Firearms.[5]

FBI WILL BEEF UP
BOSTON OFFICE FORCE

In the wake of a recent rash of bombings . . . according to Rex Davis, director of the Treasury Department's Bureau of Alcohol, Tobacco and Firearms—the local arm of the FBI—the Greater Boston area is one of three cities . . .[6]

Even in TV schedules: *The Untouchables,* the FBI against the mob.[7]

The SDS—Students for Democratic Action—attracted white, upper-middle-class college students opposed to war and the military-industrial complex. They harassed army recruiters and munitions manufactures and they mocked "the System." Many worked with the poor, black and white, in the ghettoes. A subgroup calling itself the SDS Weathermen decided that success required destruction of America's power structure.[8]

Kansas City's SDS spokesman was Arnold Stead, an expelled college student with unkempt hair, a bushy beard and soiled jeans. "Make bacon of the pigs," he screamed during one of his streetcorner diatribes, "and pork chops of the hogs."

Two banks were bombed. Then the home of a university trustee who'd publicly criticized SDS protesters, then the home of a county prosecutor, then a downtown boutique. Agents scoured crime scenes with police and sent the evidence to ATF's lab because GCA-68 had done more than simply reinstate the registration requirement for machine guns, sawed-off shotguns and silencers; it added weapons of war to the list. Now bazookas, mortars, land mines and bombs had to be registered.

Innovation rarely emanated from ATF headquarters. It was the field agents who noted that the statutory definition of "destructive devices" included "any explosive, incendiary or poison gas bomb." Since none of the terrorists constructing these weapons during the 1960s had registered their bombs, they were fair game.

The break in the bombing cases came in the early-morning hours of June 29, 1970. Plainclothes officer Thomas Saunders of the KCMoPD's Intelligence Unit spotted Arnold Stead carrying a paper bag through the city's posh Country Club Plaza. "Arnold," he called out, "come here a minute."

Stead turned to run.

Saunders drew his service revolver. "Halt!"

Stead's paper bag contained a pipe-bomb with a short fuse.

ATF agents and city detectives formed teams, canvassed stores, found the shop where Stead had purchased black powder and located the Sears Roebuck outlet where he'd bought foot-long lengths of pipe with endcaps. ATF's scientists pronounced fragments from the bomb scenes identical to those purchased by Stead and those the Weatherman had in his paper bag when Saunders arrested him.

The team canvassing Stead's neighborhood discovered two FBI agents in the apartment directly across the street with powerful telescopes aimed at the defendant's windows. The G-men admitted that on three separate days, they'd watched Stead and another Weatherman, Randy Gould, drill fuse holes in short pieces of pipe.

Gould had written, "I think the only thing that keeps me

sane is the intense desire to see the pig destroyed. I want to be there to see the pig bleed. I want to enjoy every moment of it."

The G-men knew about the pipe-bombings—the crimes were in all the papers—and they knew that holes had to be drilled in the pipes to accommodate the fuses. They also knew that *after* they'd witnessed this act by prime suspects, there had been three more bombings. The ATF agent asked, "Why didn't you tell us?"

"It's not our case," one G-man replied.

The city detective patted the Treasury man's shoulder. "Aw hell, at least they'll make good witnesses at the trial."

One FBI man said, "We'll let you know if we can testify."

Before the trial, an ATF agent handed each of them a subpoena. They'd testify.

Most law enforcement officers *wanted* to believe that the FBI lived up to its motto: "Fidelity, Bravery and Integrity." For some, disillusionment solidified in Omaha.

It was very early on the morning of July 2, 1970, when a small bomb exploded in the offices of the Component Concepts Corporation. Special agents Tom Sledge and Dick Curd joined police detectives at the scene to begin ATF's investigation. Two weeks later, Agent Sledge interviewed a twelve-year-old girl the Panthers called "a gangbang." She told of seeing sticks of stolen dynamite wrapped in black tape inside Panther headquarters. She accurately described the explosives known as crater charges, and she added, "They've got it in a Samsonite suitcase with wadded papers all around it."

Sledge asked, "What else do you remember?"

"Well, it had this shiny brass thing stuck into the dynamite. A teeny-tiny thing 'bout the size of my little finger with yellow wires stickin' out of it." A blasting cap.

"That's fine, honey. Can you remember anything else?"

"Mmm, lemme see. There was some batteries and . . ." She went on to describe a common household item fashioned to trigger a booby-trap bomb.

"Did they say anything about it? About the bomb?"

"Oh yeah. Said 'This'll kill the pig.'"

Sledge gathered enough corroboration to obtain a search

warrant. Assistant U.S. attorney J. William Gallup, United States attorney Richard Dier and a federal judge agreed. Sledge summoned ATF agents, Omaha police and U.S. marshals to plan a raid.

While Sledge briefed the task force, prosecutor Dier telephoned the FBI. "ATF has a warrant to search the Panther headquarters, and I thought you people might have some intelligence concerning their fortifications."

The G-man was nonplussed. "We'll get back to you."

He didn't, but Dier did receive a phone call from the Justice Department in Washington. "Cancel that raid. We want to examine ATF's affidavit for the warrant."

"But why?" Dier asked. "I've gone over it. So has the judge."

"The FBI informs us it's based on questionable evidence."

"How would they know? They haven't even seen it."

"Hold off. We'll get back to you."

While the task force cooled its heels in the federal building, FBI agents went door to door in the Panthers' neighborhood asking everyone whether there were weapons or explosives inside the headquarters.

Two other G-men consulted their "key informant."

The raid was blown.

Dier registered strong protests with Justice.

FBI Special Agent-in-Charge Paul Young told him, "Our key informant assured us there were no weapons in that building."

Assistant U.S. attorney Gallup resigned from government service, citing this incident as his reason.[9]

On August 10, Panthers Ed Poindexter, Raleigh House and Duane Peak carried a Samsonite suitcase into David Rice's home at 2816 Parker Street. Poindexter checked the packing around the eight-stick dynamite bomb while Rice readied the detonator.

Four nights later, the same four men sat drinking beer at the Legion Club. It was nearly two o'clock when Poindexter asked Peak, "You know that old house we looked at?"

"The one where nobody lives, on Ohio?"

"Yeah."

"You remember how I showed you to arm the pig-killer?"

"Sure, man."

"Do it, baby."

It would be another two nights before the eighteen-year-old Peak retrieved the suitcase from Rice's place and drove to 2867 Ohio Street. The heat was oppressive, even for August in Omaha. Climbing the sagging wooden steps of the vacant house intensified Peak's perspiration. A dog barked somewhere behind the house. Across the street, a neighbor's TV set amplified a late-late movie. Peak pushed through the unlocked door, sat the suitcase on the floor and switched his flashlight on.

Setting the booby-trap detonator seemed to take a very long time. Peak closed the case, locked it and walked to the door. No sound; the dog was quiet and the late movie must have ended. No one on the street. Peak hurried to his car and drove away quickly. He didn't want to be around if a stray cat knocked that suitcase over.

At 2:23 A.M. the police dispatcher's telephone rang. "Hey, man, there's a woman screamin' her ass off at 2867 Ohio. Sounds like somebody's killin' her."

"Who is this?"

The caller hung up.

Four radio cars with flashing red lights converged on the abandoned house to rescue a victim. Four officers rushed to the rear. Patrolman Larry Minard and two others entered the front with Officer James Sledge—a younger brother of Special Agent Tom Sledge, who'd secured that unserved search warrant on the Panther headquarters; a warrant that would have given ATF the very dynamite that now nestled snugly inside the Samsonite suitcase on the floor of the darkened house.

The policemen searched, but found no one. No victim, no suspect. Just an old suitcase. Officer Minard lifted it.

Nine volts flashed from battery to blasting cap.

A brilliant red-orange flash!

Three officers were knocked off their feet. Two were blown through doorways. Larry Minard—a policeman for seven years, a husband and the father of five—was dead before the roar had echoed through the deserted street.

Neighbors' windows shattered. Debris sailed into the night sky, fluttered onto rooftops and sidewalks. And then, for a long minute, there was dead silence.

One officer struggled to his feet amidst the wreckage and limped through the heavy pall of smoke and plaster dust to his cruiser.

Within minutes, Ohio Street was a restless sea of flashing lights, blue uniforms, white jackets, fire trucks and sweating cops who did their best to cordon a mob of babbling spectators. Medics treated some at the scene. Others were rushed in wailing ambulances to hospitals.

Overcast skies reflected the morning mood of deputy sheriffs, police detectives, state troopers and federal investigators assembled for a special meeting of Domino—an informal Omaha venture hosting regular monthly meetings of lawmen to discuss problems and foster interagency cooperation. This meeting had one mission: to catch the cop killers.

Preliminary discussion was brief and pointed. The weapon, the method and the target suggested extremists. Panthers and Weathermen murdered policemen this way. The Negro voice on the dispatcher's tape suggested Panthers.

The FBI representative stood up. "We have excellent informer coverage of the Panthers," he said, "and our key source advises us that two white males were observed running from the scene shortly before the blast."

Some officers expressed doubts about the Panther theory. After all, if the FBI knows . . . Besides, it's unwise for mere cops to dispute the agency that influences city officials, the same bureau that confers courses at its academy—courses that impress the civilians on police promotion boards. But Omaha police wanted the men who'd slain their officer. They'd work with ATF and let the chips fall.

An early-morning drizzle forced investigators to cover the ground with tarpaulins. Their painstaking search involved rooftop sweeps and sifting mounds of rubble through a series of screens, each with a smaller mesh; and handling each fragment, tagging and bagging anything that might later turn out to be important. One policeman preserved a tiny piece of wire he'd found, blown through the basement window of a house across the street. Everything was shipped to ATF's lab.

Six days later, ATF agents and Omaha detectives arrested the bombers. At Rice's home, they found dynamite, blasting caps and a battery. When investigators mounted Elmer Cecil's front steps, he met them with a sawed-off shotgun in his hands. They disarmed him and charged him with that crime too.

The lab found explosives residue on the suspects' clothing and in their car—traces identical with the material used to fashion the death bomb. Wirecutters taken from one defendant were positively matched as having snipped that tiny slice of copper wire the policeman recovered from the basement window across Ohio Street.

Incredibly, twenty minutes after the arrests, an FBI agent telephoned ATF's resident agent-in-charge, Dwight Thomas. "Just thought you'd like to know," the G-man snapped with military precision, "we solved the murder." He hung up before the astonished Thomas could muster a reply.

Duane Peak confessed. Poindexter and Rice got life. Appeals, all the way to the Supreme Court, were denied. The FBI's "key source" on whose word they'd sabotaged Agent Sledge's raid was unmasked—a petty crook with a credibility rating of zero.

In January 1995, the Nebraska Parole Board recommended that Poindexter be eventually made eligible for release. Governor Ben Nelson and Attorney General Don Stenberg, members of the pardons board, said they would not commute his sentence.[10]

Kansas City Panther leader Pete O'Neal fled to Algeria to avoid serving his sentence. In 1972 he accepted a $1 million hijack ransom from Delta Airlines. Algerian police confiscated the money. Twenty years later, O'Neal was asking whether he might come back home, but he still didn't want to serve his four-year prison term.

Former Kansas City Panther Keith Hinch graduated from college with a B.A. in economics and received a Ford Foundation grant to study at MIT.

Panther founder Huey Newton beat all the assault and

murder charges against him, but he did serve two years under California's gun law for possession by a convicted felon. Co-founder Bobby Seale made an unsuccessful run for mayor of Oakland, California, moved to Pennsylvania and dropped from public view.

The FBI regarded itself as America's guardian against terrorists, but congressional investigators used the FBI's own records to reveal that—despite the millions they spent, the army of informers they paid and the hundreds of agents they devoted to probing domestic terrorism—the G-men accomplished virtually nothing.[11]

Unless you consider withholding evidence and sabotaging Treasury's efforts.

Several differences between the two bureaus probably account for ATF's successes. Treasury agents worked terrorists for their crimes, not their politics, and its agents had a mantra: "Left or right, black or white, we just treat 'em all alike." Then, too, ATF worked in *genuine* cooperation with police and never hogged the "glory" of victory.

In 1972 a new federal law was enacted, aimed directly as bombers. It provided new tools for investigators and stiffer sentences than those sections of GCA-68 that ATF agents had adapted to their need. But Congress decreed that ATF and the FBI would have joint jurisdiction over this new statute.

Out on the street, joint jurisdiction proved a curse. A bomb would explode, the police would go to work, but ATF and FBI agents didn't know which bureau should investigate. Eventually, Washington realized that guidelines were needed.

Treasury was represented at these negotiations by top ATF executive John Krogman. Pallid, and hardly a match for the savvy bureaucrats of the FBI, Krogman actually came away boasting of the job he'd done. According to the interdepartmental agreement:

- Postal inspectors would investigate mail-bombs and bombings of post offices;
- FBI would investigates bombings of federal property other than Postal and Treasury facilities;

- ATF would investigate bombings directed at all other targets *except* that when ATF agents established that a bombing was committed by "terrorists," the FBI would take over.

If that seems like a workable arrangement, consider this: When a bomb explodes, no one knows who set it off unless the bomber leaves a note. Absent one of those signed confessions, the FBI rarely accepted investigative responsibility. The job fell to ATF. But once the Treasury agents had solved the crime, proving the guilt of domestic terrorists, G-men stepped in eagerly to make the arrests—and the press announcements. The weakness of ATF's leaders had deplorable consequences.

The FBI's compulsion to build a reputation on the work of others leaves those who know the truth wondering whether the hypocritical G-men *really* solve any of the cases they claim credit for. But their motive is plain and practical. Using the media, they've built a public support that generates enormous appropriations. With 10,000 agents, the FBI currently spends almost 10 percent of all the funds spent by states and the federal government supporting more than 800,000 local, county, state and federal law enforcement officers across the United States.[12]

Years were coming when the National Rifle Association's egregious falsehoods would combine with ATF's weak leadership—an ironic alliance that made it easy for Congress to slash the Treasury unit's budget. Had ATF enjoyed recognition for its agents' accomplishments—laurels so often stolen by the FBI—it could have overcome the NRA's assaults. Better funded, it would have imprisoned even more terrorists and gunmen.

Fewer criminals, less crime; less crime, fewer victims. It would be nice.

Bottom line: How many more will die by the year 2000?

8

Underworld Armorers

LOCKHART: I'm going to kill you.
VIC: Why? I never saw you before. A
           man's got a right to know why.
LOCKHART: The Dutch Creek Massacre.
VIC: I wasn't even there.
LOCKHART: My brother was, and a dozen other
           kids just like him. Those Apaches
           slaughtered them, and they used
           repeating rifles you'd sold them. As
           far as I'm concerned, it's the same as
           if you'd pulled the trigger yourself.
                  —from *The Man from Laramie*

Every year, police across the United States drain half a million guns from the underworld weapons pool.[1] Every day and every night, thousands of amateur peddlers and professional armorers slink into back rooms and back alleys to refill that pool. Supplying untraceable guns—the indispensable tool of the outlaw's trade—these greedy men are wellsprings that nourish violent crime.

Karen Belvedere was bathing three-year-old Davie in her middle-class Queens, New York, apartment when the front door suddenly splintered. Terrified and breathless, the twenty-seven-year-old mother clutched her son's damp head to her breast as heavy footsteps drew near. A man with a pistol stepped inside. "I gotta get outta New York. I need money." He emphasized his demand by pressing the muzzle of his gun to Davie's temple.

Karen shrieked, "No!" Her final horror was the sight of

Davie's cherry-red blood splattering across her snow-white porcelain tub. Then she died.[2]

Her killer's Raven revolver shared its ancestry with one taken from a gunman wounded in a shootout with police; and another confiscated from two West Side drug dealers; and a fourth, purchased in the dingy doorway of a decaying tenement by an undercover ATF agent. All were legally sold by Jim's Surplus Store in Nicholasville, Kentucky, to fifty-seven-year-old baby-supply salesman Sam Barnes, who—like most of the NRA's "honest, [otherwise] law-abiding citizens"—had no prior criminal record. Agents and police officers nailed Barnes as he emerged from the Holland Tunnel just before dawn on February 13, 1981, with a fresh cargo of lethal Valentines.

The narcotics traffic is different. A drug dealer's wares are quickly consumed; the gun peddler's product can be used again and again. One of the handguns ex-con Sam Bynum brought from Virginia to the Big Apple was linked by ballistics examiners to sixteen homicides.[3]

Then, too, the victims of drug dealers are volunteers.

Federal law says gun dealers have to get a license and keep records; their customers must sign forms certifying they're not convicted felons. When everyone complies with the law, every sale—except the occasional transaction between private parties—leaves a trail. ATF can trace crime guns for police. Criminals using false identities or lying about thier criminal records can be snatched up, disarmed and isolated from their would-have-been victims—in prison. This system of recordkeeping erects a barrier against violence.

One of ATF's jobs is to deal with the greedy men who punch holes in that wall.

Audrey Decker was typical. He was a janitor at a Kansas City school and he had a license to deal in firearms. An informant tipped me that Decker was selling off the books—without asking for ID or keeping records. So I made "a routine inspection," made sure he understood the law and gave him a fresh copy of the statute in case he'd lost the one that came with his license. "Here's my number," I said. "Call if you have any questions."

Five days later, Decker took a revolver from a drawer,

tucked it into his waist and grinned at Don Smithson, the customer sitting at his kitchen table. "Gotta be careful," Decker said. "There's a guy at the door I don't exactly trust."

The man at the door was Donald Long. Decker had already sold the stranger several pistols without even asking his name. Long admitted wanting "guns the cops can't trace back to me, in case I gotta ditch 'em." Now Decker sold him two more handguns.

Long was an undercover agent. So was Smithson. Decker pleaded guilty.[4]

Decker's "reason" was typical. "If I don't do it," he whined, "somebody else will." That's the alibi drug dealers offer. It's the same excuse used by the man who sold movies of a limp, sobbing six-year-old being brutally raped by a hulking pervert. "If I don't sell 'em," he told NBC's Tom Brokaw, "someone else will."[5]

No one knows how many gun lovers have been encouraged to sell firearms illegally by the National Rifle Association's persistent drumbeat that "Gun laws are un-Constitutional. They violate the Second Amendment." The Supreme Court quashed that argument decades ago. Then the NRA claimed that the law was unconstitutionally vague; that was settled after agents arrested a man for selling pistols at gun shows. He parroted NRA rhetoric: "I'm not a dealer; I'm a collector." The court said that "any person of ordinary intelligence would have no difficulty in ascertaining from the Gun Control Act that if he had some firearms on hand with the purpose of selling some, his conduct is prohibited unless he is licensed and that, therefore, the act is not unconstitutionally vague."

The NRA relayed this decision to its loyal followers— three years later.[6]

NRA propagandists portray offenders as harmless hobbyists. Perhaps that's why Marilyn Buck's lawyer told jurors that she'd bought the revolvers seized from her by ATF agent James C. Smith "for her personal pleasure and target practice." After all, the twenty-six-year-old blonde came from one of the best families in Austin, Texas; a high-school honor student, she'd declined invitations from Ivy League colleges to attend the University of California at Berkeley.

Special Agent Dale Littleton showed that she'd bought the guns under phony names. No one mentioned how the weapons she'd purchased were used by the Black Liberation Army, because BLA assassins had slain policemen from New York to San Francisco. That sort of knowledge might inflame impressionable jurors.

They convicted her anyway. She got ten years, but escaped from prison; six years later, the FBI charged her with driving the getaway car in a $1.7 million armored car robbery in which a guard and two policemen were murdered.[7]

Personal pleasure and target practice?

Agents want to believe that some people would never stoop to arming criminals, but ATF's list of penny-ante peddlers includes schoolteachers and doctors. Manuel Rodriguez, chief of El Salvadore's military forces, was caught trying to sell machine guns to the Mafia. General Carl Turner, the provost marshal general—top cop for the entire U.S. Army—was imprisoned after abusing his position to traffic illegally in guns.[8]

Regardless of intellect, the average peddler—whether he's a licensed dealer selling under the counter or a freelancer hawking hardware from the trunk of his car—is stupid. They're a problem because there are so many of them. Often, they're "fingered" when a crime gun is traced to their door and they can't say to whom they sold it. Naturally, that little detail—the rape or murder committed with the weapon—can't be revealed to jurors because it might "inflame their emotions" against the peddler.

Agents hate these cases. Catching the average underworld armorer offers all the challenge a chemist would encounter if he were assigned to mix a milkshake.

There are, of course, some exceptions.

Edwin Wilson was a dashing American patriot who'd distinguished himself against our country's enemies for two decades. Born in the heartland of Iowa, he served with the Marines in Korea, spent fifteen years operating cover firms for the CIA, then joined Task Force 157 and utilized more than fifty well-placed spies to monitor Soviet shipping.

111

Nearing fifty, the 6'4" former spy had grown wealthy. None of the high-ranking White House officials or influential senators he entertained at his $4 million, 1,600-acre Virginia estate had the slightest suspicion that their heroic host promoted terrorism.

Wilson already boasted of controlling interests in a hundred foreign and domestic corporations when he started an even more lucrative business; he bought an Army vehicle equipped with night-surveillance devices for $60,000 and sold it to Libya's Muammar Qaddafi—the patron of Carlos and other international terrorists—for $990,000. He paid less than $3 million for 500,000 timing devices for bombs, then sold them to Libya for $35 million. He dispatched a $2,000-a-week expert to show Qaddafi's killers how to conceal explosives in ashtrays, lamps and flower pots.

All went well until he tried to get an Army Redeye missile—a weapon any madman could use to knock an airliner out of the sky. One of his duped employees, Kevin Mulcahy, had believed that Wilson's firm was legitimate. Now he telephoned the FBI.

Hours later, Wilson phoned Mulcahy from Switzerland. "Knock off the calls to the FBI. I'll explain when I get back." Wilson and another ex-CIA man, Frank Terpil, were busy at the moment recruiting three Cubans to assassinate Qaddafi rival Umar Muhayshi.

Mulcahy, expecting lightning arrests in the wake of the documents he'd turned over to the FBI, went into hiding. But nothing happened. Months later, Mulcahy was found dead. A sheriff said he'd committed suicide by poisoning his own wine.

On October 3, 1978, plants in Houston, New Orleans and Canada shipped 40,000 pounds of explosives, under falsified Customs declarations, through Lisbon to Libya. Front men insulated Wilson from direct involvement.

The Justice Department probe was bogged down. An FBI agent confided to *New York Times* reporter Seymour Hersch, "No one is cooperating with us. . . . We've been working on this for a long time."[9]

ATF special agents Dick Pederson and Dick Wadsworth spent five months undercover, acquiring a comprehensive knowledge of how Wilson and Terpil functioned in the misty world of international intrigue. Now they needed hard evidence.

Thus far, no one had even established that a federal crime had been committed.

T-man Wadsworth spent the 1979 Memorial Day weekend sifting files in the U.S. Attorney's office. Among the papers originally handed to the FBI by Kevin Mulcahy was a scribbled note by California explosives manufacturer Jerome Brower listing weights of RDX plastic explosives shipments ordered by Wilson.

ATF agents found incriminating records at Brower's plant. Federal prosecutor Lawrence Barcella agreed that the agents had proof of a crime. Pederson and Wadsworth interviewed Brower again. Brower lied again.

On January 4, 1980, Philadelphia detectives conducting a routine vice inquiry arrested Bradley Bryant and Roger Barnard at the Sheraton Airport Inn. They found ski masks, a dozen Kentucky driver's licenses under different names, a gun and a silencer. The officers notified ATF.

Barnard and Bryant were already suspected in thefts of sophisticated equipment from the Naval Weapons Center at China Lake, California, and ATF knew that two China Lake employees had worked for Wilson, training terrorists in Libya.[10]

A week after the Philadelphia arrests, New York police nabbed Wilson's partner, Terpil, with some machine guns. The IRS was ready to assess a $2.8 million lien against Terpil's estate in an exclusive Washington suburb. On April 25, Pederson and Wadsworth arrested Terpil at a law enforcement trade show in Maryland. A grand jury indictment charged him, explosives dealer Brower and Edwin Wilson with shipping high explosives across a state line [abroad] "with knowledge the material would be used to kill, injure, intimidate and destroy." Wilson and Terpil were also charged with offering an American $1 million to assassinate a Qaddafi enemy. Terpil was held on $100,000 bail.

Wilson was safe in Libya.

A few weeks later, outside a London mosque, two men murdered outspoken Qaddafi critic Mustafa Ramaden and tossed the .38-caliber murder weapon into the street as they fled. ATF traced the revolver to Joseph McElroy, a broker agents had encountered in other subterranean marketplaces. Convicted, he cooperated.[11]

In Bonn, Germany, the former finance attaché of the Libyan embassy was assassinated. He'd refused Qaddafi's order to return home. His killer said he was acting on orders from the Libyan government. ATF traced the assassin's .357 magnum through a circuitous route to former Wilson employee Wallace Klink; and through him to Reginald Slocombe, president of Wilson's shipping firm. Slocombe admitted that the gun was one of five he'd smuggled to Rotterdam and driven to Bonn where—under Wilson's orders—he delivered them to a contact in front of the Libyan embassy.

Retired Energy Department employee Paul Cyr admitted to agents that he'd supplied Wilson with a fully automatic M-16 rifle—that Wilson delivered to Libya.

Wilson's dupes were wising up. His cover stories were unraveling. His influential friends were talking to ATF. His panic was plain when he phoned his European office manager, Peter Goulding. "I have everything under control," Wilson snarled. "I can control you too. I know your weakness. . . . I'll have your wife killed."

In October, a man posing as an IBM recruiter in Fort Collins, Colorado, shot Faisal Zagallia in the head. Qaddafi's World Revolutionary Committee claimed credit. The gun was found in a ditch and traced to Eugene Tafoya. Items in Tafoya's New Mexico apartment included the phone number of Wilson's London office and items linking Tafoya to the bombing of a Qaddafi enemy in Canada.[12]

Wilson's partner, Terpil, made bond and fled the country. The state of New York tried him *in absentia* on the machine gun charges and sentenced him to serve seventeen to fifty-three years.

U.S. marshals—the officers responsible for apprehending fugitives—devised a clever ruse that lured Wilson onto a flight bound for the Dominican Republic. Then the marshals prevailed upon Dominican authorities to refuse him entry. As the airliner taxied down the runway, Wilson suddenly realized that the plane's next stop was New York City.

Sure enough, marshals were there to greet him. Sentenced to thirty-two years imprisonment on firearms and explosives charges, he was shipped to the government's maximum-security penitentiary, where he remains today.[13]

One of ATF's most difficult, most frustrating and ultimately discouraging cases began in 1977 when agents observed a pattern in a series of killings. The victims were government witnesses and persons whose current situation suggested the advantages of cooperating with Uncle Sam: Jersey loanshark Vince Capone, wiretapper Frank Chin, Tamera Rand and Chicago crime boss San Giancana. All were slain with .22 pistols. The bullets came from different guns, but each slug bore a unique set of striations imprinted by a silencer—markings different from those produced by any previously known silencer.[14]

On Easter Sunday of that year, Mob chief Jerry Catena's lieutenant, John Lardierre, was cut down by shots to his head, chest and abdomen in the parking lot of a suburban motel, but this time ATF had a lead: The killer had abandoned the murder weapon.

Agents traced it to a Florida gunshop. Records identified the purchaser as John Bruno. "Bruno" turned out to be Frank Chierco of Manhattan—already under indictment for buying forty-eight guns under a phony name in another Florida city with Frank Amato and John Viserto. Viserto headed the Purple Gang—hit men for the Tieri-Genovese Mafia family. When agents arrested him in his $3,000-a-month apartment overlooking the Palisades in Fort Lee, New Jersey, they lifted a .38-caliber stainless steel revolver from his ankle holster and added another charge: possession by a felon. Viserto got three-to-five on the gun charge and fifteen more for a drug-smuggling scheme uncovered by the Drug Enforcement Administration. Frank Chierco died before his trial.[15]

No one was any closer to solving the .22 silencer slayings.

An ATF analysis of intelligence and lab findings regarding the eight murders opined that the hits demanding respect in Syndicate circles were committed by Genovese gunmen; those requiring less respect were carried out by the Purple Gang. Some of the guns had been acquired by Viserto's group; Viserto had been seen with Genovese mobsters; and all eight crimes bore the unique signature of those special silencers—a signature produced by the machinery used to make them.[16]

Frank Bompensiero had used one of the silencers to silence Tamera Rand. Acting Los Angeles mob chieftain Jimmy Frarianno asked who'd made them.

"Bomp" shook his head. "Tony was telling me they got a bunch of them in Chicago."

"I know," Fratianno said. "Last time I was in Cleveland, Blackie [mob boss James Licavoli] told me he saw Jackie Cerone, and he told him they had a guy in Miami making them."[17]

Thirteen months later, Bomp's Mafia membership was canceled in a phone booth by four lead pellets from a .22 pistol. All four bore those same strange markings. The FBI was shaken. Bompensiero had been one of their most secret informers.

ATF followed dozens of hot trails, but the first leg of the last journey began at noon on April 27, 1978, when a Miami smuggler introduced undercover Special Agent Ralph Altman to Frank Amirato, a 200-pound Mafia soldier reputed to have a source for silencers. Amirato checked Altman's "references" in Chicago. His inquiries were inconclusive but, gauging Altman's demeanor, the racketeer relied on his sixth sense and sold the ATF man some machine guns and narcotics. Altman promptly introduced him to "my drug contact"—a DEA agent who'd pursue the drug angle.[18]

It was unbearably hot in Amirato's Florida construction company office on July 6 when Amirato said, "Any time you want someone hit, I can get it taken care of for you."

"Thanks," Agent Altman said, standing near a fan that rotated on a rickety wooden chair, "but I like to take care of my own. Anything new on the silencers?"

Amirato lit a fresh cigar. "Matter of fact," he said, puffing a cloud of smoke, which the fan whipped away, "I got something going up in Chi that oughta work out pretty good."

The next night, the two men met at the Pine Grove Restaurant in Rosemont, a Chicago suburb. They slid into a padded booth and Amirato introduced the undercover agent to a slender man of thirty with receding brown hair, "my good friend, Jackie Gail." Agent Altman and Gail began the obligatory process of getting acquainted over cocktails. They spoke the imprecise jargon peculiar to mobsters—dropping nicknames of criminal acquaintances, hinting vaguely of shrewd scores.

Working undercover is the only way to gain evidence when all the "witnesses" are other crooks who won't talk, or can't talk, or wouldn't be credible if they did talk. Playing the role among career criminals requires all the preparation, expertise and gall of impersonating a physician at a medical convention. The difference is that the real doctors wouldn't kill you for making a little mistake.

It seemed that Agent Altman had passed the test. Amirato told him, "You can talk to Jackie here just like you talk to me. He's my contact here and he's got a really nice piece for you. You know," Amirato said, pointing his finger and cocking his thumb like a pistol, *"phhht.* You can meet him across the street and get it."

A lot of thoughts crowd an agent's mind at a time like this. Altman didn't like the idea of crossing the street for the silencer. It seemed unnecessary. If they suspected his true identity, the dark street would be a fine place to kill him. It's common practice for Mafia men to dine with an intended victim and treat him kindly until the executioner steps up and pulls his trigger. The agent's choices came down to two: accept Amirato's invitation, or go home and forget about the case. And the .22 silencers. And the murders.

Special Agent Ralph Altman crossed the street with them, then waited with Amirato in the hotel bar while Gail went "to get the silencer." Sipping his drink, Amirato babbled, "I'm number two in our organization and Jackie's next in line. He's good people, believe me. The piece is going to cost you a thousand; it costs us $900, and there's a century for Jackie."

"Damn," Altman said. "We've had some unexpected expenses, and I can give you $700 now and pay the rest later."

"No problem." Amirato waved magnanimously. He repeated his offer to "have a hit done" and touted remote-control automobile starters to avoid death by car bomb.

Even real criminals aren't safe among their own kind. "They only cost fifteen hundred," Amirato said. "It ain't much to be safe." He'd installed one on his own silver Cadillac. He prattled about the Mob's protection—police and politicians—and resumed his praise of Jackie Gail. "He was with us on the hit in Memphis." It was one of those remarks that drive undercover agents mad: the half-revealed secret, coupled with an underworld code of conversation that prohibits asking for details.

Gail joined them and informed Altman that "the piece is outside, in my girl's car." He handed Altman the keys.

Amirato walked with the agent to the station wagon, Illinois license number YA5529. Behind the rear seat, Altman found a suede carrying case containing a Colt "Woodsman" semi-automatic pistol, serial number 306499S. Threaded to its barrel was a smooth, shiny silencer, seven and a half inches long, one inch in diameter.

Back in Florida, Amirato introduced the agent to a man who introduced him to a Sunoco gas station owner who was also a licensed gun dealer. The dealer said he'd "get somebody" to sign the government forms for guns he sold Altman, and he admitted having converted semi-automatic .30-caliber carbines into machine guns.

On the night of July 29, Special Agent Altman flew back to Chicago and drove to suburban Rosemont's Garlic Press Restaurant. He waited at the bar until Jackie Gail tapped him on the shoulder. "Let's go outside for a minute."

As they approached the parking lot, Gail said, "The pieces are in a paper bag, in front of your right rear tire." Then he turned around and walked back inside.

Altman crossed the darkened lot, stooped beside his undercover G-car and found the sack containing two .22-caliber Ruger pistols, serial numbers obliterated, each fitted with a shiny silencer. He locked the guns in the trunk of his car and rejoined Gail inside. They talked for an hour before exiting to Gail's champagne-colored Lincoln Continental, license number US6476, where the agent paid for the weapons.

An hour later, Altman surrendered both guns at ATF's Chicago office to Special Agent Tony Wietrzychowski. Weitrzychowski, at thirty-nine, had worked as a police officer after college until he'd joined ATF, seven years before. A distinguished expert on the pistol range, he'd worked his share of undercover assignments and arrested scores of gunmen, but he'd never seen anything quite like these silencers. He wondered if he'd ever learn who was making them. He never guessed that the answer wouldn't please him.

Agent Altman had his final meeting with Gail on September 19. It was cool in Chicago. They hadn't seen one another for a month. Gail asked where he'd been.

"Closing some deals on the West Coast," the agent said.

"Did you do that pot deal with Frank?"

Altman shrugged. "He wasn't around when the stuff came in and we couldn't get hold of him. Hell, man, we couldn't sit on the stuff."

Gail said, "My source for explosives just got back to town."

"Look, Jackie, these silencers are important to us but we've had some problems with Frank on a few deals."

"With Frank? Amirato?"

"He wasn't around for the marijuana deal, then he sold us some PCP that was shit. Then we had a deal going down for 800 guns—we had $250,000 in cash—and the dude he brings in to do the deal says he wants fifty big ones up front. Hell, man, you know I don't do business that way."

"Do you think Frank's screwing you?"

Altman seemed to consider the possibility. "Noooo, I think it's Frank's source."

Altman and Gail parted, promising to meet again in a week.[19]

When they did, Altman showed Gail something new: his credentials. "ATF, Jackie. You're under arrest." Nine months later, Amirato pleaded guilty to twenty-one counts and received twenty-six years imprisonment. Jackie Gail got fourteen. Four others were given terms totaling twenty-five years. ATF agents fanned out across Miami with investigators from DEA and the U.S. Customs Service to wind up operations that netted two silencers, fourteen machine guns and narcotics valued at $250,000.

Three of the gun traffickers they arrested were federally licensed dealers.

An intensive probe of Jackie Gail's movements and associates forged the final link in Special Agent Ralph Altman's risky odyssey from Miami to Chicago, but the September 1980 climax turned bitter for the agents and the detectives who'd assisted them. The clandestine manufacturers of those unique silencers were Richard Madeja and Joseph Ahrens.

Both were cops. Both went to prison.

On January 20, 1983, mob fixer Allen Dorfman was executed to keep him from spilling secrets to the government. Each of the seven slugs removed from his skull carried that unique signature.[20]

Weapons peddlers go to prison, but Shakespeare said it a long time ago: "The evil that men do lives after them."

Sadly, ATF is doomed to the distraction of wasting its limited funds and precious agent energies on simple investigations to plug the ratholes where outlaws get guns—resources they'd rather use against bombers, arsonists and the gunmen themselves—but it's a job that must be done unless we want our criminals to enjoy easy access to weapons they'll use on the rest of us.

Convicted bank robber Ray Minnick—termed by the FBI "a dangerous, cold-blooded individual who has made a life of crime"—was wanted for ten bank robberies and the attempted murder of a policeman. ATF and FBI agents seized twenty-six guns in his Baltimore home; ATF agent George Rodriguez found a hundred more at Minnick's tan ranch-style house in Cortland, Ohio; another twenty were found in his car and house in Millersburg, Pennsylvania. FBI agents finally nabbed him near Hershey, Pennsylvania.

Minnick had no difficulty getting guns. He'd acquired his arsenals at flea markets and gun shows, mostly in Ohio.[21]

Back in 1920, police across the United States counted 4,477 murders by firearm. Since then, the number of cops and civilians slaughtered by gun-wielding home-based killers exceeds the total of American servicemen slain in all the foreign wars in our nation's 219-year history.[22]

In 1992 gun homicides reached 15,377.

Totals can be tabulated. Grief cannot.
The toll rises every year.

In towns and cities across America, police still drain the weapons pool.
Merchants of murder refill that pool.
The NRA makes life easier for the criminal quartermasters.
And ATF does its best to make their lives more secure—in prisons.

9

"Unsolvable
Crimes"

Variety is the mother of Enjoyment.
                    —Benjamin Disraeli

When Disraeli wrote that line in *Vivian Gray,* he wasn't
thinking of bombing investigations where—aside from the
"political" acts committed by terrorists—the enormous
variety of motives and suspects leaves no room for enjoyment.

Traditionally, two kinds of crime were considered impossible to solve: the Mafia execution, because nobody will talk
and all the suspects have perfect alibis; and the bomb-
murder because, like lightning, it's obvious where it hit and
what it did but no trace of it remains. ATF disproved both
beliefs when they joined with Connecticut State Police to
solve the slaying of Dan LaPolla, a government witness
whose home exploded one September day in 1972 when he
opened his booby-trapped front door. Twenty agents pursued more than fifty leads in distant cities and it took three
years, but they sent four Rhode Island racketeers up for life.
The investigators had help, of course—from forensic chemist Elliott Byall who'd flown to the scene, from explosive
analyst Ralph Cooper and from explosives technician Al
Gleason, who'd reconstructed the death device.[1]

ATF has three secrets that help them solve these cases.
Three secrets, and luck.

The science practiced by Al Gleason and his colleagues is
one of those three secrets. When Florida's millionaire
tobacco heiress Margaret Benson was murdered by car
bomb, author John Greenya wrote, "The hot, tired detectives and special agents all stood a little straighter when the

122

gray-haired Gleason stepped out of his car." Gleason did a walk-through of the area and gave the order that revealed ATF's second secret: "Pick up anything that doesn't grow."[2]

The fact is, bombs *don't* destroy all evidence of their existence. Fragments salvaged from the streets and rooftops surrounding the seat of the blast enable trained technicians to reassemble the device's components; it's like taking the movie of an actor being hit in the face with a pie and running the film backward so the splattered contents return to the plate. Conducting the scene search can involve heavy equipment, as it did when agents had to explore tons of debris that had once been the Jupiter Knitting Mill in South Carolina. But they found an unexploded stick of dynamite and traced that to the construction worker who'd stolen it and sold it to Ralph Cobb. A fugitive hunt that ranged from Texas to Maryland caught Cobb, and he provided the proof that also convicted the man behind the crime—mill owner Nick Michael.[3]

ATF's third secret is cooperation: a genuine, two-way partnership with state, county and local agencies where no one sluffs off the hard work that's required or hogs the credit that comes with success. Agents offer their experience and worldwide reach in the pursuit of clues along with specialized expertise and equipment; police contribute their abilities combined with a unique knowledge of who's who in the local zoo.

Cooperation was the key to ending a 1977 mob war involving bombings, murder by machine gun and running gun battles on the streets of Rochester, New York. ATF supervisor Neil Kern organized a team with officers from the city and surrounding communities that landed the gangsters in prison for 137 years.[4]

During those very same months, in faraway Pierce County, Washington—where racketeer Johnny Carbone's men were firebombing "uncooperative" taverns, shooting a state liquor agent, sending a thug to threaten a man by holding a knife to the throat of his baby and beating a sixty-eight-year-old potential witness into unconsciousness—agents encountered a problem that spoiled their policy of pure cooperation: the sheriff was on Carbone's payroll. Agents had to come and go like spies in a foreign country, but they were aided by state police and detectives from neighboring Tacoma. Kansas City agents nailed the gunmen who'd shotgunned the state officer, but the big break came when Carbone enforcer "Waco" Caliguri hired a highly recommended Chicago torpedo to plant dynamite at each corner of the Night Moves Tavern so the place would collapse, killing the merry patrons crowded inside. The "torpedo" was Paul Russell—one of three ATF men who'd penetrated Carbone's organization, undercover. Carbone and his crew received sentences totaling 162 years. Sheriff Janovich got twelve years.[5]

The range of reasons for bombing is endless, from the cold cash that motivated tobacco heiress Margaret Benson's son in the case mentioned above, to the women—owners of a chain of California prep schools—who hired a hit man to bomb former teachers for complaining to the state about conditions at the schools, to L. V. Wade's explanation for blowing up a Nashville woman's car: "I got tired of people trying to do me in," he told Special Agent Troy Hamner, "and I decided to do someone else for a change."[6]

For a change? Wade was an escaped murderer.

Motives vary, but the range of techniques employed by agents is equally broad. When an explosion showered an infant's crib with shards of debris and broken glass in a North Carolina parsonage, Special Agent Charles Mercer relied on sheer persistence. He spent five years patiently piecing clues together on the trail of threats and shotgun blasts aimed at the Reverend Robert Nichols's family, but he finally broke down the stubborn wall of provincial secrecy and convicted the town's leading citizen, whose influence in the congregation had been altered by the minister. Afterward, a reporter asked Mercer, "Was it an interesting case?"

"I don't think that's a good term," Mercer replied. "There's too much tragedy involved . . . for the families involved. Especially the victims."[7]

Luck played a role one still, muggy July night in Orlando while agents following up on a vague tip regarding some labor-union bombings watched the offices of the Overland

Trucking Company. A dark sedan cruised past the place twice, then turned into Overland's lot. A fuse sparkled in the darkness and curved in a graceful arc to the roof of the building. The car lurched toward the street. The nearest agent started his car, grabbed his microphone—"Bomb! They're turning east!"—and flicked his headlights on while his partner raced to the building to shepherd some employees working overtime to safety. Down the street, other G-cars darted from concealment to block the bombers' escape just as an orange flash banished the darkness and a thunderous roar filled the air. It would take agents five years, but Teamsters Local 385 president Paul Parker and eleven others received prison terms exceeding a hundred years.[8]

Another labor-union case illustrated a callous indifference to humanity common among the cowards who bomb. A black sedan glided down Falcon Drive in Cleveland, Tennessee. Its passenger hurled a bundle across the lawn of Kinzel Bates, a laborer at nearby Ready-Mix Concrete whose "crime" was crossing a Teamsters' picket line to get to work. The explosion blew in the wall of six-year-old Becky Bates's bedroom. Glass and masonry pierced her pink cotton sheet. Had she not been infected by the fear following threats phoned to the Bates home, she might have died an agonizing death instead of leaving her room that evening to crawl into bed with her parents.

A fingerprint on an unexploded bomb set by the same group identified Sid Dickson, a known associate of Teamsters Local 515 business agent James Gallihan. He and an accomplice went to prison without talking, but two years later, when Special Agent John Franklin and his supervisor confronted Dickson in prison with more evidence they'd gathered—enough to charge him with additional bombings—Dickson responded, "Where do you want me to begin?" Special Agent Colvin Little went undercover posing as one of the bombers' former cellmates, contacted Teamsters business agent Gallihan and got enough evidence for a search warrant.

The Gallihans weren't home. Agents waited nearly six hours before posting guards at the entrance to the long road leading into the suspect's acreage and executing the warrant. They were still finding machine guns, grenades, silencers, explosives and Gallihan's Ku Klux Klan regalia when, in the gathering dusk outside, a car approached the roadblock. Special Agent Robert Eckard, his badge clipped to his breast pocket, stepped into the lane and raised his hand. The shiny black Ford accelerated. Eckard shouted, "Federal officer!" and got off one quick shot before the car, driven by Gallihan's goon, Dave Moffa, crushed his leg and tossed him into a ditch.

Special Agent George Bradley, around the curve just sixty yards from the house, heard the car, the shout and the thud of metal on man. The Ford slewed around the curve too fast and skidded past Bradley and into a ditch. Moffa jumped out, crouched beside his open door and started shooting. Bradley snapped off two quick shots and leaped into the tall grass beside the road. The one-minute gunfight left Moffa dead beside his car, his pistol by his hand. A .45-caliber M-3 submachine gun with five fully loaded magazines was found, fortunately beyond his reach, in the trunk of the Ford.

Gallihan, Local 515 president David Halpenny and others went to prison. Two years later, Bob Eckard—surgery having failed to repair his crushed knee—retired. Fellow agents gave him a muzzle-loading rifle he'd admired and the bureau presented him with the Award for Valor.[9]

When agents are confronted with the reality of a bomb, they have to begin with the realization that *anyone* might be guilty. Like the multimillionaire president of the JRM Coal Company, imprisoned for orchestrating a 1982 campaign of bombings and shootings designed to exploit union members in Kentucky. Or veteran state bomb investigator and one-time FBI informer Howard Godfrey, who planted a pipe-bomb on a busy road near his Auburn, California, home, telephoned an anonymous threat—"I'm going to kill a trick-or-treater with a bomb."—and volunteered to head the investigation.[10]

One big surprise came when Special Agent Jerry Taylor flew in from San Francisco to examine a bombed car—the third in a series of Salt Lake City explosions that had already killed a woman and a bishop of the Mormon

Church. Authors Steven Naifeh and Gregory White Smith reported in their book, *The Mormon Murders,* that "Jerry Taylor was the two things every cop wanted to be: *professional*—totally, uncompromisingly, shit-kicking professional—and *tough*—really tough, not TV tough. . . . *No one* knew bombs like Jerry Taylor knew bombs. Cops in fifty states knew that, and they respected it."

Detective Don Bell told Special Agent Taylor that the latest victim, Mark Hofmann, "said he came back to his car and found a package on the driver's seat. When he opened the door, the package fell on the floor and he reached to catch it. That's when it blew up."

Taylor sighed and smiled. "You've got your bomber." Pointing to the right side of the seat, he told the startled detective, "That's where the bomb was when it went off. This man's lying when he says it fell onto the floor as he entered the car. Had the bomb exploded on the floor, it would have blown straight down and there wouldn't be any depression here." The agent pointed to a portion of the console dividing the two sides of the front seat. "And the driver's door was still open." Taylor based this conclusion on Hofmann's injuries and his experience with dozens of cases in which victims in cars with the doors closed had shot up through the roof, often only halfway, caught at the waist. "Otherwise, the blast would have sent Hofmann up like a rocket," Taylor explained.

"Here's what happened," the agent theorized. "He gets in the car. The bomb's probably in the back. He kneels on the front seat, reaches over and brings it toward the front, but it slips or he drops it and *boom!* No doubt, my friend, Hofmann's your bomber."

Hofmann pleaded guilty and was sentenced to life. He'd murdered his victims because they'd gotten wise to a series of master forgeries purportedly relevant to the history of the Mormon Church—documents he'd sold for enormous prices, clipping one victim, Provo attorney Brent Ashworth, for more than $400,000.[11]

Sometimes no one has any reason to harm the victim. On a bitterly cold morning in January 1975, fifty-seven-year-old Peggy Rhodes left her cozy Kentucky farmhouse to find her cat. Pulling her shawl close against the cutting wind, she picked her way down the icy slope to the barn where her pet liked to hunt mice. Stepping along the earthen floor between the stalls, she called for kitty. When she opened the door to the tack room, she tripped a detonator. The blast sent Peggy Rhodes's stocking cap sailing 150 feet.

State police asked ATF to enter the case.

Agents found no motive for killing Mrs. Rhodes, but her husband was insured for $150,000. The beneficiaries were James Johnson and James Simon, owners of an auto dealership Mr. Rhodes had sold them a few years earlier and a firm that had fallen on hard times. Agents searching the crime scene inch by inch came up with a fingerprint belonging to Steve Monroe, who was already suspected in another bombing. The lab identified the explosive as the same type Monroe had recently purchased. Two accomplices admitted helping him make the bomb. Special Agent Bob Bridgewater, who'd interviewed Monroe, testified, "At one point, he seemed very emotional and he drooped his head. He seemed to be in deep thought. He said, 'Why did that woman go to the barn?'"

Apparently, he'd only intended to make her a widow. He got life imprisonment.

Car thief Carlos Lloyd and Bowling Green businessman David Walker got eighteen and ten years, respectively, for hiring Monroe to do the job. Walker swore that the insurance beneficiaries Johnson and Simon had promised him $10,000 and a new Thunderbird to kill Mr. Rhodes. Telephone records confirmed a call from the auto agency to Walker's unlisted phone and agents verified Walker's meeting with the two men at a restaurant where Walker claimed the deal was made.

Johnson asphyxiated himself in his garage. His note said, "I didn't plan to kill her."

At Simon's trial, the prosecutor informed jurors that Walker had been convicted of lying to a federal agent, and Simon testified that he'd been outside the restaurant in the parking lot when Johnson spoke with Walker. While jurors deliberated, the defendant approached Special Agent William Rockliff outside the courtroom. "No hard feelings. No matter what happens, I understand. You're just doing your job." Tears welled up in Simon's eyes. "But goddammit, I just didn't do it. If I'm guilty of anything it's just for being so goddamned dumb."

Simon was acquitted.

Outside the courthouse, Rockliff told *Louisville Times* reporter Tom VanHowe, "You know, there are no absolutes in this business. Simon came into that courtroom an innocent man. He stood before the mast, and when it was over he walked out the same way he went in—innocent."[12]

In keeping with the variety of these cases, some bombers escape justice.

St. Louis, Missouri, sweltered on July 24, 1970. Phillip Lucier, president of the Continental Telephone Company, lunched with two of his executives at a restaurant in the Pierre LaClede shopping mall and office complex. They divided the check, left a tip and emerged into the searing sunlight. "Wait here," the portly Lucier told his younger aides. "I'll open the windows and get the air conditioner going." He climbed into his sleek, black Cadillac and turned the key.

A mighty blast shattered the placid drone of the sleepy, suburban lot.

Phillip Lucier left a widow and eight children.

ATF offered to assist the police, but homicide took precedence over a federal charge carrying, at that time, a maximum penalty of ten years. Besides, the crime was front-page news. The cops brushed the agents off with requests to handle a few minor chores and run down some distant leads. As the months passed and the case slipped from the front pages, ATF's involvement expanded in direct proportion to slackening police efforts. The major problem was an absence of motive. Lucier was a warm, likable, highly respected family man. Agents probed his associates, employees and former employees. Lucier had a financial interest in the Western Town House Corporation; agents investigated construction unions and the corporation's competitors. They combed the St. Louis underworld, pursuing rumors that Lucier had refused mob requests to use his telephone company in an illegal wire service—gossip that proved unfounded. No one had a reason to murder Phillip Lucier, but the man was dead.

Given the motive, the agents could have solved the case quickly because they had a witness. A man cruising the LaClede lot for a parking space had seen a car that seemed ready to pull out. He waited, but the man in the front seat of Lucier's Cadillac made no move to depart. The witness found another spot, and as he strolled toward the restaurant, he saw a man in the front seat of Lucier's car lean forward, his face near the windshield while his hands seemed busy beneath the dashboard. Hypnotized, the witness helped a Chicago artist sketch the suspect's likeness. The media publicized the portrait, but every look-alike the agents found in Missouri and Illinois had an alibi.

Informers were pressed. Undercover agents roamed felon haunts. All ATF needed was a suspect.

Five years later, special agents Dale Wiggins and John Liedtke were assigned to do a cold-case review. For days they pored over typed reports, glossy photos and the huge collection of newspaper stories, leafing through pounds of newsprint filled with facts they already knew and a smattering of misinformation. It all seemed an exercise in futility until one agent spotted a tiny squib reporting a quirk of fate: "Attorney Schwartz Escapes Injury."

The brief story under that headline told how, with no assigned parking spaces in the LaClede lot, the lawyer couldn't get into his accustomed slot when he returned from an early lunch with a client. Agent Wiggins and Liedtke bolted from the office.

Schwartz began by pointing out that his black Lincoln—like Lucier's black Cadillac—sported a four-digit license plate and a telephone antenna. Then he told the agents about two clients, confidence men who'd bilked New Orleans mob suspect Santo DiFatta out of $150,000. DiFatta had made threats, and killing Schwartz would send a strong message to the men who'd cheated him.

"My God," one of the ATF men said, "why didn't you tell somebody about this?"

"We did," Schwartz said. He and his clients had given the

whole story to FBI agent Howard Kennedy within days of the murder.

Wiggins and Liedtke braced Kennedy at the FBI office. "Um, yeah," the G-man said. "I remember. Met 'em out at Forest Park. Told me all about DiFatta and the threats."

Wiggins was furious. "Why didn't you tell us or the police?"

"Well," Kennedy replied, "it wasn't our case. Besides, DiFatta was giving us information on a bank fraud we were investigating."

The best ATF could do, reaching back for five-year-old memories and records, was prove that DiFatta had been in St. Louis the day after the bombing. They subpoenaed him, put him in a room with a score of people waiting to testify before a grand jury and sent their witness from the LaClede parking lot into that room. "Let us know if you see anybody in there that looks familiar."

The man came out within minutes. "I positively recognize one man. He's the guy I saw in Mr. Lucier's car that day."

DiFatta allowed the agents to take his fingerprints and photograph, and he asked questions. "What if I was the bomber, or what if I was the bomber with my attorney, or what if my attorney was the bomber? Could he go in and lie to the grand jury and make me stand alone?" And, "Just where would I be if . . . let's just suppose that I was the bomber . . . that I was in the car or my attorney was involved with me in this . . . or even if my attorney acted alone—could they frame me for this?"

The agents shrugged.

"Could they put my fingerprints in the car that was bombed?

The federal statute of limitations on bombing had expired. ATF gave its evidence to the county prosecutor. He didn't think he could get a murder conviction at this late date, but he gave the agents' file to *St. Louis Post Dispatch* reporter Ronald Lawrence. In response to his articles exposing how the FBI had concealed evidence to further their bank-fraud investigation, FBI special agent-in-charge Harlan Phillips said, "To say that we deliberately withheld information is certainly not true. If we come across information that we think is helpful to another agency, our policy is to disseminate that information as quickly as possible."[13]

If anyone believed him, it only proves that people—like bombing investigations—come in all varieties.

The oddest bit of variety is a weapon that would give law enforcement an enormous boost in solving these cases: taggants—microscopic, color-layered chips of plastic that could be mixed with explosives by manufacturers at a maximum cost of $10 million a year. Magnetic and fluorescent, they could be detected at bomb scenes via magnets or ultraviolet light. The codes shown by the color layers would identify the maker and lot number from which the destructive device had been constructed—enough to trace it, much as ATF traced firearms. The bureau convened a conference of experts from government and industry in 1972. Two years later, the bureau was granted a charter to establish an advisory committee, and in 1978, a senate subcommittee issued a report:

> In summary: The technology is here; the cost of implementing identification and detection tagging programs is almost ridiculously modest . . . there is every reason to believe that the tagging program would afford significant protection to the public by deterring many would-be bombers; and there is no question in the mind of law enforcement experts that tagging would help them in tracking down bombers and getting convictions.

During a brief test period when taggants were experimentally mixed with a minuscule percentage of the explosives distributed by U.S. companies, some of that dynamite was used to murder the driver of a pickup truck. The taggants led to the killer and he was convicted. But some manufacturers questioned the costs, and the NRA objected to placing taggants in smokeless black powder—the main ingredient in pipe-bombs—because "taggants might have a damaging effect on gun barrels and gun accuracy."

The NRA and the underworld won another battle as the

plan was defeated.[14] They replayed that victory in August of 1996 when they pressured the House of Representatives into slicing a taggant plan from the president's anti-terrorism bill.

A variety of people in this country have a variety of priorities that are not what Disraeli might have called "the mother of Enjoyment."

10

Ladies
and Gentlemen
in White Coats

> When I am in the company of scientists, I feel like
> a shabby curate who has strayed by mistake into a
> drawing room full of dukes.
>
> —W. H. Auden

They're the magicians of law enforcement. Others speculate, they prove. Prove some people guilty; prove some
suspects innocent. They master the fruits of man's quest to
understand the world and improve our future, and they use
that knowledge to help us have a future. They're assigned to
the ATF directorate of Science and Information Technology, and they're indispensable members of the bureau's
team.

ATF's is the government's oldest law-enforcement lab. Its
first chemist, Louis Starkle, was transferred from the Department of Agriculture in 1886. When chemist Robert
Watson came there in 1948, it had two instruments: a
spectrophotometer and a photometer, used to analyze the
coloration of whiskey. In 1978 the lab was moved from the
top floor of the IRS Building in Washington to the expanded
ATF National Laboratory Center in Rockville, Maryland.
Four years later, a Justice Department study ranked it
number one, on a par with Justice's own FBI lab. In 1984
the ATF facility became the first federal laboratory to win
the approval of the American Society of Crime Laboratory
Directors, tough-minded scientists who only approve labs
that meet their superstrict standards.

Small wonder. The lab's manual states that, rather than simply processing a conveyer-belt succession of cases:

> Carrying out either pure or applied research is considered an essential function in the development of the full capabilities of scientists . . . a program of library reading and research combined with laboratory investigation and experimentation.
>
> Scientists shall be encouraged to devote a part of their time to . . . the development of new and the improvement of existing methods of analysis.

The results have been spectacular. ATF pioneered law-enforcement applications of neutron-activation analysis (NAA) to establish the common origin of substances. Questioned materials are placed inside a microwavelike device and bombarded with neutrons, then put into another chamber that reads the radiation. Mud from the fender of a contraband-laden truck in New York was matched to a particular farm in Georgia; marijuana seized in different cities was shown to have been grown in the same field. A sawed-off gun barrel was matched to the weapon from which it had been cut.[1]

The most dramatic application of neutron-activation analysis was the ATF lab's invention of the gunshot residue test. The old paraffin-nitrate test used by police for decades simply detected nitrates without an ability to differentiate between various substances containing those chemicals, like gunpowder, or fertilizer, or urine. This process, utilizing flameless atomic absorption, detected barium and antimony—components of a bullet's primer cap. In a California case, it proved that slain deputy sheriff Merrit W. Deeds and two murder suspects had not fired weapons but that John Shirey had fired a gun he'd held in both hands.[2] In Virginia, the test proved that Patrolman Paul Ridley had not fired the gun that wounded Caroline Scott.[3]

ATF's innovators adapted NAA to the detection of explosives residue—handy in detemining whether a suspect has handled bomb components. Then in 1992, scientists from the National Institute of Standards and Technology developed a faster, less expensive method: micellar electro-kinetic capillary electrophoresis (MECE), and ATF forensic chemist Ed Bender announced the bureau's intention to purchase MECE equipment for explosives analysis.[4]

ATF had done quite well adapting neutron-activation analysis in hundreds of explosives cases, like the Webb City, Missouri, bombing, where the process detected explosives residues on the hands of two suspects *and* established a match between soils on the suspects' boots and soil from the spot where the bombers had parked their getaway car.[5]

Neutron-activation analysis wasn't ATF's only innovation. They pioneered the use of voiceprints, and in 1989, when a blood-spotted glove was found near a broken window through which an abortion clinic arsonist had made her escape, ATF proved her involvement by leading the federal community in the utilization of DNA blood typing.

Currently, DNA testing can even match hair samples if the roots are present, but that wasn't the case back in the 1970s, when ATF agents arrested gun shop employee Richard Hoinville for bombing a public service company substation in Colorado. Their lab proved that the substation's chain-link fence had been cut by Hoinville's wirecutters; microscopic examination matched fibers from that cut fence to fibers on Hoinville's jacket *and* to fibers on the tape around the bomb; then it matched rat hairs on that tape to rat hairs in the pocket of that jacket. Hoinville, leader of the one-man Continental Revolutionary Army, went to prison with a heightened respect for the revolutionary achievements of science.[6]

An even more "hair-raising" case began when agents arrested licensed gun dealer Ronald Kleason for lying about a New York felony indictment when he bought a shotgun in San Antonio, Texas. In Kleason's trailer, agents found a five-foot power saw with blood and hair clinging to its sawblades and a nametag with a bullet hole. The nametag's owner was one of two Mormon missionaries reported missing in Austin, and locks of hair they'd given their girlfriends matched hairs from the saw. It took a jury five minutes to find Kleason legally sane and two hours to convict him of double homicide.[7]

ATF's scientists often assist in the field, as they did in April 1985, when agents and state police raided the 224-acre compound along the Arkansas-Missouri border occupied by the neo-Nazi CSA (Covenant, Sword and Arm of the Lord) to seize ninety-five contraband machine guns, silencers and bombs along with 107 other firearms. When agents found a 12-gauge shotgun with peculiar cuttings on the outside of the barrel, bureau experts showed how the weapon had been redesigned to fire grenades.[8]

More often, the scientists and technicians help without leaving their offices, and nobody knows guns like ATF's experts. That's who the Texas Rangers and the FBI called when they were working a series of Bonnie and Clyde style bankrobbers who'd been operating for thirteen years. Members of ATF's Firearms Technology Branch inspected bank photographs and identified the weapons the bandits carried. ATF-Dallas sent agents to check dealers' records; guns were matched to two suspects. Arrested by Rangers and G-men, both confessed.[9]

A longer investigation began when New Haven, Connecticut, detectives gazed down at the corpse of Perry Farnham and clenched their fists in their overcoat pockets because Farnham had been a key witness in their probe of oil thefts by racketeers. They commenced their ritual of photos, fingerprints and neighborhood canvass with little hope of success because mob hits are rarely solved. The triggermen have no personal motive. Who can finger them? Who would?

State ballistics examiners noted the uncommon slugs removed from Farnham's body and consulted ATF. Bureau specialists identified the weapon as a .45-caliber Model SM-10 manufactured by RBP Industries of Georgia. Special Agent W. Lee Stead found that only three such firearms had been shipped to Connecticut—all to licensed dealer David Wantroba in suburban Ansonia. According to Wantroba's records, he'd kept one for himself, sold one to his sister and sold the third to his brother-in-law. "Mine's at my mother's house in Florida," he told Special Agent Pete Gagliardi. His sister's gun was lost, he said, while rafting in the Housatonic River, and the third firearm had been stolen. No, the theft wasn't reported to police.

Agents were intrigued. Wantroba's gun business was just a sideline; his main business was the Wantroba Fuel Oil Company, and the Farnham murder was tied to stolen fuel oil. They kept after the brother-in-law until Ferrara admitted he'd never even seen the gun. "Wantroba gave me fifty bucks to sign the government form."

"Are you being straight with us now?" Gagliardi asked. Ferrara swore he was being truthful. Gagliardi asked, "Will you prove it? Will you help us?" The agent wired Ferrara for sound and sent him to discuss the investigation with Wantroba. The gun peddler told Ferrara he'd converted one of the weapons into a machine gun and sold it to James McVeigh—a forty-five-year-old ex-con, a self-educated, well-spoken Jeckyl-Hyde sort known for his violent rages. A search of McVeigh's home yielded guns, but not the murder weapon. McVeigh phoned his wife, said he'd be home at six and vanished. Police found his office door open, a teabag in a cup of tepid water, but no McVeigh. Was he dead?

Agents apprehended him in Maryland with two pistols and $30,000 in cash. Wantroba pleaded guilty to multiple offenses under GCA-68, and McVeigh's ten-year federal sentence kept him on ice until the police got him convicted of murder.

There'd have been no convictions without a suspect, and there'd have been no suspect if ATF's experts hadn't pointed out which trail to follow.[10]

One of the most astonishing developments pioneered by ATF scientists was an ink-tagging program that enabled ATF to date a piece of writing. Using thin layer chromotography, bureau scientists dated an agreement and some promissory notes, proving that a Tennessee lawyer perjured himself in a tax evasion trial. Other writings—diary entries by a corporate president implicating former vice president Spiro Agnew and other officials of Baltimore's government in a kickback scheme—were proved authentic. ATF's collection—over 6,000 inks gathered from around the world—was used more recently to prove the authenticity of documents penned by the Nazi "Angel of Death," Dr. Joseph Mengele.

Another ATF collection includes nearly 6,000 firearms—some contributed by manufacturers and importers, others confiscated from the agents' criminal clientele—which are used for reference to assist lawmen everywhere. The few fortunate visitors can see the .25-caliber cigarette-pack gun, a .22-caliber cigarette-lighter gun, and others disguised as canes, cameras, pens of all kinds and tire-pressure gauges. There's even a seventeen-inch .22-caliber working replica of the Thompson submachine gun. Firearms enthusiasts are saddened by the sight of a delicately engraved Purdy shotgun that would be worth about $20,000 today if some insensitive thief hadn't hacked off its barrel, and almost everyone feels a chill when they see the assassin's kit: a cut-down rifle equipped with a silencer and fitted into an innocuous attaché case with the trigger built into its handle.

The most frequently utilized helpers at headquarters are the men and women of the bureau's National Firearms Tracing Center. During the first three months of 1984, traces solved numerous robberies, a Las Vegas kidnapping, a Detroit mail robbery, a would-be cop killer in Virginia, the identification of a serial rapist in Washington, D.C., and six murders. In a West Virginia case, tracing cleared an innocent suspect and identified the real killer. A Trenton, New Jersey, trace put a murder weapon in the hands of a so-called thrill killer suspected of more than twenty homicides. A North Canton, Ohio, trace led to bandits who'd slaughtered two gas station attendants, execution style, to prevent them from fingering the robbers.

In 1988 tracing identified a *victim*. Fort Lauderdale police requested a trace on a pistol found in a Dumpster with some bloody sheets. The gun had been sold to George Kehoe. Officers learned that Kehoe was missing, found a girlfriend who fingered men the victim had feared, and the killer was caught. Kehoe's body was fished from a canal near Boca Raton.[11]

On New Year's Eve, 1978, a man walked into an Indiana train depot and shotgunned three railroad workers. Two died. The killer dumped his weapon in a park where it was found. Police requested a trace. Its purchaser, fired railroader Rudy Bladell, was picked up and he confessed.[12]

In 1994 ATF traced more than 80,000 firearms for local, state and federal law-enforcement agencies. More were requested; many failed due to sloppy records kept by careless dealers and deficient records maintained by dealers who deliberately defy the law. Tracing revealed which dealers shouldn't be trusted with a license—by identifying those who wouldn't keep records *and* by pointing agents to the sources of criminal weaponry who supplied illicit traffickers. Back in 1973, with New York City's Sullivan law requiring that gun buyers be photographed, fingerprinted and approved by the police, it was tough for crooks to arm themselves, but traffickers supplied black market peddlers with weapons acquired easily in South Carolina. Among these were two used to shoot a cop in a cruiser, two seized from Black Liberation Army members after a gun battle with police and two confiscated from members of a Chinese street gang. Gun shop owners Edward and Sylvia Abbott of Greenville, South Carolina, got five years' imprisonment for selling more than a thousand guns illegally to out-of-state residents. Had they obeyed GCA-68 by shipping the weapons to a licensee in the buyers' home states, the firearms would have been delivered in compliance with the laws of the purchasers' home state, and local police would have access to the sales record. Greenville's gun laws were extraordinarily loose. Not surprisingly, their 12.6-per-100,000 murder rate far exceeded Boston's 5.7 or Pittsburgh's 4.2. Another South Carolina dealer illegally sold 20,000 firearms to an out-of-stater, most of which were resold in New York.[13]

Of 840 Detroit crime guns traced by ATF, only seventy had been sold in Michigan; 770 were bought beyond the reach of Michigan laws.[14] Were it not for the traffickers who supply these weapons to the underworld, and the gun fraternity's tolerance of this greedy breed, GCA-68 would function smoothly; fewer criminals could get guns (unless they're stupid enough to carry a stolen pistol that can link them to a theft) and crime would drop.

ATF's scientists and technicians continue to expand their leadership in forensic research. They're guiding development of Ceasefire, a computerized scanner that makes quick comparisons of bullets and shell casings—an innovation that's already proved its value in Atlanta, Boston and Washington, D.C., by linking bullets to guns used by criminals in murders, assaults and other violent crimes. In 1994, under Director John Magaw, they initiated a program with the Army Corps of Engineers and the Nuclear Defense Agency that includes blowing up vehicles under controlled circumstances at New Mexico's White Sands Proving Ground. Code-named Dipole Might, its goal is to create a computer model that will help agents solve terrorist car-bombings and truck-bombings like those perpetrated at the New York World Trade Center and the federal building in Oklahoma City.

11

The Birth of
a Bureau

Oft expectation fails
And most oft there
Where it most promises.
     —William Shakespeare

In 1970 ATF was still a division of the Internal Revenue Service, an agency that viewed the world through tax-colored glasses; an enormous bureaucracy led by men with little use for a unit no longer needed to protect the alcohol revenue. Agents prayed for an escape from the narrow focus of chiefs who chanted, "We're not policemen; we're tax collectors."

An answer to the agents' prayer wouldn't come for another two years. Ironically, that answer began with attacks aimed against them. But the new bureau would come into the world handicapped. Rather than create an agency designed to defeat violent crime, Treasury conceived a clone of the parent IRS. ATF's special agents came with their branch that regulated and collected taxes from legitimate industries. Then, too, ATF began its existence with a ready-made enemy—an NRA powerful enough to have instigated this unprecedented amputation from an established arm of the government. Finally, tragically, the fledgling bureau was born with a congenital defect: its leaders.

In 1970, from the IRS perspective, the ATF agents' growing shift from bootlegger cases to gun cases diminished the unit's value day by day.

Agents complained, "Those IRS people don't understand law enforcement."

Example: The Gun Control Act provided that ex-convicts

who'd turned over a new leaf might get "relief" from the law that forbade their possession of firearms—that is, if an investigation found no recent criminal activity, he might regain his right to have guns—*unless* the crime for which he'd been convicted involved the use of a weapon. When a man applied who'd served time for stabbing someone with a bread knife, ATF turned him down.

IRS attorneys overruled them, saying "a bread knife's not a weapon."

"It is when you stick it into somebody," an ATF man replied.

"No it's not. It's still a bread knife. Grant the man's relief."

While most IRS executives saw their ATF division as a contentious lot, the tax man held on. No bureaucrat willingly surrenders any authority or resource. But when the agents' actions sparked criticism—some from Capitol Hill—that was different.

The first "incident" occurred after agents hunting the man who'd blown up police headquarters in Shaker Heights, Illinois, discovered that the bomber had learned his bomb-making expertise from library books. Months later, three agents investigating three separate bombings—in Ohio, California and Wisconsin—asked local librarians whether certain suspects had borrowed books on explosives. The American Library Association fired off a salvo that landed in a Senate subcommittee. "This activity," the librarians said, "chills a citizen's freedom to read." It didn't take much of a furor to chill the IRS. Orders came down: The "practice" of questioning librarians was discontinued. Agents objected. Revenue chiefs responded, "We're not policemen, we're tax collectors."[1]

Case closed.

The next shot came from the National Rifle Association. Member Ron Shaffer, a licensed dealer based near St. Louis, was caught violating the Gun Control Act. The NRA magazine informed followers that Shaffer, "age twenty-five, has just begun a term of ten years after being convicted primarily of selling practice hand grenades."

They left out a few details. Shaffer had demonstrated one of those "practice grenades" for undercover agent Dwight

Thomas at a river bank. It sent mud and water hurtling sixty-five feet into the air. Agent Thomas asked him, "What are they good for?"

"They could be used as booby traps," Shaffer replied. "You could throw them through the window of a house, or into a group of four or five guys."

The NRA left out other crimes proved at Shaffer's trial—like hundreds of guns sold without making the required records. Sixty-five of them already recovered by police had been used to commit felonies, including ten murders. Shaffer told the undercover man he had a "secret stash [of guns] with no paper required."[2]

ATF furnished all of this to their IRS bosses, the IRS forwarded it to inquiring congressmen and the NRA. There were no long articles in the NRA's *American Rifleman* magazine reporting these facts to their followers.

Next, NRA member Kenyon Ballew was shot and paralyzed during an ATF raid. The NRA sunk their teeth into this one. A six-page article in their magazine screamed, "Gun Law Enforcers Shoot Surprised Citizen, Claim Self-Defense." Members were told that agents had smashed through the door, shot Ballew (who was "merely holding" a replica cap-and-ball pistol) and frightened "his near-naked wife" half to death. The article quoted her: "We didn't open the door because we were taking a bath."

They weren't taking a bath. Agents found the tub crusted with a dry green slime, residue from having cleaned a fish tank there. Nor was the woman Ballew's wife. The NRA neglected to mention this tidbit. Conservative gun lovers in the early 1970s might not sympathize with ladies found stripped to their panties in a bachelor's apartment.

For months, the federal prosecutor considered charging Ballew with the hand grenades the agents had found, but it was finally determined that Ballew was permanently crippled. The U.S. attorney decided not to prosecute.

Then Ballew lodged a civil lawsuit against the government.

For three years, the IRS was muzzled by court rules prohibiting pretrial publicity.

The NRA milked those years with monthly reminders of

the raid and sympathetic stories of the "Boy Scout leader who displayed an American flag in his window."

When Ballew's lawsuit came to trial, the sworn testimony bore small resemblance to the NRA version of events. The case had begun when Special Agent Marcus Davis got a tip that a man named Ballew was making hand grenades in his Silver Spring, Maryland, apartment. Local police added their suspicion that Ballew was the man who'd sniped at policemen responding to emergency calls near his residence. Agent Davis swore out an affidavit, the court issued a search warrant, and uniformed policemen assisted in the raid. Announcing the standard "Federal officers with a search warrant" as they knocked at the metal door to Ballew's apartment, all they heard was the sound of heavy objects sliding against the entrance. A battering ram was used. Special Agent Bill Seals climbed over the furniture barricading the door and found himself suddenly confronted by a nude man aiming a handgun at him. Seals and the officer who'd come in right behind him ducked and fired. One slug exploded the fishtank, filling the air with glass, water and tiny fish. Fragments of another bullet pierced Ballew's skull. He dropped his .44-caliber cap-and-ball pistol, a working replica of the deadly weapon that had killed thousands during the Civil War. It discharged into the ceiling. The hysterical, near-nude woman made a dash for her lover—or for the gun. She was hustled into the hallway. And agents found the grenades they'd come to seize, illegally re-armed with black powder and primer caps.

The court rendered a verdict:

> Federal agents acted reasonably and in exercise of due care in procuring the search warrant, in planning the search and in actually carrying it out. . . . When agent was confronted with plaintiff [Ballew] pointing revolver at him, he was justified in shooting first before plaintiff fired at him. Plaintiff, who heard law enforcement officers at the door and, rather than admitting them and submitting to search of his premises, attempted to barricade the door and

prevent entry and pointed a loaded revolver at the agents as they entered was contributorily negligent.

Judgment for the government.

That decision confirmed probes by Ballew's own congressman, the U.S. attorney and ATF—the agents had done their duty without exceeding their authority—but the NRA persisted in drumming their distortions into the minds of trusting followers.[3]

The Supreme Court's decision in the case of *Sullivan vs. The New York Times* held that officials can't win a libel suit without proving—in addition to the falsity of someone's statements about them—that the lies were printed with malice and reckless disregard for the truth. Nevertheless, several lawyers urged Special Agent Bill Seals to sue the NRA. They'd take the case "on contingency"—Seals wouldn't have to pay a cent unless they won. "It's an easy win," one attorney assured the agent, "lots of malice and we can prove *total* disregard for the truth."

Seals couldn't be bothered; he had a job; he was busy.

For years after that, the pitifully crippled Ballew was wheeled to gun shows and put on display—head hanging, face slack, mouth drooling—with a sign hung around his neck: "Victim of the Gun Control Act." The sight of that cold exploitation was enough to make Bill Seals sorry for the man he'd had to shoot.

But all that came later. In the days following the raid, Congressman Dingell, the NRA's man from Michigan, regaled his colleagues with a tale of a "stormtrooper exercise" when agents smashed through "the door of a man's home, the man is shot in the head, his wife [sic] is thrown half-naked outside as the man lies bleeding on the floor." Dingell put the screws to the IRS.

A short time later, Dingell was parroting NRA complaints over a training film ATF produced for police, showing how the Gun Control Act could aid them. Dingell didn't like the way the movie "implied" that this new law outlawed machine guns when those weapons were already illegal under the old statutes. Apparently, the NRA hadn't told him how the old law was gutted by that *Haynes* decision, holding the registration requirement unconstitutional. Worse yet, Dingell said, one scene depicted bikiniclad women on a "gangster's" yacht. Was the IRS producing pornography?

The IRS acted swiftly and decisively; the film was destroyed.

But the tragic trio—the Library Incident, the Ballew Raid, and the Dirty Movie Imbroglio—convinced the Internal Revenue Service that it was time to let go.

On July 1, 1972, a separate agency of the U.S. Treasury Department was created: the Bureau of Alcohol, Tobacco and Firearms. That ugly, cumbersome name was retained because the revenue employees who regulated legitimate industries and collected taxes accompanied law-enforcement personnel into the new agency.

In St. Louis, Special Agent Judd Doyle predicted that the news would be greeted "with mixed demotions." Agents expected strong leadership from bureau headquarters.

What they got was the "good old boys."

Rex Davis was named director. He'd held that title in the ATF division of the IRS, but that's all it was—a title. With no line authority. The chain of command began with the IRS commissioner and bypassed Davis, moving directly through seven regional IRS commissioners to assistant regional commissioners for ATF; and from each of them to ATF special agents-in-charge.

In the twenty-seven years since Director Davis had joined as an agent, his interests had shifted to taxation and regulating the legitimate industry. That's how people advanced under the IRS. Now as director of the bureau, with ultimate authority, he still focused his energies on his revenue-regulatory responsibilities. Law enforcement was relegated to an assistant director, but even he was not really "in charge."

William "Big Bill" Griffin had been assistant regional commissioner for ATF in the old IRS Southeast Region. A broad-shouldered, 6'4", no-nonsense leader, he'd served with the army in World War II, studied education at the University of Kentucky, played pro football with the Chicago Bears and L.A. Rams and joined ATF as an agent in

1948. Charisma and strength of character brought him to the top job in that region where agents suppressed more of the liquor industry's moonshining competitors than anywhere else. His influence reached, via that industry's powerful lobby, all the way to the White House. When ATF became a bureau, he chose to remain in Atlanta and run things by remote control. The unassertive Rex Davis accepted Griffin's hand-picked yes-men for the top law-enforcement positions. They answered—unofficially but slavishly—to Big Bill.

He'd chosen them well for their purpose. A domineering chief with no need for subordinate decision makers, Griffin had eliminated rivalry, dissension and competition in his region by weeding out anyone who might challenge him. His underlings were competent technicians who knew their specialized jobs, knew their limitations and knew their place. These were the men he chose for key slots in Washington.

But Big Bill Griffin's victory resulted, in no small measure, from machinations in play even before ATF became a bureau. The Nixon administration was moving to subvert federal law enforcement.

With the death of J. Edgar Hoover, President Nixon named lawyer L. Patrick Gray, a former office manager from his election campaign, to head the FBI. Gray departed when congressional hearings revealed that he'd destroyed documents implicating Nixon people in the scandal that became known as Watergate—the burglary of the Democratic party's national headquarters in the Watergate office-apartment complex.[4]

Vernon Acree, who'd sneaked tax data on White House enemies to Nixon staffers (while he headed the IRS division responsible for ensuring the Service's integrity), was named to head the U.S. Customs Service.[5]

Carl Turner, appointed to head the U.S. Marshal's Service; would go to prison for illegally trafficking in firearms while he was chief provost marshal of the U.S. Army.[6]

Ex-New York City police sergeant John Caulfield was inserted as the new ATF bureau's assistant director in charge of law enforcement. It was his reward for making illegal payoffs to conceal crimes committed by presidential aides.[7]

Even before the exposure of Caulfield's crimes, agent morale was sinking. They didn't like the good old boys from their own Southeast Region, but they were downright contemptuous of Caulfield's crudeness and his penchant for the regal treatment.

On the day of the Watergate burglary, Caulfield was in Los Angeles for the annual convention of the International Association of Chiefs of Police. Agents ordered to meet his flight watched him come off the plane wearing a purple pullover and rumpled slacks, looking as if he had too many drinks on the plane. Caulfield ordered an agent, "Pick up my bags."

The agent told him, "I don't pick up bags."

A second agent, Frank Vargofcak, gave Caulfield the same answer.

A third agent took the assistant director's claim checks and went for his luggage.

The next morning, when news of the burglary hit the papers, Caulfield was seen huddled with assistant secretary of the Treasury Pollner and Customs chief Vernon Acree in the hotel restaurant. All three dashed to telephones. All three exchanged their return reservations to Washington for flights to Nixon's summer White House at San Clemente.[8]

It could have been worse. Back before ATF became a bureau, IRS commissioner Randolph Thrower had rejected the Nixon administration's first choice for the assistant directorship, the one Caulfield would get after ATF was removed from the IRS. That first candidate was G. Gordon Liddy: former G-man, former Treasury appointee who'd been fired for insubordinate conduct in promoting the NRA's peculiar notions of gun laws. Thrower, a former FBI agent himself with more knowledge of crimefighting than his typical IRS underling, called ATF "a proud outfit . . . highly professional and tough as nails." White House aides insisted he accept Liddy.

Thrower told them, "If Liddy's in, I'll resign."[9]

Nixon's men found another job for Liddy—as chief burglar of the office of a psychiatrist (who'd allegedly

treated a White House "enemy") and as the bungling
architect of the botched Watergate burglary that would
bring down Richard Nixon's presidency.

Had Thrower accepted Liddy into ATF, the Watergate
burglary might have been managed by a competent crook.
Might never have been discovered. White House plans to
subvert federal law enforcement might have succeeded,
leaving Liddy—staunch as a Nazi in his willingness to
break the law—as the head of ATF's special agents.

The exposure of Caulfield's role as a payoff man left the
good old boys in charge.

ATF's first six months as a bureau saw agents arrest Mafia
bosses in Bayonne and Rochester, a Capo in Los Angeles,
mob enforcers in Baltimore, Cleveland, Detroit, New York,
and in Boston where they'd used a bomb to murder
government witness Dan LaPolla.[10]

Director Davis asked Congress for a 1974 appropriation
that left 38 percent of his vehicle fleet beyond the government's standards for obsolescence. He requested nothing
for new agents or equipment. Treasury had slashed his
original wish list because he'd earmarked a full third of his
manpower for work that yielded a mere 8 percent of the
bureau's arrests: enforcement of the liquor laws. Big Bill's
empire.[11]

The next year, Davis regaled the Senate appropriations
subcommittee with tales of his agents' exploits: bombings
solved; one investigation that cleared a hundred major
burglaries and robberies across five states; the half-million-
dollar kidnap plot foiled; four murders solved; the scheme
to assassinate three Ohio officials scotched. And then, with
the legislators expressing hearty enthusiasm, Davis requested less—considering inflation—than he'd received
the preceding year. Again, Treasury had cut his request.
Davis had wanted $5.4 million to investigate bombings,
$48.5 million to enforce the gun laws and $14.1 million—
the sum slashed by Treasury—for Big Bill to hunt
bootleggers.[12]

At the 1975 budget hearings, Senator Montoya asked
Director Davis for ATF's conviction rate in bombing cases.
Davis replied, "I would say somewhere between 40 and 50

percent." The out-of-touch director was giving them the percentage of last year's indictments which had, *thus far,* come to trial and brought convictions.[13]

The true conviction ratio, had Davis had the sense to check, was 95.2 percent.

The positive influence of one powerful lobby—the liquor industry—gave way to vicious opposition from the National Rifle Association. In 1977 a tiny faction within the NRA seized parliamentary power, disenfranchising 99 percent of the members who had heretofore elected their leaders. Harlon Carter was voted in as executive vice president to boss day-to-day operations at NRA headquarters and control their publications. He was elected by one of every 2,000 members; or 0.0012 percent of America's hunters; or 0.00006 percent of all gun owners—i.e., by a bare majority of those 1,200 gunlovers dedicated enough to spend money and vacation time to attend their annual convention.

Later, the press would tell how Carter had retired from the U.S. Border Patrol amidst accusations that he'd stolen 40,000 rounds of government ammunition. The crime was never solved. United Press International reporters revealed that Carter had once been convicted of murdering a boy, but the verdict had been set aside on one of those technicalities conservatives complain about.

Lying got off to a quick start a month later when Neal Knox, director of the NRA Institute for Legislative Action, told members (falsely) that a proposed Maryland law would prohibit citizens from carrying guns on their own property. He said he'd had to wait ninety days for his own state handgun permit. The *Baltimore Sun* reported on February 29, 1980, that Knox's permit had been ready in twenty-three days and he'd actually picked it up on the forty-fifth day.

When NBC-TV scheduled a documentary titled "The Shooting Gallery Called America," letters poured into their studios: "We watched [the program] and we can give you our opinion in two short words: It Stunk." And, "Why is it every Commie skunk . . . wants to take guns away from honest Americans?" And, "You subversive bastards ought to be shot!" But none of these letter-writers had really seen the program. It had been rescheduled. It wasn't aired until several weeks later.

Something remains unexplained at the very heart of those "honest, law-abiding citizens"; it's how NRA headquarters came to falsify their records so no one could learn where they'd obtained a stolen gun. The mystery began in November of 1977, when ATF inspectors, making a long-overdue routine inspection of the gun group's own federal dealers' records, found a Colt AR-15 rifle, model 604, serial number 039840, listed in the NRA's records without naming the gun's source. The NRA ledger showed it simply as received "pre-1958."[14]

On the face of it, the entry was legal. The old gun law had only required licensed dealers to keep such records for ten years; the new statute hadn't become effective until 1968, so licensees didn't have to keep book on anything they'd received before 1958.

Problem: Colt never manufactured a model 604 AR-15 until 1960.

Problem: They hadn't produced the gun numbered 039840 until 1964.

Problem: Colt AR-15 model 604, serial number 039840, was reported stolen from its owner, who was not in the NRA, in 1976—one year before the inspectors found it in the NRA's arsenal with a record concealing its origin.

Unexplained (or falsely explained) possession of stolen property permits an inference of guilty knowledge. Inferences aside, falsification of the federal dealers' records is a felony. The NRA's record was wrong. An eighteen-year lie "explaining" the concealment of where the gun came from is no simple bookkeeping error. But they weren't charged with the obvious and easily proved felony. They were charged with failing to register some neutered machine guns that "could have easily been restored to full automatic." Federal Judge Oliver Gasch ruled that the guns couldn't be reconverted into machine guns unless the owner had considerable expertise and expensive gun-smithing tools. Apparently, he felt that the NRA didn't possess these resources because he dismissed the charge. Two mysteries remain: Why the NRA was never charged with falsifying their records, and the source of the stolen Colt.

In the years to come, ATF agents would function despite their weak leadership—indeed, largely *because* that high-level frailty prevented feeble chiefs from infecting the field with their impotence. In Washington, bureaucrats and legislators were prone to assume that those who reach the top of any agency's tree are that agency's best and brightest. More than one hard-eyed professional felt that, "if these men are ATF's best, their agents must be even less competent."

Knowledgeable police officials across the country looked through the other end of the telescope. Those who met the bureau's leaders left with a new understanding: ATF's agents are dynamite but their executive suite's loaded with blank cartridges.

The problem would persist for decades.

12

Strike Force

> To confront organized crime effectively all law
> enforcement agencies must pool their knowledge
> and coordinate their actions.
>
> —Ramsey Clark

ATF had been a one-crime agency with one target: bootleggers. While the bureau's tunnel-visioned executives saw the
1968 gun law as another narrow specialty, agents saw
opportunities. Robbery gangs foiled police methods by
wearing masks so victims couldn't identify them, or operating in cities distant from their homes where detectives
wouldn't recognize their *modus operandi,* but experienced
bandits had felony convictions. They couldn't work without
guns, and GCA-68 prohibited an ex-convict from even
holding a firearm. Burglary rings and "fences" (the criminals who bought their stolen weapons for resale) were
"dealing in firearms without federal license." Hate groups
amassed illegal arsenals. Terrorists used bombs. Hired
killers used sawed-off shotguns or silencers. All were now
legitimate targets for ATF. And guns laws often worked
where all else had failed.

By the early 1970s, the government had established
Organized Crime and Racketeering strike forces—agents
from ATF, DEA, FBI, IRS, the Labor Department and the
Secret Service working with career federal prosecutors—in
Mafia centers across the country. Gun laws and ATF's skill
at forging cooperative relationships with other agencies
proved effective against the mobs. In New York City, ATF
supervisor Alex D'Atri outfitted himself with silk suits, a
diamond pinkie ring and a gleaming limo to impersonate a

gang leader. His agents played the roles of chauffeur and bodyguards. A year of eating with mobsters on the Upper East Side and drinking with them in Little Italy netted twenty-five racketeers. Another undercover infiltration of Gotham's crime families—even better because this one was a joint project with the NYPD—ended with predawn raids by 240 ATF agents and policemen. New York's Finest called the thirty-six arrests for crimes ranging from theft and drug traficking to robbery and murder "the largest roundup of syndicate hoods in twenty-five years" and elected the T-men to their prestigious Legion of Honor.

In Kansas City, where I supervised ATF's organized crime squad, our cases were less spectacular than New York's, more typical of what the bureau did nationwide.

Special Agent Duane R. Nichols ("D.R." to his friends) saw another target: the mobsters known as "masterminds." These men planned major burglaries and high-stakes robberies, recruited the mechanics to carry them out, provided the guns and fenced the loot—all for a percentage of the profits. In Kansas City, profits were shared as tribute with Nick "The Boss" Civella, an alumnus of upstate New York's infamous Appalachian Crime Convention.

Civella's chief mastermind, Robert Jones, specialized in bank robberies and jewelry-store heists. At forty-one, with eight felony convictions earned on his climb up the ladder, experience and caution shielded him from arrest. The FBI tried, but elaborate surveillances failed and their informers came up dry. The only "witnesses" to Jones's crimes were the underlings he hired; they couldn't sway a jury even if they lived long enough to testify.

Agent D. R. Nichols, a stocky, thirtyish man with a full and pleasant face who'd served four years with the U.S. Marines and won top honors at the University of Missouri before joining ATF, set his sights on Jones. The mastermind's crimes didn't create any tangible evidence of guilt, and Nichols knew he'd never find a credible witness, but an undercover operation might succeed. The problem was finding a way for an agent to penetrate that iron wall of insulation that surrounds a Mafia pro.

Nichols combed police files and strike force dossiers and brought his findings to a small group of ATF agents and detectives from the Kansas City, Missouri, Police Department (KCMoPD)—officers with whom the agents conferred frequently, routinely sharing intelligence, mounting joint operations and working in tandem. When they'd wrapped up a case, they'd charge a defendant with whichever crime, state or federal, carried the toughest penalty. "Getting the bad guy" took precedence over running up anybody's scoreboard.

"Here's the situation," Nichols said, loosening his wide tie painted with a mallard duck, and the discussion began. An hour later, all were agreed: They needed an *entree*—a known criminal with impeccable underworld credentials. They talked some more and came up with a plan. The plan depended on a man named Gillispie.[1]

Jack Gillispie's criminal record opened with an auto-theft conviction at age fourteen. At thirty-three he was on parole, having served ten years of a twenty-nine year term for assault and burglary. The underworld called him "Square Deal" because, in all his criminal career, he'd never cheated a crook or informed to the law. The FBI said he'd pulled a $40,000 diamond theft in Wichita and two bank extortions—getting a bank officer to deliver the vault's contents under threats of death—but they couldn't prove that the tall, suave, blond gang leader had done anything since leaving prison other than selling clothing at a classy Kansas City men's shop.

Gillispie was intelligent. He'd send sidekick Snake Reese out as a double agent to contact police, pose as an informer and find out what the detectives wanted to know. If they *weren't* seeking information on Gillispie, the gang leader knew his operations were still secret. Detectives acknowledged a grudging admiration for Square Deal Gillispie.

Not too long after that initial conference, KCMoPD detective Ross Adamson got a tip from an informer named Tommy that Square Deal had guns for sale. The detective asked, "Could you bring in a buyer?"

"Um, well . . ." Tommy seemed dubious. "I don't know."

"I'm talking about an ATF agent."

Tommy wasn't eager for such an active role. "Well . . ."

Adamson slapped him on the back. "Let's all get together and talk about it."

Tommy shrugged. "Sounds okay."

Adamson phoned D. R. Nichols. Nichols came to the meeting with Special Agent Virgil Walker, a Marine vet who'd earned his degree in police science while working full-time as a detective for the Galesburg, Illinois, Police Department. Tall and solidly built at thirty-two, Walker was an expert pistol shot who'd scored equally well in undercover assignments. The informer, Tommy, eyed Walker's modish hairstyle, assessed the agent's phlegmatic manner and smiled. "Let's give it a try."

Detectives would feed false information to Gillispie's spy, Snake Reese, while Walker did the undercover work.

A few days later, Tommy phoned Walker. "Gillispie just left. He gave me a list of the guns."

"I'll be right over."

The handwritten sheet cataloged twenty-eight rifles and revolvers with retail prices totaling $3,468.40. Tommy told Walker, "He said he'd be back this afternoon."

Long journeys begin with a single step. Gillispie was a steppingstone to the mastermind, Jones. Walker nodded. "Tell him I'm interested. Mind if I keep this list?"

"Be my guest," Tommy answered. The Gillispies of the world are a vindictive lot, but Walker's self-assurance was contagious and the little tipster felt brave.

At eight that evening, Gillispie's polished black Cadillac pulled into the narrow street of modest frame bungalows and halted at the curb in front of Tommy's home. As the informant and Virgil Walker descended the steps to the sidewalk, they recognized Snake Reese seated beside his boss. Gillispie got out of the car and Tommy performed the introduction: "Jack, this is Virg."

Walker and Gillispie exchanged nods.

The gang leader's 6'2" frame was draped in a well-tailored dark blue suit. His blond hair was neatly trimmed and swept back. "Who are you?"

"I work for Nate," Walker said, casually dropping the name of a mob fence. The value of using the hoodlum's name as a status giver had been carefully weighed against the risk that Gillispie would actually check with Nate

Brancato, but this was planned as a short-term phase of an overall operation. Besides, Walker reasoned, who'd believe that anyone had the brass to make such a claim if it weren't true?

Gillispie nodded toward his Cadillac coupe. Snake Reese opened the door and held the front seat forward so Walker could climb in back. Gillispie got in the driver's seat. "Did you see the list I gave Tommy?"

"Yeah, I saw it."

"Well? Are you buying?"

Walker took time to light a cigarette. "I might."

"I'll have to have two grand for them."

The agent gazed out the window. "How hot are they?"

"Around here, not at all. They came from Idaho."

Gillispie had just admitted to two crimes: interstate transportation by a convicted felon and interstate transportation of stolen firearms. Walker said, "I'll take a look."

Snake Reese sat sideways, chewing his gum and staring over the seat at Walker, his legs crossed, his nervousness betrayed by the jiggling of one glossy shoe.

Gillispie said, "Stick around. I'll set it up for tonight." Snake opened the door and Walker stepped out to stand with Tommy as the gleaming car swept around the corner.

Was the ringleader suspicious? Would he telephone Nate?

At nine that evening, Gillispie called Walker at Tommy's house. "Can't set it up till tomorrow. That okay with you?"

"Yeah," Walker replied, "that'll be all right."

"I'll phone you there around nine or ten tomorrow morning."

That night, Square Deal Gillispie telephoned Nate Brancato and asked, respectfully, for confirmation of Walker's bonafides. The agents wouldn't learn of that call for months.

The next morning, at five before ten, Gillispie demonstrated his penchant for the unexpected. Instead of phoning, he drove to Tommy's house. "Come on," he said to Walker, "I'll take you to see them now."

Reese sat in silence, chewing his gum during the drive.

Gillispie's eyes flicked constantly to his rear-view mirror. He pulled into a drive-in restaurant and waited until all the cars behind him had driven by. Ten blocks farther, he stopped at a grocery store and scrutinized the passing traffic again. Then he drove swiftly to I-495 and headed toward the state line.

Agents attempting a covering surveillance were forced to pull off. Traffic was too light for them to remain inconspicuous behind a tail-conscious pro.

Speeding past the Kansas grasslands, Gillispie asked, "How do I know you're not an agent?"

Walker's mental warning system teemed with questions. Had Gillispie checked around? If he'd discovered somehow that "Virg" wasn't working for Nate, he'd know that Walker was either a cop or an informer. Informers are shot and rolled into anonymous graves; an undercover agent's chances depend on how frightened or how crazy the criminal happens to be. Walker remained "in character," keeping the cool head that often makes the difference between the hero's funeral and staying alive for the eventual pension check. The gangleader had asked a question. Walker cleared his throat. "How do I know you're not one?"

"Agents don't sell guns," Gillispie said.

"Yeah," Walker agreed with apparent reluctance. "Well, all right." He remained calm, confident.

Gillispie asked, "You interested in anything besides guns?"

"Maybe. What have you got?"

"I can get a truckload of TVs."

"I'll have to check with my money man."

"I can let you have caps of coke for eight bucks. You can sell them for ten."

"I don't take big chances for little profits." Walker recalled the tale of how Square Deal had once tied a string around a cockroach and forced a cellmate to swallow it. Then he'd pulled up the string, drawing the wriggling bug back through the hapless prisoner's gullet, and he made him swallow it again, and again, and again.

Where the hell were they headed?

Gillispie turned off the interstate and drove south. "The guns are over here but I can deliver them to you on the Missouri side."

"I'll take a look and let you know if I'm interested."

Gillispie entered a dead end, U-turned, scanned the road and meandered through a residential district. "The only way they can tail me is with an electronic device," he said, "and I don't let nobody get close enough to my car to plant one." He pulled into a gas station, made a call, returned and drove directly to a dirt road. A few miles up the lonely lane, he entered a rutted driveway to a weed-grown farm.

Walker noted the location and the name on the mailbox, and he memorized the license numbers on four cars parked beside the barn. He also prayed that he'd live to report them.

Four men and a woman approached the Cadillac.

Gillispie told Walker, "Wait here." He and Snake got out. The others crowded around. The woman took a tan gym bag from the rear seat of a brown Buick, brought out a paratrooper-model carbine and handed it to Gillispie. He inserted a banana clip—twenty rounds of .30-caliber ammunition—and passed the gun to Reese. Snake kept Walker covered as he climbed from the car, but the agent sighed with relief when he saw Gillispie's wares spread across the rough barn floor for his inspection: brand new weapons with price tags labeled "Northway Sports Center, Idaho Falls, Idaho."

Walker examined them and said, "They're okay, but I'll only give you eighteen hundred."

Gillispie nodded his agreement and drove Walker back to Tommy's house. "I'll call you in an hour."

"Where do you want to make delivery?"

"I'll call you. How about half an hour?"

"Good."

Walker didn't know it, but he owed his life to the Mafia fence Nate. When Gillispie had asked about "Virg," there was a long pause before the suspicious mobster said, "I don't talk about such things."

Once again, Gillispie did the unexpected. Instead of calling in half an hour, he drove up to Tommy's house. "You got the money?" he asked Walker.

"Not in my pocket, but I can lay my hands on it."

Gillispie waved his hand out the window. The brown

Buick came around the corner. They loaded the guns into Tommy's pickup. Walker retrieved the cash from his undercover G-car and handed it to Gillispie.

Gillispie sent Snake to try his double-agent ploy with detectives. "I heard a guy named Virg bought some hot guns."

"Give us a description," the officers said eagerly. "See what else you can find out." When Snake left, they called D. R. Nichols. The agent saw Gillispie's suspicions as a signal for quick action. Gang members were plucked from homes, cars and the men's shop where Gillispie pretended to work. Snake Reese began babbling immediately. He was taken to another room.

Gillispie—self-possessed, neatly groomed, faultlessly tailored—smiled condescendingly and assured the agents, "This is all a big mistake. As soon as it's straightened out, you'll see how silly it is." He refused to call a lawyer and cooperated politely as Special Agent Patrick Kelly completed the ATF personal-history form. "Social security number?" Kelly asked.

"Four-nine-seven," Gillispie began easily, then he froze.

Undercover agents rarely participate in arrests. They're saved for the psychological moment, and this was it. Virgil Walker had entered the squad room and it was evident that he was not a prisoner. He belonged here. Gillispie's face turned ashen. His hands trembled.

Agents Nichols and Walker lodged Gillispie in the county jail for the night. They were leaving when a skinny trusty, one of the inmates trusted to perform menial tasks around the jail, asked Gillispie in mock civility, "Will you be spending the night with us, sir?"

The agents smiled at one another.

The trusty's face exuded innocence. "Would you care for a cup of coffee before you retire to your room?"

Gillispie's morning-after dishevelment proved that a dozen years behind bars had not rendered him sanguine regarding imprisonment. His finely tailored jacket was soiled and wrinkled, his shirt wilted, his blond hair roughly combed. Any confidence he may have brought to the courtroom seeped away as the judge read the charges and possible penalties: "Interstate transportation of stolen firearms; up to five years. Interstate transportation of firearms by a convicted felon; up to five years. Dealing in firearms without a federal license; up to five years. Possession by a felon; up to two years. Conspiracy; up to five years." The gangleader's shoulders sagged another inch with each count of the indictment: five crimes; a possible twenty-two years. As marshals led him from the courtroom, he caught Agent Walker's eye. Criminals invariably develop a deep respect for agents who beat them fairly on their own turf. "That's a pretty high bail the judge set: $50,000, secured."

"Pretty steep," Walker agreed.

"Look," Gillispie said as they stood in the marble corridor with deputy marshals waiting a few feet away, "get me probation and I'll tell you anything you want to know."

Walker raised his eyebrows. "Probation?"

"Yeah. I don't want to do any time on this."

Agent Walker smiled and shook his head. The marshals led Gillispie away.

Over the ensuing weeks, Walker waited. It was vital that the defendant make the first move. It came on December 11 when all the gang members took their lawyers' advice and pleaded guilty. Federal Judge Earl O'Connor told the defendants they'd be sentenced after he received reports from the Probation Office. His reputation for severity toward recidivists was well known.

Gillispie turned to Walker and whispered, "Can I see you?"

The agent looked at him for a moment, shrugged and nodded. When the other prisoners had been taken away, the marshals brought Gillispie to a small office. "Well," he asked the agent, "what do you want to know?"

"Nothing."

"Nothing? But I want to cooperate. I want you to tell that judge I helped you."

"If you really want to assist your government," Walker said evenly, "you'll introduce one of our agents to Robert Jones."

Gillispie looked at Walker for a very long time. Then he nodded. Phase Two of Agent Nichols's plan—the plan to nail Jones and cut one head from the chimera of Kansas City's mob—was underway.

Square Deal Gillispie's underworld passport was golden and his criminal credit rating was broad enough to embrace the agent who'd pose as his cousin from Chicago. They met the mastermind, Jones, at the Rumkeag Lounge in Independence.

Jones wasted no time. "I have a good one in Vegas. A bank. And believe me, it's a cinch." He drew a diagram of the layout and staff. "Only five females in the morning. You can open the side door with a pipe wrench. I figure it's good for two hundred thou'. I'll take 10 percent."

Gillispie looked to his "cousin."

Special Agent James Cannia shrugged. "We'll fly out and take a look, but we'll have to be clean going on the plane. Can you get us some pieces when we get there?"

"Guns are no problem." Jones grinned. "You'll like this job. I cased it for a month. Nearly pulled it off myself."

Gillispie invested his new mission with all the enthusiasm he'd previously poured into his criminal career. He told the agents about another mastermind—"Tiny" Lindsay in Dallas.

Agent Walker asked ATF-Dallas for a rundown.

Agent Larry Arnold reported, "He's Jerry Wayne Lindsay, while male born one-four-forty-one. Lives at four-two-one Gaston, apartment fourteen. He's a monster, Virg—six-nine and 280 pounds. Did jobs himself till everybody got recognizing his description. Now he sets jobs up."

"Any priors?" Walker asked.

"Probation for unlawful flight in 'sixty-five and three years for burglary in 'sixty-eight. That's it."

A week later, the towering Tiny sold guns to Gillispie and an undercover agent while trying to interest them in some jewelry-store jobs. The agent told him, "We'll look them over." Before leaving Dallas, they introduced him to a buddy he could do more business with, a man known to his real friends as ATF Special Agent Lloyd Grafton.

Back in Kansas City, Agent D. R. Nichols was keeping all of these operations on track while maximizing utilization of Gillispie. He felt like the circus performer who keeps the dinner plates spinning on tall rods—watching for a wobbly platter, giving it another spin before it crashes to the floor. Cases had been perfected against three masterminds: Lindsay in Dallas, Jones and a small-time planner named Rudy Langer in Kansas City. Now Charles Lindbergh Pierson was offering plans for a bank burglary, complete with keys to four of the bank's doors—keys he'd obtained from an inside source.

Strike force attorney Phil Adams had Gillispie's sentencing postponed.

Agent Grafton called from Dallas. "Tiny's getting antsy 'cause we're not pulling the jobs he comes up with. Now he's got an armed robbery—the owners of Bright-Williams Ford. Says if we won't help, he'll get some other guys and do it himself."

"Do your best," Nichols told him. "We're wrapping things up here but we need more time." Premature disclosure of Gillispie's cooperation would endanger him and send the rats running.

Grafton couldn't dissuade Tiny Lindsay, so two undercover agents agreed to assist in the robbery. The targeted victims, Mr. and Mrs. William Bright, were moved to a safe retreat; a detective and a policewoman assumed their places. Detectives and agents surrounded the fashionable residence, and when the bandits struck, lawmen corralled them. Tiny and a confederate were held on high bonds. ATF's undercover men were "released on lower bail."[2]

Jones was out in Vegas and he was growing uncomfortable. Gillispie and his "cousin" seemed reluctant to heist a victim Jones had fingered for them, a man known to have $10,000 with him in his hotel room.

ATF agents conferred with their police partners. Nichols summarized the situation: Each operation had been carried as far as possible without allowing anyone to commit a violent crime. It was time to pull the plug.

Proof of conspiracies to rob or burglarize banks in Kansas, Oklahoma and Nevada was furnished to the FBI. Jones got eighteen years on firearms and counterfeiting convictions. Tiny Lindsay drew ten years. Others ended up with terms ranging from three to eighteen years. The bonus was that Gillispie's lawyer, Stanford Katz, was handed eight years for sending a robbery team to steal a $100,000 Graf Zeppelin stamp collection from a Leawood, Kansas, man.[3]

In 1973 I escaped my paper-pygmy duties as area supervisor in Kansas City with an assignment to the strike force, coordinating ATF's organized crime investigations across a seven-state area. Mafia power rests on its ability to kill, so I set my sights on the city's most notorious executioners: Felix Ferina and Anthony "Tiger" Carderella. They were felons. Agents of the Federal Bureau of Narcotics—at the time, an agency of the Treasury Department—once got them ten years for trying to kill a witness in a drug trial.

Carderella and Ferina were diminutive men, barely topping five feet in height, but the fear they inspired was evident during their ritual appearances at a victim's funeral. Mourners opened a respectful path. Family members restrained grieving relatives while the bold executioners strode to the coffin, cast a contemptuous glance at their handiwork and turned without a word to depart.

The job of gathering intelligence and helping agents with their cases consumed most of my time. My sporadic efforts toward the notorious executioner team bore no fruit until the day two teenagers passed hit man Felix Ferina on the street. The boy with the wispy mustache and wild-looking hair took umbrage to "a funny look that old fart gave us." They sat on the curb across from the house Ferina entered—his girlfriend's house—chanting, "Come on out, ya old creep. Come out and talk to us."[4]

Ferina—short, slim, hawk-faced, partial to shirts with horizontal stripes and tight trousers and pointy-toed shoes that accentuated his slight build—was a quiet man who lived with his aging mother and whiled away most days playing cards at the syndicate's local headquarters, the Northside Social Club. His afternoon visits with Dorothy Bruno were special. He endured the boys' taunts for fifteen minutes before he ran out with blood in his eyes and a gun in his hand. The boys scrambled to a neighbor's house. Their call, recorded on the police 911 line, sounded breathless, "Some dude tried to shoot us!"

Uniformed officers responded and recovered the gun

from a table just inside the girlfriend's front door. Ferina glared but he wouldn't talk to them. The officers notified ATF. A day later, I had the gun, the patrolmen's statements and the boys' identification of Ferina from my six-photo lineup. It was time to interview the suspect.

The home he shared with his widowed mother was a modest cottage in one of Kansas City's blue-collar neighborhoods. Both parents had emigrated from Italy. His father sold washing machines and died of cancer. The future hit man quit school in the ninth grade and squeezed in some jobs—bartender, salesman, barber—between a string of arrests for carrying a gun, gambling, burglary, bombing, blackmail, counterfeiting, robbery and murder. He was proud of his dapper attire and that five-page rapsheet listing thirty-three arrests with just one conviction: for the attempted murder of that government witness. Tests administered at Leavenworth Penitentiary rated his I.Q. at a low normal 90 on the Beta scale but he scored at the 79th percentile in finger dexterity—a handy skill for a triggerman.

Ferina recognized me when he answered his door; four years earlier I'd earned a sort of underworld celebrity by catching Mafia underboss Carl Civella with two guns. Ferina said, "Come on in," and offered me a chair in his parlor: pale blue silk drapes hung precisely to the surface of plush gold carpeting; the gold-brocade-on-white Italian provincial furniture had clear plastic slipcovers. "What can I do for you?"

"First I have to advise you of your rights."

"Ahhh, I know all that."

"It's the rule." I recited the *Miranda* litany.

Ferina waved his hand and assured me he didn't want to call a lawyer.

I said, "It's about that incident with the two boys."

He sat back on the sofa and crossed his slim legs. "I thought you'd be around on that."

His mother, her body bent with age, hobbled into the room and spoke to Ferina in Italian. He turned to me, "She says, 'Do you want coffee?' Come on, have some."

"Thank you." I bowed to the old lady. "That would be nice." It occurred to me again, as it had many times, how we all get accustomed to the peculiarities of our jobs. Factory workers get used to odors and noises; medical folk grow familiar with blood; and I—the guy who trembled so hard I'd spilled coffee in my cup the first time I sat near a real gangster in a public diner—now felt comfortable chatting with a man who lived by killing.

Ferina said, "You know, every time something happens to me, they try to make a federal case out of it."

Mrs. Ferina returned with two delicate china cups and saucers. Steam wafted from the coffee. She placed them on the veined white-marble coffee table, left the room and returned with silver cream and sugar bowls. With a skeptical glance at me, she retired to her kitchen.

"You know," Ferina said, passing me the sugar bowl, "it's stupid to think I'd run around in broad daylight with a gun. I know I can't have guns."

"Sounds to me like you just lost it."

"C'mon now, those kids were impertinent little bastards and I just ran out to chase 'em away. Here's what I had." He drew a spectacle case from his shirt pocket and pointed it toward me.

"Why'd you do that?" I took a sip from my cup. Good coffee.

"Jeez, a man can't be too careful with kids these days. They mighta had a gun."

"Hm, so you charged two potentially armed ruffians holding your spectacle case?"

"You don't believe me?"

"That's all you were holding?"

"That's what I'm gonna say." He paused, caught himself. "That's what it *was.*"

Arresting him on the spot would start a chain of requirements mandated by the Speedy Trial Act. A month later, after my reports were written and the prosecutors were ready, the grand jury handed down an indictment. Ferina answered his door at seven-thirty in the morning wearing bright yellow pajama bottoms.

I said, "I've got a warrant for your arrest, Mr. Ferina."

He shrugged. "All right. Come on inside while I get dressed. Want some coffee?"

By the time he came back downstairs, his mother was

bringing in the cups, but now they chattered against their china saucers in her trembling hands. When we'd finished our coffee, I applied the obligatory handcuffs. As I walked the middle-aged executioner down the front steps, his creased Italian mama murmured, "Poor boy. Poor, poor boy."

The teenagers told the jury what they'd seen. The policemen testified to recovering the revolver just inside the girlfriend's door. I recounted my interview and Ferina's statement: "That's what I'm gonna say—uh, that's what it was." The girlfriend swore he'd never touched the gun. Ferina prevented any mention of his prior record by electing not to take the stand.

While the jury was out, Ferina approached me in the corridor, a near smile on his habitually solemn features. "I'll say this," he said, extending his hand, "you stuck to the truth."

He meant it as a compliment. I was insulted. "What the hell did you think I'd do?"

The jury returned in twenty-eight minutes. "We find the defendant not guilty."

I caught a few of them leaving the courthouse to ask how they'd arrived at their verdict. A solid farmer, the sort whose unshakable bias can dominate others, shoved his jaw forward. "I'm a member of the National Rifle Association, mister, and we know all about how the government uses them gun laws to harass honest citizens."

Ferina's partner, Tiger Carderella, did a burgeoning business as Kansas City's leading record retailer. The windows of his Independence Avenue shop were festooned with fluorescent green and orange banners. One proclaimed: "We Buy in Quantity and Pass the Savings to You." Actually, Carderella employed professional shoplifters to loot competitors and paid them a third of the albums' value. But he did buy in quantity—that was true enough. He and Ferina were similar in size and background, but their personalities differed. The stiletto-thin Ferina was respectful yet solemn. Tiger Carderella, fuller in the face with a body tending toward roundness as he neared fifty, was gregarious. He liked to talk. The first time he invited me into the backroom office of his shop, I asked him, "Why all the mirrors?" Aside from the convex spotter at the doorway from the shop, a wide plate of one-way glass let him watch aisles where customers browsed.[5]

"Shoplifters," he explained tersely.

"You've got a nerve."

"Hey, why should I let people rip me off?" He sprinkled bits of Mafia trivia among idle questions about my progress on the Ferina investigation—that case hadn't come to trial yet—and he told me how two blacks had robbed his store at gunpoint. "They emptied the register, but I had a thousand bucks in my pocket and they wouldn't touch me. This 'killer' image isn't too bad, ya know. Women go for it too. Young women." He leered.

When I rose to leave, he accompanied me back through the store. I lifted an album from a rack and looked pointedly at the cellophane—torn where another shop's sticker must have been removed.

Tiger grinned sheepishly. "Handling hot albums isn't a federal rap."

"Do they come across state lines?"

"If they do, no shipment's worth more than five grand." Interstate transportation of stolen property valued over $5,000 is a federal offense, and Tiger wanted me to believe that he avoided offending federal law.

My intermittent probe of Tiger was fruitless. Then Sebastian Circo, a small cog in the mob's gambling machine who'd apparently displeased his munificent superiors, was invited to an informal meeting at six in the morning on the city's North Side. He arrived early, hair slicked down and freshly shaved, and drove his old white Chevy across the sidewalk to park beneath a bridge.

Another car squealed around the corner, hopped the curb, skidded to a stop. Two men wearing green stocking masks stepped out and drilled Circo with holes. Gunshots reverberated, but no neighbor heard them. Nobody saw anything. This was the old Italian neighborhood where the Mafiosi grew up and lived before they moved to posh homes in the suburbs. These were streets where they still conducted business.

A patrolman found Circo, his head and left arm hanging through the car window as if he'd tried to leap at his attackers. Bright blood flowed in wide red paths down the dirty white door panel.

Police photographers and technicians pursued their practiced ritual. Detectives fanned out, found two masks cut from dark green pantyhose in a sewer on Pacific Street. With them lay two revolvers; neither was listed as stolen. I was asked to trace them.

The .38-caliber Smith & Wesson had been shoplifted from the Wal-Mart in Warrensburg, Missouri. The manager had spotted suspicious characters that day and called police. A highway patrolman stopped the car as it hurtled toward Kansas City; he found no loot but cited the driver for speeding and noted his passengers' names. Allan Garner, thirty-three, with an undistinguished pedigree of minor arrests; Richard Stevenson, twenty-one, with a few petty arrests. But Raymond Toliver's rapsheet listed terms served in Sing Sing and a few midwestern prisons. He'd been out for two years.

I traced the other murder weapon, a snub-nosed Colt Cobra, to a Woolco store in Topeka, Kansas. It was "missing from inventory," its loss attributed to shoplifters.

Reliable sources named the hitmen: Ferina and Carderella. IRS Special Agent Allen Malcolm told me that Toliver—one of the shoplifters stopped by police after the thefts from the Warrensburg Wal-Mart—boosted records for Tiger Carderella. I passed the tip to police and they interrogated the ex-con but he wouldn't talk.

It was two months later, after a January morning in the overheated strike force office reviewing reports regarding a gang war for control of lucrative vice rackets around the army's Fort Leonard Wood in southern Missouri, that I massaged my burning eyes and decided to cruise for the views. I drove to the supermarket lot across from the side door to Tiger's record shop, poured some coffee from my thermos and relaxed to the music from my G-car radio. A gray Plymouth drew to the curb. Two men lugged stacks of record albums through that side door. I noted its license number: J3W-402. I was refilling my thermos cap when Tiger's beanpole stockboy stuck his head out, looked up and down and stuffed a little green bag into the metal drum beside the door. When the Plymouth departed, I drained my coffee and ambled past shopping carts pushed by young mothers with bundled-up babies and middle-aged wives in heavy cloth coats, across the street to the metal trash barrel. Abandoned property is fair game.

The green bag contained junk mail addressed to Tiger's shop and fifty-two album pricetags—the kind chainstores used as inventory control devices; when customers paid at the checkout counter, the clerk would detach the bottom portion of the tag as a running account of goods sold. But the bottom halves of these tags were intact. No clerk had removed them. No customer had taken them through a checkout counter. They bore the names of seven stores, from a Montgomery Ward's in Emporia, Kansas, to a Team Electronics in St. Paul, Minnesota. They weren't proof of any federal crime, and the detective I called told me they didn't have a judge they'd trust to issue a search warrant without tipping Tiger. I passed the pricetags to an IRS man. Maybe they'd help prove a tax case.

License number J3W-402 was registered to Michael Massey, age twenty-six. He hailed from a respectable family in rural Pratt, Kansas, where his dad managed a local firm and served on the chamber of commerce. Young Michael had a few arrests for shoplifting. Men he'd been arrested with had mob connections. His mugshot didn't resemble the men who'd been driving his Plymouth.

He was affable when I visited his sparsely furnished apartment, but he "don't know anything about record albums at Tiger's" and he couldn't remember who'd borrowed his car that day. I asked whether he ever stored things at his place for his friends.

"Hey"—the clean-cut young man had a nice smile—"you think I'm crazy?"

"Ever do business with Tiger?"

"Mmm." He nodded. "Yep, you do think I'm crazy."

"What do you mean?"

"Look, if people want to hustle, that's their business, okay? But it's dangerous to get involved with guys like Tiger."

I went to the door, turned back. "See ya."

"I hope not." It was a good-natured reply.

I hoped not, too. Seemed like a nice kid, but the guys he'd been arrested with would eventually put him on the treadmill of arrest, jail, arrest, jail—or worse.

As it turned out, he'd end up worse.

In May, someone phoned a bomb threat to Tiger's shop. He called the police, who notified me. He had no idea who might have made the threat. "Tell you what," I said. "Why don't you make me a list of people who don't like you?"

"Nah. It'd be too long."

"Okay, give me permission to tap your phone. We'll record the next threat."

He grinned. "That might have some disadvantages."

KCMoPD Sergeant Billy Trolloppe phoned me on an oppressively hot July day. Detectives had milked every lead, squeezed every informer and poked into the city's darkest corners a dozen times. They were getting nowhere on the Circo hit. "Why not try for him on a gun charge?" Trolloppe asked. "Any conviction's better than no conviction."

IRS Special Agent George Warmouth told me that Ray Toliver admitted to him selling the guns his crew lifted from that Warrensburg Wal-Mart—one of which was the murder weapon—to Tiger. No problem. Just get three thieves to stand up in court and point their fingers at a man who killed people with all the aplomb of a gas jockey wiping a bug from your windshield; then corroborate their testimony with independent evidence. Toliver's sojourns to four prisons suggested a disinclination to aid the cause of justice, and the other two were terrified of Tiger.

For the next two weeks I toured the Kansas and Missouri towns the Toliver team might have worked. I brought my photo lineup to drug stores, shopping centers and department stores, showed them to sales clerks and store detectives. I buttonholed cops in police stations and checked their files.

On a cloudy February afternoon in Warrensburg, a prosecutor wound up the state's case against Toliver for the Wal-Mart theft that included one of the Circo murder weapons. The judge declared a recess. Four bored spectators scattered about the cavernous courtroom stretched and shuffled out. Toliver and a lady friend stepped onto the square landing at the head of the wide, varnished stairway. I followed and leaned against the railing across from them. The burly booster watched me; he had to be wondering why a stranger in suit and tie was taking notes during his trial. He left his girlfriend, crossed the landing with a cigarette and asked for a light. I got my pack out and lit both smokes. He asked, "You a lawyer?"

"No."

He gazed at the floor, then raised his head in an "Aha!" gesture. "I know who you are."

I smiled and said nothing. Ask for something, and he'd drive a harder bargain.

"You're Moore, the ATF agent that's been asking people about me."

"Yep."

"What're you doing here?"

"Watching."

"What for?"

The time was right. That ancient courthouse, the drab brown of the courtroom, the gray winter day—a gloomy combination that might make a man reflect on the less hopeful aspects of his life. "I'll be at all your trials, Mr. Toliver. I've given evidence of your crimes to prosecutors in Independence and Raytown and Topeka and Kansas City. They'll all file charges and I'll come to watch all your trials."

His jaw dropped slowly. A frown creased his broad brow.

"And then"—I flicked my ashes into a squat sand urn—"I'll file federal firearms charges. With your record, you'll be sentenced as a habitual criminal—twenty-five years, just for lifting a gun."

His jaw clenched, his fists balled. "How come you're hassling me, man?"

"Hassling?" I repeated, sounding offended. "I get paid to investigate crimes."

"Federal crimes, yeah, but you're picking on me special."

"I can't conceal evidence of state crimes."

His hard expression turned crafty. "You'd cover for me if I told about selling them guns to Tiger."

"I'm with ATF, pal. We don't cover for anybody. I could put in a good word for you." And then, casually, "Did you sell those guns to Tiger?" Trying to look relaxed, I raised my cigarette and contemplated its tip. Actually, I was looking past the smoke, keeping a wary eye on those huge fists, readying myself to make sure that if someone flew over that railing onto the stairway below, it wouldn't be me. After a moment's silence, I looked up. His face had crumbled into weary resignation. He spilled Tiger's techniques and named other teams. Everything he knew.

Toliver's capitulation prompted his crewmates Garner and Stevenson to talk. It was enough for an arrest, but strike force attorney Mike DeFeo told me what I already knew: The unsupported word of three thieves wouldn't get a conviction.

Months later, after I was promoted and transferred to Interpol in Washington, strike force attorney David B.B. Helfrey researched some statutes and reviewed my Carderella reports. Although Tiger had kept each interstate shipment below the $5,000 threshold that violated federal law, Helfrey discovered he could proceed based on the aggregate amount of the overall conspiracy. He asked ATF Special Agent Dave Neiman to reopen the investigation.

The pricetags I'd retrieved from Tiger's trash barrel were part of the corroboration, but when the case came to trial, Agent Neiman had amassed a ton of proof: photos taken by the KCMoPD tac unit showing boosters delivering hot goods to Tiger's shop; copies of Western Union money orders Tiger had wired to his roving bands of thieves; more witnesses. Anthony "Tiger" Carderella was convicted of receiving stolen property and "engaging in the business of dealing in firearms without a federal license."

No NRA members on his jury.

The judge gave him five years—not "justice" for the Circo murder but, as Sergeant Trolloppe said, any conviction's better than no conviction. Tiger went free on bond while his lawyer filed an appeal.

Michael Massey, the affable young man whose gray Plymouth had been used to deliver some hot albums to Tiger's shop, was found in the front seat of a stolen Lincoln Continental with $1,030 in his pocket and four .25-caliber slugs in his brain. His murder was never solved.[6]

Felix Ferina's mother passed away. Convinced that she'd hidden a fortune around the house, he tore the place apart, board by board. Mobsters and agents alike said he turned odd. At fifty-five, he looked eighty. A few years later, he was found murdered "by person or persons unknown."

Tiger Carderella did his five years and left prison flat broke. By February of 1984, he'd distanced himself from fellow Mafiosi, but his flamboyant lifestyle ran up debts of a quarter-million dollars. One morning, police found his Cadillac abandoned beside a freight-company building and towed it to their impound lot. Seventeen days later, a passing officer noted an odor emanating from its trunk. Inside, they found Tiger—smothered to death by a towel pressed tightly against his face. He was fifty-eight.[7]

Strike force lawyers combined FBI wiretap evidence with mountains of proofs uncovered by IRS agents to get Nick "The Boss" Civella and other top-ranking gangsters prison terms averaging thirty years for skimming from their Las Vegas casinos.

Special Agent D. R. Nichols, who'd ramrodded the mastermind investigation, turned down several promotion offers before accepting a supervisor slot in Kansas City, where he still serves. Special Agent Virgil Walker, who'd worked undercover with Square Deal Gillispie to nail those masterminds, became an instructor at ATF's undercover school, teaching the course that agents and detectives from every important city, state and federal law-enforcement agency competed to attend. He retired in 1990.

In 1991, Dave Neiman became the special agent-in-charge of the Explosives Enforcement Branch at ATF headquarters.

When Square Deal Gillispie came up for sentencing, federal judge Earl O'Connor said, "You took a big chance for the government, and now the government will take a chance on you." He was granted probation. He's living somewhere in the world now with a new identity.

Strike force attorney David B.B. Helfrey replaced Michael DeFeo, the brilliant chief attorney who'd led the Kansas City strike force from its inception through its most active days. DeFeo took on a number of high-profile jobs for the Justice Department, eventually rising to become assistant attorney general of the United States.[8]

* * *

The strike forces grew from Attorney General Robert F. Kennedy's Buffalo Project in the early 1960s—a venture uniting agents from all the major federal agencies to fight the mob in upstate New York. Indictments of mobsters soared from a negligible nineteen in 1960 to 1,166 in fiscal 1966.[9]

United States attorneys are the chief prosecutors for each federal district, appointed by the president on the recommendation of the district's senior senator from the political party in power. Strike force attorneys were career men and women, hired by and responsible to the Justice Department in Washington. Some U.S. attorneys resented the strike force lawyers' independence from their control, their authority to seek indictments, and their penchant for prosecuting powerful criminals without the U.S. attorney's approval. One such U.S. attorney was Pittsburgh's Dick Thornburgh. When President Ronald Reagan made him attorney general of the United States, one of Thornburgh's first acts was to terminate the strike force attorneys' independence. Now no mobster may be brought to trial—regardless of his crimes or the evidence gathered by agents—without permission from the local, politically appointed U.S. attorney. Usually it doesn't make much difference. But now, of course, the U.S. attorney gets to make the press announcements.

13

Significant Criminals

> When written in Chinese, the word "crisis" is
> composed of two characters. One represents
> danger and the other represents opportunity.
> —President John F. Kennedy

There's more than one way to catch a crook.

Within law enforcement, ATF is known for two qualities: genuine, two-way cooperation with other agencies, and excellence in the field of undercover work. Both attributes were tapped in the mid-1970s when the bureau launched its most progressive project since it was freed from the IRS.

Burl Causey owned a hefty slice of the rackets in Georgia, but he had a problem named District Attorney Larry Salmon—a relentless prosecutor who brought charges against Causey's henchmen any time the cops came up with a prima-facie case. The gangster couldn't buy him and he couldn't scare him off. If the D.A. were murdered, Causey's gang would head the hit parade of suspects. Causey and car thief Hugh Don Smith were discussing this problem when Smith asked, "How about Bunny Eckert?"

"Eckert?" Causey mused. "Yeah, I've heard a lot about him."

Arthur "Bunny" Eckert's reputation as a hit man was firmly established throughout the Southeast, and having a hired gun do the job would enable everyone in Causey's gang to build themselves airtight alibis. A few days later, at Causey's request, Smith arranged a meeting. "Mr. Eckert, this is Burl Causey."

Causey grasped the tall man's hand. "Glad to meet you. I've heard a lot—"

"Sure. Likewise." He was businesslike. Cold.

"How's things in San Antonio?"

"Warm. You got a job for me?"

"What's the hurry?" the cautious Causey asked. "Let's get to know one another."

A few days later, Causey's twenty-five-year-old son parked across from the sun-drenched courthouse. "There he is, Mr. Eckert. That's Salmon coming down the steps. The guy in the blue suit."

"I see him."

"Enough?"

"Plenty. Let's go."

That night, Burl Causey gave the handsome gent from San Antonio a pistol, a sawed-off shotgun and a $500 down payment. The balance of $7,500 would be paid upon delivery of the prosecutor's perforated corpse. It was a generous stipend for this sort of job, but Eckert's professional reputation justified prime wages.[1]

Less notorious killers come cheaper. A San Diego laundromat owner paid just $2,000 to the man he hired to slaughter one competitor and one deputy sheriff. A Tulsa crook paid a mere thousand dollars for the bombing of a judge's car, even though the bomb would have to be planted during the night and the explosion would occur when the jurist left home to drop his eight-year-old daughter at school on his way to work. For the same paltry sum, a Richmond, Virginia, dealer in stolen property contracted for a triple-header: a deputy sheriff, a county investigator and an informer.[2]

Public officials weren't the only targets. Austin, Texas, carwash owner Elizabeth Saunders offered $5,000 for the instant death of her boyfriend's inconvenient wife. An Arkansas man paid $2,000 for the murder of the guy who was dating his ex-wife, and a Trenton, New Jersey, auto mechanic came up with $1,500 to have his girlfriend's estranged husband rubbed out. A few frustrated lovers go cheap. Kansas housewife Lois Campion paid a paltry $600 to have her husband disposed of.[3]

None of these plots were consummated because every one of these (and scores of other) would-be remote-control killers made the same "fatal" mistake: dealing with undercover ATF agents posing as hired killers. The men and women who wanted to buy murder were jailed; their almost-victims lived. Racketeer Burl Causey, for example, never met Bunny Eckert. Special Agent Michael Baylor filled in for the notorious assassin.

In 1981, ATF agents caught the real Arthur "Bunny" Eckert with eighteen guns. In exchange for his plea of guilty, he received six years' imprisonment.

The Golden Dragon Restaurant on Washington Street was crowded with San Francisco gourmets and tourists lured by the restaurant's international reputation. Among them sat the leader of the notorious Wah Ching street gang. Solicitous waiters glided among tables, alert to the slightest sign of a diner's desire.

Outside, it was growing dark. Colorful banners of vertically arranged Chinese characters waved slowly in the autumn breeze. Couples paused at quaint shops along the narrow, cobbled street to browse vitalizing mixtures and medicinal roots. Others gazed longingly at treasures of ivory and jade displayed in shop windows.

Two automobiles eased to the curb in front of the Golden Dragon. The drivers kept their engines running. Three men alighted. Inside, masked and wielding guns, they shoved past the startled maître d' and strode boldly into the elegant dining room. Scanning the complacent patrons, they spotted the Wah Ching leader and raised their weapons.

The murmured mixture of English and Chinese, the occasional laugh, the muted clink of crystal and silver were utterly devastated by the roar of the fusillade. During a brief moment of silence, the assassins retraced their steps. The Golden Dragon came alive—this time with screams and groans and the belated scurrying of terrified diners. Six dead men and women lay sprawled on the plush, patterned carpet. The Wah Ching leader and ten others bled from nonfatal wounds.

This was the latest skirmish in a long-standing war

between the well-established Wah Ching and an upstart gang calling itself the Joe Boys. Police Chief Charles Gain formed a task force and asked ATF to lend a hand.

Surveillance of a Joe Boy hangout produced a photo of Walter Ang, which was used to finger him as a bank robber. Police and FBI agents raiding Ang's home found receipts in the name of Walter Pang. ATF discovered that "Pang" was a name Ang used to buy guns. The bank case fell through but he was convicted under the Gun Control Act.

A few weeks later, habitues of Chinatown's nightclubs noticed a new face. The stranger often dined with the Joe Boys. A self-assured Asian, he'd come to San Francisco from Hawaii. Before that, he'd earned a bachelor's degree in political science. The credentials he'd left at home identified him as Special Agent Cornell Lee, ATF.

The undercover man nudged casual conversations this way and that way until one Joe Boy mentioned their armorer, Humberto Rodriguez. When the topic of the Golden Dragon massacre came up, Lee confided to Joe Boy leader Wayne Yee, "I've got a deal in the islands I need handled, but it has to be done by people from the mainland."

Yee scrutinized Lee through the smoke rising from his cigarette. "It might be possible." The next day, the undercover agent was introduced to one of the Golden Dragon hit men. The killer applied for "the job on the islands," offered his experience as qualification and recommended the other members of his team by name. Then he introduced Lee to Rodriguez, who obligingly sold the agent a fourteen-stick dynamite bomb armed with two DuPont number-six blasting caps for two hundred dollars.

Lee alluded to "pressing business back home."

Joe Boys leader Wayne Yee asked if there was someone local he could contact, "in case I come across something you'd be interested in."

"Sure." Lee smiled. "I have a good friend here. We'll meet him tomorrow."

The next morning, Lee introduced the gang chief to his friend, Mel Young. Mel forgot to mention that he was a special agent with the Drug Enforcement Administration.

Column distillery raided by ATF in Chicago.

Mash vats for illicit distillery.

Mouth of escape tunnel at an illicit distillery.

ATF agents dismantling a distillery.

Academy instructor monitors agents during a training exercise.

Prohibition agent's badge.

Badge carried when ATF was a division of the IRS.

Some items carried by ATF special agents.

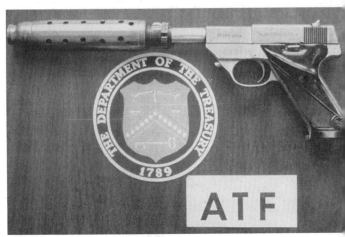
Silencer-equipped .22 pistol.

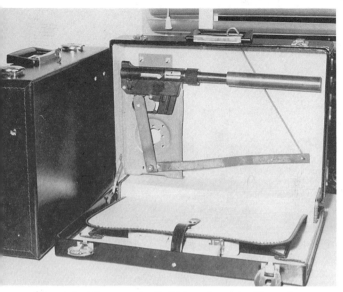

Assassin kit: sawed-off rifle equipped with a silencer and fitted into attaché case; the trigger is located beneath the handle of the case.

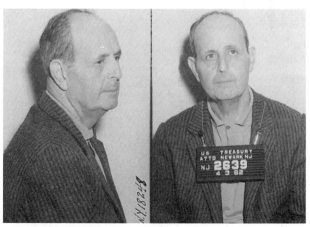

Bootlegger Angelo "Slim" Di Orio.

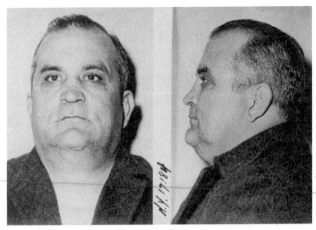

Bootlegger Jimmy "The Weasel" Roselli.

Eliot Ness.

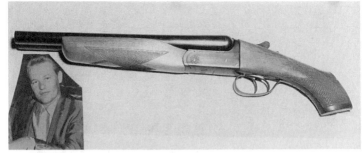

Killer for hire Charles V. Harrelson and the sawed-off shotgun seized from him in Kansas City.

Mafia executioner Felix Ferina (right) being brought to ATF office by the author.

Telephone company executive Phillip Lucier died when his car was bombed.

Kansas City Mafia underboss Carl Civella, after his arrest by the author.

Agents watched nervously but, minutes later, the biker was off on a high—a trip induced solely by the power of his own mind.[13]

By the time the Raiders' undercover penetration had run its course, they had racked up more than a dozen convictions, not to mention an unprecedented intelligence that aided lawmen in other cases.

Marcus Hook was a peaceful Pennsylvania town off the beaten track, about forty minutes from Philadelphia. Six policemen were ample for the needs of its three thousand residents until the Pagans moved in and declared war on the Warlocks. The police asked for assistance. ATF responded. The gangs signed a peace treaty at the Ridley Township police station and Pagan spokesman Dino Robinson told the press, "We're hoping that close scrutiny by the Treasury Department will slack off now. If we're not at war, we're not going to have [any weapons] around for them to bust us on."

All remained tranquil until John Marron, national president of the Pagan Nation, made Marcus Hook his headquarters. The gang acquired scores of properties around the town, including a forty-room mansion known locally as the Castle. Townsfolk saw these scurvy thugs fighting among themselves and selling dope, but none suspected the scope of their depredations. The Pagans' tightly structured organization—heavily involved in auto theft, extortion, robbery, hijacking, gunrunning and the wholesale narcotics trade—had 1,300 members scattered in semi-independent chapters from California to Massachusetts.

Marron, called "Satan," stood at an unimposing 5'8". Long brown hair flowed freely from a high forehead; thin whiskers sprouted from pallid cheeks. At thirty-eight, his list of arrests—guns, drugs, fraud and rape—included few convictions. Virginia police wanted him to answer charges of one murder, two robberies and three maimings but they couldn't find him. He was a wraith, sighted briefly, only to dematerialize when the law came looking.

Two Marcus Hook taverns where Pagans had brawled were burned to the ground. Victims in the growing plague of rapes—girls and their families—were silenced by midnight phone calls, assaults and gunfire. Mayor Harry Roberts hired more police officers, but the city council rejected his counteroffensive. One councilman asked, "Do you think I want them blowing up my house?"

County police called ATF. Agents learned quickly that their most effective strategy—total teamwork among all concerned agencies—would have to be adjusted in this case: The daughter of Chester's mayor was caught with a gang member selling drugs to an undercover narcotics agent; and a roadblock set up to prevent a scheduled gang battle netted one Pagan with a copy of the police teletype message. Satan had compromised some female police clerks and perhaps a few cops, but which ones?

Agents maintained their normal contacts with local departments regarding routine business, but some casual meetings were covers for secret conferences to inform chiefs of an embryo operation. Department heads in Upper Darby, Springfield Township, Aston Township and the Pennsylvania state police made cautious approaches to selected subordinates, offering a volunteer assignment. The Drug Enforcement Administration was enlisted. A cadre of fifteen investigators formed a special squad, maintaining confidentiality even from fellow officers and their parent agencies. Other than these fifteen, only seven persons—police and federal executives—knew of the operation.

Investigators shunned two-way radios and telephones. Communication was limited to personal meetings. When a gang member was arrested for any offense from disturbing the peace to theft or assault, a member of the special squad chatted with him, probing discreetly. Intelligence was shared among team members. Informers were milked in a manner that never revealed the existence of a special operation. Surveillances were mounted. Suspects were secretly photographed and their associations documented. The team's greatest secret was the penetration by federal undercover men—DEA agents looking for drugs and ATF agents.

Drawing upon expertise and intelligence from other ATF offices, Treasury's bearded and well-costumed actor-agents came with documented backgrounds and criminal credentials that won them acceptance among bikers. They ate with the gangs, drank with them, gathered tidbits from adroitly manipulated conversations and collected an arsenal that began to take up considerable space in ATF-Philadelphia's evidence vault: fourteen handguns, eleven sawed-off shotguns, six silencers, three machine guns, four pen-guns and sixteen other firearms.

An ATF agent posing as a New York Mafia hoodlum made contact with the Pagans.

Farmers were starting their spring planting when 130 local, state and federal officers swooped to snatch up forty-eight defendants, including some unlikely weapons suppliers: Jules DiLeo, employed by the Naval Development Center in Bucks County; James Shockley, a fifty-three-year-old guard at the Delaware county prison; and former deputy sheriff Frank Mongiello. All were convicted.[14]

Marron, alias Satan, got twenty years for the Virginia murder.

Intelligence gathered at Marcus Hook led to other arrests.

Pennsylvania Pagan James Miller used phony checks to buy guns in Arizona. Agents nailed him on his way to California. He got sixty-one years' imprisonment for his string of offenses under the Gun Control Act. Three Virginia Pagans were nabbed bringing explosives across a state line to blow up a Baltimore rival's clubhouse.

Back in Pennsylvania, the mayor of Darby realized he'd lost control of his police department. Haunted by a belief that some of his officers were involved in burglaries and other crimes, he went to Chief Gallagher of the Delaware County Criminal Investigation Unit and begged for action.

Gallagher turned to ATF.

Wallace Hay, the special agent in charge of the bureau's Philadelphia district, told Gallagher, "We'd like to help but we can't work outside our jurisdiction."

"It's not just burglary and corruption," Gallagher said. "They're breaking the gun laws, too."

Hay stood up, reached across the desk and shook hands. "We'll take a look."

The Marcus Hook roundup looked like the end of the investigation. It wasn't. It was a mere prologue for the hunt for bigger game. In the atmosphere of victory following the roundup, in which it seemed investigators already knew everything, witnesses had talked. Bikers facing long prison terms had babbled freely. Every intelligence resource was now focused on the county's most pernicious problem: corruption.

The biker raids hadn't breached the cover of the pseudo New York gangster, Special Agent Randy Davis. Hay ordered him to concentrate on the prime suspect: Darby police sergeant Anthony Terra. Four weeks later, Terra invited the agent into the back room of a tavern he owned and showed him a submachine gun. "Want to buy it?"

"It's not on file anywhere, is it?"

"What do you mean 'on file'?"

"You know, registered with ATF. My people don't want—"

"What the hell, you think I'm stupid?" Terra seemed insulted. "Of course it's not registered."

The undercover man examined the weapon and handed it back. "No thanks."

"What's the matter? You don't believe it's clean?"

Davis lit a cigarette, tossed the match in an ashtray on the rickety table. "My friend says you're okay but I don't know you that well. Maybe you're gonna sell me the gun; maybe you're gonna have me busted when I leave with it."

"All right," Terra said with a laugh, "play it cool. To tell the truth, I like you. I like the way you operate."

The two met regularly, neither man seemingly in any hurry. The renegade cop ran a business that promised perpetual profits, and ATF was out to smash the entire crime ring. Terra's vending-machine corporation owned one tavern that fronted for gambling and loan sharking. The money rolled in but Terra coveted the opportunities for expansion available through the Mafia. He made the undercover T-man a proposition.

"You want to buy in? Be my partner?"

"I might. What do you have in mind?"

Terra's terms were acceptable. Davis bought in with cash provided by county CID and the FBI. G-men, delighted with the evidence ATF had already given them regarding crimes within their jurisdiction, were eager at the prospect of getting more.

Now, as a partner in Shortstop Vending, Davis was freed from the underworld taboo against asking direct questions of those with whom one transacts illicit business. Now he asked pointed questions and insisted on precise answers. Agent Davis's apartment and the Lincoln Continental he drove were equipped with court-authorized bugs. His circle of acquaintances widened to include Philadelphia underworld figures, and their conversations ran the gamut from arson and hot guns to securities theft, insurance fraud, narcotics, gambling, police and political corruption. An employee of the FBI's Washington headquarters admitted to Davis his participation with Terra in an armed robbery. The agent identified a clerk in the U.S. attorney's office who was passing secrets to the mob.

Special Agent Davis endured his risky double life for two nerve-wracking years. Terra went to prison for arson and firearms crimes. Most of the other defendants were prosecuted in state court where more severe penalties were exacted. The Pagan terror was terminated. The flyspecks of filth had been picked from the ranks of law enforcement.

The file on Marcus Hook was closed.[15]

The Significant Criminal Enforcement Project aimed agents at the most violent outlaws they could find throughout the United States. Bureau chiefs liked the specially earmarked reports flagging investigations they could point out to officials at Treasury and members of Congress, but, like many agents who remained in the field, these executives had been weaned on the IRS numbers game. It was easier to measure success by counting total cases. Agents could net a school of small fish with the resources it took to catch one really smart, dangerous criminal. Then, too, field managers found frustration among that firmly entrenched segment of southern investigators recruited during the moonshiners' heyday—men who'd been hired by short-sighted executives seeking little more than raw courage, fleetness of foot, endurance and skill at tracking suspects through dense forests.

"Don't bother me," one old-school agent snapped sarcastically to his boss, "I'm working one of those magnificent criminals."

In 1979 SCEP was shelved.

* * *

Agents working the most dangerous outlaws still earned peer respect among their colleagues, but their achievements went unappreciated by bureau leaders for more than a decade—until Congress enacted the Armed Career Criminal Act. Under this 1984 law, anyone with three or more violent felony convictions would, if caught with a gun, be imprisoned for *any term not less than fifteen years*. Incarceration was mandatory, with no probation, no parole, no early release.

Pushed by Congress, cautious bureau leaders tested the waters with three pilot projects. Delighted agents pumped informers, went undercover and tailed likely suspects to take 102 armed career criminals off the streets of St. Louis, Detroit and New Orleans. Satisfied, ATF's hierarchy launched Project Achilles in 1986, so named because, although crooks could wear masks and intimidate witnesses, even kill their victims to avoid arrest, they couldn't pursue their "careers" without illegally possessing a firearm. The gun was their Achilles Heel.

Police hailed the new project, and it met their fondest dreams:[16]

- By age thirty-six, David Eubanks of Indiana had accumulated thirty-four felony convictions. Sheriff's deputies caught him with a .22 Marlin rifle. A federal judge let him off with the minimum sentence: fifteen years; no parole, no probation.
- At thirty-five, Michael Brady had convictions for robbery, car theft and rape. Given twenty-five to forty years for armed robbery in 1977, he was on the streets again two years later. On January 19, 1990, arrested while armed with a handgun he'd used to commit a rape, he received fifty years' imprisonment; no parole, no probation.
- California probation officers called Richard Morris "one of Orange County's most desperate and vicious criminals." ATF Special Agent Tom Miller informed the court that the gun found in Morris's apartment had been used to murder an East Pasadena market owner. Morris denied committing that crime and no one could prove otherwise. He got

fifteen years for possession of the pistol; no parole, no probation.

- Eric "Chill" Bryant, twenty-five, led a gang that robbed jewelry stores in Georgia and North Carolina. He got sixty-four years; no parole, no probation.
- Warren Bland, suspected of murdering three little girls and an eighty-one-year-old women, had once received two life sentences for kidnapping, rape and assault with a deadly weapon. He also had convictions for homicide, robbery and oral copulation. Free again and sought for the kidnap, rape and murder of a seven-year-old girl, he got himself a gun. That earned him life in a federal prison; no parole, no probation.

In June 1990, a nationwide ATF sweep across eleven states netted 160 members of the Los Angeles-based Crips and Bloods street gangs—gunmen involved in murders, driveby shootings, drug trafficking, robberies, credit-card fraud and money laundering.

A thirteen-year study demonstrated that years when gun laws were vigorously enforced saw reductions in violent gun crime, but gun violence rose following those years when ATF's efforts were diminished. [See Appendix J.]

NRA followers, still determined to deny the value of any firearms law, argued that crooks should only be prosecuted for the violent acts they committed. But talk's cheap, and convicting criminals is more easily said than done. During 1988 (according to U.S. Bureau of Justice Statistics Special Report NCJ-140614), America's seventy-five most populous counties experienced 14,288 murders. By 1993, 8,063 (56 percent) of these cases had been disposed of through 9,576 prosecutions. Of these defendants, 63 percent were convicted of murder or voluntary manslaughter and sentenced to terms averaging fourteen years; 10 percent were convicted of a lesser crime (8 percent were sentenced to probation or jailed for less than a year); and 27 percent were acquitted. This leaves about 4,700 homicides that never resulted in any charges against anyone.

ATF's Armed Violent Offender Program targeted gun-toting criminals with three or more prior felony convictions for violent crimes or drug trafficking; any conviction for a violent felony where a weapon was used; conviction for any crime where the victim was injured or killed; or who were armed felons released from prison or probation within the past five years.

Police were asked to list outlaws who met these criteria in ATF's computerized Violent Felon File, part of the National Crime Information Center. Law enforcement agencies were also asked to notify ATF when anyone so listed was caught with a firearm or suspected of possessing one. ATF's communications center would call back within ten minutes and an agent would be dispatched to pursue the case.

On August 7, 1991, U.S. Senator Arlen Specter convinced his appropriations committee to give ATF an additional $18.1 million to expand the program.

Fifteen days later, agents mounted a nationwide sweep, rounding up nearly 600 Achilles targets. A year later, a series of Los Angeles raids conducted with the LAPD netted 145 felons, 168 guns, narcotics valued at $250,000 and cash totalling $121,624.

By October, 638 career criminals had been given 10,768 years' imprisonment—among them an ex-con with fifty-seven prior arrests, sent up for thirty years after agents, acting on a tip, caught him with a gun in a Tulsa bar.[17]

Since the statute specified no maximum sentence, eleven men received life terms.

These were good days in ATF.

It doesn't take much to make an agent happy.

14

Fire

In working to achieve [the freeing of America from
the fear of crime and violence], we must begin to
measure one another in terms of contributing to
each other's success. In no other area is this
philosophy more critical than in the . . . investigation of criminal bombings and incendiary fires.
The nature of these incidents strikes at this
country's very foundation and demands a coordinated, unified approach.
                              —ATF Director John W. Magaw

The mid-1970s saw arsons resulting in a thousand deaths,
ten thousand injuries and $2 billion a year in insurance
claims, and the arsonists were getting away with it. A
hundred arson investigations typically produced nine arrests, two convictions, and 0.7 criminals sent to prisons.
State and local authorities lacked training and resources.
There was no one to help them.[1] ATF's work to increase the
frequency of justice was prompted by a 1975 fire that
consumed the Santiago family in Philadelphia.

It was autumn when Randames Santiago moved his
family into the plain brick row home at 4419 North 4th
Street, the first Hispanics in this previously solid black-and-
white neighborhood.

A week later, someone bombed his old station wagon.

Then came the anonymous calls: "Get out, spic!"

That's why, on the night of October 5, a young friend
named Nelson Garcia was posted as a lookout on the
Santiagos' enclosed front porch. The fifteen-year-old boy
tried to stay awake, but at one in the morning the street was
silent, the house was quiet and he dozed.

A window crashed. Firebomb!

Nelson leaped to his feet. The porch was ablaze. *"Fire!"* he shouted in Spanish. There were voices on the street but he couldn't make out what they were saying. He raced through the house to the back yard, looked for a water hose. There was none. He jerked the gate open, ran up the alley to Cayuga Street and came around to the front. Fire engines were already screaming down the narrow street.

Police reports show that Nelson ran back into the burning building, found Mr. Santiago—his face burnt black—and shouted above the roar of the flames, "I saw Red Wilkinson!"

Man and boy stumbled outside. Fire spewed from windows. Jet-black clouds billowed into an orange-tinted sky. Neighbors filled the brilliantly illuminated street and rushed toward the house, only to be driven back by intense heat. Helpless, they listened in horror to shrieks of terror and agony from inside: Mrs. Santiago and four children.

Firefighters battled valiantly against the wind-whipped inferno, but at dawn the smoking ruins yielded five charred corpses: Isabella Santiago, thirty-seven; Nancy, fourteen; Isradames, thirteen; Heriberto, six; and a neighbor's son, Eddie Carrucini, age fourteen.[2]

Nelson Garcia told homicide detectives he'd seen a black neighbor, Red Wilkinson, throw the firebomb. Wilkinson's friends knew the auto mechanic as a nice guy with a wife and baby, but the twenty-six-year-old suspect was taken into custody and twenty hours later he'd confessed to the multiple murder. Common-pleas court judge Lex Bonavitacola suppressed that confession, believing that Wilkinson's I.Q. of 75 rendered him incapable of understanding the *Miranda* warning. But Nelson Garcia told the jury his story and others testified that Wilkinson had purchased a gallon of gasoline that night. He was convicted of wholesale homicide and sentenced to life imprisonment.

The trial had faded from the front pages when a delegation representing the Spanish Merchant's Association and the Council of Spanish Speaking Organizations visited Wallace Hay, special agent-in-charge of ATF's Philadelphia district. "The police won't listen to us but this case can't be closed," they told Hay. "One black bomber? After all the threats and harassment against the Santiagos' 'Spanish invasion'? Impossible! There must be others.''

ATF had jurisdiction in arson cases but this one had been solved quickly. Police hadn't requested assistance and murder charges took precedence, so ATF had deferred to local authorities. Now Special Agent Hay telephoned the district attorney's office and the Philadelphia police department. No, they weren't seeking additional suspects. Yes, they'd closed their investigation. Intrigued by his visitors' arguments, Hay rapped his knuckles on his desk. "We'll look into it."

He assigned special agents Bill Albright and Walt Wasyluk—two experienced men in their early thirties—to find out whether Wilkinson had any accomplices. The chief of the homicide squad wouldn't let Albright and Wasyluk see the police reports of the Wilkinson investigation, but he offered one of his detectives to assist the agents in their quest. The ATF men shrugged—some cops see their files as sacred and why get into a squabble when it's not necessary?—so ATF subpoenaed the city's seven-inch-thick file and told the detective from the original investigation, "Come on. Let's get started."

No one else seemed willing to cooperate. The Santiagos' neighbors and shopkeepers had one answer to all questions: "I dunno nothin'."

Albright and Wasyluk persisted. A mother and four children had perished in those flames. They wanted answers. They practically moved into the neighborhood, ringing doorbells, passing the time of day in grocery stores and corner taverns. When "I dunno nothin'" became depressingly repetitious, they made the rounds again. Albright hailed men leaving their homes for work and chatted with housewives walking to market. Wasyluk buttonholed people at bus stops. They strolled the sidewalks with citizens sandwiching questions between comments on the weather and the high cost of living. Folks began waving and smiling. "Hi, Bill. Hi, Walt." They liked the friendly agents. But they wouldn't talk about the bombing.

Weeks passed without a single lead.

Between their street forays, the agents took turns studying

the weighty police file. They noted some disturbing inconsistencies. Nelson Garcia's statement to detectives had Red Wilkinson throwing the firebomb with his left hand; Wilkinson was right-handed. Garcia said he saw Wilkinson light the Molotov cocktail with his cigarette; experts pronounced this unlikely if not impossible. Garcia's signed statement placed Wilkinson at one location when he tossed the bomb; his trial testimony put the man at a different spot.

Albright asked Wasyluk, "What if nobody helped him?"

Wasyluk pictured the retarded man serving life in a dank cell and frowned. "What if the poor bastard's innocent?"

They recalled that some of the people who "dunno nothin'" seemed afraid. And although both agents had friends among Philadelphia's police—patrolmen and detectives of unquestioned integrity—they knew the department's reputation.

Frank Rizzo, former police commissioner; former cop known for courage and pragmatism, made a prediction while running for mayor: "I'm gonna make Attila the Hun look like a faggot after this election's over." During his 1972–1979 term as mayor, he backed up his invitations of police brutality by insulating his officers from accountability.

A 1980 U.S. Justice Department report would belatedly illustrate the Rizzo police department's use of force:

> While Philadelphia police were no more likely than New York police to make arrests or to come face to face with armed people, they were *thirty-seven times* as likely as New York policemen to shoot unarmed people who had threatened nobody and who were fleeing from suspected nonviolent crimes.

The ATF men learned of one man in the Santiagos' neighborhood who might inspire fear among neighbors: thirty-five-year-old Democratic committeeman Ronald Hanley, known for an overbearing arrogance and oft-frenzied behavior. Could Hanley be covering for cops who'd railroaded an innocent man into life imprisonment?

Agents Albright and Wasyluk arranged to interview Nelson Garcia themselves. A member of the Spanish neighborhood organization insisted on being present "to protect the boy." The three men sat with Garcia around his parents' dining-room table. Albright said, "You saw the bomb come through the window, you stuck your head out through the broken glass and that's when you saw Wilkinson. Is that right?"

"Yeah." The boy licked his lips. "That's it."

"But the window was on fire. Wouldn't you have burned your face?"

"Before. I stuck my head out before."

"You said the bomb broke the glass, Nelson. The window must have been closed."

The teenager hemmed and hawed. The agents cataloged inconsistencies in the story he'd told detectives: the left-handed throw by a right-handed Wilkinson; lighting the gas-soaked wick with a cigarette; the discrepancies regarding Wilkinson's position when he supposedly tossed the firebomb.

"Oh God!" Garcia burst into tears and buried his face in his arms. "I'm so sorry." He admitted he'd been asleep. He hadn't seen Wilkinson until he'd run into the street after the house was ablaze.

Still, this didn't prove Wilkinson hadn't thrown the Molotov cocktail. Seven trial witnesses had corroborated vital elements of the case. Albright and Wasyluk visited them. The first two told of being taken with their wives to the Roundhouse—Philadelphia's drum-shaped police headquarters—and held for twelve hours. The women were threatened with the loss of their children. The men were treated to more direct persuasion.

One was plunked into a hard chair in a tiny, soundproof interrogation room. A beefy detective stood before him, removed the rings from his huge fingers, slid them into his pocket and asked the "witness" how much gasoline he'd given Wilkinson.

"Me? None." The man sat erect, meeting the officer's gaze.

A crashing fist sprawled him across the floor. They picked him up, plopped him into the chair again. "How much gas did you give Wilkinson?"

"None."

The fist hurled him from the chair again. They propped him up and repeated the question. "I don't know," the man said, "how much did I give him?"

"A gallon."

The man signed a statement. The detectives assured him there were other witnesses and that "Wilkinson's guilty as sin."

The ATF men had had no cause to work with the homicide squad prior to this investigation. Now they discovered that the inspector in charge of the squad held two unshakable beliefs: that every investigation should develop a confession; and a *real man* can always get a confession. Albright confronted the detective assigned by the police lieutenant to "assist" in their investigation. The man walked out of the ATF office and never returned.

Word flashed through the neighborhood grapevine: "Bill and Walt aren't giving up. They want the truth." One by one, hesitant and frightened neighbors whispered answers to the agents' questions about Committeeman Ronald Hanley. The man was brutal; he'd even beaten his own wife with a dog chain. The Hanleys were divorced now.

On a sunny summer morning, the two agents waited outside the city's welfare office. When Doris Hanley emerged, they introduced themselves and walked with her along Broad Street. Her story chilled them.

On that fateful October night, Hanley had come home late from a political rally and announced that he was going to "take care of those spics." He awakened their nineteen-year-old boarder, David McGinniss, and ordered him to siphon gas from the family car. The two of them poured it into a whiskey bottle, fashioned a wick from an old baby diaper and left the house. Hanley returned laughing. He told a horrified Doris, "The place went up like a Christmas tree." When the radio reported that Isabella and the four children had perished, McGinnis wept.

The agents talked to more people. On the night of the bombing, Wilkinson had gone out to buy cigarettes. He was returning home when he saw the fire and turned in the alarm. Firemen answering the call recalled Wilkinson helping them uncoil their hoses.

Detectives had snatched him off the street, rushed him to

the Roundhouse and beat him with blackjacks. They jumped on his legs. They screamed into his face, "You'll never see your wife and baby again!" Twenty hours of torture yielded what the inspector in charge expected: a confession, procured by "real men." And then, for fifteen months, Red Wilkinson had suffered the indignity of an innocent among felons, the hopelessness of being consigned to nonexistence for the rest of his life.

McGinnis broke down and admitted helping Hanley. He also told agents how he'd gone to the prosecutors before Wilkinson's trial and told them the whole truth. They threw him out of their office. Albright and Wasyluk uncovered improprieties that occurred during the trial. Among them, jurors had been secretly informed of Wilkinson's confession, the one Judge Bonavitacola had suppressed.

The ATF men brought their evidence to the office of the district attorney. The D.A.'s men listened with clenched teeth and told the agents, literally, to "stick that stuff up your ass."

Bill Albright and Walt Wasyluk had conducted themselves above-board with everyone—first by confronting the homicide detective, then by offering their evidence to the city prosecutor. Now they gathered up their reports quietly, departed with cold determination and visited the U.S. attorney.

One month later, the sixth victim of the fire, Red Wilkinson, was freed.

The bombers were convicted on federal charges of denying the Santiagos their civil right to live where they pleased. U.S. District Judge Joseph Lord termed McGinnis "a malleable young man" and gave him twenty-two years. He sentenced Hanley—"the vilest kind of human being I can imagine"—to life plus thirty-three years.

Six members of the Philadelphia homicide squad were sentenced to federal prison for fifteen months—the same span Wilkinson had suffered for a crime he didn't commit.

The D.A. allowed two of his assistants to resign.

Special Agent-in-Charge Wallace Hay used the Santiago case to justify forming ATF's first arson task force, a team effort with IRS agents, U.S. postal inspectors, state fire marshals and local police. During the task force's first months they imprisoned a slumlord, an insurance adjuster, a lawyer and two notorious racketeers. Since then, arson task forces have been established in sixteen major cities. ATF organized four arson response teams: specially trained agents and scientists armed with the most modern equipment, ready to respond at a moment's notice to suspected arsons causing death, injuries or substantial property damage anywhere in the country. The bureau's intensive two-week course trains police detectives in the intricacies of arson investigation.

Agents never know where a "routine" case will end. Sniffing around the smelly remains of a burned-out stable near Chicago led ATF past the arrest of the arsonist and across the sunny fields of high society's horsey set to solve the killing of Thoroughbreds for insurance and the seventeen-year-old unsolved murder of candy heiress Helen Brach, the wealthiest woman in America.[3]

In 1996 ATF's top priority was a series of sixty-four black church burnings across the South, hyped as racially motivated by those who couldn't understand why anyone would burn a black church for any other reason. Two Klansmen were arrested in 1995, but thirty arrests by mid-1996 yielded defendants with motives unrelated to race: two black contractors, trying to hide the fact that they'd failed to finish some work on the church before the money ran out; a black burglar, covering the clues to his crime; a white firefighter who wanted to be a hero; a known pyromaniac; a female mental patient; a dozen teenagers, black and white; two ten-year-olds; a pair of seven-year-olds.

The firebombing of the Inner City Church in Knoxville, Tennessee, touched off a firestorm of controversy when agents questioned church members, subjected some to the lie-detector, and subpoenaed church records—all this despite earlier threats signed "skinheads for white justice" and racial slurs scrawled on outer walls. Pastor David Upton's screams echoed back to ATF in the form of a call from Vice President Gore asking for an explanation. So the agents explained: five-gallon pails of kerosene and eighteen unexploded Molotov cocktails had been found inside the church, a locked brick building with no signs of forced entry. Added to that, two natural gas lines had been turned on by someone who just happened to know where they were. The vice president agreed that agents must pursue the evidence they find.

Tony Nacaroto was a hard-working forty-six-year-old immigrant who owned Pike Beef & Beer until a high-ranking Philadelphia mobster named John Calabrese muscled in and burned the place down for the insurance. IRS agent Alan Hart handed Tony a grand jury subpoena on behalf of the federal strike force.

Tony told him, "I'll talk. I'll tell them everything."

Tony repeated his intentions to anyone who'd listen. Honest but impractical.

Racketeers are practical. Calabrese owned interests in extortion rings and the inside sources who tipped the mob to easy burglary targets and robberies. DEA rated him a Class I narcotics violator. Tall and bulky, this busy executive had no patience for petty problems. He gave freelancers Vince Zabala and Robert Harris a $10,000 contract to murder Tony Nacaroto. A most practical solution.

On a balmy October evening in 1976, Zabala and Harris climbed into the dented auto Zabala had bought at auction and registered under a phony name—a gold Plymouth with blackwall tires and no trim, formerly the property of the Pennsylvania state police—and drove to a parking lot in Cherry Hill, New Jersey, where they could watch Tony Nacaroto's tan Chevrolet. The hit men were comfortable without conversation. They'd worked together often: the Boyertown bank robbery, an armored car job at the Echelon Mall, a load of copper from the contractor erecting a post office in Bellmawr, New Jersey.

Nor was this their first murder for hire. Given a contract on Nick Mellillo, they'd had a friend lure him out "to pull a job"; the friend delivered Mellillo to his executioners. Bill Mitchell was easy too. They'd simply invited him to a mutual friend's apartment on Woodhaven Road in Philly, and when good-old-buddy-Bill arrived, they beat him to death with a blackjack. The fact that buddy-Bill had been a loyal accomplice in previous scores was no more relevant than Nick Mellillo's standing as their partner in diamond heists and mail-truck robberies. Calabrese suspected they were talking to the wrong people. It looked like a problem.

The practical solution: murder.

To Zabala and Harris, Tony Nacaroto was just another job.

At nine-thirty that October night they saw a man key the driver's door of the tan Chevy. Stepping from the gold Plymouth, Zabala called out, "Mr. Nacaroto?"

Tony eyed the two medium-size men wearing suits and ties. "I'm Tony Nacaroto."

"We're FBI agents, Mr. Nacaroto. We've come to take you to Philadelphia. It's about the grand jury."

"I was just going—"

"This won't take long. We'll drive you." The Plymouth looked official. Zabala opened the passenger door and held the front seat forward so Tony could climb in back. Harris drove. They crossed into Philadelphia and kept going.

"Hey," Tony said, "where we goin'?"

Zabala turned, smiled across the seat. "Look, Tony, we're not FBI men. We work for Calabrese."

Tony shrank back and looked helplessly through the window into the darkness. They were out in the country now. Not much traffic.

"C'mon," said Zabala, folding his arms on the back of his seat, "don't be scared. Calabrese just wants you to go away for a while. He'll give you a hundred grand, just to disappear till all this blows over."

Tony looked outside again and shrugged. "Okay."

The tension in the front seat eased.

But Tony Nacaroto had brought something more than his broken English from the old country—something he couldn't lose as easily as his accent: integrity. "No!" he said. "I'm-a-gonna stay right here where I live. I'm-a-not-goin' anywhere. And I'm-a-gonna tell the FBI that I been kidnapped."

Zabala pointed his .22-caliber pistol across the seat. "Shut up, stupid." Then he telephoned home and told his wife to take their kids out shopping.

When the two killers shoved their victim into the kitchen

of the Zabala farmhouse, Tony might still have believed they'd try talking him into running away. He asked for a drink of water. His abductors just stood there. Harris turned to Zabala for an answer to Tony's request.

"A drink of water," Tony repeated. "Okay?"

The squat, balding Zabala replied, "You won't need it." Standing just eight feet away, he drew the pistol from his belt, leveled it at a bug-eyed Tony and jerked the trigger six times. Five bullets buried themselves in Tony's chest and arm; a sixth bored into a kitchen chair.

They rolled Tony's corpse into a quilt, trundled it out back to Zabala's orange pickup and covered it with bales of hay. They wiped Tony's blood from the kitchen floor, pried the misdirected slug from the chair, drove the truck to a junkyard and left it there overnight. Next morning, with the sun shining brightly on autumn foliage surrounding the junkyard beside the Bible Ark Chapel, they dug a five-foot pit behind a rusting van, shoved the bundle that had been Tony into the hole and covered him with dirt. They hosed the blood from the pickup, dropped the murder weapon into the Schuylkill River and reported their contract completed.

A few weeks later, Tony's landlord reported him missing.

Contract killers are rarely caught. The men behind them have even less to worry about. Two years passed and the mobsters forgot all about Tony Nacaroto.

It was the spring of 1979 when Vince Zabala found himself firmly wedged in a very deep crack. On a cool pleasant evening he drove to a secluded spot where no one would see him sitting in a G-car talking to ATF Special Agent James Henley. The agent candidly displayed his iron-clad case against Zabala, promised him a lifetime behind bars and opened a door. "We'd rather capture a general than a soldier." If Zabala assisted his country in its war against the syndicate, a federal prosecutor might make helpful suggestions to the judge who'd be sentencing Mr. Zabala.

The killer stared straight through the windshield. "Yeah? Like what?" Being a practical man, Zabala was open to a practical solution.

"It depends, Vince." Henley saw skepticism in Zabala's face. "I'm not hedging. It has to depend on what you give us. For nothing, you get nothing. For a little, you might get a little. Go the distance and we'll meet you halfway."

The night air turned cold. Zabala shivered, rolled up the window. "Can I walk?"

"Go free? No way. With what we've got, you'll have to do some time."

Zabala knew what was coming. The moment his indictment was announced, Calabrese would see him as a potential traitor. The mob chief's practical solution would come in the form of men like Zabala himself. He'd never live to serve a life term. "Okay." He went the distance, implicating Calabrese and ten others in interstate transportation of stolen property, thefts from interstate shipments, one meth lab, sixteen armed robberies, two arsons and three homicides. Agents moved Zabala to a Harrisburg hotel.

A killer's tale is one thing; proof is something else. Agents began the delicate task of digging up evidence of years-old crimes without alerting the underworld that someone was spilling secrets. Pull the missing-persons report on Tony Nacaroto; verify Nick Mellillo's disappearance; examine insurance investigators' reports regarding the arson of a mansion on Winding Way in Lower Merion, Pennsylvania: Calabrese had paid a $708 insurance premium on April 23, 1974, the place burned twelve days later, Calabrese collected $400,000. Everything corroborated Zabala's account. The tedious task of reconstructing past events in a discreet fashion dragged through the winter. Postal inspectors provided reports of mail-truck robberies. DEA agents were brought in to probe Zabala's disclosures of illicit drug labs. It was another spring before ATF agents with shovels and a backhoe exhumed the bodies of Mellillo and Tony Nacaroto. Dental charts confirmed their identities. Carpeting from the apartment where William Mitchell had been murdered was sent to ATF's lab; they found human blood.

Next, agents interviewed selected suspects. Most refused to answer questions; they couldn't guess the extent of ATF's knowledge, and agents wouldn't show their hand. Not at this point. But a hood involved in an armored-car heist talked; and the accomplice in the Mellillo murder confessed. Agents made Zabala available to the New Jersey State Police Intelligence Unit and the Philadelphia Police Department's Organized Crime Squad.

Zabala's partner, Harris, agreed to a polygraph exam. ATF Special Agent Jerry O'Reilly advised him of his rights, explained the procedure and asked, "Did you deliberately withhold information?"

Harris said, "No."

"Did you deliberately lie when you said you didn't take part in any killing?"

"No."

"Did you make up anything you told us?"

"No."

O'Reilly reported, "After careful review and evaluation of Mr. Harris' physiological responses to the relevant questions, it is the opinion of this examiner that there are sufficient indicators of deception in Mr. Harris' answers."

Translation: Harris lied.

Agents spent the whole summer and the next winter checking motel registers, car-rental records and jail logs. They interviewed hundreds of witnesses and verified testimony given by a score of songbirds across seven states. It was January 20, 1981—four years after Tony Nacaroto's brutal slaying—before a warrant was issued commanding "any ATF agent" to arrest Big John Calabrese for obstruction of justice and conspiracy to deny Mr. Nacaroto his constitutional right to be a federal witness. Maximum penalty: life.

Ripples spread all along the East Coast as agents used the intelligence they'd gathered to shut down old rackets, recruit new informers and generate fresh leads to still more cases. Vince Zabala got his deal: fifteen years in prison. A state jury acquitted Harris of Tony Nacaroto's murder, so ATF put him in a federal pen for his role in using a firearm to commit a federal crime—to wit, denying Tony his constitutional right to testify.

Big John Calabrese, facing life imprisonment, now posed the same threat to the mob that Tony Nacaroto once represented. The same threat, inviting the same response from the mob that triggerman Zabala avoided by becoming a witness. But Calabrese didn't talk. And six weeks after his indictment, this Mafia restaurateur and member of the Andorra Country Club was gunned down in the streets of South Philly.[4]

It was the practical solution.

Treasury's efforts against arson continue to expand. ATF man Thomas Horbert conducted a study with the FBI's Behavioral Science Unit to profile arsonists and bombers; his work had led to several convictions. Following a joint experiment with the Connecticut state police, ATF supplied various departments with dogs trained to sniff out the accelerants used to start fires.[5]

The most recently released report, covering 1994, shows 545 arson incidents that caused $370.5 million in property damage, injured 174 victims and killed fifty-four. ATF agents submitted 260 case reports to prosecutors that year charging 474 alleged arsonists; at year's end, 263 had already been indicted or convicted. A typical case description listed in ATF's *1994 Arson and Explosives Incidents Report* reads:

> On March 4, 1994, a suspect was indicted in Plymouth [MA] on charges of arson. He has since pled guilty to the charges and been sentenced to 9 to 15 years' imprisonment. The suspect was the subject of an investigation conducted by ATF, the Whitman Police and Fire Departments, the Quincy Police and Fire Departments, and the Massachusetts State Fire Marshal's Office into more than 35 arson fires that have occurred in Quincy and Whitman over the past few years. The suspect, who was under surveillance, was arrested prior to his indictment as he was about to burn a church rectory. His girlfriend was also arrested. She pled guilty as well and was sentenced to a term of probation.

For ATF, cooperation isn't something the agents merely utilize. Unlike some federal agencies, it's *this* bureau's policy to credit every participating agency for their contributions to success.

Today, thanks to the project launched by Special Agent-in-Charge Wallace Hay after Red Wilkinson was freed in the Santiago case, an arsonist's odds of being caught and sent to prison have soared 2,500 percent.[6]

15

The Circus

All his professional life, it seemed to [the spy, George] Smiley, he had listened to similar verbal antics signaling supposedly great changes in Whitehall doctrine . . . always another reason for doing nothing. He had watched Whitehall's skirts go up, and come down again, her belts being tightened, loosened, tightened. . . . Each new fashion had been hailed as a panacea: "Now we shall vanquish, now the machine will work!" Each had gone out with a whimper. . . . He had toiled in back rooms while shallower men held the stage. They held it still.

—John LeCarre

When ATF became a bureau in 1972, agents saw hope on the horizon—hope that they'd finally shed the IRS attitude and philosophies to become, at long last, a law-enforcement agency first and foremost. In Washington, the core of the agency known as "NO" (for national office) was christened "BHQ," for bureau headquarters.

By 1977 agents were calling it Burro Hindquarters.

ATF was born with two congenital defects: its revenue/regulatory branch that accompanied agents into the new bureau; and a pathetic lack of leadership.

Regulators adopted the IRS principle called "voluntary compliance." With only 544 inspectors, they couldn't collect that annual $13 billion in taxes *and* compel obedience to the law by 19,148 breweries, distilleries, wineries, alcohol fuel plants and explosives licensees *plus*—in their spare time, perhaps—155,573 licensed gun dealers.[1] Director Rex Davis had a dream he called "one bureau," where revenue folk and agent folk shared goals and tactics, as if

208

the criminals his agents sought were wayward taxpayers. That's why the administrator preparing ATF's official mission statement designed it, he said, "to minimize the distinction between what Criminal Enforcement [the agents] and Regulatory Enforcement [the tax collectors] do in the program."

Special Agent John W. Kern responded for all agents, utilizing an emphatic style born of long-standing frustration:[2]

> This is the real problem we see in this document and in the current posture of this bureau. We consistently perpetuate the fiction that Criminal Enforcement and Regulatory Enforcement work closely. . . . We *do not*, we *will not*, and we *cannot* perform the same function. . . . Our missions are different; our enforcement philosophies are different; and our programs are different. The Criminal Enforcement Firearms Program is different from that of Regulatory."

Kern's memo had no effect on Director Davis's beloved "one bureau" concept.

Change creates anxiety and uncertainty among the employees of any organization. From the repeal of Prohibition through 1977, ATF had been reorganized seventeen times—four times in the five years since becoming a bureau. One innovation eliminated the regional directors, known among agents as the Seven Chinese Warlords for their practice of running their fiefdoms arbitrarily independent of one another and independent of their impotent headquarters. Now with the seven warlords removed as a barrier between headquarters and the field, ATF directors and their assistant directors for law enforcement could impose uniform standards to enhance efficiency; they could improve effectiveness. They could take charge. They could lead. They could, but they didn't.

Violent crime fell when ATF agents were most active, and vice versa—i.e., it surged upward when agents were less productive.[3] Strong leaders could have transformed ATF into the world's most effective enemy of violent crime, earned the public support that generates congressional support, countered the lies leveled by the NRA and garnered the appropriations that perpetuate success. Instead, Director Rex Davis and his successors, elevated to executive levels by their old revenue chiefs, focused on that side of ATF they saw as paramount: regulation and revenue. Law enforcement was left to Big Bill Griffin's marionettes, men he ran by remote control from his Atlanta office, men who floundered when Griffin retired—men who became known, bureauwide, as the Good Ole Boys.

Throughout the late 1970s and early 1980s, Assistant Director Miles Keathley bossed bureau law enforcement. Once husky, now paunchy with a close-cropped military-style haircut and a beet-red complexion, good ole boy Keathley made decisions. If his decrees demonstrated fear and appeasement of those critics he couldn't muzzle, his decisions were nevertheless law within ATF.

Example: Agents identified every violent felon in the USA and entered their names—along with descriptions, criminal records, residences, cars and license numbers—into Treasury's computer. The data was available to any Treasury officer. A Customs inspector at a remote border crossing queried the license number of an approaching auto, got a hit and showed the printout to the felon. The ex-con complained. Keathley's decision: Erase all those violent felons from the computer.

Example: Several special agents-in-charge (SACs) requested authority to offer rewards for information in bombing cases. Keathley's decision:[4]

> We could be leaving ourselves open to numerous victims asking that they be afforded the same opportunity to have their case, no matter how significant, advertised as well. To the gun dealer who had twenty guns stolen, his case is just as important as a major bombing incident. Therefore, we will not exercise this practice since it could place us in a very precarious situation.

Example: When ATF's tracing section documented dozens of devastating crimes committed with untraceable guns acquired at flea markets and gun shows, agents and deputy sheriffs distributed copies of the Gun Control Act to peddlers at one California gun show and asked recipients for their names. The NRA screamed. Rather than respond with facts and evidence, daring the gun lovers to justify illegal trafficking, Keathley made another decision: He forbade agents to conduct any investigation "relating to a gun show or flea market, unless there is reliable, definite information that guns involved have shown up in crimes of violence, or there is a significant, willful violation of the Gun Control or Explosive [sic] Act. . . . The chief, Investigations Division, will be contacted prior to active investigation action in even these instances. . . . The final decision will be made by the assistant director."[5]

Mr. Keathley never told his agents how to get "definite information" regarding "significant, willful violation" without making an investigation, but eight months later, he'd report that his guidelines had resulted in few authorizations granted and "no unfavorable publicity."[6]

If Keathley and his good ole boy buddies were soft on outsiders, they were ruthless toward insiders. The National Association of Treasury Agents (NATA) was founded by retired ATF agent Bill Pace to rescue those it thought had been treated unfairly: like the agent who was disciplined for wearing a shirt and tie at a fish fry where good ole boy executives appeared in their shirtsleeves; or the New Orleans incident where a SAC improperly denied his agents the overtime pay they'd earned.

When a personnel supervisor voiced an opinion that penalties for misconduct were being imposed arbitrarily with no semblance of evenhanded uniformity, Ellen Drummey and I were ordered to study the matter. We examined every allegation of impropriety investigated by Internal Affairs (IA). This peek at ATF's most secret files was instructive:[7]

- On April 19, 1977, an agent in upstate New York patted a suspect down, then struck the man with the barrel of his gun. IA's report went to the local district attorney. The agent pleaded *nolo contendre* to felony assault. His partner, who'd failed to report the crime, was allowed to resign.

- In 1976 a supervisor borrowed $250 from the office expense fund. He repaid it long before IA commenced its inquiry, but he was reduced in rank and transferred.
- The agent who attended law school at night had never put his studies ahead of his duties, but he hadn't obtained the bureau's permission to take courses; he got five days' suspension. (All suspensions are without pay.)
- An agent interviewed a witness one evening after having a few beers with a district attorney and several FBI agents; he'd shown no effects of intoxication, but the witness reported smelling it on his breath; he got a ten-day suspension.
- In California, three agents shared a beer with an informant, a prostitute. Later, she claimed she'd been raped. Chemical tests and lie detectors disproved the rape allegation, but two agents were suspended for ten days and the third was given fifteen days for consuming alcohol while on duty.
- The agent who charged thirteen personal phone calls on his bureau credit card got a four-day suspension after he repaid Uncle Sam for the calls.

None of the accusations leveled at agents during the three years covered by IA files we reviewed approached the proven crimes committed time and again by members of Congress, judges and clergymen from any church you can name, but Ms. Drummey and I noticed that penalties were usually exacted in inverse proportion to the offender's rank.

A Dallas ATF agent told a writer for *Argosy* magazine how he'd joined officers at the Texas School Book Depository after JFK's assassination, found the sniper's nest, notified the senior search officer and—at the request of police captain Will Fritz—he'd traced the murder weapon through its sale by the NRA to assassin Lee Harvey Oswald. That interview occurred thirteen years after the assassination and the agent hadn't revealed any secret but, for failing to get bureau permission to grant the interview, he received a five-day suspension. The SAC who disclosed *confidential* information to a reporter got off with a written admonishment in his personnel file.

An agent who, over a period of weeks, claimed nine hours' duty when he hadn't actually worked was suspended for forty-five days. The SAC who claimed fifteen hours over a period of days while attending to purely personal business outside the office received no penalty whatsoever.

ATF organized its Internal Affairs unit in 1972. Its first case probed a Denver agent and his supervisor who'd sold some guns—evidence, no longer needed for trials—and falsified certifications that they'd destroyed the weapons. IA presented the evidence to the U.S. attorney with a recommendation that the crime be prosecuted.[8]

The prosecutor was nonplussed. "I thought the agencies preferred to handle these embarrassments internally to avoid the scandal."

One of the IA men replied, "ATF's job is putting crooks in jail."

Both agents went to prison.

IA's investigators were feared but respected until good ole boys began using IA to intimidate subordinates who'd complained of favoritism or sexual harassment. When a female who'd applied to become an agent complained she'd had to rebuff sexual advances by an SAC, IA investigators reported false allegations that were used to deny her the job. She requested a hearing. The judge held that Deputy Assistant Director Daniel Hartnett's testimony "consistently misrepresented or exaggerated information"; that IA chief Frank Nickell's testimony was "not credible"; and the IA man who'd conducted the woman's pre-employment investigation was "nervous, evasive and not a credible witness." The SAC was transferred to a smaller post and the woman got the job with back pay, but it was two years before ATF gave her an assignment that met Treasury's equal-opportunity guidelines.[9] Deputy Assistant Director

Hartnett would inherit Keathley's crown and later be forced into retirement by exposures of false statements made following the Waco tragedy of 1993.

Keathley created the Program Review Division when Treasury noted the bureau's lack of an internal mechanism to ensure that field managers complied with national priorities. Neither I nor any of the agents ordered into this unit suspected that we were mere window dressing. We believed, naively, that we existed to inspect district offices and evaluate the SAC's performance. But, like IA, we were used. Our findings were ignored.

In the IRS tradition, ATF measured effectiveness by the number of cases a SAC "recommended for prosecution." It didn't matter whether these cases ever came to trial; U.S. attorneys could decline prosecution for reasons ranging from insufficient evidence to a vague and undefined "not in the best interests of the government," and no good ole boy was about to rate the value of a case on the basis of an outsider's opinion. If an SAC recommended a case for prosecution and sent the report to federal prosecutors, he and the agent who'd made the case got credit—rather like giving a basketball player two points every time he took a shot, regardless of whether he ever scored.

Keathley dispatched two of us to St Louis. "SAC Elder's caseload has fallen," he said. "Find out what's wrong with him."

SAC Elder was a slender, soft-spoken southern gentlemen who didn't happen to be a good ole boy. "What's wrong with him" turned out to be increased efficiency. Rather than emulating his predecessor—Jimmy Welch, who'd sent every crappy case that crossed his desk forward with his hoofprint recommending prosecution—Elder only submitted quality investigations. The total "recommended" had dropped from 134 to 123, but the cases prosecutors took to trial had climbed from Welch's 71 to Elder's 105.

Keathley seemed displeased by our report.[10]

SAC Jimmy Welch was short and built like a cannon ball with a moon-round face habitually split by a jolly grin. His favorite saying: "I can do any job in this bureau." Our team crossed his trail in Chicago. Among their findings:[11]

- During 1977, Welch commanded 116 special agents; these agents utilized $58,728.01 in investigative expenses and paid their informers a total of $25,139.15.
- The fruits of all that manpower and resources: 147 cases recommended by Welch for prosecution; 21 defendants convicted; 11 men imprisoned; their sentences added up to a grand total of 13 years.

Within weeks of the report detailing Welch's "accomplishments," Keathley promoted Welch to deputy assistant director, the bureau's number-three position.

The Gun Control Act of 1968 created a recordkeeping system that enabled ATF to trace crime guns. A phone call to the weapon's importer or manufacturer reveals where they shipped it; a call to that wholesaler leads to a retail gun shop where, if the dealer obeyed the law, ATF finds the form the purchaser filled out when he bought the gun. If that first owner disposed of the firearm, agents interview successive owners until they find the one who had it at the time of the crime. Special Agent Lyman Shaffer's 260-day odyssey began when San Francisco detectives requested a trace on the pistol used by the infamous random killer they code-named Zebra. Lyman followed the firearm's trail to Hawaii and back, through loans, theft, street people and a hockshop. If he'd known of the pawnshop sale and its recent record, success would have come in days rather than months, but how could he know? Thousands of traces failed and thousands of violent outlaws continued their criminal careers despite the existence of recent sales records because the first chain of ownership was broken by a purchaser who lied, or couldn't be found, and no one knew that a new record existed somewhere.[12]

Search Group, a commission of local, state and federal lawmen studying this problem, recommended that licensed dealers send ATF quarterly reports listing the serial numbers of guns they sold.[13] ATF proposed a regulation requiring such reports—no customers' names; just the gun numbers. The NRA branded it "registration by regulation."

NRA president Lloyd Mustin asked, "And why is tracing supposed to be so good, like motherhood and the American way of life?"[14]

The firearms fraternity bombarded politicians with calls and letters. Congress killed the regulation, then sliced $4.2 million—the amount it would have cost to implement the plan—from ATF's appropriation, even though *that* $4.2 million wasn't part of the bureau's current budget request. Representative Ashbrook rose on the floor of the House to call ATF's proposal an attempt to usurp congressional powers by imposing registration through regulation. The NRA won that vote too: 314 to 80.[15]

Representative Risenhoover stood up to praise the work of ATF's special agents. "But," he added, "if they can't get a director in there who can be a lawman . . . I'm going to vote against all their appropriations."[16] Weeks later, Director Davis resigned.

Esquire magazine reported:[17]

> Treasury's top brass has now shelved their original idea of finding a proven innovative and independent crime fighter to run ATF. According to a well-placed source, "We've decided not to look for anyone who's a threatening figure to be the new director. We're looking for someone already in the civil service—not a major law enforcement type—which is the way we'd go if we felt we could get away with upgrading ATF."

On February 12, 1979, Treasury named fifty-one-year-old G. R. Dickerson as director. A lifetime member of the NRA, Dickerson expanded Keathley's ban against investigating anything at a flea market or gun show; now the order embraced licensed gun dealers.

At the office I headed covering Maine and New Hampshire, police informed us that a gunshop owner had obtained his license by lying about a pending felony indictment for shooting a man. Falsifying an application is a felony. I forwarded an agent's request to investigate. The request was denied. When a sheriff reported another licensed gun dealer, allegedly dealing in stolen guns, who'd lied on his application to conceal a grand larceny conviction, we requested permission to investigate. The response: "Request Denied."[18]

Ultimately, we were ordered to ignore every crime within the bureau's jurisdiction—illegal sales, possession of machine guns, even bombings—*everything* except interstate trafficking. The new program was called "interdiction." A verse appeared on the blackboard in the squadroom of a California ATF office:

> We don't arrest, we don't convict.
> All we do is interdict.

No one had bribed an ATF agent since Prohibition. Now no one had to. That ten-dollar gun dealer's license granted immunity from investigation. Today the license costs more, and President Clinton has ordered that applicants be fingerprinted and photographed to keep criminals from getting a license under a ficticious name.

Agency appropriations depend largely on reputation, but some opinions count more than others. A congressional subcommittee asked 1,600 prosecutors and police chiefs to rank the federal bureaus in terms of practical assistance—i.e., how useful they were; a majority named ATF number one.[19] But congressmen who'd never known ATF beyond the Beltway were limited to a view of the good ole boys at bureau headquarters. Judging from the support they gave ATF, that closeup did not inspire confidence.

Today, fortunately for the country, ATF has a strong, professional leader.

16

The Spring
of '81

Reputation is what men and women think of us;
character is what God and angels know of us.
                                    —Thomas Paine

The 1995 bombing of the federal building in Oklahoma
City was the sort of crime we'd have expected in Belfast or
Beirut, but the threat of terrorism has been with us for
decades from people who don't care whether their victims
are nice people, or good or bad, or very important, or
nobody, because bodies become mere punctuation marks in
their explosive statements.

ATF agents have devised numerous strategies to deal with
these criminals because each suspect is unique, every plot a
little different, and failure brings death. Although the FBI
calls itself our protector from terrorism, the Treasury agents
have scotched more schemes and caught more of these
would-be killers than any other agency.

Several cases reached a critical stage in the soft spring-
time months of 1981.

Pulaski, Tennessee, is the birthplace of the Ku Klux Klan.
Twenty miles away, in Nashville—a beautiful city of culture
and commerce—a grandmother subsisting on social security invited three tall men to discuss current events at her
comfortable, suburban ranch-style home. They arrived in
moderately priced autos; the newest was thirteen years old.
Bill Foutch was an art dealer. Bob Vance worked as a
security guard. Charles Boyer played the guitar for a living.
Gladys Girganti, the gray-haired grandmother, listened

intently as guitar player Boyer explained the group's latest community-improvement project to the security guard, Vance.

"The temple in West Nashville"—Boyer's voice betrayed his enthusiasm—"and the transmission tower for that Jew-owned WSM-TV, and a couple of those kike pawnshops downtown. We're gonna blow 'em up." He was twenty-six with a ruddy complexion. The anchor tattoo on his left forearm branded him an ex-sailor without revealing his discharge for desertion. A convicted felon too, he called himself a "patriot." And a Nazi.

Vance, the security guard, doubled as Grand Dragon for the Confederate Vigilantes of the Ku Klux Klan. "The temple's pretty isolated but those hockshops—if somebody happens to be walking by the blast might kill them."

Bill Foutch, the blond-haired, blue-eyed forty-eight-year-old entrepreneur of art, pursed his lips. "Every war has its casualties." Family members, unaware of his Nazi connection—would describe Foutch as even tempered and well mannered "with an inquiring mind." The relative who'd stored two large cartons for him never examined their contents: detailed plans for the extermination of Jews by bombing and decapitation.

Gladys Girganti, hardly the typical Tennessee grandmother, nodded at Foutch's assessment: Deaths would be regrettable but essential for the preservation of Christianity and the United States. Raised and widowed in Michigan—her husband a Klansman—Gladys's bookshelves bristled with hate literature, and her five-drawer filing cabinet was crammed with correspondence from like-minded "patriots" around the country.

Grand Dragon/security guard Vance agreed to join their project.

Another cauldron of venom was about to boil.

There were more meetings to map strategy, and then, on an overcast afternoon, Gladys drove Vance to the Almaville exit of Interstate 24, where they met two Klansmen in their twenties. The younger men drove Vance to a gas station where a man handed him a metal ammunition box filled with dynamite and time fuses. Vance had volunteered to assemble the big bomb—the one for the temple.

May 25, 1981, was Memorial Day, dedicated to men who'd died defending liberty and justice. That's the day Vance brought his handiwork to Gladys's home where she and the guitar player, Boyer, examined the fuse leading to a blasting cap stuck into a bundle of dynamite cylinders and nodded their approval. The trio left Gladys's home in Vance's gray pickup and drove slowly along Harding Road—slowly, because the bomb lay between their feet. They turned between the high, wrought-iron gates and followed the blacktop driveway past well-tended lawns toward the imposing, modern concrete temple.

Rabbi Randall Falk glanced from the window of his quiet study. There was nothing odd about a pickup truck coming up the driveway. Deliveries were common, even on sunny, placid holidays. But then two sedans sped through the gates, overtook the pickup and forced it to a halt. Rabbi Falk saw men jump from the cars.

"ATF!" one shouted at the passengers in the truck. "You're all under arrest. Get out with your hands in plain sight."

Boyer, handcuffed and advised of his rights, said, "I'm just here because these people wanted to hire a band for a rally."

The plump granny said nothing.

Other agents and the Nashville detectives they'd been working with rounded up the rest of the plotters, including the suppliers of the dynamite.

Bob Vance reflected on his wisdom in listening when ATF had called on him a few months ago. "We don't care how many rallies you people hold," Special Agent Charles Lowe told him. "You've got a right to make speeches but violence is out of bounds." Yes, Vance mused, he'd been wise to listen, wise to call the agent after that meeting at Gladys's home where the musical Boyer had explained the plot, wise to keep ATF informed of the terrorists' progress and wise to wear the transmitter Lowe had attached to his body. The schemers were on their way to prison and Bob Vance was a free man because nobody got hurt and nothing had been destroyed.[1]

Foreign strife—like the shah of Iran's ouster by the Ayatollah Khomeini—sometimes spawns men who would vent violence on Americans.

Patrons of Reza Almaneih's picture-framing shop on Redmond Avenue in San Jose, California, saw him as a polite, neatly groomed, soft-spoken man of thirty. They'd never guess that he'd styled himself the leader of the Iran Free Army.

Amir Ehadee, an agent of SAVAK, the shah's secret police—had helped Almaneih plant a small bomb in a trash can at a Berkeley high school. A student was injured. But the SAVAK man grew frightened when Almaneih spoke of detonating greater bombs, so he phoned a friend in the Santa Clara Sheriff's Department. The officer called ATF and said, "I think you ought to talk to this guy."

The first thing an agent has to do when confronted with a bizarre tale of terror is to separate fact from fiction. This one asked Ehadee, "What's Almaneih doing now?"

"Crazy things. He's got lots of money and he wants guns."

So an agent posing as a Mafia member visited the framing shop. Almaneih welcomed him, placed a $50,000 order for plastic explosives and machine guns and handed the undercover man a $5,000 down payment without having seen a single weapon.

The agent was convinced. He sent SAVAK man Ehadee back to the shop wired for sound. Among the suspect's ravings, one remark set the ATF man's teeth on edge. "President Carter has to die, even if I have to tie explosives around my waist and make myself a human bomb."

The Secret Service was notified. Surveillance was strengthened while Treasury agents worked to identify accomplices. Then Almaneih revealed his new plan: to conceal a huge bomb in Room 142 of San Jose University's old science building. "This time," he ranted, "I want to see bodies carried out." A second, smaller explosion would shower survivors with leaflets, "so people will know the Iran

Free Army means business." Murdering students would make America realize the depth of Almaneih's hatred for the Ayatollah Khomeini, who'd taken over Iran from the shah.

Warrants were obtained. The FBI was invited to join Treasury's ATF and Secret Service agents and the sheriff's deputies who'd been working with them. They surrounded the framing shop unobtrusively. An ATF man parked out front backed his G-car too close to Almaneih's van and entered the shop.

The suspect was repairing a picture frame.

"That your truck out there?" the agent asked. "I just scraped your fender."

Almaneih rushed outside. Two Treasury agents strolling down the sidewalk sidled close and made the arrest without incident. In the back room of the shop they found several powerful bombs.[2]

While Almaneih was being led away in California, ATF agents on the East Coast were investigating plotters from the opposite camp—supporters of the Ayatollah Khomeini calling themselves the Islamic Guerrillas of America. One critic of their cause was shot to death on the front step of his Bethesda, Maryland, home by an assassin dressed as a mailman.

ATF agents spent months poring over gunshop records in Washington suburbs. Suspicion focused on employees of the Iranian Interest Section of the Algerian embassy. (Iran's own diplomatic post was closed when the Ayatollah Khomeini promoted the takeover of the U.S. embassy in Tehran.) An intensive surveillance was mounted. There were late-night meetings with frightened informers on dark, foggy sidestreets. The break came when ATF agents arrested Al Hunter for using a false name to buy firearms. Hunter named their leader, cab driver David Powell, and revealed secret details of meetings inside the Bait-Ul-Allah mosque on NW Crittenden Street in Washington—meetings the agents had watched from a distance. The broad plan to recruit followers from penitentiaries and indoctrinate them for worldwide religious warfare had reached the stage of getting guns for bank robberies and the slaughter of enemies—or anyone else who got in their way. "Unbeliever's" lives had no value whatsoever. Then Hunter confessed to driving the getaway car for David Belfield, the Bethesda killer in the mailman's uniform. ATF's chief polygraph examiner, Jack Barnett, pronounced Hunter's statements free from deception and Treasury agents uncovered corroborating evidence in Maryland, Virginia and Plattsburgh, New York. Since some of the crimes they'd solved lay within the FBI's jurisdiction, G-men were brought in to assist.

On December 8, ATF agents arrested guerrilla leader Powell while ATF-FBI teams swept across the nation's capital rounding up the others.[3]

KKK Grand Wizard Richard Savina, a burly man of medium height with straight brown hair, drove his ten-year-old American Motors station wagon through the sunny Maryland countryside, his eyes flashing as he discussed his favorite topic with Ed Eifert. "Man," Savina said, "that would be just right. Go up there in a helicopter with a napalm bomb—two fifty-five-gallon drums—and drop 'em on those Freedom Marchers around the Lincoln Memorial." Elaborating to his eager listener, Savina said, "I want to make a nail-bomb, see? The nails are just on one side so you can toss it in a crowd and get everybody. Next time they have a nigger concert at the Civic Center, just put it where you're gonna put it and keep going. That'll get about thirty thousand niggers right there."

The Baltimore wizard considered himself knowledgeable on race-mixing, the "Jew conspiracy," guns and bombs. He was also a federally licensed gun dealer. Fortunately, beyond the broad areas of ignorance he expressed to Eifert, he lacked knowledge of certain specifics. He didn't know, for example, that some of his illegal gun sales had been made to undercover ATF agents. Nor was he aware, when he handed Eifert a Molotov cocktail to toss at the home of Maryland's NAACP leader, that Eifert was an officer of the Baltimore County Police Department working with ATF.

Agents didn't have to wait for the NAACP man's house to be bombed. On the morning of May 21, 1981, Savina was arrested.

"Sell guns off the books? Make a bomb? Me?" Surely the agents were bluffing.

At the same hour, in Philadelphia, agents entered the Main Line Coin and Stamp Company at 20th and JFK Boulevard and displayed their credentials to security chief Charles Sickles. "We're ATF agents, Mr. Sickles. You're under arrest for crimes under the Gun Control Act of 1968."[4]

Sickles, the slender, six-foot Imperial Wizard of the Adamic Knights of the KKK, had been getting guns through straw purchasers, men without criminal records who'd fill out the government forms as if they were the real buyers. He'd falsified forms himself, denying his prior felony conviction, bought more weapons at gun shows where he and some fellow Klansmen worked as security guards and distributed these armaments to followers in the clandestine organization.

Sickles's blue eyes went wide. "What's this all about? May I get my pills?"

"Who's your doctor?" an agent asked as he picked up the .357 magnum revolver lying on the desk beside the tablets. "We'll have to check with him first."

At the same hour, in Wilmington, Delaware, an ATF man and a police detective knocked on Al Weakland's front door. They knocked several times before he opened up. They arrested the ex-con for possessing firearms and advised him of his rights.

"I'm not in the Klan," Weakland babbled, "and I don't know Sickles very well. I just worked on his car once."

The agent smiled. "Who asked you?"[5]

Patrons of shopping centers in Greensboro, North Carolina, knew that Nazis and Klansmen were on trial downtown for killing some "communists," but they had no way of guessing that miles away, in Ashville, people were planning to give them "a week of terror like no city has ever seen."

Forty-eight-year-old Frank Braswell was slender with receding brown hair, a worn face and sincere eyes. A husband and father who attended church every Sunday, he had the look of a tired insurance man. No one visiting the comfortable living room of his modest mobile home would suspect anything sinister unless Braswell was entertaining his friends. One afternoon they sat with "Major" Mike Swain, a soldier of fortune sent by national Nazi commander Harold Covington to help them, and discussed their plan: If their comrades were convicted of killing those communists in Greensboro, they'd blow up the chemical fertilizer plant and a petroleum tank farm situated beside Interstate 40; and they'd bomb the court house; and they'd plant fifty-five-gallon drums of napalm—set to be detonated via remote control—in the shopping mall. "Let's face it," Braswell told Major Swain, "downtown area, right around four in the evening when it's good and crowded. Tell me, what's wrong with that?" Even if the jury freed their fellow Nazis, "What's wrong with doing it anyway? I want to." None of Braswell's friends disagreed.

There's an eerie, almost incredible quality to the tapes of this conversation. "The main thing we want, Mike," Braswell said, lighting another cigarette from the butt of his last one, "we want a lot of damage. We want to keep the firefighters, the hospitals busy for quite a while. But we want the maximum psychological effect out of it that we can get."

After the explosions, they wanted Swain to fly them to South America. The major sent by Nazi chief Covington quoted a price: $15,000. Swain's docile girlfriend, seated beside him on the couch, said nothing.

At future meetings, each Nazi got his assignment. Braswell had dynamite hidden under a trailer at the Spruce Pine Airport. If they needed more, his men could steal it from a nearby warehouse.

But the scheme failed. No one was hurt. "Major Mike Swain" was an ATF special agent who'd gone undercover and fooled Commander Covington into believing his dedication to Nazism. "Jill," the girlfriend he'd brought along, worked for the FBI.[6]

Covington told new members that his National Socialist (Nazi) Party "is not a hobby or a game. It is a serious political movement which is going to change American society from top to bottom . . . through fire and sword."[7] Recruits pledged loyalty to Adolph Hitler, swearing "swift and merciless justice [to] the enemies of my people." Their

SS sought the "fanatical National Socialist who is willing to obey orders without question and, if necessary, risk death and imprisonment." With an unfathomable optimism, Covington hoped to enlist "men of above-average intelligence."[8]

ATF has learned that most Nazis and Klansmen are harmless frauds—brash-mouthed bigots excited by bombast spouted at secret meetings—but the hooded robes and swastikas also attract criminals and mental defectives. While the herd pays dues and devours hate literature, this cadre of criminals wearies of empty words. They urge one another to *"act* for God and country." Feverish plotting evolves into practical preparation. None will voice the caution that might denote cowardice in the eyes of their comrades.

George Clayton Wallace joined the Nazis in prison after compiling an impressive resumé of convictions: armed robbery, grand theft, possessing a machine gun, burglary and escape. Released from prison, he eked out a precarious living on the streets of Sacramento peddling pistols to criminal friends until he conceived a plan to combine his Nazi beliefs with profit: kidnap, torture, rob and kill the owner of Finegold's Restaurant and Hotel Supply Company. Unable to implement his scheme alone, he confided in one of his gun customers. "Do you know a good man who could give me a hand?"

The customer paused. "Yeah," he said at length, "I know a real good man."

Ex-con Wallace met the "real good man" two days later at a North Highlands tavern. He explained his scheme, described the preparations he'd already made, paid for the beer and grinned across the booth. "How about it? You want in?"

The real good man laid a set of leather-cased credentials on the table. "I think not, Mr. Wallace. I'm an ATF agent."

The heroic representative of the Master Race passed out in a cold faint. Detectives who'd been waiting in the wings revived the skinny felon and charged him with conspiracy to commit homicide.[9]

In Paterson, New Jersey, Nazi Stanley LaBruna saw ATF men closing in to arrest him for selling machine guns. He drew a gun. Special Agent Barry Letts rushed him to deflect LaBruna's bullets from fellow officers. The young agent endured several operations without regaining the full use of his hands. He had to retire.[10]

Michael Eugene Perdue wore wraparound sunglasses and drove a flashy Cadillac. Gold chains were visible in the tangled black mat protruding from his open collar. At thirty, he'd assumed the macho pose of a born adventurer, but he had to travel, had to meet new friends to maintain this image because those who knew him saw a short, balding homosexual, a Marine reject, an ex-convict. Perdue dreamed of riches and power, but all he possessed were guile and imagination. These might be enough to make his dreams come true. Maybe he'd become a king.

He set his sights on Dominica, a sixteen-by-twenty-mile island north of Martinique in the Carribean with a population of 80,000, 41 percent of whom were illiterate. Their hundred-man army had never been called to battle. Their fifty policemen were untrained in the use of firearms. Given the proper political support, a small force with superior weaponry could walk ashore and take over.

Ex-prime minister Patrick John's corrupt regime had been ousted from power, but if this tough-talking American could pull off his scheme to take control of the country, John would be delighted to resume office. He offered Perdue $150,000 in cash and economic concessions guaranteed to ensure a lifetime of luxury.

Perdue's plans included using lumber exports to finance a modern airport that would encourage a lucrative tourist trade. He'd plow these profits into a gambling empire to generate greater fortunes. He figured the United States would lend Dominica $60 million to build schools, roads and hospitals. Touring the southern states, he enlisted financiers and volunteers for his expedition. Seated in his Cadillac on a dimly lit New Orleans street, he invited knights of the KKK Imperial Wizard Stephen Don Black to sign on. The prospect of lording it over a defenseless population of blacks was appealing. Black agreed to furnish men and explosives.

Wolfgang Droege signed up in hopes of making Dominica

his base for a lucrative smuggling operation to supply American drug traffickers.

Perdue prowled the darker dens of the New Orleans waterfront making discreet inquiries before approaching Mike Howell to charter his marine research vessel, *The Mañana.* Howell's first mate, John Osberg, became Perdue's final recruit.

When all was ready, Perdue handed boat owner Howell the final $10,000 charter payment, but first mate Osberg, a tall man with the blond hair and blue eyes of his Scandinavian ancestors, was uneasy about loading the implements of war from a crowded New Orleans wharf. "Anybody might notice and get suspicious."

Perdue saw his point. "Got any ideas?"

Osberg stroked his bushy mustache. "I know a secluded cove on the north shore of Lake Pontchartrain." He drew a map.

Perdue said, "That'll do," and he tucked the map in his pocket.

Hours later, two trucks loaded with Perdue's weapons stopped side by side at Osberg's site: a gloomy, mosquito-infested swamp surrounded by water on three sides. There, with the would-be invaders separated from their guns, they were quietly confronted by a task force of federal, state and local lawmen.

Boat owner Mike Howell had called ATF the moment Perdue broached his reckless scheme. Special Agent John Osberg and his colleagues laughingly called their coup the "Bayou of Pigs," but Dominica was vulnerable, its ex-prime minister was part of the plot and Perdue *had* acquired an arsenal and assembled an army.[11]

Perdue's plan was violent. Philadelphia's enigmatic black organization called MOVE was founded on principles of nonviolence. In their primitive lifestyle, soap was taboo. Women delivered their babies alone, chewed off their umbilical cords and licked the infants clean. Rejecting civilization, they set up their own society in a densely populated section of the city. They dumped garbage in the back yard of their ramshackle, three-story house to ferment with the feces of their dogs and cats and breed rats—"sacred rodents" they wouldn't kill. The neighborhood reeked with their nauseating stench. Health inspectors were halted by gun-toting sentinels. Neighbors retched. Police laid siege. After six steaming weeks, MOVE agreed to vacate. The barricades were removed.

But inside that crumbling old house, there was conflict. Donald Glassey, a tall, bespectacled University of Pennsylvania graduate, desired peace; but the majority agreed with cofounder Vincent Leaphart, a short, angry handyman who insisted that MOVE had a perfect right to do as they liked and live as they pleased on their own property. There were ways, he said, to bring the Establishment to its knees.

One MOVE gun buyer tripped a line, one of many ATF maintains submerged in the murky world of contraband weaponry. An agent was sent beneath the surface for a close look. In July agents and detectives raided an apartment in the city's Mount Airy section to seize forty-one freshly fashioned bombs and some documents—random pieces of a jigsaw puzzle for which agents had no guiding picture. Eight MOVE members, charged under the Gun Control Act of 1968, were released on bail.

The deadline to vacate that smelly house passed. MOVE refused to leave. At dawn on a sultry August morning, flak-jacketed policemen massed outside the barricaded fortress. A police captain used a bullhorn to read a court order. MOVE responded with obscenities through a loudspeaker. Pleas by a black church official and a noted black activist fell on deaf ears. When officers commenced their raid, gunfire erupted from the MOVE house. Patrolman James Ramp fell mortally wounded. The firefight raged for hours before tear-gassed suspects were dragged out to be freed on bail.

ATF began tracing the arsenal confiscated inside. An undercover operation was launched. The attorney general authorized wiretaps. As bits of intelligence were being pieced together, MOVE cofounder Glassey told agents of the plot to bomb hotels in Boston, Washington, Chicago and the great cities of Europe. Wholesale homicide would continue until the U.S. government compelled Philadelphia to leave MOVE alone.

Two members were convicted. Leader Leaphart and the others fled.

The three-year hunt led ATF to Rochester, New York. Two weeks of ultradiscreet surveillance in the ancient ghetto of clapboard houses uncovered each fugitive's hideout and the abandoned Citgo gas station where they lounged on sunny afternoons. Each MOVE man's identity had to be confirmed. When Special Agent Walter Wasyluk of the Philadelphia office spotted a wiry man with tinted glasses and a spade-shaped beard exit a house on Lewis Street, he handed his partner the binoculars, grinning. "The game's afoot, Watson. I'd know Leaphart anywhere."

At dawn on May 13, 1981, fifty-five agents and twenty policemen were stationed at strategic locations. Wind-driven newspapers tumbled through the Citgo gas station at Union and Lewis streets. Laborers left their homes carrying lunchboxes. Children dawdled on their way to school. Housewives walked to market and trudged home with heavy grocery sacks. It was nine-thirty when Leaphart and four MOVE men strolled to the vacant gas station where they lounged about, enjoying the sweet spring morning.

A radio signal alerted the tense lawmen.

Three young pedestrians sauntered down the street toward the Citgo station and the fugitives, hands in pockets, chatting and laughing. A sedan with four black men approached the intersection on Lewis Street, only to be overtaken by a police cruiser with lights blinking. They stopped thirty feet from the mildly curious fugitives. The black patrolman opened his summons book and asked for the driver's license. A huge van lumbered to the corner from the opposite direction just as a U-Haul truck turned from Union Street to stop beside the flaking Citgo gas pumps. Its driver asked Leaphart for directions.

Suddenly the U-Haul's rear doors flew open to disgorge twenty agents with shotguns. Another twenty leaped from the back of the huge van. The policeman who'd been writing a ticket, the occupants of the car he'd stopped and the three casual pedestrians leveled revolvers at the fugitives. "Halt! You're under arrest."

Other agents raided homes where two MOVE men had spent the night. No shots were fired. All the fugitives were apprehended. Leaphart was so startled by the lightning capture, it was half an hour before he mustered sufficient composure to insult the officers.[12]

People who think themselves safe from armed bigots should consider certain facts: The Nashville Nazis targeted "that Jew-owned WSM-TV," but the station wasn't owned by Jews. The man Cleveland's "Aryan Avenger," Frank Spisak, shot and killed because he "looked like a Jew" was Irish Catholic Timothy Sheehan.[13] ATF agents raiding the Kentucky headquarters of the Death Knights of the KKK found dossiers on lawmen, politicians and white women the bigots suspected of "fraternizing with Negroes." The Death Knights' Exalted Cyclops and several accomplices were convicted of actually shooting at two women outside their homes, plus bombing and perjury.[14]

The FBI liked these cases, liked them so much that, notwithstanding their minor assistance in no more than three investigations, they issued an official report taking full and exclusive credit for almost all of them. The sad news is that 85 percent of all the cases the G-men claimed in that report were actually ATF's.[15] The nice news is that the FBI might really deserve credit for 15 percent of the cases they claimed.

ATF agents prevented untold destruction, saved an unknown number of lives, and sent fifty vicious criminals to prisons for terms totaling nearly six centuries:

The Nashville Conspirators

> Gladys Girganti. . . . . 15 years
> Charles C. Boyer. . . . . 6 years
> Bobby Joe Norton. . . . . . . 5 years
> Codefendants received lesser terms

The Iran Free Army

> Reza Almaneih. . . . . 30 years

The Islamic Guerrillas of America

David Powell. . . . . 5 years
[Five years' imprisonment was the maximum
penalty for most GCA-68 offenses]
Clarence Griffin. . . . . 4 years
Others received lesser terms for weapons offenses.
Several were convicted of other crimes including
murder (the FBI made important contributions to
some of these cases); and three defendants became
fugitives, believed to have fled the United States

The KKK—Maryland, Delaware, Pennsylvania and New England

Richard L. Savina. . . . . . 15 years
Charles Sickles. . . . . 5 years on each of 11
                            counts, to be served
                            concurrently
Five others received lesser terms

Nazis in North Carolina

Frank Braswell. . . . . 15 years
Codefendants received lesser terms

The Would-Be Invaders of Dominica

Michael Perdue. . . . . 3 years
Stephen Don Black. . . . . . 3 years
Joe D. Hawkins. . . . . 3 years
Others received lesser terms; one was acquitted
because jurors believed that he thought he was
aiding a CIA venture

Death Knights of the KKK

Ralph D. Morgan. . . . . . . 18 months for assault-
                            ing an ATF agent;
                            turned over to the
                            state of Kentucky for
                            trial on firebombing
                            charges; one defendant
                            in that case received 8
                            years, another was
                            acquitted

Invisible Empire of the KKK

William Riccio. . . . . 10 years for possession of a sawed-off shotgun

Paterson, New Jersey, Nazi

Stanley LaBruna. . . . . . . 30 years for shooting Special Agent Barry Letts

MOVE

Nine defendants received 30- to 100-year terms for murdering Officer Ramp; two were imprisoned for federal weapons offenses.

17

A Wonderful Plan
to Kill ATF

When we are on the defense, we yield nothing.
We never back down. We never give an inch.
When we are on the offense, we take all we can get,
—NRA Executive Vice President, Harlon Carter

In ATF's war on crime, the National Rifle Association was an enemy every bit as relentless and remorseless as the Mafia. They paid politicians and they lied freely—not only to the public but to their own members. They exploited the Second Amendment to the Constitution the way mobsters take the Fifth; and their selfish crusade for personal convenience in the pursuit of their hobbies ignored their victims—the casualties of crimes that could have been prevented through effective enforcement of gun laws.

It's one thing to feel a twinge of sympathy after reading about a crime, but the depth of the NRA's depraved indifference can't be comprehended without facing the consequences of violence—emotions that aren't limited to people who have suffered a personal loss. On November 9, 1985, Dr. Michael R. Mantell, chief psychologist for the San Diego Police Department, testifying before the House of Representatives Committee on the Judiciary, quoted policemen who'd come to him for counseling after a crazed gun owner slew twenty-two children, parents and other innocents at a McDonald's restaurant in that city.

- "I didn't feel anything then. It was a job keeping the area cleared. A lot of people wanted to gawk. I thought I was doing just fine. Another day, another dollar. When I got home, my wife was so worried, wanting to do something for me, wanting me to talk. I went in to look at the kids. When I saw my six-year-old in her little pink nightie, I started to cry."

- "They were so damn still. I stood there for hours watching. My mind was filled with such trivia, like what I was going to do tomorrow, a report I had to fill out. Once I got home, I started to throw up and for three days the only thing I could keep down was liquid."

- "You know, I really love those people. I felt like they were part of my family. They were so helpless. They needed someone to protect them. I thought about who they were and made up stories about each. Like how much the man and woman with the child loved each other and were glad to be together. The old man had been famous, and was loved by his family. I stayed, really toward the end pretending to be busy because I didn't want to leave them. I got so scared when the coroner began to take them to the morgue. I really didn't want to leave them or let them go into the dark. It was as if we were all together; and with all that activity, they were still alive. I didn't realize what I was doing then. I must have been crazy. That's what really scares me. Am I crazy? . . . Hell, they were bodies, bodies are nothing; and I was talking to them in my mind; they were like friends."

- "Hell, I got so shitfaced I couldn't think any more. The cop bars were packed that night, whatever anybody else may tell you. But we didn't tell stories, everybody was so quiet. We just didn't talk, just sat there for hours. I got home, couldn't sleep or eat. Finally around 3:00 A.M. I got up and ran the streets for two hours as fast as I could. Even then I felt restless . . . just couldn't be still, and I am a relaxed kind of person."

- Another officer exhibited no symptoms until a few weeks later, when he responded to an auto accident in which children were killed. "I lost it. I couldn't breathe, I was shaking. I wondered if I was going crazy. I started to cry. . . . Somehow I managed to get the job done. It was horrible. I don't know if I want to continue seeing all the crap of the world."

In 1979, determined to emasculate the Gun Control Act of 1968 (GCA-68), the NRA wrote the Firearms Owners' Protection Act (FOPA) and had it introduced by two of its tame legislators; Senator James McClure and Representative Harold Volkmer.

The *Daily Democrat,* in Volkmer's home state of Missouri, editorialized:[1]

> We don't know who McClure is. Unfortunately, we know who Volkmer is: a dunderheaded Democrat from Hannibal, a brash and oftentimes unthinking representative . . . and we are not surprised that he is continuing his long-standing tradition of mediocrity.

Equally obscure and insignificant, Senator McClure hailed from Idaho where his constituents had enacted a state law requiring handgun buyers to get a police permit, but the folks back home played second fiddle to McClure's love for the NRA—and their cash.

FOPA would have allowed felons convicted of kidnapping, assassination or extortion, Klansmen caught with sawed-off shotguns, terrorist bombers and Mafia killers nabbed with machine guns to rearm themselves as soon as they got out of prison. Licensed gun dealers could sell anything to anyone "without paper"—i.e., without asking for identification or making any record of the sale—if the weapon came from a "collection," which was defined as any guns they kept separate from their regular inventories. Further, ATF couldn't check those sales records dealers did keep without "substantial evidence" that the records themselves violated GCA-68. Since robbery and murder weren't federal crimes, the bureau could no longer trace crime guns for police departments.[2]

It's hard to see why the NRA needed FOPA when ATF director G. R. Dickerson had already prohibited investigations of dealers without his personal authorization. NRA propaganda suggested that agents enjoyed arresting these "honest businessmen" when in fact—despite the damage done by petty peddlers arming local crooks, working small-timers was never a sought-after assignment. Agents earned peer respect by nailing outlaws who were tough and dangerous; proving crimes committed by dirty dealers was, for the most part, an elementary exercise against amateurs whose arrogant defiance of federal law was matched by overconfidence and, quite often, by stupidity.

Agents saw Dickerson's mandate as proof that lobbyists were running the bureau.

Morale sagged.

The timing was unfortunate. Since 1974, when GCA-68 prosecutions topped 2,500 a year (achieving the potential to reduce violence), a four-year surge of trials had sent thousands of predators to prisons. While violent offenses committed with other weapons continued their decades-long climb, robbery and assaults committed with guns fell. Murder-by-firearm dropped 15 percent. Now in 1979 and 1980, under Dickerson's discipline, murder soared to exceed the pre-1974 level.[3]

FOPA failed to pass in 1979 and again in 1981, but it hardly mattered. By then bureau inspectors were only visiting 5 percent of all licensees anyway. And yet, even among this small slice of the nearly quarter-million gun dealers, the inspectors found 2,100 operating in violation of GCA-68. They referred 740 for criminal investigation. Dickerson allowed agents to open three cases.[4] In 1981 Treasury issued a report on the director's management of ATF. Director Dickerson would say, later, "I chose not to read it."[5]

In May of 1981, the NRA marshaled its forces for a *coup de grace*. NRA lifetime member Ronald Reagan's administration recommended that ATF be abolished and reabsorbed by the IRS. The NRA produced a movie shamelessly distorting the bureau's conduct in several cases. Agents were angered by the film but some expressed a form of gallows humor:

        08OCT81
    FM: ATF DETROIT
    TO: ALL ATF STATIONS
    SUBJECT: PROJECT OUTLAW

AT APPROXIMATELY 5:30 A.M. THIS DATE, SPECIAL AGENTS OF THE DETROIT DISTRICT OF-

FICE ACCOMPANIED BY STATE AND LOCAL PO-
LICE BEGAN TO EFFECT ARRESTS REGARDING
DEFENDANTS IN THE ABOVE CAPTIONED
PROJECT. . . . A JOINT INVESTIGATIVE EFFORT
BY ATF, THE WASHTENAW COUNTY SHERIFF OF-
FICE, ANN ARBOR AND THE YPSILANTI POLICE
DEPARTMENTS IN WHICH ATF WAS THE LEAD
AGENCY . . . ARREST WARRANTS HAVE BEEN
OBTAINED FOR FORTY-FIVE (45) INDIVIDUALS,
FORTY-ONE (41) OF WHOM ARE CONVICTED
FELONS [with] A COMBINED TOTAL OF OVER ONE
HUNDRED AND SEVENTY-EIGHT (178) PREVI-
OUS FELONY ARRESTS AND ONE HUNDRED
TWENTY-EIGHT (128) PREVIOUS FELONY CON-
VICTIONS.
[The teletype message listed the fugitives still wanted
regarding this case, and concluded:]
NRA HAS BEEN CONTACTED ABOUT MOVIE
RIGHTS BUT HAS SHOWN NO INTEREST TO
DATE.

SAC HAERA   10:23EDT   FPJ

A short time after acknowledging that he'd chosen not to
read Treasury's review of his performance as director,
Dickerson was out. His replacement, Stephen R. Higgins,
was a sincere and likable chap who'd worked his way up the
ladder through ATF's revenue branch. His knowledge of law
enforcement matched most agents' familiarity with taxing
the tobacco industry, so he left criminal investigations to
the good ole boys and their heirs. One assistant director for
law enforcement, Phillip McGuire, would make some significant improvements in how the agents functioned, but
with McGuire's retirement, the office regained its somewhat
seedy reputation.

The Reagan White House wanted to abolish ATF. Treasury answered with a proposal of its own: to merge ATF's
agent cadre and law-enforcement responsibilities into the
U.S. Secret Service. Their agents met the same pre-
employment qualifications, took the same civil service test

and studied at the same agents' academy. Treasury produced evidence that the move would not only save taxpayers $39 million a year, it would improve effectiveness and efficiency in counterterrorism, presidential protection, the suppression of bombing and counterfeiting and enforcement of GCA-68. The Federal Criminal Investigators' Association approved of the plan, recognizing Secret Service management as the best among all the federal investigative agencies.[6] The National Association of Treasury Agents polled ATF members; 84 percent favored the idea[7] despite notification that 625 special agents would lose their jobs— a stressmaker that motivated some (like Special Agent Ariel Rios, whose story was told in Chapter 1) to strive for an excellence that would make their dismissal inconceivable.

Congressional committees debated the proposal until 1982 when the NRA, realizing that slaying the ATF beast would pit them against the competent executives of the government's most prestigious service, hastened to revive the crippled bureau. A compliant Senate supported the abrupt about-face. The proposal was dead.

The NRA revived FOPA with a version that would whitewash the black market in firearms: Anybody could sell everything to everybody without asking for identification or making any record whatsoever—unless agents could prove beyond a reasonable doubt that the sales were made with the *"principal* objective of livelihood or profit." Any peddler who'd say he sold guns for extra cash to buy a six-pack or another gun would be legal. If he was making an "occasional sale" or selling from a "collection"—neither term was defined in the proposal—that was legal too.[8] Buying a gun from an unlicensed peddler eliminates the ex-con's risk of imprisonment for denying his felony conviction when he executes that government form one signs when making a purchase from a licensee. Without sales records, the bureau's ability to trace crime guns would be diminished.

Congress enacted FOPA in May of 1986.

It was just another sunny autumn morning in the tiny town of Richmond, Vermont, population 3,159. Inside the

Crickmore family's attractive chalet, snuggled among the hills on five acres of rolling hills where their Morgan horses roamed, fifteen-year-old Paulette was getting ready for school when her father whispered, "Now just be quiet, honey. I don't want you to miss your bus, but Mom's been up all night with the baby and we don't want to wake her up." Father and daughter embraced for their morning ritual of a hug and a peck on the cheek. "I love you." He smiled. "Have a nice day."[9]

"I love you too, Daddy. Have a nice day."

Just like every other morning.

Waiting for the school bus, the petite ninth-grader with the big smile and big eyes and short dark hair feathered at the sides was still excited by her first week at Mount Mansfield Union High School in nearby Jerhico. A touch of frost tinged a leaf here and there, hints of the brilliant foliage that would soon cover the countryside. Paulette loved nature—animals, picking wildflowers—and she liked music. The little black case she carried onto the bus contained her flute.

But Paulette broke her normal routine this ordinary morning in 1986, only months after enactment of the NRA's pet law freeing gun peddlers from the licensing and recordkeeping requirements of the Gun Control Act. She got off the bus in town at eight o'clock and walked to a store to cash her babysitting check. Sweet and trustworthy, she enjoyed steady work by the parents of Richmond's toddlers. Now she planned to take a later bus to school, but she misjudged her time and missed it. Still, it wasn't terribly far and Jerhico Road was busy at this time of day. Several people noticed the slim student with her white shirt, Chic jeans and white sneakers lugging her blue bookbag and clutching her flute as she hiked along the highway at eight o'clock in this peaceful, pleasant region of New England.

It was the quiet innocence of Vermont that had convinced Alan and Tammy Crickmore to bring their family here from Connecticut. "We moved to get away from the hardness," Mr. Crickmore would say, "and Paulette . . . she was very sensitive. Very opposite of the fifteen-year-olds in a more urban environment." He took a job as a plant supervisor. "We didn't have any close neighbors and we don't allow our kids to be out, but there were school activities and Paulette went to a lot of church functions. . . . We kept her from growing up real, real fast. She was very unworldly and that was great. I loved it. She had plenty of time to grow up."

At four that afternoon, the bus rolled past the Crickmores' chalet without stopping. Tammy phoned her husband at work. "Paulette didn't come home."

The father was only slightly annoyed until he called the school. His daughter hadn't attended classes all day. "Whoa," he whispered to himself, "that's not Paulette." Something was terribly wrong. "So I came right home and reported her missing and, of course, a fifteen-year-old girl, and some people thought, well, she's just run away somewhere. But no way. For a kid to run away they've got to be mad about something and we've always had a lot of communication. If there was something wrong, I'd know it because my kids aren't afraid to say it."

The family began calling Paulette's friends. None of them believed she'd run away. Some had been in the habit of bringing their problems to this quiet, understanding girl, and Paulette had talked several of them out of running away when things got tough at home. One girlfriend said her brother remembered Paulette getting off the bus in town.

Officer Bob Small of Richmond's two-man police force didn't take the matter lightly either. He launched an immediate search.

Alan Crickmore would say, "I was scared to death. When your child is abducted, you don't know if she's been sold into slavery, being sexually abused, or whether she's alive. . . . You never know till the body's been found."

Support rallied from every corner of the state. When a search was announced in any area, hundreds of citizens turned out to trudge through forests on the coldest, rainiest days. Contributions for a reward fund topped $10,000. People were shocked. It couldn't happen here.

Couldn't happen? The average American's likelihood of being murdered that year was thirty-five times greater than a New Englander's chance of winning the Tri-State Megabucks lottery.[10]

Alan Crickmore took time off from work. "A friend and I must have searched every back road in the state. Dead ends and logging trails. Just looking for . . . anything. I talked to mystics. One said she was being held captive and one said, 'Well, I feel that she's dead.' One fear I had all the way through, and I said this at the outset, I just hope they don't find her body in deer season." Feverish activity filled his days and fond memories flooded his mind constantly. "You know, she'd ask me to do something that I didn't really agree with and I'd say no, and then I'd say something like, 'You'll probably hate me now.' And she'd cry. She'd actually cry and she'd say, 'Daddy, I don't hate you. I know you're just doing what's best for me.' She understood. Yep, she knew I couldn't say yes all the time."

By November, with dead leaves dropping from the trees, the Crickmores were still clinging to the hope that their pretty, naive little girl had been kidnapped. "We hoped she was still alive and they would let her go, or she would get away," her daddy said later. But a deer hunter found Paulette in the woods just off River Road in Duxbury. Dead, with three bullets in her decomposing body.

Suspicion focused on thirty-four-year-old Edwin Towne Jr., a brutish-looking man with a bearlike build and unkempt beard who'd reportedly been hauling bricks down the Jerhico Road when Paulette disappeared. An ex-con with a criminal record in four states, Towne had two convictions for kidnapping and rape. A state trooper stopped him on I-89 in South Burlington and found a gun in his car. It wasn't the murder weapon, but the police called ATF. Special agents joined the investigation, and two searches of Towne's ramshackle abode turned up more firearms. An ATF agent filed charges for an eight-page federal indictment; with his record, Towne would qualify for enhanced sentencing. Then a ballistics lab reported that a .32-caliber revolver found by a state policeman in the foundation of Towne's shack during one of the searches had fired the bullets that killed Paulette. Agents traced it through several owners to the man who'd sold it to Towne—at a flea market.[11]

Paulette was just one victim in the year of FOPA. Murder rose 8.6 percent while *gun* murders shot up 10.5 percent. Child victims (under the age of ten) hopped 9.9 percent.[12]

Alan Crickmore had dropped his NRA membership years earlier. "Any time there's a whisper, and legislation *has* been introduced," he'd say, "the NRA sends a team of lobbyists to go into Montpelier and they just run the state. It's ridiculous. They shouldn't sell them at flea markets."

Paulette is not forgotten. Her daddy keeps a picture of "my very special little girl" on his desk at the office. "She'd get teeny-bopperish and giggly and loud sometimes," he muses. "Pajama parties. Have lots of kids here, or stay over at friends.'"

Tammy Crickmore experiences intense memories any time she sees a flower. "She loved them so. Flowers and animals and little kids. She'd talk about what she'd do when she got older. Work with kids. Be a teacher or something."

"And she would have," Alan says. "She would have been great."

Towne is in Leavenworth, still serving the seventy-year sentence he got on ATF's firearms charges. If he finishes that before he dies, Vermont has a seventy-year-to-life term waiting—the best they could do since they don't have the death penalty.

ATF survived the NRA assault—an unfortunate outcome for law enforcement and the country at large, since a consolidation of Treasury's investigative agencies would have improved effectiveness enormously at a greatly reduced cost[13]—but GCA-68 was seriously mauled.

Ultimately, it comes down to one question: Who's most in need of protection? And protection from whom? FOPA—the Firearms Owners' Protection Act—was a boon to animals like Towne who can't sign the forms at a gunshop without risking imprisonment.

Were it not for the NRA's victory in getting it passed . . .

18

The *Un*-Terrorists

> As sure as God is good, so surely there is no such
> thing as necessary evil.
>
> —Robert Southey

Americans are seeing more and more people who think
they have a right, based on some personal belief, to destroy property and endanger—even kill—innocent victims.
When such people blow up buildings, most of us call them
terrorists, but there were cases where the FBI disagreed.

ATF agents had a good year in 1985. They solved New
Jersey's Pine Hill massacre, where a hit man with a silencer-
equipped pistol mistakenly murdered his target's
neighbors—man, wife and three-year-old daughter. When a
lawyer and a South American general offered $800 million
in military munitions to Iran, agents went undercover to get
the evidence they needed, posing as Irish Republican Army
gun runners and flashing a bankroll of $10 million in cool,
crisp currency. They halted a Pensacola woman's habit of
homicide—she'd poisoned a husband and a fiancé, and
drowned her physically impaired son, before attracting
ATF's attention by trying to fry another fiancé in an auto-
bombing. They disarmed and imprisoned Posse Comitatus
members who'd threatened to kill IRS agents; they nailed
Alabama's KKK organizer and four accomplices for bombing the Southern Poverty Law Center; they convicted an
East Indian Moslem who'd bombed a hotel to kill a Hindu.
They climaxed a three-year investigation of the Order,
leading two hundred state and federal raiders against a
heavily fortified compound in the Ozarks, seizing eighty-
two machine guns, bombs and silencers, and sending the

neo-Nazi leader and five cohorts to prison on weapons charges. In fact, they sent so many home-grown terrorists shuffling into prisons, the parade aroused all the fanfare of illegal aliens crossing the Rio Grande.[1]

These were fine achievements, but the one case seen by Congress and the media as proving ATF's true worth among America's investigative agencies involved a series of ten bombings in and around the nation's capital.

The case was rife with ironies. The first occurred shortly before the first bombing. It involved a sound in the rear of a yellow Honda hatchback crossing the bridge spanning Chesapeake Bay, twenty miles south of Baltimore in the dead hours between midnight and dawn of January 14, 1984: the clinking of a Dr. Pepper bottle jostling babyfood jars, ironic because the containers were firebombs, intended for an abortion clinic.[2]

Mike drove. Well built and handsome, he'd graduated from high school with scholastic honors, the state's wrestling championship and an appointment to West Point. At thirty-one, the typical yuppie in casual clothes, his boyish face smiled easily. He was not smiling now.

It was warm in the car. He rolled down the window. "Okay?"

"Hm? Oh, sure." His companion, Tom, was five years older and twenty pounds lighter with wide-lensed glasses, heavy eyebrows that curved downward like a misplaced bandit mustache, and a mobile face that expressed watery submissiveness or glowering rage with equal ease.

A slow drizzle produced a quarter inch of ice on the highway. Moving at about 45 mph, they saw a tractor-trailer jackknifed on the iron bridge at Kent Narrows. Mike braked. They skidded. Tom whirled to steady their bombs against the inevitable impact. They smashed into the blue van ahead of them. Then stillness and the keening wind.

Mike apologized and exchanged the obligatory information with the van's driver. The Honda's grill was pushed in, one headlight and both tail lights were out, the engine stalled and its driver's door was crunched inward but, despite the damage that would make the car memorable to witnesses or liable to being stopped by police, they limped onward to complete their mission.

Entering Dover, Delaware, they passed sleek motels and shopping plazas illuminated in the golden glow of sodium-vapor streetlights, passed the downtown turnoff and parked in a shadowy gloom where the blacktop needed repair and sparse, mercury streetlamps flattened all colors into a drab monochrome. Tom used his hunting knife to stab holes in the gasoline-filled cans and babyfood jar caps. Mike stuffed a white rag with yellow dots into the mouth of the Dr. Pepper bottle. Minutes later, they backed up to the Reproductive Care Center. Across the road, one feeble light in a used-car office. No life in sight.

Mike opened the hatchback. Tom grabbed the log and bashed it through the clinic's door. Mike hurled a cinder-block through the plate-glass window. They tossed cans and bottles inside. Mike got back into his car. Tom lit the Molotov cocktails and threw them into the building. Fire followed the flow of liquids dribbled from the jars and cans, licked the walls, reached for the ceiling. Instant inferno! Tom slipped, fell, crawled, pulled himself into the car. They escaped.

Deputy Fire Marshal James Melvin viewed the blackened walls, warped heat ducts drooping from the ceiling, a plastic chair melted in a corner. He photographed the scene, preserved the log and jar lids and began the routine questioning of an employee. "Has the center had any financial problems?"

She answered, "No."

Money's a common motive for arson. Suspects include racketeers, competitors, former employees, exparamours—anyone with a real or imagined reason for revenge. Buildings are torched to conceal burglary, tax evasion, embezzlement and murder. Even if the motive were known, it wouldn't have helped much. Ten percent of the population opposed abortion. That's 2,174 Doverites, 54,981 Delawarians and 18 million Americans—most of whose identities were unknown. A mathematician could prune this thicket with Justice Department statistics: percentages were higher for Democrats than Republicans; for persons over fifty, from the Northeast, earning under $7,000 a year, who hadn't finished high school; higher for blacks than whites; for women than men. But even if police could name everyone meeting these criteria, casting a net on this basis would fail. Mike and Tom were white, male, well under fifty, born away from the Northeast, educated beyond high school and earning over $7,000 a year. Neither voted Democrat.

Deputy Melvin asked ATF to lend a hand. Agents followed the few clues. No success.

Three days later, at the quiet birthday party for a fellow church member, Tom enlisted a third member for his infant Army of God. The shy, immense man called Grizzly had studied chemistry in college. He knew about explosives.

Shortly after midnight on February 17, Tom linked eight pipe-bombs like sausages. Wearing gloves, he and Mike taped them and wiped them down. Hours later, in Norfolk, Virginia, Mike wheeled his "new" used car behind the two-story Sovran Bank. Tom set the bomb against the wall, directly beneath the Hillcrest Clinic. Mike placed a wooden sign on the sidewalk: "AOG" on one side, "Hillcrest Murders" on its reverse. Tom set the timer and connected the battery. One bomb exploded. The others ruptured and fragmented. Were it not for the "AOG" sign, police would have assumed the bomber had targeted the bank.

Forensic chemist Richard Stroble, with nine years' experience in ATF's lab, reported:

- The black powder was a mixture of sodium chlorate and sucrose; the source of the sodium chlorate was oxygen sticks (Solidox), manufactured for use in propane welding systems.
- The PVC [white plastic] pipes were manufactured by Bristol Pipe Company on March 30, 1982; with endcaps, their overall dimensions were fourteen inches, diameter three inches.
- The endcaps were manufactured by Lasco, Inc. Six were pierced by small holes.

247

- The timer was a Sunbeam kitchen-type sixty-minute timer. Glue appeared on the front knob. An imprint in the glue corresponded to wire found at the scene.
- Wires included multistrand speaker wire and single-strand wire. The battery was an EverReady nine-volt alkaline Energizer.

Agents would thumb through tons of sales slips at stores handling these items, but their best lead was the "Hill-crest/AOG" sign—unique because it was painted on a slab of high-quality hemlock known as Hemfir manufactured by Dant & Russell of Oregon and cut with a power saw. Agents visited the nearest distributor, Erdman Lumber in Baltimore, for a list of purchasers. Anyone who'd bought Bristol pipe, Lasco endcaps, Solidox, Sunbeam timers and Hemfir planks would become a suspect.

It's always nice to have a suspect.

Best Company had sold 10,000 Sunbeam timers. A computerized record from the chain's Norfolk outlet for one February morning seemed promising:

> Transaction #3472: 1 unit, cash
> Transaction #3502: 1 unit, cash
> Transaction #3503: 9 units, cash

The cashier remembered a six-footer, medium build, shirt and tie; she'd never seen him before, or since.

One Maryland hardware store stocking Bristol pipe had eight thousand sales slips for February alone. Manufacturers' names weren't noted unless customers specified a particular brand.

Ross Heating and Plumbing had bought twenty-one Lasco endcaps and Bristol pipe for a project that utilized Hemfir planks. Blueprints showed all these materials were used, but scraps were sufficient for the pipe-bombs and AOG sign. Employees were investigated; none qualified as suspects.

AOG? Two years earlier, ATF had imprisoned an Army of God—Don Anderson and two accomplices—for bombing Virginia and Florida clinics. Teletype to ATF-Houston:

INTERVIEW ASSOCIATES OF DON ANDERSON, WAYNE MOORE AND MATTHEW MOORE. ELICIT INFORMATION RE ARMY OF GOD. REQUEST KNOWN FACTS RE ASSOCIATES IN ILLINOIS, PENNSYLVANIA, KENTUCKY AND GREATER WASHINGTON, D.C.

None of these leads contributed anything toward solving this clinic case.

A six-month-old threat to bomb that Norfolk clinic had been reported to the FBI, which has jurisdiction over bomb threats. Their report detailed notification by local police and the words on Hillcrest's answering machine: "I'm calling from the Rock Church and we're gonna close your doors with a bomb." The FBI agent's recommendation at the end of this one-page report: "Open and close."

Mike decided he'd still help Tom get information on clinics but he'd no longer assist in the bombings. Tom was casing a Maryland clinic when he found a wallet. The description of its owner, Lou Burns, resembled Tom's. The photo on Burns's drivers' license could pass for a bearded likeness of the clean-shaven Tom. He kept it.

The $100,000 predawn firebombing of the University Professional Center in College Park, Maryland, prompted Investigator Sergeant C. D. Davenport to request ATF assistance. The block was cordoned. Smoldering ruins dazzled under harsh lights. Some agents, like archeologists excavating an ancient Egyptian village, sifted and scrutinized every fleck and granule from the mountain of twisted steel, crumbled concrete and charred timbers. Others canvassed neighbors. One, awakened by breaking glass, had seen a slender man silhouetted against flames: 5'7" or so, slender, brown haired, wearing jeans and a dark jacket. No, she wouldn't recognize him again. Inside that window lay two five-gallon cans. With no evidence that the three recent crimes were connected, a teletype went to ATF-Newark:

RE: LA BELLA PURE VEGETABLE SALAD OIL. DETERMINE NAMES, ALL PURCHASERS IN 5-GALLON CAN CONTAINERS IN DELAWARE, MARYLAND, VIRGINIA AND D.C.

One clinic worker resented an agent's questions. "No! We're not having financial problems. And no one here has any enemies. It's *obvious* who's responsible. Don't you *want* to investigate pro-life terrorists? You're incompetent. How come the FBI isn't here?"

An anonymous caller told the *Washington Times,* "We are a right-wing group. . . . At 1:25 A.M. today we destroyed the Women's Reproductive Clinic. . . . We will continue to destroy these clinics. . . . I repeat, this is a warning." Minutes later, someone phoned the *Washington Post* to claim responsibility for the Army of God. The *Post* called the FBI.

There were still no leads.

The FBI referred them to ATF.

The next evening, FBI headquarters answered a question posed by FBI-Norfolk, weeks earlier:

TERRORISM SECTION DOES NOT CONSIDER THE "ARMY OF GOD" AS A TERRORIST GROUP, AND THEREFORE, NO FBI INVESTIGATION APPEARS WARRANTED AT THIS TIME.

ATF-Newark reported nine outlets for La Bella Salad Oil in the targeted areas. Agents visited them all. "Who works here? What do you do with the empties? Has anyone asked for cans?" After all, the bomber had used two of them.

Erdman Lumber had 2,100 accounts. Some customers bought items every day. Agents identified every purchaser of Hemfir lumber. Each was asked, "What do you do with extra pieces after you've cut a plank to specs? How about PVC pipe?" None of these efforts helped.

A priest reported a man named Fred who'd told him of a discouraged right-to-life activist, Farraday, who'd once threatened to bomb a clinic. The priest didn't know Fred's last name but he'd picked up some clues during their conversation: Fred was married, had children, lived in an upper-middle-class neighborhood, and "I got the impression he worked for a school. Not a teacher. Perhaps a counselor. Oh, and I saw his car. Small, white and square-shaped."

"You have a good eye for detail, Father," the agent said,

closing his notebook. "We lost a chance to get a fine agent the day you joined the priesthood."

Agents listed every employee of local school systems, ran the names of every married "Fred" through motor vehicle computers, copied yearbook photos of those owning small white cars and showed the pictures to the priest. He picked Fred Trimble. Trimble knew nothing more about Farraday. Farraday had one arrest for picketing a clinic. His description: 5'10", brown hair and eyes, 263 pounds, a bear of a man—with alibis for the dates of the bombings.

On March 5, FBI-Baltimore received a tip about the Dover firebombing. Their report to headquarters— "Attention: Terrorism Unit"—stated they'd relay the lead to interested agencies. They never did.

ATF's status report: "This investigation is at a standstill. All witnesses have been re-interviewed; all suspects have been dismissed." It closed with the phrase that ends every ATF report until a case is solved: "Investigation continues."

ATF's lab processed threat letters received by the bombed clinics for handwriting, typewriter identification and latent fingerprints. As new suspects were developed anywhere, their prints and penmanship were submitted for comparison.

FBI agents solicited updates from ATF. The FBI's Terrorism Unit circulated these reports to other FBI offices. They shared nothing with anyone outside their own bureau.

With the permission of an unsuspecting machine-shop owner, Tom gathered metal turnings accumulating beneath a lathe. Grizzly's books explained how these metals, once ignited, burn with an intense heat, difficult to extinguish.

At eleven o'clock on the night of the Fourth of July, the whitewashed, once-elegant brick building housing the National Abortion Federation in Washington was bombed. Police called ATF. The few leads were exhausted within days. A man claiming to represent the Army of God telephoned *Washington Times* columnist Bob Robinson: "The bombings will go on until some changes are made."

Members of Mike's church sat around drinking coffee after the Sunday sermon. A man said, "This bomber will kill someone. How could he live with that?"

Mike reminded them of the Savior's rage when he over-turned the moneychangers' tables in the Temple.

A woman responded, "The Lord was confronted with men defiling the house of God, not an ordinary crime like murder. Even then, he didn't destroy anything."

Another woman recalled Jesus' statement, "Render unto Caesar . . ."

Mike was troubled. His friends shared his horror of abortion but what would they say if they knew what he'd done?

Tom sat in his workshop, writing on lined paper in a three-ring binder:

So just what do you need for your bomb? Dad has already made up your shopping list for you. . . . [He cataloged equipment.] Hopefully, your IQ falls in the bright-normal range and you are a nonsmoker. . . .

PVC pipe . . . makes a fair bomb but steel is far superior. Before you decide to blow up the world, realize that only 2 oz. fills a standard U.S. grenade. This means your first little 3 lb. batch of goodies will fill two dozen grenade bodies. . . . [After specific in-structions for re-arming deactivated hand grenades], On to bigger things. . . . Another of the beautiful things with these smaller bombs is that it can be easily taped to a 20 or 30 portable l.p. gas cylinder. Now you're talkin'!

He gave an exhaustive treatment of small bombs, then:

So you're greedy and want more, huh? Before I go any further let Dad bring out a point or two. I am totally unashamed to openly confess that I believe in the Lord Jesus Christ. . . .

If ever one dies at my hand may God have mercy on me for it will not be on purpose. . . . My conscience commanded that I tell you what I have that you may also fear God. . . .

I would also say from personal experience that if you don't get a minimum return of $1,000 damage for

each dollar spent . . . that you are doing something
wrong. . . . One 25–28 lb. bomb placed on a sidewalk
or a driveway at a distance of a few yards will

Here, the manuscript ended. Other pages listed clinic
owners and employees' names and addresses with directions to their homes like, "last home on end, old colonial,
Mercedes, boat, 2 other cars . . . 36 miles from home."

After midnight on July 7, the spires and cupolas of
Annapolis, Maryland, were lashed by winds and a drench-
ing downpour. Lightning bolts lanced the veil of rain like
celestial flashbulbs. Thunderclaps split the air and rumbled
away. A fuse sparkled inside a garbage bag beside the Bay
Ridge Professional Building. The roar of eight pipe-bombs
taped to an explosives-packed canister gouged a four-foot
crater in the brickfront. One metal fragment flew 1,557
feet—three blocks. Another jagged shard pierced the cab of
a pickup parked 150 feet away, traversed its front seat and
passed through the driver's door.

Police called ATF. Searchers bagged metal hunks, a valve
from a canister, strips of black electrical tape and sent them
to the lab with several fifty-five-gallon drums filled with
debris from the seat of the blast. Destruction of the target:
$100,000, plus damage to nearby homes.

A message to the *Washington Times* claimed credit for
the Army of God.

Witnesses who'd seen a Datsun parked nearby were
shown photos and color charts. They chose a marine-blue
model produced in 1980. Dealers in Washington and surrounding states named purchasers. Agents toured used-car
lots. Lists, names, record checks, a hundred dead ends.

The FBI's Washington Field Office (WFO), ordered to
keep their headquarters apprised of progress, reported to
Director Webster: "WFO has maintained liaison with the
Bureau of Alcohol, Tobacco and Firearms (ATF) . . .
regarding captioned matter. To date, a subject has not yet
been identified and no evidence of a national conspiracy to
bomb abortion clinics has been developed."

Privately, ATF agents voiced discontent. One groused,

"What'll we get after all this work? A mob guy? Somebody we can take pride in catching? Hell, no! We'll get the kind of dipshit who'd try to cut traffic accidents by torching gas stations."

Clinic victims accused agents of dogging the case. Pro-lifers accused them of trying to destroy their movement.

On the placid Saturday morning of November 3 in downtown Washington, Tom jiggled the doorknob of the American Civil Liberties Union office to make sure it was closed. In a back room, an ACLU worker heard "a scratching sound at the door" and debated going to see what it was. Moments later, shrapnel penetrated the door to pierce a desk where the ACLU worker would have been had she approached the entrance.

A caller phoned radio station WTOP, claiming credit for the Army of God. Station personnel called the FBI, which referred them to ATF.

Adrian Cretchmer telephoned ATF. "I hear you been lookin' for me."

Special Agent Simon Wolf said, "We'd like to talk to you. Can we get together?

"Nope."

"Where are you living?"

"I got a lean-to in the woods."

"You have an apartment. Why are you sleeping in the woods?"

"The KGB's after me."

"Oh? Why?"

"They're scared of me 'cause I can make myself invisible. I walk in and out of their embassy any time I want to."

"Well, I'd really like to get together and . . ."

"Can't take the chance, mister. Just the other night, I took a walk 'bout three in the morning. Woke up 'cause it was cold in the lean-to. And one of those damned Russian satellites took a shot at me. Missed me and blew up a car."

ATF's Forensic Branch evaluated this conversation and reviewed Cretchmer's mental records. Conclusion: He couldn't construct a complicated device and pursue a single goal long enough to carry out these crimes.

"Investigation continues."

Debris from the ACLU bombing included traces of the same explosive compound used in the clinic cases and a thumbprint on a strip of black electrical tape. The best evidence yet.

Penny Smith, a pretty nurse with long brown hair, worked at a Wheaton, Maryland, clinic where picketers came "almost every Saturday," she'd tell agents, "and they were nasty. I had a problem with how they could call themselves Christians with some of the things they'd scream. 'Don't kill your baby' and 'Don't be a murderer.' They call it counseling."

Pastor Bray of the Reformation Lutheran Church says his group "stressed the need to identify with the vulnerability of the child."

Reporters, TV crews and policemen watched a hundred demonstrators—singles, couples, grandparents, babies in strollers—as they sang and prayed and blocked the clinic doors. Police made arrests. Pastor Bray would say later, "When it was time for our group, I asked my mother to bring Jonas, my one-year-old son . . . to demonstrate that it was real children we were concerned about."

Channel Four zoomed in to photograph Bray and his son for the six-o'clock news.

Shortly after dawn on November 17, Tom bombed that clinic. Minutes later, he blew up Planned Parenthood just blocks away. Damage to the two facilities and their neighbors: $500,000.

Two years later, that bleak morning would remain fresh in the mind of Head Nurse Penny Smith. "It was just numbing to see an office and medical center just literally burned to the ground. Just rubble. Walking through, we tried to salvage what we could, and walked out with smoke and smudge. Every time I smell smoke I think of that. There was a lot of anger, and 'How dare they?' Other doctors offered assistance and office space, so we were operational a day later."

Across the country, clinic workers lived in fear. Some fought the black dog of depression on a shrink's couch at $45 an hour.

Canister fragments found at Wheaton came from a twenty-pound carbon-dioxide tank manufactured by the Marison Company for Coca-Cola twenty-four years before. The Planned Parenthood scene yielded cylinder slivers manufactured in 1942, with traces of sodium chlorate, magnesium, and black electrical tape.

With the bombs growing larger and coming faster, reinforcements were needed to trace purchasers of the bomb materials—common substances, available to anyone. Assistant Director Philip McGuire summoned 500 agents to join the hunt.

A few suspects looked promising.

- Suspect Thistle had indicated knowledge of the bombings and tried to recruit acquaintances into "some kind of pro-life organization, more active and more secret." A West Pointer who'd served in Vietnam, he fit bomber's description and refused a lie-detector test: "Hell no. The needle would probably go sky-high." A lodge member reported, "He has no friends. He's filled with hate against queers and women."

- Homosexuals *and* women? Clearly a man of limited inclinations.

- Suspect Bennet, a pro-lifer, talked about firebombing and worked for the owner of Erdman Lumber, a supplier of Hemfir; he lied when he told the polygraph examiner he had no knowledge of the crimes.

- Suspect Payne, an Annapolis anti-abortionist, fit the general description and said he "talks to God." Occasionally he left town, telling neighbors he counseled a group in Cherry Hill, New Jersey. He was employed at the Naval Academy where steel canisters were recently discarded, replaced by aluminum canisters; he became furious with crewmates who disagreed about abortion. Three stores within walking distance of the academy sold PVC pipe. He owned army explosives manual. On the day of one bombing, he failed to show up for scheduled visitation with his child. He told co-workers, "When all

else fails, use lots of black electrical tape." Polygraph results: "Either he's deliberately distorting results, or he's too unstable to be tested."
"Investigation continues."

ATF-Philadelphia pursued prosaic inquiries like phone calls to a family-planning center; "This is the Army of God. Close up now, bitch!" And threats to two pro-abortion organizations in Cherry Hill, New Jersey: "This is the Army of God. You will be hit soon."

A man phoned a Washington TV station. "Look, I don't want to get involved in this but I was out jogging past that Wheaton clinic about ten minutes before the bomb went off, and I saw a guy standing in the parking lot. I recognized him from your coverage of the demonstration there, last Saturday. He was the only guy holding a kid in his arms."

Videotapes showed one man holding a child: the Reverend Bray. His wife, Jayne, was raised a Quaker. They had a three-year-old daughter, the year-old son he'd held at the demonstration, and Mrs. Bray was expecting. Special Agent William Seals, assigned to investigate Bray, was less than enthusiastic. "Gimme a break," he told his supervisor, "an anonymous phone call?"

"We have to check everything. If this guy actually was at the scene at that ungodly hour . . ."

"Is that one of your puns?"

"What?"

"A minister, out at an ungodly hour?"

"Call it 'The Case of the Curious Clergyman.'"

Seals's first report on Bray: part-time pastor; housepainter; openly sympathetic to motives of persons who damage clinics; solid citizen; comfortable home in suburban Bowie, Maryland; pays his bills; arrests at demonstrations but no criminal record. "Investigation continues."

Detective Katherine Stavely and Fire Marshal Carvel Harding, members of the team organized by ATF, visited the Brays' neat colonial in Bowie. Jayne Bray and her husband called Planned Parenthood people "accessories to murder . . . as guilty as the butchers." Pastor Bray was glad these clinics weren't killing babies now. Property damage

257

was "less important than the destruction of innocent human lives." But no, he knew nothing that would help to identify any bombers.

An agent brought bomb-scene fragments to Charles Talbot, manager of the F&M Fire Protection Company in Hyattsville, Maryland. Talbot pointed to the neck of a canister. "These one-inch openings are made for soft drinks or beer. The ones with an inch-and-an-eighth opening come from extinguishers." Talbot would say, later, that the agent "didn't know a darned thing about these cylinders. But he pulled everything we knew out of us, and he watched us testing them out in the shop, and he read all kinds of books about it. He got to be an expert."

Talbot mentioned a man who'd bought thirty-four discards the previous July. "Next thing you know, we had three agents here for a whole day, going through the records." He thought the woman agent was pretty. "Just a slim girl but when she took off her jacket to sit with those records, she had this .357 magnum on her waist that was just as big as she was."

The invoices included thirty-four empties sold in July to "Lou Burns." Serial number CC-20L-2186, found on a sliver at the Planned Parenthood crime scene, appeared halfway down on page 565 of the records. Burns had bought the bomb tank. Clerks described him as a white male, dark hair, thirty-five or forty years old, maybe 5'8" and thin. "He wore construction type clothes" and drove a full-size car, maybe a Ford, dark green, older with dents, and Maryland license plates. He'd said he was an artist making a modern sculpture for the Hirschhorn Museum. The curator of the Hirschhorn reported no sculpture used or contemplated involving carbon dioxide tanks.

A real artist from the Anne Arundel County Police Department sat with F&M employees to create a likeness of Lou Burns. Copies were given to every agency assisting in the investigation.

Agents eliminated most of the Burns, Berns, Byrnes and Barnes in the greater Washington area via drivers' license descriptions—too young, too tall, wrong hair color. The rest were visited. None resembled the sketch. Every ma-

and-pa hardware store selling Solidox pellets had been contacted. Department stores and discount outlets had sold thousands more cans. Day by day, purchasers were investigated. And eliminated.

On December 5, Tom rented unit 161 at a storage park and completed a lease agreement as Lou Burns, 102 Woodland Court, Laurel, Maryland. He and Mike stored bomb components there.

FBI-Baltimore asked ATF whether the Army of God had claimed credit for the latest bombing. "Yes," the ATF man replied. "You guys want the case?" The FBI agent declined and reported the conversation to his headquarters.

With their scientists telling them four clinic bombings were connected, the pressure on agents was heavy. That pressure intensified when Tom bombed the Hair Success Beauty Salon in a Suitland, Maryland, office building, putting beautician Valarie Williams out of business for four months. The family planning center upstairs was unscathed. Metal fragments pocked a Baptist church next door; one landed 442 feet away. Damage: $150,000. Debris yielded PVC pipe, black electrical tape and pieces of a compressed gas cylinder, #48187DE, one of those Lou Burns had bought from F&M.

Suspects were re-interviewed—even the clergyman Bray who'd been fingered by an anonymous phone call to a television station. Bray's wife, Jayne, was an attractive blonde with green eyes, just inches over five feet tall, and nine months' pregnant in December. "They were friendly," she'd say of the agents, "and we invited them in and talked." The agents sat on a couch, the Brays in apricot velour barrel chairs. Fine-boned with delicate features, Mrs. Bray spoke with a vigor that dispelled any notion of fragility. "We are happy to talk with you," she said, one hand making a chopping motion into her other palm, "but we're not going to assist you in your investigation. You want to talk about abortion, we'll talk about abortion."

The agents didn't want to talk about abortion.

Pastor Bray warned, "Beware of defiling yourselves through a Nazi-like following of orders."

Agent Seals said, "Any one of those bombings might have killed someone."

"Might kill someone?" Jayne Bray asked. "Four thousand people a day *are* killed. By abortions."

Seals shook his head. "The end result of these bombings is nil. Women just go to different clinics, and the ones that have been bombed are being rebuilt."

The Reverend Bray smiled. "My method of protesting is nonviolent."

Seals, tall and bulky with broad shoulders, projected a strength that was offset, somewhat, by a full, pinkish face and soft voice. But the folksy air that projected genuine sympathy for someone in trouble could vanish in a flicker that asked, without words, Do you really expect me to believe that? He asked the minister, "Were you involved in any of these bombings?"

"No."

"If you knew anything, would you tell us?"

"I don't know."

"How would you feel if some innocent person were killed?"

"That would be . . . those abortionists are butchering innocent children every day. That would be, er, acceptable."

Throughout this investigation, Seals had seen naked hostility, angry denials, darting eyes and perspiring foreheads. The Brays were relaxed, cordial and candidly approving of the crimes. The agent was puzzled. He didn't mention the tip from the anonymous midnight jogger.

There were more interviews. Mrs. Bray would say, "It was always Mr. Seals. He was always your friendly guy. He wears cowboy boots and he has this southern accent and he'd say, 'You know we're against [abortion] too. Lots of people [in ATF] are against it too.' And the other guy would just sit there kind of sternly, you know. They looked about like you'd expect agents to look. Like you see on TV. And he was always a pleasant man. We talked about his family and his kids, and we invited him to dinner because he lived in Virginia and he always had to come out here late at night. And we'd say, 'Bring your wife and come for dinner.' I'd bring out pictures of abortions but he'd say, 'That's not the issue.' The conversations were never that long. They were always friendly."

There wasn't a single shred of evidence against Bray. Some agents were convinced he was innocent. Seals wanted proof, one way or the other.

Bill Seals was an agent who'd seen every side of the job— the good, the bad and the worst. He'd served with the Louisiana State Police and army intelligence before joining ATF in 1969. He'd been shot at. He'd been pilloried by the NRA for shooting member Kenyon Ballew, who'd pointed a loaded gun at him when the agent came with a warrant to seize illegal grenades. Seals's last high-profile case was a one-day wonder.

On December 8, 1982, Norman Mayer parked a van at the base of the Washington Monument and threatened to detonate 1,000 pounds of dynamite if his antinuclear demands weren't met. His criminal record dated back thirty years, he'd had military explosives training, and ATF found where he'd tried to buy dynamite in Kentucky. Police negotiated the release of persons trapped inside the monument. At seven-thirty that evening, Mayer drove away. Police marksmen fired. The van veered and overturned. Seals raced across the browned grass pell-mell and dove head-first through the broken window to prevent Mayer from pressing his detonator. The International Association of Chiefs of Police and *Parade* magazine named Seals one of the top-ten lawmen for 1982—an uncommon honor for a federal agent.

Now Seals's investigation raised eyebrows in Bowie's Christian community. Contractor Bob Green, who sometimes employed Bray, asked the minister, "Why are these agents asking questions about you?"

"They're confused," Bray assured him. "They don't have their facts straight. They're just trying to blame somebody."

To Green, the investigation seemed incredible. Bray wasn't "just a Sunday Christian. Like, for me it's easy to send money to World Relief. But to take someone into my home, that's another thing. But [Bray] brought in these Ethiopian refugees and went out and got churches to sponsor them. I have an awful lot of respect for that guy."

Jayne Bray would smile when she told an interviewer that her husband "liked a lot of stray cats. We had some real doozies sometimes, but he seemed to attract that type of person. The type of people that sometimes you had to force yourself to like." Laughing softly, she recalled, "One time there was this guy, a paranoid schizophrenic staying with us. My husband liked the guy, a nice enough guy, and he would come by, wander in and out, and he had no place to stay. So he said, 'Okay, Harry, come on over.' One night"— she laughed again—"we heard this noise around three A.M. and we smelled something. Harry was cooking. My husband comes out and here's Harry's jeans hanging over our living-room lamp. He'd washed them out in the bathtub and wrung them out by throwing them against the wall, so there was all this blue spatter all over the wall. And my husband says, 'Well, let's just put these in the dryer.' Others came by. They weren't very stimulating, but he'd sit and talk with them. He always liked people that were different. He liked Tommy Spinks. Tommy was a different sort of character. Marched to a different drummer. Wasn't the same old cookie-cutter, you know?"

On December 28, ATF released the Lou Burns sketch to the media with a physical description and a caption: "This person is believed to have information which is important to the investigation."

Pro-choice organizations prodded politicians and their shrill cries echoed in the media: "Call in the FBI!"

Five minutes into 1985, a bomb gutted another Washington clinic, shattering 302 windows in an apartment house across the street. While searchers salvaged black electrical tape and fragments of a gas cylinder, Mayor Marion Barry appeared in a tuxedo. He looked about, turned to reporters and issued a fresh call for FBI action.

Ten hours later, the duty agent at the FBI's Washington Field Office notified Director Webster and Assistant Director Revell. A memo to Revell stated that the chief of their Domestic Terrorism Unit "was telephonically advised." Revell penned a note on the memo: "Pls insure [sic] that I am immediately informed of any future bombing of Abortion clinics in the Wash. Metro area." In fact, G-men had pumped every informer they owned, digested everything uncovered by ATF and added such tips as their own agents held secret from everyone. Conclusion: too few clues and no suspects.

Congressman Don Edwards led a contingent of colleagues calling for the FBI to take charge. As a former G-man himself, Edwards should have known that the pirates of the police community don't steal tough cases until they've been solved—not if they can wriggle free. The FBI demurred, citing restrictions imposed on them in the wake of the COINTELPRO scandal: revelations of illegal break-ins and wiretaps aimed at groups as disparate as the Students for a Democratic Society and the National Organization of Women.

The FBI's excuse was untrue.

Confidential guidelines approved eighteen months earlier permitted the FBI to use any legal tactic against anyone "likely to be involved" any time they had a "reasonable" belief that terrorism "has been, is being or will be committed."[3]

The FBI officially defined terrorism as "the unlawful use of force or violence against persons or property to intimidate or coerce a government, the civilian population, or any segment thereof, in furtherance of political or social objectives."

FBI Director Webster said this case didn't meet that definition. G-man Lane Bonner explained that the clinic bombings didn't qualify "because no organized group or conspiracy has been identified."

Put succinctly, the Army of God clinic bombers were *un*-terrorists because their identities were unknown.

The *Wall Street Journal* complained that "the President stays silent . . . [and] will not commit its most symbolically and practically important agency to the battle." The *Washington Post* scoffed at Director Webster's statement that "the clinic attacks don't merit the Bureau's attention." Webster told President Reagan he'd respectfully decline to accept responsibility for the probe. The White House announced that ATF was carrying the ball "because they have primary jurisdiction in explosives cases."

On January 2, ATF fingerprint expert Ben Wilson peeled back a strip of tape from the New Year's Day bomb and found a human hair. Minutes later, chemist Ray Keto found two hairs between layers of black electrical tape. At that time, hair comparison wasn't a positive form of identification, but it was a clue. The hairs were sent to the FBI lab.

Special Agents Seals and D'Angelo "showed up with this woman with her little kit to get a hair sample," Jayne Bray recalls. "It was, 'You can do it in the comfort of your home or we'll subpoena you.' And we said, 'Get the subpoena,' you know. So they, er, issued the subpoena."

John D'Angelo recalls Mrs. Bray as indignant, but her husband put her at ease. "That's okay, honey. They're just doing their job."

On January 8, while Tom celebrated his birthday, D'Angelo found something of his own to celebrate: an invoice at the Inland Leidy Chemical Company for two 110-pound sacks of potassium nitrate sold on September 27 to Lou Burns—purchaser of the bomb canisters from F&M Fire Protection. Digging deeper, agents found 220 pounds of sodium nitrate and fifty pounds of iron oxide sold to Burns. Clerks couldn't remember him and he'd paid cash, but he said he represented SurCo and he gave an address. No one at 102 Woodland Court recognized the name. Agents hip-deep in records at Maryland Chemical in Baltimore found 300 pounds of sodium nitrate sold to Burns on July 12. He'd claimed to work for Shields Industries and he'd paid cash. Lou Burns was now known to have bought thirty-four casings and chemicals equaling the destructive power of 4,500 hand grenades. He wouldn't quit until ATF caught him.

At Inland Leidy, where "Burns" claimed to work for Shields Industries, agents found an invoice dated two days earlier showing fifty pounds of sulfur sold to Ken Shields. Coincidence? Another alias? After a thousand leads had petered into iron-clad innocence, it was clear that this case required the optimism of a jewelry salesman in an Amish village.

Shields Industries was listed in the phone book. It was owned by Ken Shields, an accountant with no criminal record employed by Warrenton Wire and Fabrication Company in Virginia. His sideline, Shields Industries, employed three men, none named Burns, reclaiming silver from X-ray film. That process utilized potassium nitrate, but the man who'd bought that chemical called himself Burns. And Shields, at 6'4" was too tall to be Burns. One of Shields's friends, a roofer named Thomas Spinks, fit the description and, working with contractors, he'd have access to PVC pipe. Spinks was added to the growing flock of suspects kept under surveillance. As with the others, specimens of his handwriting were sought from banks, businessmen and public records, then dropped at ATF's lab with a mugshot and fingerprints taken by Maryland State Police when they'd charged him once with assault. The package was added to stacks submitted by agents across the country.

Agents in cars, aided by a helicopter, tailed the Reverend Bray's green Chevy station wagon from his home to an Exxon gas station, then to the McCormick Paint Company, then to a Fica gas station on Greenbelt Avenue. One agent drove on past. Another parked where he could watch. The helicopter hovered.

"What's he doing?" one agent radioed to the "eyeball."

"Getting out of his car."

"He just gassed up half an hour ago."

"He's got his hood up. Putting water in the radiator. . . . He's looking around. Now he's putting gas in the tank."

"Again? That wagon must get great mileage."

"He keeps looking across the street. Uh-oh, Metropolitan Family Planning Institute. Maybe he's picking his next target."

"Or a place to picket."

"So why the big covert deal, screwing around with a gas tank he just filled up?"

"Hey, pal, we just watch 'em. We don't read their minds."

Pastor Bray didn't resemble the Lou Burns sketch. His handwriting was unlike the Burns signatures on chemical invoices. His thumb hadn't made the print on the tape that was part of the ACLU bomb. Nothing he'd said to agents was remotely incriminating. Then the FBI called.

"The hair of Mr. Bray is microscopically identical to the hairs your people found on that tape from the New Year's Day bomb." The chance of another person's hair matching perfectly in twenty-five characteristics is one in umpteen thousand. But Bray wasn't Lou Burns. Neither was Ken

Shields—he was too tall and he'd been at work when Burns picked up most of the chemicals. Nor was either man—family men with good reputations and steady jobs—"the type" to commit these crimes.

Agents met Mr. and Mrs. Shields at a Holiday Inn restaurant. The waitress took their orders: coffee for the agents, soft drinks for the Shieldses.

Mr. Shields asked, "What's this all about?"

"Do you buy chemicals?"

"Oh, sure." He told how he reclaimed silver and sold the ingots. He used nitric acid, sodium carbonate and potassium nitrate.

"Nothing else?" The older agent chewed his pipestem.

"That's all. Why?"

The other agent handed him an invoice for fifty pounds of sulfur while the waitress served their refreshments. "We're curious about this." The clerk's notation stated, "Order placed by Ken Shields."

"Oh, I'd forgotten about that." He'd intended to start a mail-order chemical business, buying in bulk and repackaging for sale in smaller containers. "A guy can make a pretty good profit that way."

"So the signature is yours?"

"Oh sure."

Was he too calm? There's no standard reaction to a visit by Treasury agents. Totally innocent people sweat and stutter; some of America's worst criminals act friendly and mildly perplexed. The younger agent asked, "Did you pick up the sulfur yourself?"

"Um, yeah. A friend drove me over."

"Who was the friend?"

"You mean the one that drove me over to pick up the sulfur?"

"Yes. What's his name?"

"Tom Spinks."

The agent handed Shields an invoice for 270 pounds of burnt umber and potassium nitrate sold to Lou Burns from SurCo. Shields said he'd never heard of either name.

"Did you use all the potassium nitrate in your business?"

"Well, no." He'd moved his business and left fifty pounds

of the chemical at his old location. That's all that was left, and the only order he'd picked up personally.

"Except for the sulfur."

"Oh yes, the sulfur."

"The one you picked up with your friend, Mr. Spinks."

The older agent seemed intrigued. "How do you repackage chemicals? Where do you advertise? How do you market it?"

Shields looked sheepish. He hadn't thought about that.

"What happened to the sulfur?"

"We put it in the shed behind Tom Spinks's house. I guess it's still there."

"How about this?" The younger agent showed him the invoice for 300 pounds of sodium nitrate sold to Lou Burns, care of Shields Industries. Shields shook his head. He didn't know anyone named Lou Burns.

Another invoice was placed between the Shieldses' soda glasses: 220 pounds of potassium nitrate sold to "Lou Burns representing SurCo" and a penciled notation that SurCo was the new name for Shields Industries.

Shields said he'd never heard of Lou Burns or SurCo.

The younger agent gathered the papers into his government-issue briefcase. "If you're telling us the truth, Mr. Shields—and I'm not saying you're not—but if you are, there've been an awful lot of coincidences here."

Shields agreed. Astonishing coincidences.

"Tell me," said the older agent, taking the cold pipe from his mouth, "what did you and Mr. Spinks talk about while you were driving to Inland Leidy Chemical?"

"Gosh, I can't remember that we talked about anything in particular."

"Did Mr. Spinks ever talk about abortion?"

Shields called abortion "reprehensible."

"What do you think about the bombings we've had?"

"Property has no value compared to human life."

"How about Mr. Spinks?"

"Well, he's more strongly opposed to it than I am."

"What's he think about the bombings?"

"How would you feel if a child was snatched from your arms?"

Driving back to their office, the older agent turned to his partner. "Let's talk to him again tomorrow."

The next day, Saturday, the agents asked Shields to "tell us more about Mr. Spinks."

Shields began slowly, paused, took a deep breath. "Back around the end of '83, Tom told me, 'These clinics have to be destroyed.'"

The agents sat calmly, the older one with legs crossed, his unlit pipe held in his lap. "Go ahead."

"One day he said God had instructed him to take care of the clinics. A couple months later, he asked me what chemicals he'd need to make explosives."

Even as Shields poured forth his confession, Tom Spinks was under surveillance in Maryland. He wore a camouflaged field jacket with matching cap. Watchers couldn't help noticing how his dark green Mercury, rusty dents and Maryland license tags might have been mistaken for a green Ford by the F&M worker who'd helped Lou Burns load those canisters into his trunk.

At ATF's crime lab, Ben Wilson worked through the weekend with stacks of fingerprint cards submitted by agents across the country. He compared the card sent by ATF-Cleveland with the whorls and ridges imprinted on black tape from the ACLU bombing, and sighed. No match. He reached for another.

It was a busy day in the nation's capital with 8,500 military personnel—acting as chauffeurs or arrayed as honor guards—flourishing through Saturday's segment of President Reagan's four-day inaugural pageant; and pro-lifers massing for their annual march along Pennsylvania Avenue; and a hundred ATF and FBI agents getting ready for a 7:00 P.M. briefing and their scheduled all-night watch over thirty-seven potential targets in greater Washington. This would be a symbolic day for another bombing.

After a year of mind-numbing canvasses, interviews, crime scene searches and record reviews—months of dead ends and frustration—everything was coming together at once for ATF. Shields was spilling Spinks's boasts of the bombings, his use of "Lou Burns" and "SurCo," the Solidox and carbon dioxide canisters he'd seen in Spinks's workshop. Facts gathered at scene searches and lab findings confirmed his details, but the word of an accomplice needed corroboration.

Spinks was tailed from his home to Doug's Hobby Shop in Waldorf, Maryland. He left seven minutes later. Most of the team followed. One agent entered the shop, showed his credentials and asked a few questions.

At the lab, Ben Wilson focused his magnifying glass over a fresh card. This one had similarities. He compared those unique bifurcations.

The agent at the hobby shop phoned his office. Spinks had bought two gallons of highly flammable model-engine fuel and two waterproof wicks, identical to those used in two bombings. Five minutes later, the office phone rang again. "It's Ben Wilson, and I got a match with the print from that ACLU bomb. Name's Spinks, Thomas Eugene, white male born—"

"Thanks, Ben."

Thirty-five minutes later, a U.S. magistrate issued two warrants.

Spinks would later say, "They pulled up in all kinds of vehicles, about twenty agents with their guns drawn." One agent jerked open the Mercury's driver-side door. "Thomas Spinks, we're special agents, ATF. We have a warrant for your arrest for conspiracy to commit bombing. Step out of the car please." Later, "I was a bit afraid. I asked for a Bible and the officers got me a Bible. I couldn't sign the fingerprint card."

Advised of his rights, he requested a lawyer.

Shortly after five o'clock, Shields was arrested at a Warrenton laundromat. He refused to make any statement.

A cavalcade of cars clogged Spinks's street to disgorge twenty-three agents, policemen and scientists. Uniformed officers were posted around the neat, yellow colonial to bar the curious and guarantee the integrity of any evidence that might be found. Agents seized pipe-bombs taped to Molotov cocktails and two bombs in metal cylinders. Between the shed and the fence, Special Agent Mark Stephenson brushed an inch of snow from two five-gallon cans, lying on their sides, and shone his flashlight on their labels: La Bella Pure Vegetable Salad Oil.

Forensic chemist Mary Lou Fultz—with a doctorate in chemistry; she'd taught at two universities—pronounced tape from Spinks's workshop "indistinguishable" from tape used on the College Park bomb. A scrap of cloth matched the wick from a Molotov cocktail used at Dover.

Forensic chemist Rick Stroble summarized the rich lode. "We found Solidox, Bristol pipe, Lasco endcaps, Sunbeam timers, a Hemfir plank, gas cylinders purchased by Lou Burns, Playtex gloves that matched gloveprints on several bombs, and 210 pounds of chemicals."

Special Agent Simon Wolf found the Lou Burns cards in a dresser with a receipt for unit 161 at the storage park. A warrant there produced more timers, 800 pounds of chemicals and twenty-eight carbon dioxide cylinders resting like rusted torpedoes.

Vacuum sweepings from Spinks's Mercury contained potassium nitrate and paint chips matching paint on the carbon dioxide tanks.

Agents found Pastor Bray's name in Spinks's notebook. Mrs. Spinks said she'd seen Bray accompany her husband into the workshop. A supervisor radioed agents tailing Bray, who'd just left his brother's home. "Arrest him."

Agents met Jayne Bray when she returned home. She assured them there were no explosives in her house. "If you want to come in, get a search warrant." Then she asked, "How did you find us?"

Agents saw this as a spontaneous admission of guilt. Mrs. Bray would later say she'd merely wanted to know how ATF could lay its hands on her husband when they wanted to arrest him. "I wanted them to admit they'd been following us."

Later, she saw her husband on TV, "and there he was," she'd say, "handcuffed, being taken into some building. And he's talking with this agent and they're smiling and talking."

Evidence against Spinks and Shields was ample, but after the submerged investigation erupted from covert surveillances and cautious interviews, nothing more was found to implicate Bray. Some agents doubted his involvement.

Bowie was the epitome of middle-class suburbia just outside the Washington Beltway: eleven square miles of forests, fields, shopping centers and developer-planned neighborhoods. Two decades had seen its population soar from 1,100 to 33,000. The median citizen was 28.8 years old, earned $32,373 a year; 94 percent were white; 41 percent had children; six out of seven owned single-family homes with neat lawns and mature trees valued above $100,000. There were twenty-nine churches. A cultural light-year from the slums that spawned lawlessness, the typical resident's hazy perceptions of crimefighters were fed by movies and *Reader's Digest*. They'd spoken to county policemen who patrolled their neighborhoods but few had ever met a detective. Now they'd encounter the fabled agents of the federal government, portrayed on TV by attractive actors who always knew whom to suspect so they could solve incredible mysteries in an hour, between commercials.

Church member Bob Green was stunned by Bray's arrest. Still muscular in middle age, Mr. Green was a cautious, self-employed contractor, proud of his craftsmanship and his honor but—aside from his wife and five children—his greatest pride lay in his American birthright to make up his own mind. "Pastor Bray told me they had, in fact, gathered some facts that [were] all wrong, so I didn't think a whole lot was going to happen. Then they arrested him."

Typical of Bray's acquaintances, Mr. Green was among the supporters jamming the courtroom for Bray's arraignment. The minister was bound over for trial and released on bail. The president of a right-to-life chapter told a reporter, "I know he's innocent." Former lieutenant governor Sam Bogley stated, "I don't think anything has come out today that caused me to lose any trust and faith in Pastor Bray."

Bob Green phoned home. His son told him, "Dad, the girls are petrified. Some men came to the door looking for you, and then they went out and parked in the street." Green would say his daughters "had heard stories about how they arrested Pastor Bray, you know, falsified these charges. And [they're] scared to death that the same thing is going to happen to me. So I was furious that they would do such a thing."

Contemplative and well read, Mr. Green saw protesters as "kind of like the Boston Tea Party," but bombing was beyond the pale. "The first guys were from somewhere else. Supposedly they'd brought them in from all over the country. I told them I'm not involved and I don't want to play cops-and-robbers games. I'll cooperate, tell you all I know, and you're welcome to check it out. Check me out."

He couldn't know that his name appeared in Tom Spinks's secret notebook.

Bob Green was "furious about what was going on. I honestly believed that Pastor Bray was arrested solely because he was an activist. It was believable because I was being investigated and I knew absolutely nothing. . . . If they could get him, they could get me. One agent told me, 'We found a code book and your name's in there. Your code name was The Carpenter.' So I said, 'You can't be serious.' But they were dead serious." He thought his reputation would satisfy them, but "after they made their little investigation, they kept coming back." Cleared, finally, "I started asking questions myself. I'm just thankful that they were very candid with me."

Another church member, Steve Clements, submitted to the lie detector. The report:

> Clements says he cannot believe Bray is involved. [After he began to suspect Spinks's involvement] he went to his pastor, Mr. Bray, for counseling. Clements said he told Bray he thought he knew someone who might be involved in the bombing. Clements said Bray asked him if he had any proof. Clements replied he did not but he was suspicious of the person. Clements said Bray told him without evidence, he [Clements] may be subject to a libel suit."

One by one, as suspects passed the polygraph, the agents' attitudes changed. One of Green's employees, Little Jim Walker said, "It was all, well, we were all buddy-buddy."

Formality gone, barriers came down.

Bob Green recalls, "A lot of these guys told me they had

heated conversations back in the investigative circles. The agents were disturbed that people saw their investigation as motivated by anyone's opinion about abortion. It was strictly a matter of bombings. They were investigating crimes."

One agent asked Green, "What if I told you your man Little Jim was involved?"

"I'd be just as shocked as when you told me that Pastor Bray was involved."

But Spinks had asked Little Jim to drive the car while he committed a bombing; "I didn't know that either," Green said. "The man worked for me every day. We talked about the investigation on a regular basis and he never volunteered that information. So when the agent sitting here in my living room told me that, I was devastated. I couldn't trust my own judgment of people. And of course, if Little Jim said that, that meant Tom Spinks did in fact do the bombing. And of course, if that's the case, that means Pastor Bray is probably involved."

Bill Seals still felt that Bray was involved; his hair matched bomb-hairs in twenty-odd characteristics. Then the FBI lab called again. Another match: Bray's brother.

"Identical to Bray's," Seals asked, "or the ones we found on the tape?"

"All of them."

Second samples were obtained from both men. Same results. FBI expert Gary Podolak would testify that this was a first for him. "It's only rarely been found in our laboratory since its inception about thirty years ago." Even hairs from identical twins were "readily distinguishable."

Pastor Bray maintained total innocence. There was no proof. ATF was hounding him, retaliating for his prominence in the battle to save babies.

Church members launched a massive campaign, with printed stationery and flyers, rallies, a special post office box for contributions to the defense fund.

By now there was an alternative explanation for each piece of evidence against Pastor Bray—all except the anonymous phone call placing him near the Wheaton clinic just before it was bombed. That and Bill Seals's intuition.

Ken Shields had clammed up completely.

Then Spinks rolled over, told everything, implicated Bray, described the pastor's participation in the Dover firebombing. But some criminals lie to protect their real accomplice or implicate someone who'd refused to join the plot. Treasury trained its agents to play devil's advocate: remedy the weaknesses in your case, or prove the suspect innocent and move on to find the guilty man.

The trial was scheduled to start in one week.

Baltimore's federal courtroom 7C was small, almost intimate. Pale white walls and doors, blond woodwork. Clerks', witnesses' and jurors' chairs were cushioned with a cranberry fabric that lent some warmth to the room.

Assistant U.S. Attorney Bob Mathias, twenty-nine, a product of Yale University and Harvard Law School, was the sort of lawyer prestigious law firms offering three times Uncle Sam's salary competed to recruit. He, his wife and daughter were practicing Catholics but, he'd tell an interviewer, "My personal opinion of abortion is irrelevant. This is a trial about terrorism."

Pastor Bray's supporters thronged the pews, eager for the purifying ordeal of a trial.

Reporters in the front row considered themselves the only unbiased spectators.

Starting with the Dover arson, prosecutor Mathias paraded agents, fire investigators and scientists before the jury. Spinks confessed to all his crimes and swore that Bray accompanied him in Dover and Norfolk.

Defense lawyer Muse's relentless cross-examination attacked the government. "They wanted Mr. Bray. They said, 'No deal unless we get Mr. Bray, correct?'"

"They wanted everybody," Spinks said. "The government is very thorough."

ATF's Ben Wilson told of finding Bray's fingerprint on the page of Spinks's notebook containing notes on one target. Michael Rennert—thirteen years as an ATF document examiner with a master's degree in forensic science and training with the Secret Service, the FBI, Georgetown University and other colleges—testified that Bray penned another target's address in Spinks's notebook. Spinks's confession was supported by forensic chemist Mary Lou

Fultz's finding that the cloth from his workshop matched the Dover firebomb, but it didn't prove Bray had been with him.

Prosecutor Mathias called Forest Stuber to the stand. "Directing your attention to January 14, 1984"—the day of the Dover firebombing—"where were you?"

Stuber was en route to a hunting trip with some friends. The roads were icy.

"And what, if anything, happened that morning?"

"As I was going across the Kent Narrows Bridge, there was a semi—a tractor-trailer—jackknifed across the road. I stopped about fifty feet behind the truck, and a car ran into the back of me."

"And what happened after the car ran into you?"

"I got out of my truck and we exchanged insurance information."

"And did you at that time observe whether there were any passengers in that car?"

"Yes. There was one passenger and one driver."

"Showing you what has been marked for identification as Government's Exhibit 60, I would ask whether you recognize that."

"Yes." It was the information he'd received from the other driver.

"And what name did that individual give you?"

"Michael D. Bray."

The next witness, insurance adjuster James Wright, identified Exhibit 58—a claim for insurance benefits. The form described Bray's Honda, the location of the accident—an hour from Dover—and the time, 4:30 A.M. The bombing occurred two hours later.

"What does the form say as to the identity of the passengers?"

"It lists one, Thomas Spinks."

"Is there a signature on the form?"

"The signature of Michael Bray."

Document examiner Rennert certified that the signature was genuine.

The jury convicted Michael Bray of possessing bombs and "willingly, knowingly and maliciously conspiring to bomb the clinics."

Harry Hand of the Pro-Life Nonviolent Action Project told reporter Ruth Marcus, "We stood by Mike all the way because we believed in his innocence . . . Everything that came out . . . pointing toward Mike's guilt were things that we were not aware of."

Judge Harvey, calling terrorist bombings "the most cowardly and despicable of all criminal acts," gave Spinks fifteen years, plus $53,944 to be paid in restitution to his victims. Bray got ten years and $43,782 in restitution. It would have been more, the judge said, were it not for Bray's exemplary character. Ken Shields pleaded guilty and received two years. Bray won a new trial due to faulty instructions given by the judge and tendered an "Alford plea," acknowledging the government could win a new trial. Sentenced to six years, he served four.

Seven years later, at a congressional hearing, Bray was asked whether the *Washington Post* had quoted him accurately as stating, "It is justified to destroy the abortion facilities and it is justified . . . to terminate the abortionists."[4] Bray admitted making that statement.

Representative Levine asked, "Are you suggesting that you believe it would be appropriate to kill somebody who is involved in the delivery of abortion services?"

Bray leaned back in his chair. "Clearly. As far as the ethical question goes, yes."

A year later, when Michael Griffin shot Dr. David Gunn to death outside the doctor's abortion clinic. Bray wrote, "Mr. Griffin committed no murder, he performed a homicide. Michael Griffin killed; he slew; he neutralized; he terminated a serial killer."[5]

Time magazine quoted Bray as writing that abortionists should be stoned to death: "With each blow . . . by the grace of God, he may confess his sins and be saved before expiring." But some things do change; the same article noted, "The FBI launches a probe of abortion-clinic violence . . ." The G-men were admitting now that these criminals were terrorists.

Thomas Spinks served his sentence inside the government's maximum security penitentiary at Marion, Illinois. He was scheduled for release on January 22, 1995.

* * *

ATF's worth was finally recognized.

The *New York Times* headlined, "An Agency Steps Out of Obscurity."

The *Washington Post* editorialized, "The cases were solved not by tips, confessions or informers, but by difficult and classic police work."

Senator James Abdnor, a staunch NRA supporter, stood on the floor of the Senate to term the *Post*'s praise, "highly appropriate. . . . The investigation was brilliantly conducted." And

> Although recognized for many years by the nation's law-enforcement community as the premier bombing and arson investigators, the public knows little of its skills and its successes. Until the outcry attendant to the clinic bombings, the media has chosen to largely ignore ATF's effectiveness. . . .
>
> Nor is ATF's skill limited to explosives crimes. In its other major jurisdictional areas . . . ATF is more than just good, it is the best.

Congressman Don Edwards, who'd urged the president to shift the case to his old employer, the FBI, acknowledged tersely to *New York Times* reporter Robert D. Hershey Jr. that "our initial reservation has been washed away by their hardworking group of investigators." At a public hearing, he'd state that future bombers "are going to get caught because you [ATF agents] are terribly skillful at your business."

Two questions remain unanswered to this day.

Who made the anonymous call placing Bray near the Wheaton bombing, the call that put ATF on his trail? No one really saw him because he wasn't there.

The final mystery: that collision on the icy road to Dover. Spiritual people speculate that God was giving Bray a chance to reconsider—and, if the minister ignored His warning, providing indisputable proof of guilt beyond a reasonable doubt.

Or was it just an accident?

19

Déjà Vu

There is nothing more deceptive than an obvious
fact.

—Sir Arthur Conan Doyle

The FBI has grown quite bold when it comes to stealing
credit for the work of others—partly because they've become so experienced at the glory grabbing that wins them
influence and appropriations; partly because the deserving
investigators' weak leaders let the G-men get away with it.
This particular case began on the cool, cloudy Saturday
morning of December 16, 1989. A white postal van chugged
up the winding driveway to a hilltop house with a wide,
second-story portico in Mountain Brook, Alabama. Its
driver handed several letters and a package to Bob Vance.

Bob smiled. "Merry Christmas."

"Same to you, Judge."

The gray-haired justice of the 11th U.S. Circuit Court of
Appeals carried the mail to his kitchen, glanced at the
return address on the package and told his wife, Helen, "A
Christmas present from Judge Morgan. Feels like a book."
Laying it on the table, he slit the paper and lifted a flap.

The deafening explosion hurled a dozen thick nails into
his abdomen, knocked Helen from her chair, studded walls
with shrapnel and splattered cheery holiday decorations
with globs of blood.

Helen Vance, her chest seared by nails, struggled across
the tan, tile-patterned linoleum floor to cover Bob's gushing
wounds with a yellow towel. He made a few sounds, "like
when you're hit in the stomach," she'd say later, "and the
breath going out."

The barbaric murder galvanized postal inspectors to
discover who'd misused the mails, ATF agents to learn

who'd made the bomb, and G-men intent on solving the third slaying of a federal judge in the past century. Attorney General Dick Thornburgh declared this case the FBI's number-one priority.

The man they sought—a would-be lawyer with an IQ of 130—sat in his living room, calmly videotaping news coverage of the feds' frenzied activities.[1]

At nine-thirty on Monday morning, a package delivered to Atlanta's federal courthouse aroused suspicion. Clerks called the FBI and the city bomb squad; police summoned ATF. X-rays revealed a bomb. Police cleared the building and removed the package. Postal inspectors questioned mail clerks. The FBI told reporters that this bomb might be related to their investigation of Judge Vance's murder. ATF Special Agent Bob Holland rendered the device safe and examined its construction: a thick, explosives-filled pipe, its ends sealed by metal plates held in place by a connector rod.

Hours later, in Savannah, city alderman and civil rights lawyer Robbie Robinson opened a package at his desk. The blast severed his right arm and left hand and tore his chest wide open. Screaming in agony, he was rushed to a hospital, where he thrashed in pain for three hours before dying.

Postal inspectors, ATF experts and G-men converged on Robinson's demolished office. ATF Special Agent Frank Lee directed a meticulous search that yielded explosives residue, hunks of pipe and fragments of metal plates with connector rods like those noted by Holland at the Atlanta courthouse. Like the pieces recovered in Judge Vance's kitchen. The FBI-postal inspector-ATF task force was joined by U.S. marshals, the Georgia Bureau of Investigation and local police.

The next day, Agent Holland, a muscular man with a face resembling actor Jimmy Cagney's and an inch-long military haircut, drove to Ryan's Steak House in Atlanta where an association of bomb technicians were holding a meeting. He joined ATF forensic chemist Lloyd Erwin for lunch and drew a diagram of the bombs on a paper napkin.

Cunningly designed to maximize their explosives materials' killing force, the unique construction sparked Erwin's memory. "I saw a bomb like that once. Back in '72. One of

Chet Bryant's cases out of Macon. The defendant was a guy named Moody."

Seventeen years earlier, Special Agent Chester Bryant's investigation sent Walter Leroy Moody to prison for making a bomb he'd supposedly intended to mail to a used-car dealer with a demand for $65,000. But he'd stashed it in a filing cabinet at home. His wife opened it—and lost two fingers and part of a breast. She divorced him. A judge gave Moody five years. He served two.

Back at his office, Agent Holland was informed of a fourth bomb, discovered at the Jacksonville, Florida, branch of the National Association for the Advancement of Colored People. Speaking to a member of the police bomb squad by telephone, the agent learned that this bomb matched the construction of the Vance and Robinson devices. Holland's directions helped the Florida authorities disarm it.

The FBI was under heavy pressure. "It's relentless," one G-man told author Ronald Kessler. "Everything in the FBI stops. Full court press. No lead is too small to be covered by two agents." Another told Kessler, "One pressure is knowing that there is nothing you can ask for that you will not get." And yet, despite this urgency, G-men pooh-poohed the evidence Holland had come up with. They had their own theory.

Judge Vance had ruled favoring blacks in recent school desegregation cases; slain Savannah lawyer Robinson once served as legal counsel for the NAACP; the murderous bomb packages resembled a tear-gas device recently mailed to Atlanta's NAACP office. While Moody was a loner with no known antagonism toward blacks, the typewriter used to address the mailbombs was the same machine used to type letters to the court of appeals seven years earlier—letters sent by Wayne O'Ferrell of Enterprise, Alabama. And a man who'd once lived with O'Ferrell was related to Robert Edward Chambliss, the Klansman convicted by Alabama's attorney general for the bombing murder of four little girls at a Birmingham church. These were obvious facts. The bomber was a racist.

Holland, with a thousand investigations under his belt, preferred hard evidence to anyone's theory. Special Agent

Frank Lee, after more than twenty years with ATF, agreed with Holland. And so, while an army of FBI resources marched against O'Ferrell and white supremacists across the South, a few ATF agents discreetly probed Walter Moody.

In Florida, Moody had been charged with attempted murder—trying to drown some divers he'd insured before hiring them to take underwater photos; that case ended with a hung jury. Agents re-examined Moody's first bomb case. He'd appealed, producing two women who'd testified that a mysterious Gene Walker had put that bomb in Moody's home. Now ATF agents proved that in May of 1972, when the "witnesses" claimed they'd met Gene Walker in Atlanta, one of the women had actually spent the entire month in a Wisconsin hospital. Both confessed.

The FBI, scrutinizing Wayne O'Ferrell and issuing daily progress reports to the press, climaxed their Alabama efforts five weeks after Judge Vance's death. Accompanied by a horde of newsmen and TV cameras, they raided O'Ferrell's home. Networks carried scenes of G-men draining a pond and plumbing a septic tank, combing O'Ferrell's junkyard in a vain search for the incriminating typewriter. FBI agents stayed for weeks, interrogating the forty-six-year-old part-time preacher again and again. They took saliva samples, blood samples and hair samples. They gave him a lie-detector test twice. They came up dry.

Agents Holland and Lee believed the Moody witnesses now, but the unsupported word of a pair of perjurers is practically worthless. "If you're telling the truth now," one ATF agent asked, "will you help us prove it?"

The younger woman bowed her head and whispered, "Yes."

ATF concealed video cameras in the women's apartment to record Moody's visits. Aware now that his appeal was under investigation, he coached both women on the fine points of concealing their crime—and his.

Lee got a warrant to search Moody's home and truck. Agents found scripts Moody had written so his "witnesses" could rehearse their testimony. These, added to the videotaped conversations at the women's apartment and other proofs gathered by ATF, sufficed to convict Moody on thirteen counts of suborning perjury, bribery, tampering with a witness and obstructing a federal investigation. He'd get fifteen years, but long before that case came to trial, Agent Lee was back in court seeking another warrant. He'd used ATF's computer to scan descriptions of ten thousand illegal bombs. The judge who issued the warrant called Lee's affidavit "a forty-three-page tome which exhaustively explains the staggering number of similarities in the recent bombings and the 1972 bombing."

ATF agents searching Moody's home found pipes, rods, nails, glue, paint and other materials identical to those their lab experts had told them were used in the bombs.

Tom Stokes, special agent-in-charge of ATF-Atlanta, sent his agents' reports with a transcript of Moody's 1972 trial to Georgia's chief federal prosecutor. Two days later, the prosecutor telephoned Stokes. "Tom, have you read this report yourself?"

"Of course."

"Moody did it! Moody killed Vance and Robinson."

"No shit."

The main force of FBI agents joined ATF's investigation. On April 1, 1990, G-man John D. Behnke sought authorization to tap Moody's phone and bug his house. Included in Behnke's eighty-eight-page affidavit were Agent Holland's information, the evidence uncovered by Lee and his unit, Moody's denial that he'd ever owned a portable typewriter and a neighbor's statement that he'd once borrowed a typewriter from Moody. The wiretap was a waste of time but the bug paid off: Moody talked to himself. Among his 5,409 solitary ramblings were "Now you've killed two" and "Now you can't pull another bombing."

The seventy-count grand jury indictment charged Moody with murdering Judge Vance and interstate transportation of explosives to kill Robbie Robinson—both crimes punishable by death. One official called the government's case "a coffin with a thousand nails."

Pretrial publicity prompted transfer of the trial to Minneapolis. Now Moody's motive for selecting his victims was revealed. Judge Vance had turned down Moody's appeal from the earlier bomb conviction. But the killer's "reason" for the callous slaughter of Robbie Robinson and sending bombs to NAACP offices was grotesque in its warped simplicity: to divert suspicion from himself and toward the Ku Klux Klan. In other words, to provide lawmen with the obvious fact that can be so deceptive. The sixteen-day trial ended with a verdict that surprised no one. One of Moody's own attorneys shrugged. "We're lawyers, not magicians."[2] Judge Edward Devitt sentenced Moody to seven life terms, plus 400 years' imprisonment, to be followed by three years' probation—if necessary.

When the indictments were handed down and Moody was arrested, and again after the convictions, FBI director William Sessions and Attorney General Dick Thornburgh hosted mammoth press conferences. Thornburgh trumpeted the triumph as a victory for "one of the most intensive investigations and manhunts ever carried out by the Justice Department" and praised the FBI agents who'd "performed superbly in this case, devoting over 140,000 man-hours and eleven months to get their man."[3]

He wasn't "lying by commission," as lawyers would say. The FBI *had* knocked their brains out on this case. But he lied "by omission" when he glossed over contributions by postal inspectors, U.S. marshals, the Georgia Bureau of Investigation and local police in each of the areas where any action occurred. Thornburgh admitted chemist Lloyd Erwin's contribution in recognizing Moody's handiwork, even acknowledging that Erwin worked for ATF, but he had no public praise for Bob Holland or Frank Lee or any of the ATF agents who'd played the foremost role in solving the case.

ATF director Stephen Higgins attended the news conference, but only at the urging of ATF-Atlanta special agent-in-charge Tom Stokes. Higgins watched, listened and said nothing.

I've seen it happen time and again. Every time the FBI is caught grabbing the glory for work of others, they tell everyone, "Now we've changed. Things are different now. It won't happen again." It's hard to believe they'll ever change, considering the fact that their current director, Louis Freeh, already knows this whole story. He was the government lawyer who prosecuted Moody. And yet to this day, Mr. Freeh's reaction to praise for the FBI's feat in convicting Moody is a humble smile. He never disputes the FBI-generated perception that they deserve the laurels, and—as recently as December 1994 (three years after the case was closed with Moody's conviction)—the FBI persisted in its concealment by denying my request under the Freedom of Information Act for permission to examine their file. Their excuse: Releasing any of this information—even regarding those facts disclosed in the public trial—would violate Mr. Moody's right to privacy.[4]

After twenty-four years with ATF, Agent Bob Holland retired in December 1989. Shortly thereafter, he became director of the International Association of Bomb Technicians and Investigators, the worldwide organization of investigators, scientists, technicians and specialists from government and the private sector.

If the FBI's haughty theft of credit for catching and convicting Moody aroused anything among ATF agents, it was *déjà vu*.

20

Waco

> There was never a time when we didn't expect to
> be killed by the feds, whom David said were
> Babylon. While we waited for this to happen, we
> built up an army for David so the battle would be a
> big one and everyone would know the power of
> David and God.
>
> —Kiri Jewell

The tragedy at Waco or some equally appalling event was an
inevitable consequence of the paranoid anti-Washington
sentiment I first observed thirty years ago among right-wing
fanatics in the Midwest who saw government "traitors"
aiding the communist conspiracy. This decade's extremists
offer motives for "treason" that are vague, often racial,
always "liberal." But, as before, their fears and hatred are
fueled by an NRA-manufactured mistrust of "government
gun grabbers," congressmen too cowardly to seek a truth
that might cost them a gun lover's vote, and, until recently,
an executive infirmity among ATF leaders that kept them
from vigorously correcting far-right falsehoods.

Several salient facts are generally accepted: Koresh was
crazy,[1] his followers were gullible, ATF screwed up, the FBI
screwed up and scores of people—including children and
four young ATF agents—were killed. Other truths are
virtual secrets, drowned in a sea of fantasy spouted by
pompous "experts," and propaganda generated by leaders
of the NRA, the FBI and ATF.

Starting with facts that stand undisputed, Chief Deputy
Daniel Weyenberg of the McLennan County Sheriff's Department informed ATF of certain crimes and asked agents
to investigate. Special Agent Davy Aguilera headed a probe

classified by his special agent-in-charge as "sensitive"—a designation that prompts monitoring at headquarters—that spread to former cult members and weapons suppliers from New Zealand and California to Illinois and New Jersey. The evidence showed that Koresh and his followers had amassed an arsenal of illegal machine guns and explosives; and that some Branch Davidians were illegal aliens and ex-convicts—persons prohibited under federal law from possessing any firearm.[2]

Along the way, agents were advised by former cult members that Koresh's followers saw him as God, obeying him implicitly to the extent that male followers went celibate, giving him their wives, and that Koresh was sexually abusing children as young as ten. One girl was fourteen when she gave birth to a Koresh son. These reports, irrelevant to ATF's official mission, eliminated any possibility that Koresh was a misguided technical violator of federal laws. This suspect was "a bad guy." More relevant was Koresh's teaching that people who attended church on Sunday were worshiping Satan. Any agent dubious about investigating a "religious group" shivered at the prospect of Koresh's sheep invading a church with bombs and machine guns to "deal with the devil."

In retrospect, violence was a very real possibility. Koresh won leadership of the Branch Davidians following a shoot-out with his predecessor, George Roden, after both men lost a challenge to resurrect the twenty-year-old corpse of Anna Hughes. A local contractor was told to change the name on his $2,900 bill for cement mixers: "It's not Mount Carmel any more," the Branch Davidian told him. "The new name's Ranch Apocalypse." Koresh preached that Babylon (the government) would come to "get" him, then set out to fulfill his prophecy by gathering contraband weapons that were sure to attract agents. Otherwise, how *would* he prove his prediction? If he attacked a church, and it came out that ATF hadn't used the evidence they had to disarm him, what would the country say to that?

On December 4, 1993, ATF held a conference to plan tactics for executing the warrants they'd obtain—one for

Koresh's arrest, a second to search Ranch Apocalypse for
contraband firearms. Those present included Agent Aguilera, ASAC James Cavanaugh, Houston SAC Phillip Chojnacki (designated overall raid commander) and ASAC
Chuck Sarabyn, who'd serve as tactical coordinator. This
would be critical. ATF-Little Rock's agent-in-charge, Bill
Buford, was a Special Forces combat veteran with past
experience in planning and carrying out large-scale ATF
operations, but leadership selections were made on the
basis of rank rather than experience.

The planners had three options: First, inform Koresh that
they had warrants and ask him to submit. If he refused,
agents would have to either lay siege to the compound or go
home and ignore the judicial command to execute the
warrants. Second, arrest Koresh away from the compound;
then serve the search warrant. Third, make a "dynamic
entry"—i.e., storm the compound in force.

Given Koresh's prior conduct in denying state authorities
permission to enter and interview alleged victims of sexual
abuse, his defiant attitude toward law enforcement and the
presence of evidence that could send him to prison, it was
considered unlikely he'd submit to the judicial warrant.
Even if U.S. Attorney Johnston would authorize a siege-
style operation (which he'd said he wouldn't), the delay
would give Koresh and his people time to destroy all
evidence by temporarily dismantling the illegal weapons.
Then, too, agents knew that Koresh had trained his followers to commit suicide by placing the gun barrel in their
mouths, its muzzle against the soft part of the palate. And a
cyanide supply was on hand for the same purpose.

So much for the first option.

Arresting Koresh away from the compound was a tempt-
ing choice, but the only vantage point to watch for him—a
house down the road, where several agents took up residence posing as college students so they could conduct
observations—afforded only a view of the front of the
compound. He could, and did, leave without being seen on
several occasions. Cars couldn't park on the flat dirt roads
without being "made," and the idea of flooding nearby
Waco with strangers, prowling the streets with eyes peeled

for Koresh, was ludicrous. Besides, even if the arrest could be made away from Ranch Apocalypse, how would his followers react when agents arrived in Koresh's absence to make their search? When social worker Joyce Sparks came with deputy sheriffs to ask about suspected child abuse, they'd refused to answer questions.

One option remained: dynamic entry.

ATF's special response teams (SRTs)—experienced agents, all volunteers—underwent the training given all Treasury agents (the "Malibu Maze" obstacle course with its pop-up targets, judgmental pistol shooting, handgun stress and instinctive reaction), plus two weeks of vigorous training under instructors with backgrounds in the army's Special Forces or police SWAT teams. Nationwide, during the eighteen months preceding Waco, ATF's twenty-two SRTs had executed 278 search warrants, seized 794 guns and bombs and arrested 413 criminals. In all of their brief four-year history, only one agent had been injured by gunfire—a minor leg wound.

At Fort Hood, Texas, a mockup was constructed of the cult's sprawling, square, two-story compound with the four-story observation tower rising from its inner court. Interiors were mapped out from floor plans furnished by former cult members. The SRTs drilled for four days until they could—simultaneously and within thirty to forty seconds of their arrival—get inside, sew up the arsenal, safeguard the cyanide Koresh laid in for last year's mass suicide scheme, neutralize the adults and protect the children.

Agents would wear Kevlar vests and carry their weapons, but the keys to any safe and successful dynamic entry are speed and surprise.

One agent summed up what he and his colleagues had to look forward to: "Koresh and his followers are unpredictable. There are innocent women and children in there. The men—men crazy enough to let Koresh screw their wives and little girls—are heavily armed with all sorts of dangerous weapons. But the warrants are orders of the court. It's our duty to carry them out—arrest this guy and seize the illegal weapons."

On February 11, Agent Aguilera flew to Washington with

Chojnacki and Sarabyn to brief Associate Director Daniel Hartnett and others. They reviewed the reasons for deciding on a raid, rather than a siege: Koresh's ability to hold out indefinitely while he destroyed evidence and their concerns about mass suicide.

The next day, they answered Director Stephen Higgins's questions about the 10:00 A.M. timing, rather than predawn hours: The agents' information placed most of the cult men in the pit where they'd been digging daily—unarmed, and far from the supposedly locked arsenal. The conference concluded with Chojnacki's review of provisions for aborting the mission, if necessary. Associate Director Hartnett called Chojnacki a few days later, concerned that cult members might sneak back into the compound after agents arrived. Enter the pit, he instructed, to assure control over the men working there. He also sought assurances concerning the abort option. Agent Chojnacki assured him that the raid wouldn't proceed unless conditions were right.

The plan depended on that assumption that Davidian men would be working in the pit, unarmed and separated from the guns, but no one conveyed this to agents at the observation post. Surveillance reports of work in the pit grew more sporadic. No one asked the agents why.

Months earlier, Waco *Tribune-Herald* reporter Mark England, hearing of a State Department warning about possible mass suicide by Davidians, began sniffing around. Reporter Darlene McCormick telephoned U.S. Attorney Bill Johnston to ask what weapons were prohibited under federal law. Johnston suggested she contact "the Treasury guys." McCormick concluded that ATF was investigating. On February 1, managing editor Barbara Elmore phoned to ask Johnston's opinion regarding the likelihood that Branch Davidians would retaliate against the newspaper if they ran a series of articles. Johnston told her ATF was concerned about the proposed series and suggested a meeting.

Agents Sarabyn and Earl Dunagan met with her at Johnston's office. Concerned that adverse publicity might prompt Koresh to alter his routine or strike out somehow, they confided the existence of the investigation and planned raid. In exchange for delaying their series, ATF offered "front row seats" to observe the raid. Elmore said her publisher would have to make that decision and switched the conversation to her concern: the safety of *Tribune-Herald* employees and property. The meeting ended with the ATF men telling Elmore the raid would take place in a few weeks and promising to keep her informed.

Special Agent Robert Rodriguez, working undercover out of the nearby house from which the agents conducted their observations, made contact with the suspects by pretending interest in buying a horse trailer that was parked beside the compound. On February 5, Koresh invited him to a Bible session that turned into an intense one-on-one with Koresh himself. Rodriguez was forty-two, an expert pistol shot who kept himself in peak physical condition. But nothing in his past experience as a narcotics investigator for the state of Texas and nine years with ATF had prepared him for David Koresh. On February 17, during a two-hour Bible study, Koresh told Rodriguez that he rarely left the compound because the people in town didn't like him. He asked the agent to return the next day. That session lasted three hours.

Raised Catholic, Rodriguez had served as an altar boy, but now, after so many hours with Koresh, the self-styled messiah's words seemed to be making sense. Each time he left the compound, fellow agents had to help him regain reality.

"His Bible interpretations are just that, Bob—interpretations. You can interpret those passages he quotes a hundred ways. You're in there to investigate. If there's a crime, your job's to get evidence."

Rodriguez came to like many of Koresh's followers—men, women and children with no one to help them the way his colleagues counseled him—and he pitied them. Especially the children. When a three-year-old girl drifted off to sleep beside him during one of Koresh's endless sermons, the agent found himself wondering what kind of life she'd have. What would become of her and the others?

On February 21, Rodriguez accepted a Koresh invitation to listen to music at the compound. Koresh showed an anti-

ATF movie produced by a gun-nut organization and asked Rodriguez to join his church.

Galley prints of the *Tribune-Herald*'s "Sinful Messiah" series were sent to their parent organization, Cox Enterprises of Atlanta, along with a request that Charles Rochner, vice president for security, assess the potential for violent retaliation by Koresh. Rochner phoned Agent Chojnacki for an appointment. At their meeting, Chojnacki invited him to observe the raid training at Fort Hood and offered key interviews, but he refused a demand that reporters accompany the raiders. ATF couldn't guarantee their safety.

A few days later, Special Agent Earl Dunagan contacted managing editor Barbara Elmore to tell her the raid was postponed to March 1. She said the paper had made no decision on delaying their series. She notified her coworkers of the new schedule. Dunagan believed the newspaper was cooperating with requests to delay publication, but *Tribune-Herald* editors would later admit that they felt no obligation to answer ATF one way or the other.

In fact, they couldn't wait to publish. Their lawyers had reviewed their final draft for possible libel and they'd instituted security precautions: Building entrances were locked, identifying decals were removed from their vehicles and the homes of their executives would be protected. Reporters Mark England and Darlene McCormick, who'd written the articles, would leave Waco when the series started.

On February 24, SAC Chojnacki met with publisher Preddy and editors Elmore, Blansett and Lott. He thanked them for delaying publication. They made it clear that they weren't holding off in the interests of law enforcement. Chojnacki begged them to wait until after the raid. Koresh was relaxed now, he said. The publicity might agitate him and disrupt the operation. Chojnacki wouldn't give the news people the scheduled date for the raid. He acknowledged it would come "fairly soon" but declined to say whether ATF had an agent inside the cult.

They said they'd start their series in seven days.

Chojnacki asked, "Does that mean you're willing to run

this story even though we're asking you to keep it quiet for a few more days so we can do what we have to do?"

Editor Lott said, "The important thing is the public's right to know, and that's our job. We're not concerned about where it falls in or falls out of your law-enforcement case."

In truth, the "public's right to know" about Koresh a few days sooner than ATF had requested was eclipsed by another concern. Their series didn't simply paint a scary picture of the "sinful messiah"; the *Tribune-Herald* demanded action by law enforcement. Publishing after ATF had *already* acted would sacrifice exclusivity and profitability; a raid after the articles would make it seem *they'd* saved society from Koresh.

Chojnacki would admit, later, that he left "feeling hot." (Rochner recalled the agent's demeanor as "businesslike.") The editors and reporters agreed they'd heard nothing to dissuade them from publishing as soon as they'd provided for their own security. Saturday, February 27, would give them a weekend of minimal activity at their facilities to gauge the Davidians' reaction. Publisher Preddy wouldn't notify ATF of that decision until Rochner had answered all their security questions. Later, he and the editors would claim that the March 1 raid date mentioned earlier by Agent Dunagan had no effect on their decision to publish the day before, February 27.

Reporter Tom Witherspoon told editor Blansett of a tip that "something big" might happen at the compound between nine and ten on Monday morning. Blansett assigned reporters to go there on Monday.

On February 25, Special Agent Davy Aguilera assembled his evidence and composed an affidavit. U.S. Magistrate David Green issued two warrants: one commanding ATF to search Ranch Apocalypse for illegal weapons; the second ordered Koresh's arrest for crimes under GCA-68.

SAC Chojnacki asked ASAC Sarabyn whether the raid could be moved up to Saturday. Informed that essential preparations rendered this impossible, Chojnacki ordered the raid for Sunday, February 28.

Rochner told Chojnacki that the "Sinful Messiah" series would begin on Saturday.

That afternoon, Treasury officials were notified. Director Higgins told Acting Assistant Secretary Simpson that an undercover agent would enter the compound to make sure there was no change in the Branch Davidians' routine—that the men would be separated from the weapons—and added two assurances: that the raid would be canceled if there was any change in the cult members' routine; and the raid would be canceled if its secrecy was compromised.

Success depended on secrecy, surprise and several beliefs held by the raid planners, but ATF's intelligence was inadequate. The compound's population wasn't seventy-five, it was 125; and the belief that weapons were securely locked up—primarily based on the word of a former member who'd said, simply, that guns were kept in a room from which the men couldn't take them without Koresh's permission—was incorrect.

On Saturday, undercover agent Rodriguez gave Koresh time to digest the "Sinful Messiah" story before visiting the compound. Koresh seemed to dismiss the newspaper's ability to arouse anything beyond a possible effect on his fundraising.

Reporter Witherspoon confided his "Monday" tip to KWTX-TV's Dan Mulloney. Mulloney called Darlene Helmstatter, a dispatcher for American Medical Transport. She told him ATF's original request to have three ambulances standing by on Monday had been changed to Sunday morning. The two men met to play racquetball and discuss the raid.

Editor Blansett tripled the number of reporters he'd intended to send. Then he received a call from Koresh aide Steve Schneider asking to be interviewed. Blansett phoned reporter Mark England, who'd already fled to Dallas and ordered him to accompany their security man and an off-duty policeman to meet Koresh at a public restaurant. England refused.

Rodriguez left the compound that evening after a seven-hour Bible session and reported Koresh's statement to followers: "They" were coming; if this happened, no one

should become hysterical, but "remember how we've re-
hearsed. Just do as you've been taught and everything will
be fine." Koresh hadn't reiterated what action he'd instructed them to take.

Sunday, February 28, 1993

It was still dark at five o'clock when ASAC James Cavanaugh commenced observations of the compound from the
undercover house. The morning dawned cloudy, with intermittent drizzles. Cavanaugh saw a few cult members walking about, and some women emptying waste buckets. In the
house with Cavanaugh, forward observers checked their
sniper rifles, preparing to provide cover fire, if necessary,
for the raid teams. When the time came, one of the agents
living at the house would lead them and the arrest support
teams to a barn behind the compound. The other undercover agents would go to the Spoon home—the only other
house on that road—to ensure the safety of that family.

TV reporter Mulloney drove his white Bronco past the
compound twice and parked about a mile away. Cameraman Jim Peeler got lost in his white Blazer and used his
cellular phone to ask Mulloney for directions. Reporter
England halted his white Cavalier beside a state trooper's
car near the compound to ask whether he could pass. The
officer told him he could, but the road would be closed very
soon. Soon, six white vehicles carrying eleven reporters and
cameramen were cruising the roads near the compound.

David Jones stopped his yellow Buick with "U.S. Mail"
painted on its door behind cameraman Peeler, parked up
the road from the compound. Jones asked whether Peeler
was lost. Peeler, wearing his KWTX-TV jacket, introduced
himself and asked directions to the compound. Jones
pointed across the barren fields. "That's it, right there."

Peeler, oblivious of the fact that he was talking to a
Branch Davidian, told Jones that a raid was about to take
place and there might be shooting. Jones sped away toward
the compound. Peeler wondered whether he'd made a
mistake.

Undercover agent Rodriguez was discussing the Bible

with Koresh when Jones arrived and told other members what Mulloney had said. They called Koresh away from Rodriguez. When Koresh returned, he tried to resume the Bible discussion, but he couldn't talk and his hands shook. Rodriguez snatched the Bible from him and asked, "What's wrong?"

Koresh blurted, "Neither ATF nor the National Guard will ever get me. They got me once and they'll never get me again." He walked to the window. "They're coming, Robert. The time has come. They're coming, Robert." Staring out the window, he repeated, "They're coming."

Rodriguez said he had to meet a man for breakfast and turned to leave. Other cult members blocked his way. The agent gave a fleeting thought to jumping through the window but he kept his cool, repeating that he had to meet someone for breakfast.

Koresh walked up to him and, in a manner Rodriguez thought uncharacteristic, grasped the agent's hand and said, "Good luck, Robert."

Rodriguez was terrified. Did they suspect that *he* was an agent? A Koresh aide opened the door for him but, with each step on that seemingly endless walk to his car, he fully expected a bullet in the back. Minutes later, at the under-cover house, he reported to Jim Cavanaugh. The ASAC asked whether he'd seen any guns, heard anyone talk about guns, or seen anyone rushing about. Rodriguez answered no. Instructed to notify the command post, Rodriguez answered the same three questions to Agent Sarabyn.

Sarabyn asked, "What were they doing?"

"Praying."

Sarabyn relayed this to Chojnacki. After a three-minute conference amidst the bustle of preparations, they decided they could still make it if they hurried.

That decision—to move out at 9:05 A.M., bringing the agents to the compound at 9:47—was flawed no matter how Koresh might react. If the Davidians' routine remained unaltered, the men scheduled to start work in the pit at ten o'clock would still be inside the compound. If they intended resistance, they had nearly an hour to get ready.

Rodriguez, visibly distraught, wondered aloud how the raid could proceed after what he'd reported.

Sarabyn rushed to the staging area and hastened agents into the cattle trailers—common vehicles in that part of Texas—intended to transport agents to the compound without arousing undue suspicion until it was too late for the Davidians to resist. "Get ready to go," Sarabyn shouted. "They know we're coming. We're going to hit them now." There was no briefing, no discussion or evaluation of Rodriguez's information. There was no contingency plan for what to do if cult members used their massive arsenal. Surprise and a show of force had always prevented resistance. But the vital element of surprise was gone.

With the mile-long caravan of cars and cattle trailers en route, some agents engaged in nervous banter. Some felt confident. Others wondered, Why proceed when Koresh was expecting them?

Branch Davidian men and women donned armored vests and grabbed hand grenades from the dining-room table. Harvard-educated lawyer Douglas Martin wore a necklace of grenades.

Three *Tribune-Herald* reporters drove to the Spoon home adjacent to the undercover house. With no idea whether the residents were cult members, they knocked, but just then, another agent arrived at the house. Taking him for the homeowner, reporter Witherspoon said there was about to be a raid and asked permission to watch it from the front yard. The agent ordered them to leave. They were backing onto the road when the cattle trailers passed.

Agents in the trailers grew apprehensive when they saw no activity around the compound. One radioed, "There's no one outside."

Another agent answered, "That's not so good."

KWTX's Mulloney and McLemore followed the trailers up the driveway and parked behind a bus.

One of the first agents out of the trailers focused on the compound's dogs, aimed the fire extinguisher he carried for this purpose, and discharged it toward them to keep the hounds at bay without hurting them. Agents were jumping from the second trailer.

Koresh opened the front door and yelled, "What's going on?"

"ATF! Federal officers with a search warrant. Freeze!"

Koresh slammed the door before agents could reach it.

Mulloney was setting up his camera when a fusillade of gunfire erupted through the front door with such force that the door bowed outward. Several agents fell wounded.

Bullets struck *Tribune-Herald* cars at the Spoon home. Five reporters dove into a muddy roadside ditch.

Gun muzzles spat fire from every window across the broad facade of the building. Special Agent Steve Steele was shot in the lower lip and left hand. Bob White took bullets in his shoulder and neck. Curtis Williams was wounded in his left leg. Terry Hicks suffered injuries to several vertebra while moving for cover. John Williams chipped two front teeth when he dove for cover.

Gunfire rained and hand grenades exploded in the no man's land between agents and ambushers. Special Agent Robert Rowe took shrapnel in his right hand. Mike Russell was wounded in the left shoulder. Larry Shiver received multiple shrapnel wounds to his left leg and lost tissue from his calf.

One cult member sprayed the agents with a machine gun from his nest in the four-story tower. ATF snipers, firing from 285 yards away, took him down.

Special Agent Clayton Alexander was wounded in both legs. Roland Ballesteros was shot in the hand. Sam Cohen received shrapnel wounds in his right thigh.

Steve Willis had received his B.S. degree in criminal justice from Southwest Texas State University. His academic advisor, David Flores, would say, "He was a fantastic student. One of the nicest kids I ever had in my classes." Recalling Willis's oft-expressed ambition to join ATF, Flores added, "If there was someone I'd want with me in a firefight like that, it would have been him." Willis was reloading his weapon when he jerked forward and slumped onto Lowell Sprague. Sprague checked his pulse and was laying him down when he saw a bullet smash into his left temple and exit through his neck. Willis's chin dropped slowly to his chest. Sprague held him, trying to stanch the blood that gushed from the wound. "My fingers were inside," he'd testify later, "and I could feel the blood pumping. Pretty soon his heart stopped beating." Willis, thirty-two, was survived by his parents and a sister.

Special Agent Eric Evers, rounding the southwest corner of the compound—his pistol still holstered so his hands would be free "in the event of fisticuffs"—was confronted by cult member Livingston Fagan and two others. Fagan fired his AR-15 rifle four times, hitting Evers in the right arm and upper shoulder. The agent crawled to a ditch where he'd lay—trapped, bleeding and torn by shrapnel wounds—while they kept shooting at him.

ATF rules prohibited firing without an identifiable target posing an imminent threat to human life. An agent with Marine combat experience would say, "War was easier. We could kill anybody in front of us and kill them any way we could. Shoot through walls, toss grenades into their fortress. Anybody, any way we could. They were all 'the enemy.' But this was . . . hell, that crazy bastard had kids in there."

Shrapnel struck Special Agent Mark Handley in the leg, Gary Orchowski in the hand, Joe Patterson in the cheek. Mark Murray's shoulder was peppered with buckshot.

The New Orleans SRT, a crack team that had used its swift precision against scores of dangerous outlaws without anyone from either side suffering a scratch, propped their ladders against the building's east side. With one agent providing covering-fire from the ground, seven agents ascended onto the computer-room roof where they could enter a window to the cult's arms room. Special Agent Conway LeBleu, age thirty, was the son of a prominent Louisiana lawyer, named for an uncle who'd served in the state legislature for twenty years. A graduate of McNeese State University and an agent for five years, he was shot to death on that small sloping roof. He left a widow, Paige, and two sons; Scott was eleven, Cameron was eighteen months old.

Special Agent Todd McKeehan, twenty-eight, was described by New Orleans police sergeant Bruce Little as "energetic, extremely outgoing . . . always wanted to be the first to go through the door." A high-school swimmer and football player, he'd earned degrees in engineering and criminal justice at Eastern Tennessee State University. His three years as an agent were interrupted by army service when he did battle in Operation Desert Storm. He'd survived that war, only to die of Branch Davidian bullets beside Agent LeBleu on that computer-room roof. His widow's name is Leslie.

Forty-eight-year-old Kenny King, a seventeen-year veteran with ATF, was shot six times—in the chest, one arm, both legs and his abdomen. He rolled from that roof down into the courtyard behind the compound and lay there, helpless. "Come get me," he radioed. "I'm bleeding to death." His colleagues, pinned down by withering sprays of .50-caliber and .223-caliber machine gun fire, wouldn't get to him for ninety minutes.

Agent Jordan managed to "rake and break" the window to the arms room while Agent Millin stood guard beside him on the roof. Balding, broad-shouldered Bill Buford tossed a flashbang distraction device through the window and entered with Jordan and Agent Constantino. A Davidian with an assault rifle backed out of that room and fired at the agents through a wall. Some of his bullets penetrated the outer wall to Agent Millin's position on the roof. More bullets came at Millin up through the roof from inside the first floor. He was able to escape by sliding down the ladder to the ground.

Inside the arms room, unseen riflemen spat automatic gunfire through walls into the smoky gloom. Agents couldn't shoot back without risking injury to innocent children who might be on the other side. Agent Glen Jordan was wounded in the arm.

Buford, shot in the left hip, said, "I heard the thud and it felt like I'd been hit with a baseball bat." Another slug struck him in the thigh. He began to worry that he wouldn't be able to stand up and get out.

Constantino, a tall man with a dark brown beard showing traces of gray, a single father with three small daughters, covered the agents' retreat. Buford and Jordan got out the window. Jordan made his way down the ladder, staggered across open ground to a shed where agents were pinned down by vicious machine gun fire, and collapsed. Bernadette Griffin elevated his arm and compressed his wound to stanch the gushing blood for ninety minutes until the gunfire ended.

Gerald Petrelli received shrapnel wounds to his right hand, wrist, forearms and upper right arm. Clair Rayburn was shot in the hand. John Risenhoover was shot in both legs.

Buford rolled from that roof. Two agents tried to catch him, but the fall broke four ribs. Agents dragged him a few yards, but they couldn't escape the hail of bullets raining from several directions. Team medic Chisholm rushed to Buford's side and administered an IV. A bullet grazed the bridge of Buford's nose. Three more whizzed past his head. Chisholm lay beside him, shielding his head from the gunfire. Buford croaked, "Get outta here. They're not giving Congressional Medals of Honor for this one."

Chisholm refused. "I'm not going to let them shoot you any more."

A Davadian entered the arms room and shot at Constantino. The agent fired back and his attacker went down. Constantino's pistol was empty. He ran for the window, but struck his head as he climbed out. His helmet fell off. He dropped his gun. Dazed, he rolled from the roof, landing on his elbow and knee. The stabbing pain made him think he'd been shot. Two agents pulled him close to the building, where the gunmen firing through every window wouldn't be able to finish him off.

Buford saw Special Agent Robert Williams, still providing cover fire from behind a large metal object, pushed back as if he'd been hit, but he regained his balance and raised his head to resume his job. When the next bullet struck him, Buford would say, "I sort of knew he wouldn't get up." Robb Williams would have been twenty-seven on Monday, the day after the raid. A high-school football player who'd excelled in sports and art, he'd graduated with a B.S. in criminology from Florida State University. His father had been a Secret Service agent.

Pinned down by exploding grenades and relentless machine-gun fire, agents had to conserve ammunition. Their attackers' inexhaustible supply left more than a million rounds found later inside the compound.

After an hour and a half of sustained gunfire, Jim Cavanaugh was finally able to reach Koresh's lieutenant, Steve Schneider, by phone. Schneider was frantic and hostile. Cavanaugh heard yells, screams and crying through the telephone, but he worked at arranging a cease-fire. "I'm sorry to get a little sad about it," Cavanaugh would testify later, "but I had a radio mike in one ear with [the wounded and bleeding Special Agent Kenny King, lying trapped in the compound's inner courtyard where he'd fallen] pleading for his life. And I had this guy on the phone who thought he was God. And if I couldn't negotiate it, how was I going to get this guy out? And how many agents was I going to send to get him? How many people would die?"

Cavanaugh insisted agents wouldn't leave without their fallen comrades. Davidians granted permission to rescue King. Pete Mastin led Chisholm, Bonaventure and Bernadette Griffin—with hands raised—around the east wall of the compound to the courtyard. One of the Davidians pointed a rifle out the window toward Agent Griffin, a black woman, and shouted racial slurs. Griffin decided that if she was going to die, she'd die trying to help a fellow agent. She turned her back on the gunman and approached King. His injuries were too serious to permit carrying him without a stretcher. The agents laid him on a ladder and carried him out.

Undercover agent Rodriguez—among the agents carrying dead and wounded friends through the light drizzle across the flat, barren field—asked himself why God would allow such good men, families and children to endure such tragedy. Back at his truck, he picked up the Bible he'd carried and threw it away.

KWTX-TV man Mulloney was filming everything in sight. Treasury's official report, issued months later, would state, "ATF agents and local law-enforcement authorities verbally and physically assaulted Mulloney as he filmed the agents' dead colleagues lying on the ground." Despite the agents' reaction, Mulloney would testify at trial that the first shots had come from inside the compound.

Hours later, agents patrolling the perimeter around the compound were attacked by three armed Davidians. One gunman was killed, one surrendered, and one escaped to be captured later.

Koresh said that one man and a girl had been killed. Actually, three Davidian men were killed and four, including Koresh, had been wounded. One of Koresh's wives would later testify that Davidian Neal Veaga performed at least two "mercy killings" of wounded members. Forensic pathologists would report death wounds fired from less than three feet.

Associate Director Hartnett arrived at the national command center at eleven o'clock, Waco time, and dispatched his deputy, Dan Conroy, to Waco. Three hours later, Director Higgins appeared and sent Hartnett to Waco.

Jim Cavanaugh stayed on the phone with the Davidians throughout the day and into Monday. He secured the release of ten Branch Davidian children Then, on duty for nearly thirty hours, he slept. The FBI was called in to take over the siege and dialog with the Davidians. Koresh aide Schneider told reporters, "The reason we haven't continued sending children out is, we're waiting for Jim to get up. We have a very good working relationship with Jim, and we want it to continue." On Tuesday, Cavanaugh secured the release of two women and six children. Those who knew him weren't surprised. DEA's top man in Dallas credited Cavanaugh with improving cooperation among city, county, state and federal officers. Cavanaugh's own colleagues recognized the tall, easygoing father of two as a fair man and a "people person."

ATF headquarters began peppering its Texas managers with questions about the disaster. A weary Cavanaugh turned over negotiations to FBI hostage experts. During the next three weeks, ten more cultists departed the compound. FBI officials would later boast that "we" got twenty-eight people out of there.

On that Tuesday, while Cavanaugh brought the eight kids and adults out of the compound, eight ATF agents and two New York City Police Department bomb squad officers strode down a ramp into the underground garage where, days earlier, the World Trade Center had been bombed. Two agents and an NYPD man rappelled into the depths of a sixty-foot crater where cement ceilings balanced precariously on weakened pillars among buckled walls. Sifting through concrete rubble and hundreds of vehicles blasted into millions of pieces, Special Agent Joe Hamlin selected a length of axle exhibiting the pitting and heat effects of extreme proximity to the blast. It bore a serial number. It took ATF explosives expert Joe Tontarski, five chemists and two technicians from ATF-Atlanta's forensics section more than a day to convince the FBI that this blackened, twisted hunk of metal was important. Its number, punched into a computer, tagged the vehicle as a van rented from Ryder Truck Rental in Jersey City. From that point onward, FBI assistant director James Fox would eventually acknowledge that "it all fell like dominoes." The van was rented by Mohammed Salomeh; another man's name appeared on the rental contract, and a search of his apartment yielded bomb components; a card in Salomeh's wallet identified a chemical engineer carrying a receipt for a storage shed where more explosives were found.

FBI man Fox's press announcement described the arrest by G-men and NYPD detectives in dramatic detail. He credited the critical lead to "our explosives experts."

The FBI siege at Waco dragged on. Journalists quoted anonymous G-men as saying this would never have happened had the FBI rather than ATF handled the original raid.

Through seven weeks of the standoff, media people worked out of a satellite city of antennae they'd erected near the compound, cranking out continuous coverage. On Day 49 they began to pull out. Nothing was happening. Then the FBI acted—assaulting the compound with tanks, ramming holes in the building and pumping gas inside to drive the Davidians out. The result was a frenzy of executions— Davidians killing Davidians—and mass suicide by fire.

The FBI's attack—after fifty-one days of consultations with the nation's foremost experts, the use of every resource available to the United States government and the leisure to ponder their options—represented the same sort of misjudgement ATF's field managers had made in a three-minute discussion under the pressure of an impending raid.

Seven surviving Branch Davidians were convicted of possessing an unregistered explosive device, conspiring to make machine guns, using firearms in a crime of violence and/or manslaughter. Others haggled over the Ranch Apocalypse property. Some favored delaying a decision until David Koresh returned.[3]

Ignoring the 130 trial witnesses and 1,400-plus pieces of evidence from both sides, the ultraconservative press and talk shows, told the "faithful" what they wanted to believe, as illustrated by the following *Washington Times* piece:

AFFIDAVIT TO SEARCH
WACO SITE CRITICIZED

by Jerry Seper

One Washington lawyer, considered a weapons expert, said a review of the affidavit, written by ATF agent Aguil [sic], shows there was no probable cause to arrest Koresh or search the property. The lawyer, who asked not to be identified, said the ATF search appeared to be based on a desire "to punish Koresh for showing disrespect" to the ATF.

Considering the federal courts' finding that Aguilera's affidavit was amply sufficient, the alleged lawyer/weapons-expert was wise to require anonymity.

A *Cleveland Plain Dealer* editorial called the fallen agents a "clod squad."

University of Chicago professor Richard Shweder wrote that the Davidians "acquired an arsenal of guns in anticipation of the end of the world. But for the most part, they minded their own business. . . . To the bureaucratic state and its regulatory agents, this can be very annoying."[4]

Andy Rooney didn't question the dubious value of firearms at the end of the world, but he said this to *60 Minutes* viewers: "Whose fault was it that those cult members died? It was their own damned fault, that's whose fault it was. . . . There are too many unfortunate people in the world to waste time feeling sorry for the Waco wackos."[5]

Cult members' testimony and DNA tests affirmed Koresh's sexual abuse of prepubescent girls, but Republican congressman Mark Souder of Indiana stated, "The only law that [the FBI] clearly established [Koresh] broke that I can see so far is he had sex with consenting minors."[6]

Amidst the ignorance, there were valid criticisms. ATF field managers blundered by initiating the raid after Agent

Rodriguez's warning that Koresh was expecting them. Within the bureau, agents might have forgiven management errors, but they found the lies infuriating: the denials of receiving or understanding Rodriguez's warning; Associate Director Hartnett's denial that he'd been instructed to abort the raid if the element of surprise were compromised.

Director Higgins's public pronouncements changed as the days passed. On *Face the Nation,* he flatly denied ATF's awareness that Koresh had been tipped. A few days later, on NBC's *Today Show,* he said, "We would not have executed the raid if our supervisors felt like we had lost that element [of surprise]." Soon it became, "There is no one in ATF that I know of that would purposely lead agents into a situation where they knew they would be ambushed." Critics saw the metamorphosis of Higgins's statements as a grudging retreat from cover-up, necessitated by agents' public acknowledgments of Sarabyn's shouts that "Koresh knows we're coming." But while Higgins trusted his subordinates too implicitly, virtually abdicating his law-enforcement responsibilities, there's nothing in his history to suggest he'd lie. Mr. Higgins told me, "The information I had [after the initial denials] was—and I heard it from at least two or three different sources—that the undercover officer came out and said he warned them, and I asked [Hartnett] to take a look at that and the only reports I got back was, 'No, that's not true. He's changing his statements.' And so, with conflicting reports, I figured the Rangers are going to get the statements and we'll find out."

It was, after all, Higgins who'd decided to request that Texas Rangers conduct the inquiry. "We had the option . . . and [Hartnett and I] both agreed," Higgins says, "it was better to have the Rangers do it to avoid the very thing that happened. That somebody claimed we went in and tried to cover up. And then, two days later, I wrote a memo on my own initiative to Treasury saying instead of us doing the shooting review, it'd be better if you form a team of experts from outside ATF . . . and that way we won't have to worry about people questioning our objectivity."

The FBI took time from defending their own attack on the compound to give congressmen some taped conversa-

tions between Koresh and the sheriff's 911 dispatcher—
thirty minutes extracted from twenty-nine hours of
dialog—portraying Koresh as ATF's victim. But the conversations had segments lifted out of context, and its chronology had been "rearranged." Representative Jim Lightfoot of
Iowa stated he was "deeply disturbed that the subcommittee has been provided with misleading or doctored or
bootlegged information," and he saw the FBI's motive as
trying to "make ATF look bad." G-men apologized. They
hadn't intended to mislead anyone, they said. It was a
training tape, they said, created for their agents assigned to
the Waco standoff. FBI director Sessions, already facing
unrelated charges of misconduct, was fired by President
Clinton. A Justice Department inquiry absolved the FBI of
all blame.

The Society of Professional Journalists "investigated" the
Waco *Tribune-Herald*'s actions and concluded that no media person had done anything wrong.

Treasury secretary Bentsen's investigators—senior
agents of the Secret Service, Customs and IRS, a specialist
from the Federal Law Enforcement Training Center, and
two attorneys from Treasury's general counsel—questioned
508 persons, some of them repeatedly, some for more than
a full day. Findings: The element of surprise was lost before
the raid began; Agent Aguilera's investigation of Koresh
deserved high praise; other agents conducted themselves
with valor and distinction; field commanders were ill prepared to lead such an operation; top management had failed
to provide adequate training, supervision or leadership.

Treasury removed Director Higgins from his position and
ordered him to retire. Associate Director Daniel Hartnett
and his deputy, Dan Conroy, were removed and ordered to
retire. Chojnacki and Sarabyn were fired; they appealed.
The new ATF director, John Magaw (formerly director of
the U.S. Secret Service), took them back in positions with
no law-enforcement authority. Magaw was motivated by the
unpredictability of judges. In one case, an appeals court
overturned ATF's firing of supervisor John Gamboa for
twenty-one incidents of sexual harassment against Special
Agent Sandra Hernandez and returned him to his job.

Director Magaw would explain, "I *didn't* want [Chojnacki and Sarabyn] back in law enforcement."[7]

MURDERED AT WACO

Special Agent Conway LeBleu
Special Agent Todd W. McKeehan
Special Agent Robert Williams
Special Agent Steven D. Willis

21

Fallout

As thou sowest, so shalt thou reap.
—Cicero

Anyone who saw Waco as a one-time horror was unduly
optimistic. Anybody who thought Congress would seek all
the facts and act on what they found was doomed to
disappointment. Everybody who says we'd have more freedom without any gun laws or the enforcement of those
laws—giving convicts and crazy people more freedom to
arm themselves with the tools of their predatory trade—is
either credulous, cuckoo, or a bald-faced liar.

There *is* a way to get more effective federal law enforcement, at less cost, in a manner least likely to see our
government violating anyone's civil rights. Strange as it
seems, the idea's been around for decades but never imple-
mented because some people don't want it to happen.

At 9:06A.M. on the sunny Monday morning of April 19,
1995, three-year-old Joey Webber saw a blinding flash,
heard a loud wind noise, and then his arm was broken his
eardrums ruptured by concussion and his face slashed by
glass. He was lucky.

Nineteen other children in the daycare center at the
Murrah Federal Building in Oklahoma City had been killed
along with 149 men and women by the worst terrorist act in
American history. An ATF agent witnessed the destruction
from the courthouse across the street, and—relying on his
experience with ATF's "Dipole Might" (a project that
involved blowing up cars at White Sands Proving Grounds
to create a computer model that would help unravel car
bombings)—he phoned ATF-Dallas to report the cause: "an

308

'anfo' [ammonium nitrate/fuel oil] bomb, at least several thousand pounds."[1]

Sixty miles north of the city, Trooper Charlie Hanger halted a yellow Mercury for having no license plates. He might have merely warned the driver or issued a ticket but, standing beside the Mercury, he spotted a pistol under the driver's coat. He pulled it out. The gun was loaded with Black Talon "cop-killer" bullets. He arrested Timothy McVeigh for violating a law the McVeighs of the world hate most—a gun law. An Oklahoma City policeman found a truck axle bearing a number that was traced to the place where McVeigh had rented the bomb-carrying truck. Two days later, just as McVeigh was about to be released on bail from Trooper Hanger's charges, an ATF agent discovered the suspect's whereabouts. It wasn't any superagency that caught the prime suspect so quickly, it was cooperation among dozens of law-enforcement officers. Informed of the evidence and discoveries made by others, the FBI rushed to make the arrest and the press announcement: *"We* caught him!"

There's much about the Oklahoma City case that can't be told until after the trial, but the only surprise to ATF agents was the public's astonishment that the suspect was an American. Hadn't they heard the gun-toting "militias," and Nazis, and their clones—fed by rhetoric from the NRA and other antigovernment elements—condoning crime and promising violence to "protect their rights"? Hadn't anyone considered that politicians who parrotted these radical recriminations would encourage other mindless madmen?

After Oklahoma City, congressmen acted even sillier. The "Waco Hearings" of July saw NRA people posing as staff members and questioning potential witnesses "to assist" the subcommittee—and congressmen thanking them for their help. Republican congressman Bob Bar was pitifully transparent, swallowing absurd statements by Branch Davidians without question, expressing incredulity to Treasury's officials, even refusing to let one witness answer fully the question Bar had asked. Republican John Shadegg's question to one agent took six minutes to ask, and he demanded a yes-or-no answer. Criticisms of ATF's raid plan were sought and welcomed from Joyce Sparks, the

Texas social worker who'd failed to help the Branch David-ian children. But John Kolman, the well-known expert on law-enforcement raids, stood by for a full week, only to be dismissed after answering one question. Even then, Kolman was persistently interrupted and cut off by Senator Grassley.[2]

Libertarians picketed the Dallas Federal Building with signs demanding ATF be abolished for violating the Branch Davidians' rights to carry arms and worship God in their own way. The NRA shared their opinion. That was one point of view.

On the other side, thousands of citizens did more than talk, they acted: Within a month of the shootout, public contributions for the fallen agents' families reached $142,000. Residents of Waco—the people most at risk through their proximity to Koresh and his robotic followers—posted barbecue and dinner invitations on an ATF bulletin board. When agents entered a packed restau-rant wearing their ATF coveralls, everyone stood and ap-plauded. A woman living three miles from the compound wrote to Treasury secretary Bentsen, voicing support for ATF, gratitude for their dealing with "a crazyman living here with a ton of guns," and her appreciation—not only for the friendly treatment she received at checkpoints but "the protection that is being provided for all concerned."

Empathy emerged from unexpected sources. The former spokesman for the neo-Nazi CSA—Covenant, Sword and Arm of the Lord, whose leaders were imprisoned after that four-day standoff in 1985—phoned to extend condolences to the murdered agents' families and even asked if there was anything he could do to help.

Registered nurse Pat Muhl, on duty at the Hillcrest Baptist Medical Center after the raid, wrote to Secretary Bentsen praising ATF agents' kindness, professionalism, and the "special camaraderie among the group that one seldom sees. . . . It makes me sad and angry to hear the criticisms of people who were not involved. Please express to ATF for me (and others in my community) what one of the children at Hallsburg Elementary said so well, 'Thank you for protecting us, you are our heroes.'"

The congressional duty to supervise federal agencies

can't help anyone when it's carried out like those Waco hearings—by "judges" acting like prosecutors. Not if they want the truth. The legislators' apparent support of the antigovernment element certainly didn't discourage violence. Nevada "patriots" bombed offices of the U.S. Forest Service. Missouri's Citizens for Christ stockpiled bombs and machine guns until police raided their compound; soon afterward, Trooper Bobbie Harper (who participated in the raid) was shot in his home. Members of a Virginia militia group armed themselves with machine guns and plotted to steal more from a National Guard armory. Another Virginian arrested by ATF agents had documents showing he was organizing a terrorist group to kill cops and other officials if gun-control laws became too strict for his taste.[3] Any ATF agent can tell you that this sort of thing has been going on since the 1960s with organizations like the Minutemen and the Posse Comitatus.

But now, grown more violent and even more bold, twenty Freemen spouting separatist and white supremacy sentiments declared their Montana ranch a "free sovereign independent state" and declared war on government officials. Wanted on a variety of fraud charges, they even posted signs threatening to kill lawmen entering their property and offered a $1 million bounty on a district attorney. One prosecutor refused to run for re-election. A judge closed her court, admitting fear of Freemen violence. Local lawmen hadn't the manpower or expertise to root the fugitives out, and for months, they couldn't get help from federal agencies. The feds, they said, were gun-shy in the wake of congressional lambasting. Finally the FBI moved in and, after consulting top experts and fugitives' relatives, the G-men played a waiting game for eighty-one days. The Freemen's stubbornness cost Uncle Sam a fortune, with more than a hundred agents tied up surrounding that ranch when they might have been elsewhere investigating other crimes, but their professional patience paid off with the peaceful capture of the wanted men and a message to would-be copycats: "We'll wait you out; you won't escape justice."[4]

Senate Judicial Subcommittee chairman Senator Arlen Spector, the rear-running candidate for the Republican presidential nomination in 1996, became a front-runner for court jester when he probed the Ruby Ridge incident, where a shootout between Randy Weaver's family and U.S. marshals, augmented by FBI agents, ended with three deaths: a marshal, Weaver's wife and his son. ATF's involvement with Weaver was limited to having arrested him months earlier for selling sawed-off shotguns to an ATF informant he'd met at a Nazi conference. Weaver, who wrote letters calling the U.S. government ZOG—the Zionist Occupied Government—gave only one reason for never formally joining the Nazis: "I'm not a joiner." His refusal to appear for that firearms trial brought the marshals to take him in. They came with caution, because neighbors reported Weaver's statement that he "expected federal agents to come to his home, that he was not going to be arrested by anyone, and he would rather fight than go peaceably."

Weaver's renowned attorney, Gerry Spence, played on the jurors' sympathy for a man whose wife and son had been killed. Considering the fact that, like Koresh, Weaver had "invited" federal agents by breaking the law, it sounded like the boy who murdered his parents, then pleaded for mercy "because I'm an orphan." Nevertheless, Spence's talent got Weaver acquitted of the firearms charges.

Senator Specter said the jury "found entrapment" in ATF's conduct of the case, claiming support for this conclusion from a Justice Department investigation. Senator Dianne Feinstein corrected Specter's inaccuracy, reading from that report that stated, "We cannot conclude on the evidence before us that Weaver was coerced or unduly enticed into selling weapons to [the informant]." And ATF director Magaw responded:

It's a matter of, do you believe the federal agents who have sworn to tell the truth, are carrying out a career in this government, and a confidential source who you saw here today [a successful businessman with no criminal history and a track record of truthfulness in his reports]? Do you believe the agents and that informant, or do you believe Randy Weaver when everything Randy Weaver said in terms of four or five neighbors who said he threatened them? . . . If there's

entrapment, where do you show it? I believe the
reports of our agents, the investigation by our agents,
and I believe the confidential informant. I do not
believe Weaver.

Specter paid tribute to Director Magaw's professionalism
and openness, then issued a report recommending that ATF
be abolished. In fact, Specter's plan wasn't aimed merely at
eliminating a bureau. It would make the NRA's dream
come true by eradicating realistic enforcement of the gun
laws. His anemic bid for the presidential nomination died a
few weeks later.[5]

FBI director Louis Freeh offered Congress a solution to
domestic terrorism. "There's no single fulcrum point within the United States government where intelligence regarding domestic terrorism can be properly and in a
constitutional manner be accumulated under somebody's
leadership and direction," Freeh said, "and I'm a great
believer in putting somebody in charge. . . . I think there
needs to be one center and I think it needs to be under the
FBI's control." Considering the FBI's deplorable history of
constitutionality and their persistent refusal to share information with those agencies responsible for investigating
crimes, it's wise to remember that actions speak louder than
words. Centralizing intelligence would aid law enforcement
if the job were given to agents with a track record of
demonstrating the interagency cooperation that prevents
violence. Mr. Freeh's plan would glorify his bureau at the
expense of victims.[6]

The better solution—one that would enhance efficiency
by eliminating the currently duplicative and fragmented
bureaucracy, *and* improve effectiveness in convicting criminals and preventing violence, *and* (unlike most government
plans) do all this at less cost than the present system—is to
give this job to Treasury. These investigative agencies—
ATF, Customs, IRS and Secret Service—have legitimate
jurisdiction over the laws that terrorists violate *before and
during* their vicious acts: illegal weapons, bombing, arson,
gun smuggling, tax evasion and assassination. [See Appendix F for more details.]

It would work because Treasury's agents have demonstrated their ability to work in genuine, two-way (and effective) cooperation with other departments at the federal, state, county and local levels. Even without the G-men's official mandate and huge budgetary support, Treasury agents have already accomplished more in this field than the FBI.[7] Consolidated into one bureau under the most professional management, they'd do even better.[8]

Some folks argue that "small and specialized" is better. Were that true, the FBI would be more effective if we broke it up into several bureaus, each with limited duties: a bank-robbery bureau, a theft bureau, a counterintelligence bureau—each with its own separate headquarters and separate offices in each city. Other people say we must beware of creating a too-powerful police agency. But wouldn't the ubiquitous FBI—unrivaled in power and resources—be better kept in check if the government had another force capable of balancing the scales? Just as their agents "excepted" status keeps pragmatic G-men in line to do their boss's bidding,[9] the existence of an equally powerful bureau—one they couldn't run roughshod over—would compel cooperation.

Legislators sincerely out to help the country and those who crave public approval might be smart to look beyond knee-jerk allegations by gun lovers and those with nothing to lose but their hatred, and listen for people who do more than complain—citizens who speak from the heart.

Two letters might better express the sincere opinions of real people—an agent and a schoolteacher, Americans who know from experience what they're talking about.

April 28, 1995

Dear Friends in Oklahoma City:

It is 3:40 A.M. We are seated at a table in the South Western Bell parking garage eating a wonderful meal prepared by volunteers from the Oklahoma Restaurant Association. Soda pop and fruit from the Salvation Army and a friendly visit from members of the local clergy cheer on weary scene workers. My evidence team of ATF, FBI, OKCPD, and OHP agents and officers are reflecting on the latest news about the horror in the Murrah Federal Building. We started our shift at midnight with the recovery of a woman's shattered body by Oklahoma City firefighters and a search of the area for evidence.

Our conversation turns to militias of self-proclaimed patriots, bomb threats received at federal buildings, so-called talk-show hosts telling their listeners to shoot federal agents in the head. He is talking about those seated around me; people from around the country I have come to know well in the past few days.

Tired, covered with concrete dust, mud and, in some cases, the remains of fellow Americans, I am depressed and angry. . . . Sitting in silence, I look down at the table and see a folded piece of blue craft paper covered with a child's scrawling picture in a rainbow of Crayola colors. I open it and read the simple message inside. "Thank you, rescue workers, for helping the hurt people. God loves you. I love you very much. Justin, Assembly of God." We pass the basket of cards around the table. I notice banners hanging around the garage with messages of love and gratitude from churches, schools and civic organizations. Banners line the security fences saying Thank You and God Bless You. Floral sprays and wreaths line the route back to the blast scene. Team 3 returns to work with new energy.

4:30 A.M. A member of the Metro Dade Search and Rescue Team approaches my partners, OKCPD Bomb Squad Sergeant Randy Kirby and St. Louis ATF Agent Tad Heitzler. The SAR team has found something of great value that they want to turn over to law-enforcement officers for safekeeping. We stand with swelling emotion as the rescuers line up and present a torn and dirty American flag. The staff is sheered in half. The white stars and stripes are stained crimson with the blood of Americans. Human tissue adheres to the fabric. Tad, Randy and I solemnly walk past the security gate at the inner perimeter. With military precision, the police officers, deputy united states marshals and Oklahoma national guardsmen come to attention and salute our nation's colors as we pass by.

I cannot go with them because tears stream down my face. Something priceless was recovered indeed. Dr. Albert Schweitzer said, "The only ones among you who will be truly happy are those who will have sought and found how to serve." Firefighters, paramedics, police officers, sheriff's deputies, highway patrol officers, national guardsmen, FEMA personnel, Salvation Army and Red Cross volunteers; federal officers from ATF, FBI, DEA, Customs, Secret Service, postal inspectors, U.S. marshals; the elderly lady who took my hand and told me how grateful she was that we were here; the two little girls, five and nine years old, standing at the gate with their mother, passing out tiny golden angels; Wes at the restaurant who insisted on paying for our dinner over our protests; the people on the streets who took the time to stop and offer a word of gratitude and encouragement; families and friends left behind in New York, Miami, Virginia Beach, Phoenix, Seattle, Kansas City, San Francisco, Des Moines and Milwaukee; the writers of thousands of cards, notes, and letters of encouragement; people from all over the country who sent mounds of supplies and equipment; all have found ways to serve. American patriots? These are American patriots. The people of Oklahoma City and its capital city—American patriots all.

My memories of Oklahoma City will have sad thoughts of the personal tragedy; the sorrow and fear of people who never deserved such villainy. But my deepest thoughts will be of that bloodstained flag; of the goodness, generosity, and the heartfelt thanks of my brothers and sisters in Oklahoma City.

The days ahead will be dark and filled with challenges for this beautiful city. I pray God will give you the strength and love in the difficult time ahead. We are all humbled by your dignity and spirit. We are so very proud to serve you. Thank you, Oklahoma City. God bless you. God bless America.

Special Agent Kevin L. Kelm, ATF
Milwaukee National Response Team

And one more letter, this one from Trudy Stillwell White:

I teach eighth grade at St. Charles Borromeo Catholic School, about ten miles from where a terrorist bomb shattered not only the federal building in the center of our city but also the serenity of our lives. Like the rest of Oklahoma City, we heard the bomb and continue to feel its terrible shudder.

Three members of our parish community have been found dead. Teachers have attended funerals, older students have been asked to be altar servers for them, and our school cafeteria has been used for a funeral dinner. Our students have made cards, collected money and said prayers. We decorated white lunch sacks with messages to the rescue workers and filled them with snacks. We made and sent to the rescue site a giant banner proclaiming "God Bless You!" in letters fashioned from cutouts of our hands on which we had written prayers and messages.

We Oklahomans are a resilient people and so, even though two of our dead will probably never be found, the center of our city still lies in ruin, and our hearts, like our city, are scarred, we must begin picking up the pieces of our lives and trying to go on. The spring musical in which my eighth-graders will star must still be performed; I must still be sure that my math students know what the Pythagorean Theorem is; I still have to read and grade the *To Kill a Mockingbird* essays which, even more incredibly, my students must write.

On Thursday, one week and a day after the bomb, we were trying to restore some sense of normalcy to the school. The halls were a beehive of activity as students put out castles, consumer fair projects and artwork for a parent-teacher meeting to be held that night. Two of my students were sprawled in the hall painting a scene for the upcoming musical when a knock came at the side door of the school. One of them scurried to open the door to four imposing figures, ATF agents, wearing their helmets and the distinctive uniforms with which we have all become so familiar. They had been cheered by our cards, climbed on a ladder to read the prayers and thoughts on the banner and eaten our snacks. Now they were coming to say "Thank you." Instead of resting or sleeping and still dusty from their twelve-hour shift at the bomb site, these remarkable men, to whom all of Oklahoma City is indebted for their compassionate work, were coming to thank us.

We quickly assembled the school in the cafeteria where the younger children were already eating lunch. The regular cafeteria noises were gradually suspended as the children became aware of the ATF agents entering the room. After a hushed moment of incredulity, the children spontaneously rose to their feet and burst into cheers.

The men were grim and tired from their terrible work, but the welcome of the children seemed to touch them, and they stayed to have lunch and to visit. They had come from across the country, from Phoenix, Fort Worth, Lubbock and Virginia, and they told the students about their families back home and how much they missed them. They explained that the black stripe across their badges, which they wear over their hearts, were for those of their number who had died. "It shows that our hearts are sad," an agent explained. They praised the people of Oklahoma City, saying that they had worked all over the country and did not think that such an outpouring of support and love would have been as great anywhere else. Over and over again, they thanked the children for the cards, the treats and the banner.

The press of children became so great around one of the agents that he could hardly eat. When a teacher went in to rescue him, he said quietly that he could eat later and that he would talk to the children as long as they wanted to talk to him. He didn't add "for all of such is the kingdom of heaven," but we teachers, like the disciples long ago, heard the mild rebuke and stayed quietly at our table.

One of the agents removed himself from the crowd of students and sat silent and alone, watching, his face haggard with fatigue and sorrow. A group of eighth-grade girls observed him, and, with the spontaneous generosity of fourteen-year-olds, ducked across the hall into our room, emerging in a few minutes with a hastily constructed card, its bold Magic Marker letters declaring, "We love you!" They shyly approached the agent and silently handed him the card. An amazing thing happened: He began to cry. The girls stood uncertainly, afraid that they had done something wrong. After a moment, he stood, thanked them gravely and, his eyes still wet, hugged each one of them.

They stayed for about an hour, visiting with the students and the staff. They admired the castles and the artwork; they accepted cinnamon rolls from the cooks, and they told us, the teachers, to hug our children and tell them often that we love them. They never spoke of the horrors that they had seen or complained of their fatigue. They spoke instead of the generosity and kindness of others and of the great courage of our fellow Oklahomans. Again they thanked us, profusely, in spite of our protestations that it was we who should be thanking them. And then they left.

One of my students approached me, her eyes bright with tears and her voice filled with emotion. "Mrs. White," she said, "do you remember the story Father Rick told us before about how Jesus washed the feet of the disciples and Peter said, 'No Lord, don't wash my feet. I'm not worthy'? Well, I think that is just what happened today." She swallowed hard, wrapped her arms around herself and retreated into the usual inarticulate silence of the young adolescent—indeed, of most of us—when we recognize a truth bigger than ourselves.

There is much I hope my students learn this year and take with them the rest of their lives. I hope they remember to write in the active voice most of the time and, although they may not have many opportunities to apply the knowledge that the square of the hypotenuse of a right triangle equals the sum of the square of the sides, I do hope they remember it long enough for their geometry teacher to know that I did my job. I am quite sure that they have already forgotten who was the victor at the Battle of Cowpens during the Revolutionary War.

There are, however, more important lessons I hope they never forget. I hope that they have learned that real men do cry, and that it is the small kindnesses we show one another that really matter. I hope that they realize that, although there is a great deal of evil in the world, there is greater good. Above all, I hope that they remember the day Jesus came to our school. He wore a dusty blue uniform and heavy boots, and on his head was a halo formed by a hard hat with a lamp. He talked with us, shared a meal with us and washed our feet with his tears.

The nation has been amazed at the dignity and courage with which our community is facing the terrible tragedy which has happened here, and we are overwhelmed by the outpouring of compassion from people we do not even know. We are experiencing a living affirmation of the words of a hymn we sang at church on the Sunday after that fateful Wednesday, that "gladly we bear each other's pain." By doing so, we are truly Christ to one another.

Unsentimental politicians who ignore kids because they can't vote should consider the words of the German philosopher Goethe, who wrote, "Children, like dogs, have so sharp and fine a scent that they detect and hunt out everything—the bad before all the rest. They also know well enough how this or that friend stands with their parents; and as they practice no dissimulation, they serve as excellent barometers by which to observe the degree of favor or disfavor at which we stand with their parents."

Two years before Oklahoma City, in the depths of despondency following the murders of four ATF agents at Waco, children from around the country sent thousands of notes.

Dear ATF agent,
   I think that you have been such a good help to
Waco. I'm writing to tell you have a excellent
Easter. I wish you the best of luck.

                                    Bye bye,
                                    Brittany D.

Dear ATF agents,
   Thank you so much for trying to settle this
matter. Please have a very happy Easter. We
talk about your bravery all the time at St.
Paul's. I'm very sorry about your fellow agents
who have been wounded or that have deceased.
Thank you again!

                                    Your friend,
                                    Carolyn V.

Dear ATF Agent,
   Have a Happy Easter. Good Luck! Man!
                                    Your friend,
                                    Matthew S.

   We have serious problems. ATF is the nation's premier
bomb investigators but, terrorists aside, criminals have
murdered more Americans *with firearms* here at home, just
in the past fifty years, than all the soldiers, sailors and
marines killed during all the foreign conflicts in U.S.
history, including the Revolutionary War. Crime won't just
go away.
   Consolidating the fragmented, uncoordinated investigative agencies of the Treasury Department would preserve
the traditions of honor demonstrated for the past 133 years;
it would improve our government's efficiency and effectiveness in dealing with violent criminals; and it would cost
less! Some people don't want that—criminals, gun lovers,
the politicians who milk them for money and the bureaucrats who'd be displaced by the streamlining.
   "Tell your congressman" sounds trite, but it's worked for
the NRA—an organization that claims to represent a mere
1.3 percent of our population.

Afterword

The early days are gone. The silent, simple men who brought law to a harsh wilderness weren't beset by crazy cults or Mafia executioners or traitors who'd destroy the government that epitomizes democracy. And yet, armed with little beyond their instincts and their honor, those first agents left a legacy more lasting than the fading footprints of fleeting fame: tradition. And it's that tradition—preserved by Treasury and instilled into the men and women of its investigative bureaus—that's brought ATF through the pollution of the Prohibition era, the falsehoods of the firearms fraternity, the G-man's greed for glory and the pompous conceit of unworthy leaders.

The agents' future is uncertain. Will politicians cave in for the convenience of selfish gun lovers, or will our elected representatives rise above the NRA's dogma of death on behalf of that great army of anonymous Americans who'd be maimed or dead now, had ATF agents not incapacitated so many armed, criminal predators *before* they robbed and raped and murdered more? Might we even hope that

Congress and the President will opt to make all our lives safer by consolidating Treasury's special agents into a single unit?

Ultimately, the answer will depend upon whether the quiet but determined and persistent voice of sincere citizens can drown the noisy clamor of the agents' enemies.

Appendix A

Endnotes

1

Sources for the account of Ariel Rios et. al. include the author's personal experience and accounts by other agents; ATF Cases 3610-11824514R, 361011824506Y and 370609813001R; Michelmore, Peter, "From Cuba With Hate," *Reader's Digest* December 1988; *New York Times* (12/4/82); *Miami Herald* (12/3–5/82 and 1/19/83); Finn, Robin, "The Undercover Life and Death of Ariel Rios," *Hartford Courant* (Northeast Magazine); *The Agent,* a publication of the National Association of Treasury Agents, 12/82 and 9/83; ATF Mag #02144, 21 April 83; *The Eighteen-Eleven,* Professional Journal of the Federal Law Enforcement Officers Association, 4/86; The Director's Memorandum, No. 5, 1990; Memorandum to ATF Assistant Director by Miami Task Group Program Manager, 1/2/83; Congressional Record, page S13968, 12/6/82; and an interview with Special Agent Alexander D'Atri, given for the ATF training film, *The Psyche of Survival.*

2

1. Notes on the Constitutional Convention by James Madison.
2. *Organization and Functions of Alcohol and Tobacco Tax Divi-*

sion, Investigator Basic Training Publication #1487, 2/66, "History," pages 1–8. Miller, Wilbur R., *Revenuers & Moonshiners,* University of North Carolina Press, 1991; this source provided much of the material given throughout this chapter.

    Among the sources for general historical facts: *Annals of America* (Chicago: Encyclopedia Britannica, Inc., 1968); and Wallechinsky, David, and Irving Wallace, *The People's Almanac,* (Garden City, NY: Doubleday & Co., Inc., 1975); *Civil War Times Illustrated,* vol 13, no. 10, 2/75.

3. The Maurer quotes are from: *Kentucky Moonshine,* by David W. Maurer, (University Press of Kentucky). Details regarding the exploits of Special Agent James Davis and Campbell Morgan may be found in *Mountain Spirits,* by Joseph Earl Dabney (1974), and *Revenuers & Moonshiners, supra.*

4. For information regarding the Prohibition era, we are indebted to: Allsop, Kenneth, *The Bootleggers* (New Rochelle, NY: Arlington House); Kobler, John, *Ardent Spirits* (New York: G.P. Putnam & Sons, 1973); Sann, Paul, *The Lawless Decade* (New York: Crown Publishers); and Coffey, Thomas M., *The Long Thirst* (New York: W. W. Norton & Co.). Begg, Paul, *Jack the Ripper,* (London: Robson Books, Ltd., 1988). London. Facts and anecdotes from these sources are used throughout this chapter.

5. Re alcohol prices/profits, *ibid.* Re salaries: *Field Manual,* Treasury Department, Bureau of Prohibition; Ditzen, L. Stuart, "Cops, Robbers and the Good Old Days," Philadelphia *Inquirer,* 5/11/92.

6. *The Tax Dodgers,* by Elmer Irey, as told to William Slocum, (New York: Greenberg Publisher)

7. Treasury Department, Bureau of Prohibition *Field Manual* no. 1, 1927.

8. *Ibid.*

9. *Ardent Spirits,* by John Kobler (New York: G.P. Putnam's Sons); and *The Tax Dodgers,* by Elmer Irey, as told to William Slocum (New York: Greenberg Publisher); Whitehead, Don, *The FBI Story* (New York: Random House, 1956); Wilson, Frank J., *Special Agent* (New York: Holt, Rinehart Winston); and same sources as note 4.

10. Pickering, Clarence, *The Early Days of Prohibition* (New York: Vantage Press, Inc., 1964).

11. The exploits of Izzy and Moe are drawn from the sources listed in note 4, above.

12. Thorpe, George C., *Digest of Prohibition Cases* (St. Paul, MN: West Publ. Co., 1926); Lapidus, Edith, *Eavesdropping on Trial* (Arlington House); *Olmstead vs. United States,* 277 U.S. 438, 48 S. Ct. 564, 72 L. Ed. 944 (1928).

13. Ness, Eliot, and Oscar Fraley, *The Untouchables* (New York: Julian Messner, 1957).

14. Messick, Hank, *The Silent Syndicate* (New York: MacMillan Co.).

15. The Remus story is drawn from the sources listed in note 4.

16. Same as note 2, above. However, reports regarding agents and policemen wounded are incomplete. In an unknown number of cases, these incidents weren't reported to Washington.

3

1. Sann, Paul, *The Lawless Decade* (New York: Crown Publishers). The Virgil Peterson quote is from his book *The Barbarians in Our Midst* (Boston: Little, Brown & Co., 1952). Additional sources for the Torrio story include: Messick, Hank, *Secret File* (New York: G.P. Putnam's Sons, 1969); "Federal Agents Seize Crime King", *Daily Reporter* (White Plains, NY), 4/23/36; the personal reports and recollections of Special Agent Lewis West, ATF, retired.

2. The case that finally sent Torrio to prison began when IRS Intelligence agents went after Torrio for income tax evasion. The crucial break came when ATF gave them the books they'd seized from Jimmy LaPenna, who'd kept complete records of their Prohibition-era profits.

3. Blum, John Morton, *The Morgenthau Diaries* (Boston: Houghton-Mifflin Co. Inc., 1959); Messick, Hank, *The Silent Syndicate* (New York: MacMillan Co.).

4. *Ibid;* and Salerno, Ralph, and John S. Tompkins, *The Crime Confederation* (Garden City, NY: Doubleday & Co., Inc., 1969); Labor Dept., Consumer Price Index 1913–91, 1/17/92.

5. *Ibid* and Whitehead, Don, *The FBI Story* (New York: Random House, 1956). In the latter, every word of which was approved by the FBI, Whitehead states, "An unsuccessful effort was being made in Congress to consolidate all the Treasury's investigative agencies . . . into a single agency that would over-

shadow the FBI." Interestingly, not all of Secretary Morgenthau's diary survives. Curt Gentry, in his *J. Edgar Hoover: The Man And His Secrets* (New York: Norton, 1991), reports a former FBI agent's admission that he and five fellow G-men "spent weeks in the National Archives covertly removing unfavorable references [to the FBI] in the often-consulted diaries of FDR's treasury secretary . . . and then retyping and renumbering the pages to cover up the deletions." Also see *Publishers Weekly,* 7/12/91, p. 32.

6. Tully, Andrew, *Treasury Agent* (New York: Simon & Schuster, 1958).

7. Material regarding the McNabb case is drawn from *McNabb vs. United States,* 318 U.S. 332 (1943); 142 F. 2d 904 (6th Cir. 1944); 319 U.S. 784 (1942); Congressional Record 9199 (1944); and Reid, John E., and Fred E. Inbau, *Criminal Interrogations and Confessions,* 2nd ed. (Baltimore: Williams & Wilkins Co., 1967).

8. Kellner, Esther, *Moonshine: Its History and Folklore* (New York: Weathervane Books, 1971); Dabney, Joseph E., *Mountain Spirits* (1974).

9. Kellner, *supra;* Perry, Doug "Big Six," (article in *The Courier Journal,* Louisville, KY 5/5/74); AP dispatch "Big Six Henderson . . ." published 7/9/87, *Lexington Herald Leader,* Lexington, KY.

10. Memorandum from G. E. Knapp to ATF director Dwight Avis, dated 9/18/47, titled "Vital Statistics"; memoranda by G. E. Knapp to Director Avis dated 3/8/45; information obtained by Harold Shapiro, Criminal Division, U.S. Justice Department, from FBI assistant director Louis Nichols on 3/23/55.

11. Casualty statistics from ATF roster of agents killed in the line of duty compiled 10/75.

12. Tully, Andrew, *Treasury Agent, supra.*

13. Jeanes, William, "Thunder and Lightning" (article in *Motor Trend,* 6/79); Carr, Jess, *The Second Oldest Profession,* (New York: Prentice-Hall, 1972).

14. *Ibid;* Carr, Jess, *The Second Oldest Profession, supra;* Dabney, Joseph E., *Mountain Spirits* (1974); author's training and interviews with former agents. Re penalties: 26 USC 5685 provides ten years' imprisonment for anyone possessing a device that emits "gas, smoke or fumes" that may be used in evading capture for violation of liquor laws.

ENDNOTES

15. Personal recollections of ATF Special Agent James Layton, retired.

16. Facts re moonshine production in the South are from the author's interviews with agents; Carr, Jess, *supra;* Dabney, Joseph E., *supra;* and Licensed Beverage Industries, NY, NY.

17. Carr, Jess, *supra.*

18. Personal recollections of ATF Special Agent Robert Oakenell, retired, who participated in the raid; Maas, Peter, *The Valachi Papers* (New York: G.P. Putnam's Sons); *The Federal Investigators,* by Miriam Ottenberg, (Englewood Cliffs, NJ: Prentice-Hall, Inc., 1962).

19. Ottenberg, Miriam, *The Federal Investigators, supra.*

20. Facts surrounding the Appalachian Crime Convention are drawn from: Salerno, Ralph, *The Crime Confederation* (Garden City, NY: Doubleday, 1969); Buse, Rene, *The Deadly Silence* (Garden City, NY: Doubleday); Sondern, Frederic Jr. *Brotherhood of Evil* (New York: Farrar, Strauss & Cudahy); Peterson, Virgil W., *The Mob* (Ottawa, IL: Green Hill Publishers, 1983); and the author's interviews with ATF Special Agent Robert O. Rose, who participated in the investigation.

    Previous accounts have reported that NY State Police Sergeant Crosswell had been investigating Barbara since 1944.

    In view of Barbara's reputation and criminal record, this is unlikely. At the time of the 1957 crime convention, Barbara possessed a valid New York State pistol permit.

4

1. Author's personal experience and notes.

2. *Ibid.*

3. *Ibid* and the author's conversations with Special Agent Robert Sanders.

4. This account was related by Special Agent Charles Weems, ATF, retired, with W. Horace Carter in *A Breed Apart* (© 1992, Charles Weems; published by Mr. Weems).

5

1. All of the information regarding criminals circumventing state gun laws is from testimony presented by police at Hearings Before the Subcommittee to Investigate Juvenile Delinquency of the Committee on the Judiciary, U.S. Senate, 89th Congress, First Session, Pursuant to S. Res. 52, S. 1592 (A Bill to Amend the Federal Firearms Act) S.14, S1180 and S.1965; hearings on May 19, 20 and 21; June 2, 3, 8, 24 and 30; July 1, 20, and 27, 1965. Other testimony quoted in this chapter is from the same source.

2. History of the National Firearms Act from Bloomgarden, Henry S., *The Gun* (New York: Grossman Publishers, 1975); 89th Congress, First Session Pursuant to S.Res. 52 (hearings quoted *supra*).

3. Sources for the Nussbaum-Wilcoxin case include the hearings listed above; and Jeffers, H. Paul, *Wanted by the FBI* (Hawthorne Publishers); and Tully, Andrew, *The FBI's Most Famous Cases;* and *The Story of the FBI,* a booklet issued by the Federal Bureau of Investigation, US GPO: 1974, 0-357-781.

4. See source listed in note 1, above.

5. Items advertised by Service Armament Co., 689 Bergen Blvd., Ridgefield, NJ. Copies of these ads were included as Exhibit #14 to the testimony of Sheldon Cohen, IRS Commissioner, at hearings listed in note 1 above.

6. ATF Case # Nebr. 888; author's personal experience.

7. Legislative Resolution 50, passed 6/2/65 by the Nebraska Legislature.

8. See *Waffengesetz* (weapons law), Federal Republic of Germany, enacted 3/13/38 under the Nazi regime and still in force, at least until 1976 (when this author checked) per Sec. 123, Paragraph (1) of the German Constitution. Re Soviet law, see USSR-RSFSR Decree of 9/20/44; and RSFSR Collection of Decrees, 1944, No. 11, Item 69 (also last checked in 1976.)

   Concerning the NRA's knowledge of laws in Communist China, see the 9/84 issue of *The American Rifleman,* where an article on the 1984 Olympics reports the USA winning gold medals for women's air rifle, the English match and skeet shooting. The Chinese team took gold medals for free pistol, running-game target, and the standard rifle.

In all, the USA came home with six of the twenty-seven gold, silver and bronze medals awarded.

9. See note 1, above.

10. Same as note 1, above.

11. *Ibid.*

12. *Haynes vs. United States,* 390 U.S. 85 (1968). Re Kirby case: ATF Case LI #5274(NFA) St. Louis; articles by Billotte, Bill, 5/19 and 20/68, 1/10/69, Omaha NE *World Herald;* author's personal experience.

13. NRA president Glassen's speech was printed in the 6/67 edition of *The American Rifleman.* Also see "Nostalgia Helps Gun Lobby Torpedo Controls," by David C. Acheson, *Washington Post,* 1/10/65.

14. Gun-murder reports extrapolated from the Uniform Crime Reports issued by the FBI. Since many police agencies do not report the weapons used to commit murders within their jurisdiction, the percentage of guns used in municipalities where weapons *were* reported—no more, no less—was applied to the total number of homicides nationwide.

15. Of 3,073,900 burglaries, 51,178 brought jail terms; 639,270 robberies yielded 28,623 prison sentences; and 23,440 homicides ended with the imprisonment of 8,966 killers. See Sourcebook of Criminal Justice Statistics, 1991; U.S. Bureau of Justice Statistics, U.S. Department of Justice, NCJ-137369: Tables 3.127, 4.2, and 5.53.

16. Sources for the Charles Harrelson story include: Baltz, Dan, and M. J. Canville, "Surprise Ending to Sensational Texas Murder Case," *Official Detective Magazine,* 5/70; *State of Texas vs. Charles Harrelson,* Brazoria County Court, Cause #7372.

17. FBI Uniform Crime Reports and Administrative Office of the U.S. Courts.

18. Cover story, *Newsweek,* 6/24/68.

19. *Time,* 6/21/68, p. 15.

20. Facts of the Butler case are from the author's experience.

21. Sources regarding Harrelson: ATF Case #220402801501W; 220409791501Z; Verboon, Jon, "Convicted Contract Killer Arrested on Loaded Dice Charge," *Houston Chronicle,* 2/2/80; "Officers in West Texas Arrest Fugitive Wanted Here on Two Felony Charges," *Houston Post,* 9/3/80; "Wood Informant

Provides New Clues," *Houston Post,* 1/28/80; "Wood Witness Says Life Threatened," *Daily Telegram,* Temple, TX, 6/19/81; "Harrelson's Pal Refuses to Testify," *Caller Times,* Temple, TX, 6/20/81; Thornton, Mary, "Five Indicted in '79 Murder of Federal Judge in Texas," *Washington Post,* 4/16/82; UPI dispatch, "Arrests Made in 1979 Death of Judge," printed in the Portland, Maine, *Press Herald* on 4/16/82; Baltz, Dan, "Jury Convicts Harrelson in Judge Wood's Murder," *Washington Post,* 12/15/82.

22. See Appendix J.

6

1. This information and other information regarding DePugh, et. al, are from ATF Case #StL 8201(MV), intelligence files compiled at ATF headquarters by Special Agent John W. Kern; the author's personal involvement/investigations of DePugh; *The Minutemen,* by J. Harry Jones, Jr. (Garden City, NY: Doubleday & Co., 1968).

2. FBI Bureau File #62-107621; KC Field Office File #62-7797.

3. Donald, June and Maryann Telerman are pseudonyms. Their ordeal ended more than twenty years ago. It serves no purpose to publicize their true names again. The name Ed Hickey has been changed for the same reason. All of the facts regarding their experiences with the Minutemen are from evidence obtained during ATF investigations, the author's personal interviews with "Donald" and "June," and the following articles by Harry Jones Jr. in *the Kansas City Times:* "Attorney Says DePugh Held 2 Captives 6 Weeks," 9/22/70; "Tells Jury DePugh Kept Her in Box," 9/24/70; trial testimony during September 1970, at Albuquerque, NM, re *U.S. vs. Robert DePugh.*

4. See FBI files cited in note 2, above.

5. "DePugh Sentenced to 30 Months in Prison," by John T. Dauner, *Kansas City Star,* 7/21/92; "Sex Suspect's Home Yields Guns," by R. George Smith, Omaha *World Herald,* 9/18/81. The author also testified at this trial.

7

1. *Newsweek,* 2/23/70.

2. *Ibid;* "Panthers Share S.L.A. Ideas," Lofton, John D. Jr., *Kansas City Star,* 7/10/74; "Armed Raids on Police Unit," AP dispatch, *Kansas City Star,* 10/24/70; "Charge 15 Panthers in Detroit Police Slaying," AP dispatch, *Kansas City Times,* 10/26/70; "Policemen, Targets of Attacks," Cook, Louise, *Kansas City Times,* 9/17/70; the official FBI description of the Panthers was attached to FBI reports during the 1970s.

3. ATF Case #mOw-2853, and author's personal experience/notes.

4. *Omaha World Herald,* 12/15/74.

5. *Portland Press Herald* (ME), 11/25/81.

6. Lawrence, M. A., *Eagle Tribune,* 7/19/76.

7. *Kansas City Star* television schedules 2/12/74 and throughout the season.

8. Much of the information about the SDS Weathermen is drawn from articles in *Life Magazine,* 10/18/68 and 3/27/70; "The Destruction of Diana," Franks, Lucinda, and Thomas Powers, a UPI series condensed in *The Reader's Digest,* 11/70; and "It's Nice to Be Ambidextrous," by David Nyhan, *Boston Globe,* 1/25/81.

9. Facts disclosed to author (while an agent) by Special Agent James Layton and others involved in the investigation of Stead, et al. The FBI agent's testimony was reported 4/27/73 in *Kansas City Times.*

10. ATF case files and memoranda; author's contemporaneous conversations and subsequent interviews with Special Agent Thomas Sledge, Supervisor Dwight Thomas and others; FBI-Omaha file #157-18687; "Gallup Quits over Federal Halt of Raid," by Bill Billotte, *Omaha World Herald,* 9/2/70.

11. See Appendix E.

12. *Ibid.*

8

1. Source: International Association of Chiefs of Police, quoted 9/25/88, "Seized Guns Are Destroyed . . ." by Wayne Greene, Tulsa, OK, *Sunday World.*

2. New York *Daily News,* 4/22/81; New York *Post,* 4/22/81; Providence, RI, *Bulletin,* 6/8/81.

3. ATF headquarters summary report of Operation Pathway—a series of 1980 investigations that produced the conviction of sixty-seven gun runners.

4. The Decker investigation was conducted by the author.

5. Brokaw, Tom, NBC News (8/24/84); film clip of Copenhagen porn dealer who, while admitting that the acts committed to make movies of prepubescent children were "not good for them," added, "If I not do it, someone else will." Usage of this rationalization by drug dealers is too common to list.

6. Court case *U.S. vs. Jackson,* Nov. 1972, 352 Fed. Sup. 672, Affirmed 480 F. 2d 927, reported to members by the NRA in *The American Rifleman,* 4/75, as "A Court Case of Consequence," by Judge Bartlett Rummell, based on a 1972 court decision.

7. ATF Cases #481208734002C, 481212734003K, 481101733502X; "Judge to Rule in Former Austinite's Gun ID Case," by Cox, Austin *American Statesman,* 4/11/75; "Guns Found . . ." UPI, published in *New York Times,* 9/4/73 (re murder, two NYCPD officers); "Suspect in Cop Slaying," *San Francisco Chronicle,* 8/30/73; "Suspect Arrested in Fatal Robbery," UPI, published 11/6/81, Portland, ME, *Press Herald.* "New Suspect Arrested in Brink's Shootout," by Joyce Wadler and John Kennedy, *Washington Post,* 10/28/81; ATF investigation #441910818006N (re Brinks shootout).

8. Among the gun peddlers caught by ATF: a Georgia policeman, Albany, GA, *Herald,* 5/21/75; re active-duty U.S. Marines, San Jose, CA, *Mercury,* 6/16/78; re schoolteacher Richard Traylor, *Washington Post,* 5/22/80; re Dr. Chomsky, Newark, NJ, *Star-Ledger,* 3/20/80 and the Paterson, NJ, *News,* 3/23/81; re Army general Carl Turner, the Fayetteville, NC, *Times,* 5/27/75 and 5/28/75, memo from Kansas City ATF Supervisor Frank Belecky to SAC, St. Louis, re Turner's acquisition of guns from KCMoPD Chief Clarence M. Kelley, who would later become

director of the FBI [ATF's investigation revealed no improprie-ty by Chief Kelley]; re Manual Rodriguez, *New York Post*, 9/20, 22 and 2/8/76; New York *Daily News*, 5/17/76; the Mt. Kisco, NY, *Patent Trader*, 10/21/76; *New York Times*, 5/17/76 and 9/28/76; Washington *Star*, 5/17 and 1/8/76; *Washington Post*, 5/17 and 1/8/76; *San Francisco Chronicle*, 5/18/76.

9. FBI agent's quote: articles by Hersch, Seymour, *New York Times Magazine*, 6/14 and 2/1/81.

10. *Ibid* ATF Case #321005783004Y; ATF Case #4007028025 02P; the author's contemporaneous conversations with persons involved in the investigation; ABC-TV *Nightline*, 4/29/83; *Washington Post*, 4/26/80, 2/24/81, 9/12/81, 12/23/81, 2/13/82, 6/19/82, 7/22/82, 7/27/82, 8/3/82, 8/7/82, 9/22/82, 10/30/82, 11/16/82, 11/17/82, 12/18/82 and 12/21/82. *Parade Magazine*, 9/18/83; *Newsweek*, 7/20/81; the following wire service articles published in the Portland, ME, *Press-Herald*: AP 11/18/82, UPI, 1/23/83, AP 2/19/83; *Philadelphia Inquirer*, 2/3/81; *New York Times*, 7/14/81.

11. ATF Case #461301767002E; Philadelphia *News*, 6/12/81; *Washington Post*, 11/18/82.

12. *Newsweek*, 11/30/81.

13. *Washington Post*, 10/27, 28, and 29, 11/19/82.

14. *Washington Post*, 4/11/77.

15. ATF Case #420310800502R; Newark, NJ, *Star-Ledger*, 4/22/77.

16. ATF Intelligence Report titled "*.22 Silencer Killings, 7/1/76–11/1/78, Analysis*"; Anderson, Jack, and Les Whitten, syndicated column in *Washington Post*, 12/6/77.

17. Conversation quoted by Demaris, Ovid, in *The Last Mafioso* (New York: Times Books, 1981).

18. Re Amirato, et. al.: ATF Case #360701783004Y.

19. Re Jackie Gail and others; *ibid* and ATF Case #270511793001V.

20. Gun dealers' arrests reported in *ATF Information Bulletin*, 8/13/79; re Officers Madeja and Ahrens, ATF Case #270511793001V; *Chicago Sun Times*, 9/28 and 30/80; re Allen Dorfman murder: article from *Chicago Tribune*, re-printed 1/22/84 in *Kansas City Star*.

21. Re Minnick: "Officials Seeking Fugitive Find Weapons . . .", by Norman Leigh, Youngstown, OH, *Vindicator*, 1/9/88; "Elu-

sive Bank Robber Suspected in Repeat Job," by Brian Kladko, *Baltimore Sun,* 2/11/88; "Md. Bank Robber with False ID, Toupee, Sidesteps Police in Ohio," by Brian Kladko, *Baltimore Sun,* 2/7/88; "Guns, Bullets, Cash Tell Story of Captured Minnick," by S. M. Khalid, *Baltimore Sun,* 5/3/88.

22. Regarding homicide by firearm, see Appendix I.

9

1. ATF Newsletter *All The Facts,* 7/74; "Two Convicted in LaPolla Killing," *Hartford Times* (CT), 11/12/75.

2. Greenya, John, *Blood Relations* (San Diego: Harcourt Brace Jovanovich, 1989).

3. Sources regarding the investigation of the Jupiter Mill bombing are from *State,* Columbia, SC, 8/14/71; *Gaffney Ledger,* Gaffney, SC, 4/5/74; *All the Facts* (ATF newsletter), Summer 1974.

4. Sources re the Rochester, NY, gang war: Hearings before the U.S. Senate Permanent Subcommittee on Investigations, Committee on Government Affairs, "Organized Crime and the Use of Violence," May 2–5, 1980; ATF Fugitive Alert for suspect Starkweather, *Democrat & Chronicle,* Rochester, NY, 1/17/78, 6/29/78, 11/15/78, 11/19/78, 3/12/80; *Evening News,* Buffalo, NY, 7/31/78, 10/25/78, 2/16/79, 4/17/79; *Courier Express,* Buffalo, NY, 8/6/78, 2/16/79, 2/1/80; *Times Union,* Rochester, NY, 7/1/78, 7/20/78, 7/31/78, 4/12/79; *Times Union,* Albany, NY, 1/29/80.

5. Sources re ATF's investigation of the Carbone mob: U.S. Senate Hearings quoted in previous appendix note; *All the Facts* (ATF newsletter); *Kansas City Times,* 5/3/80; *New York Times,* 3/29/79; *News Tribune,* Tacoma, WA, 12/1/78; *Oregon Journal,* Portland, OR, 1/17/81; *Times,* Seattle, WA, 1/9/79, 1/28/79, 5/16/79, 5/18/79; *Seattle Post-Intelligencer,* 4/5/79, 11/30/78, 12/20/78.

6. Source re L. V. Wade: *Louisville Times* (KY), 2/4/87.

7. Sources re bombing of the Free Welcome Church: *News Reporter,* Whiteville, NC, 2/12/81, 2/16/81; *Wilmington Morning Star,* (NC), 3/6/81, 2/20/81, 2/13/81, 2/24/81; *Tribune,* Tabor City, NC, 2/25/81.

8. Bombings by members of Teamsters Local 385: ATF Inv. #360403772008R; as reported in BHQ Monthly Narrative Report; "The Revenuers Are Goin'," by Burton T. Miller, *Gun*

World, 3/75; *Sentinel Star,* Orlando, FL, 11/6/76, 3/23/78; and the author's personal conversations with officials involved.

9. ATF Investigation #410105730049T; *Chattanooga Times,* 8/30/64, 6/17/75, 6/29/74, 4/18/74, 7/19/74; *News-Free Press,* Chattanooga, TN, 11/14/73, 3/6/74, 4/10/74, 6/25/74, 7/5/74, 9/4/74; ATF Investigation #410110733001D; and author's conversations with personnel involved. [All re Kinzel Bates, et al.]

10. Re JRM Coal Co. investigation: ATF Case #33710841016; re arrest of California bomb investigator: "Specialist Who Led Probe Charged in Bombing Case," by Dan Bernstein, *Sacramento Bee Final* (CA), 11/16/89.

11. *The Mormon Murders,* by Steven Naifeh and Gregory White Smith, (New York: Weidenfeld & Nicholson, 1988); AP dispatch "Even in Prison, Utah Man Leaves a Trail of Forgery," published 10/29/95, *Maine Sunday Telegram.*

12. Sources re the Rhodes bombing: *Park City News,* Bowling Green, KY, 11/11/75; *Louisville Times,* (KY), 9/22/75, 7/9/76; *Courier Journal,* 6/3/75; and *News Enterprise,* Elizabethtown, KY, 6/3/75 and 2/10/76.

13. Re the Lucier murder investigation: ATF Case # 500711752009H; ATF Office of Internal Affairs investigation #770166; seven-page untitled report filed by FBI Special Agent-in-Charge Harlan Phillips, St. Louis, MO, dated 2/22/77; letter from St. Louis County Prosecutor Courtney Goodman Jr., dated 7/13/76; the following articles in the *St. Louis Post-Dispatch,* all under the byline Ronald J. Lawrence: "Clayton Phone Executive Was Killed by Mistake," 2/11/77; "Hypnosis Yielded Clue in Death of Lucier," 2/13/77; "Lag in Lucier Case Laid to FBI Inquiry," 2/14/77; "Bomb Maker Reported Near Lucier Blast Site," 2/27/77; "Lucier Killing Unsolved Despite Intensive Study," 7/24/80; "Criticism by Family of Lucier," 2/15/77; the author's personal conversations with case agents and the author's personal notes/recollections while assigned to peripheral aspects of the case.

14. Hearing, Subcommittee on Criminal Laws and Procedures, Committee of the Judiciary, U.S. Senate, 9/14/77; Report of the [same subcommittee] on S. 2013, U.S. Government Printing Office, Washington: 1978; ATF Annual Report, FY-79.

10

1. *American Jurisprudence,* "Proof of Facts," vol. 15, 1973 supplement.

2. "Witness Says Tests Show Shirey Fired Gun or Guns," *Press Democrat,* Santa Rosa, CA, 4/23/76.

3. "Ptl. Ridley Back on Duty," *Virginia Progress Index,* 2/26/74.

4. "Gunpowder Residue Is Key to Solving Crimes," *Mechanical Engineering,* 10/92.

5. ATF Case #370201731044H.

6. "Denver Man Convicted in Bomb Conspiracy," *Denver Post,* 7/11/74.

7. "Kleason Jury Decided 'Inconceivable Case'" by John Sutton, *American-Statesman,* Austin, TX, 6/5/75.

8. "ATF's Firearms Experts Called on to Identify, Test Variety of Firearms," by Ed Owens, *Police Chief,* 9/87.

9. ATF Case #53230803034.

10. ATF North Atlantic Region RDI's Monthly Narrative Report 3/4/81; author's conversation with ATF supervisor Lou Borelli, 7/16/81.

11. "Police Solve Crime as Backward Hunt Discloses Killer," by Renee Krause, *Fort Lauderdale News,* 4/4/89.

12. "Elkhart Man Confesses to Conrail Murders," *Ft. Wayne News Sentinel* (IN), 4/4/79.

13. "Deadly Carolina Export: Cheap Guns for North," by Paul Clancy, Detroit, MI, *Free Press,* 12/19/73; and "Guns for Sale—by the Thousands," by Richard Ryan, *The Sunday News,* 5/4/75.

14. *Ibid.*

11

1. Details surrounding the Library Incident are contained in a letter from Treasury Secretary David M. Kennedy to Sam Ervin, Chairman, Senate Subcommittee on Constitutional Rights, dated 7/29/70.

2. Re Shaffer: NRA magazine *The American Rifleman,* 11/71; official memoranda and case report; the author's contemporaneous conversations with case agent Dwight Thomas, Special

Agent James Duff and others; court transcript: *U.S. vs. Ronald Shafer.*

3. Re Ballew: *The American Rifleman,* 7/71, 8/71; official ATF files; the author's personal conversations with Special Agent William Seals and others; transcript of civil case, *Kenyon F. Ballew vs. United States of America,* Civ. No. 72-283-H, U.S. District Court, District of Maryland.

4. Re Gray: Epstein, Edward J., *Agency of Fear* (New York: G.P. Putnam's Sons); AP dispatch, "Gray Quits Helm of FBI Amid Tempest over Files," *Kansas City Star,* 4/27/73.

5. Re Acree: *Agency of Fear (supra);* Schnepper, Jeff A., *Inside IRS* (New York: Stein & Day, 1978); AP dispatch, "Customs Chief Named as Caulfield Contact," *Washington Post,* 4/14/74; Kuttner, Bob, "White House Pressure on IRS Detailed," *Washington Post* 7/17/74; AP dispatch, "Ex-Nixon Aide Tells of IRS Contact," *Kansas City Times,* 4/12/74, page 6.

6. Re Turner: author's personal experience; reports re ATF Case #SI-3437; the Fayetteville, NC, *Times* article dated 5/28/75, detailing Turner's admissions to a Senate subcommittee that he'd sold $2,000 worth of firearms to Earl Redick, a man from whom U.S. Customs agents seized the weapons, destined for Haitian revolutionaries. Turner also obtained firearms from the Kansas City police department, but ATF's investigation proved that police chief (and later FBI director) Clarence M. Kelley was not involved in any illegal transaction.

7. Re Caulfield: *Agency of Fear* (see note 4, *supra*); see sources listed in note 5, *supra.* Murray, David, "Nixon 'in' on politics in the IRS?," *Chicago Sun Times,* 7/17/74; Wieghart, James, and Frank VanRiper, "Report IRS Posts Sought for Caulfield, Liddy," *New York Daily News,* 6/13/74; Lukas, J. Anthony, *Nightmare: The Underside of the Nixon Years* (New York: Viking Press, 1976); AP dispatch, "Caulfield Aware Offer Illegal," published in *Kansas City Star,* 5/23/73; AP dispatch, "Requested by Schultz, Caulfield Resigns . . ." published 5/25/75 in *Kansas City Times.*

8. Caulfield's activities immediately after Watergate from the author's notes of conversations with agents who observed these events.

9. Re Thrower: sources cited in note 7, above, Shannon, Marga-

ret, "Before Watergate: Randolph Thrower vs. the Nixon White House," *The Atlanta Journal and Constitution,* 4/7/74.

10. Miscellaneous organized crime cases: Briefing Report, ATF Enforcement Activities, July–December 1972.

11. U.S. Senate Subcommittee on Treasury and Postal Appropriations, Hearings for the FY-74 ATF budget.

12. U.S. Senate Subcommittee on Treasury and Postal Appropriations, Hearings for the FY-75 ATF budget.

13. U.S. Senate Subcommittee on Treasury and Postal Appropriations, Hearings for the FY-76 ATF budget.

14. ATF Case #321001773009Y.

12

1. Re Jones and Gillispie: ATF Cases #370301730020Y; #370304740002V; #300203744050V; the author's personal experience and contemporaneous conversations with the case agents and prosecutors.

2. *Ibid.* and Ewell, James, "Police, Agents Smash Plot to Rob Executive," Dallas *Morning News,* 3/22/74.

3. The Katz sentence was reported as "Stamp Dealer Sentenced," *Kansas City Times,* 4/15/75; also see case files listed in note 1, above.

4. Re Ferina: ATF Case #370311730001C and author's personal experience.

5. Re Carderella: ATF Case #370306740100U and author's personal experience.

6. Hartman, Aline, and Patrick J. Dunn, "Killing Similar to Mancuso Case," *Kansas City Times,* 3/29/84.

7. Cilwick, Ted, "Suffocation, Not Choking, Caused Carderella Death," *Kansas City Times,* 2/29/84.

8. Records of U.S. Justice Department Strike Force #17.

9. Clark, Ramsey. *Crime in America,* (New York: Simon & Schuster, 1970), p. 82.

13

1. *Atlanta Journal and Constitution,* 9/11/78; *Rome News Tribune* (GA), 9/10/78, 9/11/78, 1/18/79; author's contemporaneous conversations with investigative personnel involved in the case.

2. ATF Case # 390811776009S; *Union,* San Diego, CA, 3/11/78, 8/30/78; *Tulsa World* (OK), 7/12/79, 7/26/79; *Tulsa Tribune,* 5/25/78; Muskogee, OK, *Daily Phoenix and Times Democrat,* 1/12/79; *Daily Oklahoman,* Oklahoma City, 6/20/78; ATF Case #471003784010S; *Free Lance Star,* Fredericksburg, VA, 5/27/78; *News Leader,* Richmond, VA, 5/9/78.

3. Austin, TX, *American Statesman,* 10/26/78; *Trentonian* (NJ), 10/13/78; Enid, KS, *Morning News,* 4/12/74; Batesville, AR, *Guard & Record,* 2/13/78.

4. ATF Case #481109773513N; memorandum from SAC; San Francisco, to Assistant Director, ATF, dated 6/6/78; *Star Bulletin,* Honolulu, Hawaii, 5/10/78; *Press Democrat,* Santa Rosa, CA, 3/27/78; *Reading Searchlight* (CA), 8/2/78; author's contemporaneous conversations with investigating agents.

5. *RCMP Gazette,* vol. 42, no. 10; FBI testimony in hearing before U.S. Senate Permanent Subcommittee on Investigations of the Committee on Governmental Affairs.

6. Early incidents of violence by outlaw biker gangs extracted from an undated report submitted circa 1972 by ATF-Los Angeles to acquaint headquarters personnel with "the types of individuals the ATF Omega Program is directed toward." The report contains dozens of similar documented incidents.

7. ATF Summary, "Highlights, Omega Program," covering the period from 3/73 through 5/73 and listing 34 particularly significant arrests.

8. Monthly PPP Report from SAC, Los Angeles, to Assistant Director, ATF, 5/23/83.

9. *Ibid.*

10. ATF Case #300105755001J; statement by Special Agent Raymon L. Todd; case report cover letter to U.S. Attorney Ortega.

11. ATF Case #010212801026A; *Arizona Republican,* Phoenix, AZ, 9/13/75.

12. Buffalo, NY, *Courier Express,* 3/22/76, 5/11/76, 5/14/76, 6/4/76; Buffalo, NY, *Evening News,* 3/12/76; Columbus, OH, *Dispatch,* 11/2/78; Niagara Falls, NY, *Gazette,* 3/18/76; *Union Sun Journal,* 5/11/76, 6/1/76.

13. The author's contemporaneous conversations with Omega Project Coordinator Edward L. Hopkins; Long Beach, CA, *Press Telegram,* 2/21/77; San Antonio, TX, *Light,* 7/8/73; Seattle, WA, *Post-Intelligencer,* 7/3/73; Washington, D.C., *Star,* 3/31/75; Orange County, CA, *Register,* 5/18/75.

14. ATF Case #461304767002P; Case #462203749004R; Philadelphia, PA, *Evening Bulletin,* 3/21/76; *Philadelphia Sunday Bulletin,* 3/21/76; "Profile of Organized Crime—Mid-Atlantic Region"; hearings before U.S. Senate Permanent Subcommittee on Investigations of the Senate Committee on Governmental Affairs, 2/15/83, 2/23/83 and 2/24/83.

15. ATF Case #461301787003P; Case #460408741008X; Case #462210779001Y; 462210779002B; Philadelphia, PA, *Daily News,* 9/13/79; the author's contemporaneous conversations with agents, supervisors and others directly involved.

16. Re Bland and Brady: *The Investigator,* 5/92. Re Rushing: Palleson, Tim, "Feds Throw Book at Local Crime," *Palm Beach Post,* (FL), 6/8/92. Re Eubanks: Daniels, Deborah J., "Fed Jury Convicts Local Man," Danville, IN, *Republican,* 4/30/92. Re Morris: Dawson, Adam, "Vicious Offender Gets 15 Years under Career Criminal Law," *Orange County Register* (CA), 2/4/88. Re Bryant: "Six Gang Members Get Stiff Sentences," by Eric Velasco, *The Macon Telegraph* (GA), 12/21/91.

14

1. Remarks by Lt. W. R. "Casey" Jones to 1979 convention, International Association of Chiefs of Police.

2. Re Wilkinson and Santiago case: official ATF reports; contemporaneous notes from author's conversations with agents who conducted investigation; *Above the Law: Police and the Excessive Use of Force,* Skolnick, Jerome H., and James J. Fyfe (New York: Free Press, 1993). *Time* (12/19/77) reported that this case instigated a series of front-page articles in *Philadelphia Inquirer* exposing brutality in the Philadelphia Police Department.

3. "Where There's Smoke," by Robert W. Kotzbauer, *Philadelphia Inquirer,* 5/27/79. ATF Report, "ATF National Response Teams," 1/82; ATF Case #63210841002D. Re Brach: "Death Probes Reveal Seamy Side of Horsy Set," by Sharon Cohen, AP, published 8/28/94, *Portland Press Herald* (ME).

4. ATF Case #460403791001Z.

5. "Arsonist Profile Is Similar to Suspect," by David Goldstein, *Kansas City Times,* 8/12/88; "Sniffing Out Crime," by Kitty Caparella, *Philadelphia Daily News* (undated).

6. Statistical odds computed via comparison of conviction rate when ATF entered this field (i.e., 2 percent) versus the 50 percent solution rate achieved in cases entered by ATF's arson task forces. Of those charged, the conviction rate is about 95 percent.

15

1. "Bureau of Alcohol, Tobacco and Firearms Annual Report," FY-79, page 19.

2. Memo drafted by Special Agent Bill Kern from Acting Assistant Director (Criminal Enforcement) to Assistant Director (Administration) dated 9/8/77.

3. See Appendix J, study of effectiveness, GCA enforcement.

4. Memo from Mr. Keathley to all SACs dated 6/23/78, "Use of News Media for Purchase of Information." Keathley's order to remove "Armed and Dangerous" felon entries from the Treasury Enforcement Communication System (TECS) computer was related to author on 11/14/78 by TECS chief Richard Johnson.

5. Memo from Mr. Keathley to all SACs, "Gun Shows and Flea Markets," 7/21/78. Among high-profile crime guns acquired at gun shows: reported in a memo from the director to the secretary of the Treasury on 5/25/78; the pistol used by Sarah Jane Moore in her attempt to assassinate President Ford; a handgun used to murder a Brinks guard; one carbine used by the notorious Symbionese Liberation Army and another used by the Black Liberation Army to kill a San Francisco policeman. Also *Mercury*, San Jose, CA, 6/5/78.

6. Memo from Mr. Keathley to Deputy Director, "Gun Shows," 3/28/79.

7. Details regarding Internal Affairs investigations and resulting disciplinary actions are from facts acquired during a study conducted by the author and editor-writer Ellen M. Drummey. During fiscal year 1978 alone, ATF's annual report revealed 178 IA investigations of bureau agents, regulatory inspectors, clerical and administrative personnel. Of these, 140 were cleared of alleged misconduct and 31 were subject to adverse actions. Two cases were "referred to other law-enforcement agencies" because IA uncovered crimes within the jurisdiction of those agencies; five employees were allowed to resign. A

report of the survey by Moore and Drummey was submitted to Assistant Director Miles Keathley on 2/5/79.

8. "Ex-Treasury Agent Found Guilty of Embezzling Guns," *Denver Post,* 4/4/74; "Special Message [to all personnel] from the Director," by Rex Davis, 7/3/74.

9. From the files of IA; the transcript of the hearing; and reports published by *The Agent,* Official Publication, National Association of Treasury Agents. "Treasury Agent Sues for Rights Violation," *Federal Times,* 3/14/77.

10. Author's personal experience.

11. From the files of the Program Review Division, ATF, "Review of the Chicago Division," and author's personal experience.

12. "Zebra" was the SFPD's code name for a series of random murders. Details of the gun trace were reported by Adams, Nathan, "The Tracing of Beretta A47469," *Reader's Digest,* 1/78.

13. "Gun Tracing Systems Study Report," Technical Report #5, Search Group, Inc., Sacramento, CA, 6/76.

14. Mustin's remarks from "Official NRA Journal," *The American Rifleman,* 8/78.

15. *Congressional Record,* 6/7/78.

16. *Ibid.;* author was present and heard Risenhoover's remark.

17. "Help Needed on Gunrunning," *Esquire Magazine,* 9/26/78.

18. These incidents are from the author's personal experience.

19. Hearings before a Subcommittee of the Committee on Government Operations, House of Representatives, 97th Congress, 2nd Session, 12/9/82, pages 5 and 8, re congressional poll of 1,600 officials; remarks by Rep. Fortney H. Stark, U.S. House of Representatives, *Congressional Record,* 6/13/84, re survey of 100 South Florida law-enforcement agencies by the Select Committee on Narcotics Abuse and Control asking which federal agency was the most cooperative. The cops' personal reaction to ATF was typified in a *New York Times* article ["Crazy Angelo Meets the Preacher," by Allan J. Mayer, 6/13/76], which stated:

> New York police are notorious for hating to work with most federal law-enforcement agencies. The ATF is a notable exception. . . . It's also a matter of style. "With ATF, it's always give and take,"

says Sgt. Michael Harris, who heads a Police Department squad of gun crime specialists.

16

1. ATF Case #41080581; *Nashville Tennessean,* 5/26 thru 5/28/81 and 6/10/81; Thompson, Jerry, *My Life in the Klan* (New York: G.P. Putnam's Sons, 1982).

2. ATF Case #481309802501K, *Mercury,* San Jose, CA, 2/4/81; *Tribune-TODAY* (CA), 10/9/80; *San Francisco Chronicle,* 10/11/80.

3. ATF Case #320403812009K; *Washington Post,* 12/9/81; Portland, ME, *Press Herald,* 1/11/82; ATF Newsletter, *All the Facts.*

4. ATF Case #320103810008J; *All the Facts,* 6/81; *Washington Post,* 6/21/81; *Baltimore Sun,* 7/30/81; Hagerstown, MD, *Morning Herald,* 6/27/81.

5. ATF Case #320901815501R; Wilmington, DE, *News,* 6/4/81; Dover, DE, *News,* 6/4/81.

6. ATF Case #260110791503N; Charlotte, NC, *Observer,* 3/3/81, 3/4/81, 3/11/81, 3/18/81, 3/20/81, 6/2/81, 7/7/81, 7/14–7/19/81, 7/22/81, 9/1/81, 9/16–21/81, 9/12–17/83.

7. Nazi Commander Covington's quotes are from the secret "Handbook, National Socialist Party of America," issued to followers 8/12/80.

8. *Ibid.*

9. ATF Case #480810761507W; *Sacramento Bee,* 2/23/77.

10. Passaic, NJ, *Herald News,* 11/11/77; Newark, NJ, *Star Ledger,* 11/12/77; Trenton, NJ, *Trentonian,* 3/22/78; ATF Case #420311770509R.

11. *All the Facts,* 7/8/81; *Time,* 5/11/81; *Washington Star,* 7/13/81, 7/15/81; *Hammond's Almanac,* 10/80; *Baltimore Sun,* 6/23/81; *Philadelphia Inquirer,* 6/18/81; New Orleans *Times-Picayune,* 6/10/81; Jackson, MS, *Daily News,* 5/21/81; *Washington Post,* 4/29/81; Portland, ME, *Press Herald,* 6/28/81; letter from the headquarters of the Knights of the Ku Klux Klan, mailed to all KKK members on 4/9/83.

12. This investigation of MOVE is not related to a subsequent case where police dropped a bomb onto MOVE's roof which ignited an entire block of homes—an incident that occurred years later. *All the Facts,* 6/81; *New York Times,* 7/23/81; *Philadel-*

phia *Inquirer,* 5/17/81, 7/14/81–7/16/81; 8/5/81; *Philadelphia Bulletin,* 2/11/81; UPI dispatch published 12/11/82 in the Portland, ME, *Press Herald; Washington Post,* 3/17/78 and 8/19/78; Rochester, NY, *Democrat & Chronicle,* 7/11/81.

13. *Newsweek,* 8/22/83.

14. New Orleans *Times Picayune,* 6/26/81; Louisville, KY, *Times,* 11/15/78; Paducah, KY, *Sun Democrat,* 6/12/78; ATF Criminal Enforcement Briefing Book, 1/81; ATF Case #420306810505C.

15. The segment submitted by the FBI for the U.S. Attorney General's 1981 Annual Report listed twenty-eight convictions under "Terrorism" for which the FBI took full and exclusive credit. In fact, the conviction of five Croatian National Resistance members (not detailed in this chapter) resulted from a joint operation by ATF and the Cleveland police department during which ATF Special Agent Nicholaj Dikey penetrated the terrorist group undercover and obtained a substantial part of the evidence that brought three arrests for conspiracy to commit multiple murder. Also see Johns, Walter Jr., "Plot Foiled, 3 Lives Saved," *Cleveland Press,* 9/15/80.

Among the cases covered in this chapter for which the FBI claimed total credit were those against nine members of the Islamic Guerrillas of America, the one-man Iran Free Army, and the capture of the would-be invaders of Dominica. Actually, they'd made substantial contributions to the Islamic Guerrillas investigation, and in one case they'd loaned a female agent to pose as an ATF man's girlfriend, but their participation in the other cases was limited to accepting ATF's invitation to assist with the final arrests. Also see Appendix E.

17

1. "No Reform at All," *Dunklin Daily Democrat,* Kennett, MO, 6/26/81.

2. S.1862, proposed to the U.S. Senate 10/5/79; *Congressional Record,* Senate, S4126, 4/29/81, re later version of FOPA.

3. See Appendix I, Homicides in the USA, 1910 through 1983.

4. Hearings before the Subcommittee on Crime of the Committee on the Judiciary, House of Representatives, 10/28, 30; 11/9/85; 2/19 and 27/86, Serial No. 131 (hereinafter "HR-131"), page 391, re federal firearms licensees. See Appendix H.

5. Re Dickerson's disinterest in reading report, HR-131, page 412.

6. Senate Hearings Before the Committee on Appropriations, Proposed Dissolution of Bureau of Alcohol, Tobacco and Firearms, FY 1983, page 128, regarding the FCIA assessment of Secret Service management.

7. Summary of conference call between BHQ and all SACs, 6/29/82, re RIF; and *The Agent,* publication of the National Association of Treasury Agents, 3/84.

8. Firearms Owners' Protection Act, as enacted.

9. Details of the Crickmore family and Paulette's last day are from the author's interviews with her parents, Alan and Tammy Crickmore, 6/13/88.

10. Comparison between murders in 1986 (FBI Uniform Crime Report) and published odds of winning the Tri-State Megabucks lottery.

11. Details of the Towne investigation are from the author's interview with John Churchill, chief deputy state's attorney of Chittenden County, Vermont, on 6/13/88; "Ex-Convict Pleads Innocent in Slaying of Crickmore Girl," by Ted Tedford, and Stephen Casimiro, *Burlington Free Press,* 12/9/86; and "Gun Control Not Seen as a Solution," by Yvonne Daley, *Daily Herald,* Rutland, VT, 12/9/86; author's 12/5/95 interview with Assistant D.A. Pam Johnson, who defeated Towne's appeals.

12. Crime statistics are from the FBI's Uniform Crime Reports, 1985 and 1986.

13. See Appendix F.

18

1. Pine Hill Massacre, ATF Case #63420831548. Other cases described more fully in testimony before Senate Subcommittee of Committee on Appropriations, re H.R.5294, 3/20/86.

2. Events and dialog regarding the Army of God case are reconstructed from transcripts, tape recordings, author's interviews with and letters written by suspects and witnesses, public papers, ATF case #63510841037D, FBI files #95-264908, 174-9671-X, 174A-1075, 174-3093, 174B-571-1-13, 174-3199-6-7, 174-2-22935-7, 174A-3208, 199-O-3208, 50116002, 50129002, and miscellaneous FBI memoranda bearing no file number.

3. FBI "Domestic Security/Terrorism Investigations" guidelines approved by A. G. Smith: see congressional Library Services Division, dated 4/16/83, #S-03 02319. They state that such investigations "may be initiated when the facts or circumstances reasonably indicate that two or more persons are engaged in an enterprise for the purpose of furthering political or social goals wholly or in part through activities that involve force or violence and a violation of the criminal laws of the United States. . . . The standard of 'reasonable indication' is substantially lower than probable cause. . . . A Special Agent may take into account any facts or circumstances that a prudent investigator would consider. However. . . . a mere hunch is insufficient."

4. House Judiciary Subcommittee on Crime and Criminal Justice, 5/6/92. Comments attributed to Bray are from *Washington Post,* 12/3/91.

5. *Capitol Area Christian News,* vol. 3, no. 2, 6/93.

19

1. Sources include: U.S. Court fact summaries 490 2d. 866; 390 S.Sup 1403; 874 Fed 2d 1575; 746 F Supp. 1090; 1991 WL 50169; 1991 WL 54926; 1991 WL 69418; "Mail-Bomb Murder Trial Opens," by Kevin McGee, *USA Today;* "New Counsel for Bomb Suspect," by Charles E. Anderson and Debra Cassens Moss, *ABA Journal,* 2/91; *The FBI: Inside the World's Most Powerful Law Enforcement Agency,* by Ronald Kessler (New York: Pocket Books, 1993). "Georgia Man Is Charged in Series of Bombings," by David Johnson, *New York Times,* 11/8/90. Also see Chapter 5 of this book re the murder of Judge Wood.

2. "Moody Convicted on All Counts," by Bill Montgomery, *Atlanta Constitution,* 6/29/91.

3. *Ibid.,* and "Moody Indicted in Mail Bombings," by Bill Montgomery, *Atlanta Journal and Constitution,* 11/8/90.

4. FBI denial of author's FOIA request dated 6/17/94; Justice Department response sustaining FBI denial, dated 12/16/94.

20

1. *Abnormal Psychology,* by David S. Holmes (New York: Harper Collins, 1974), page 279: ". . . cult leader David Koresh, whose

behavior indicated that he probably suffered from a delusional disorder."

2. Sources for this chapter include: interviews with agents involved in the investigation who spoke on condition of anonymity since Bureau orders prohibited extra-legal disclosures; memos and reports re ATF Case #53110921069X; documents on file with the U.S. District Court, Western District of Texas; Director's Memo No. 2, 1992; Director Higgins's testimony before the House Subcommittee on Crime and Criminal Justice (Committee on the Judiciary) on 3/9/93; fax message, Explosives Section Chief Rick Tontarski to BHQ 4/4/93; ATF News Release, 3/1/93; "Young Agent Died on Front Lines of Dangerous Duty He Loved," by Jon E. DeSantis, *Washington Post,* 3/5/93; "The Clue in the Crater," by Malcolm Gladwell, *Washington Post,* 3/6/93; "Animosity Between Agencies Surfaces," by Martin Gottleib, *New York Times,* 3/7/93; "Excerpts from Complaint Against Nidal Ayyad" from complaint filed 3/10/93, U.S. District Court, Manhattan, published 3/11/93, *New York Times;* "A Few Minutes with Andy Rooney," published in *The Eighteen-Eleven,* official journal of the Federal Law Enforcement Officers Association; "Negotiator Builds Rapport with Cult," by Tracy Everbach, *Dallas Morning News,* 3/2/93; and Report of the Department of the Treasury on the Bureau of Alcohol, Tobacco and Firearms Investigation of Vernon Wayne Howell also known as David Koresh, 9/93.

FBI Assistant Director James Fox's statement—"Clearly finding the vehicle identification number was an early break. From there it fell like dominoes . . ."—is from *The FBI: Inside the World's Most Powerful Law Enforcement Agency,* by Ronald Kessler (New York: Pocket Books, 1993), page 26.

3. *New York Times,* 12/6/94.

4. "Why the Flames of Waco Won't Die," by Richard Shweder, *New York Times,* 4/17/94.

5. "A Few Minutes with Andy Rooney," published in *The Eighteen-Eleven,* official journal of the Federal Law Enforcement Officers Association.

6. "Congressman Offers Vile Defense," by John Young, *Cox News Service,* published 8/12/95 in the Brunswick, Maine, *Times Record.*

7. "Accused Sex Harasser Gets Job Back . . ." by Christy Harris, *Federal Times,* 3/13/95.

21

1. *Newsweek*, 6/5/95.
2. House Judiciary Subcommittee on Crime, 7/95; Government Reform and Oversight Subcommittee; Senate Judiciary Committee, 10/31/95. "NRA Role Alive in Hearings," by Marcy Gordon, AP 7/19/95. John Kolman, the expert short-shrifted and rudely interrupted while answering the one question asked of him, is a former captain of the Los Angeles County Sheriff's Department; he had nine years' practical experience as a SWAT (Special Weapons and Tactics) team leader; he holds a master's degree; he has authored a SWAT text and numerous articles in professional journals; he was an adjunct college faculty member who had instructed thousands of lawmen in the methods and intricacies of raids. In short, it wouldn't have required a brilliant intellect to recognize that his opinion on this topic was more relevant than that of a kindly social worker with no knowledge of the subject who had failed—as anyone probably would have—to save the Branch Davidian children.
3. "Militia Groups Armed . . .", *Federal Times*, 5/15/95, page 12; "Around the Nation," *Law Enforcement News*, 8/20/94, page 2.
4. "Republic of Hate" aired on *Primetime Live*, 11/95.
5. Hearings, Senate Judiciary Subcommittee, September 5–8, 1995; "Specter of Defeat," *Time*, 12/4/95, page 22.
6. Hearing, Senate Judiciary Committee, 4/27/95. See Appendix E for facts on the FBI's actual performance in the field of domestic terrorism.
7. See Appendix F for details.
8. See Appendix F for details.
9. See Appendix F.

Appendix B

ATF Mission Statement

The mission of the Bureau of Alcohol, Tobacco and Firearms (ATF) is: to reduce the criminal use of firearms and to assist other Federal, State, local and foreign law enforcement agencies in reducing crime and violence by effective enforcement of the Federal firearms laws; to provide for the public safety by reducing the criminal misuse of explosives, combating arson-for-profit schemes, and removing safety hazards caused by improper and unsafe storage of explosives materials; to assure the collection of all alcohol, tobacco, and firearms tax revenues and obtain a high level of compliance with the alcohol, tobacco, and firearms tax statutes; to suppress the commercial bribery, consumer deception, and other prohibited trade practices in the alcoholic beverage industry by effective enforcement and administration of the Federal Alcohol Administration Act; to assist the States in their efforts to eliminate interstate trafficking in the sale and distribution of contraband cigarettes; to actively target and investigate those individuals who possess or use firearms in furtherance of their illegal narcotics/drug related activities; and, to suppress illicit manufacture and sale of nontax-paid alcoholic beverages.

Appendix C

Job Description, ATF Special Agent

Official Position Description for ATF Special Agents who have completed—in addition to three months' formal training at the Federal Law Enforcement Training Center—typically, three years' on-the-job training. Promotion to this level is automatic for those who maintain acceptable proficiency during the training phases.

Promotions to the senior level—special agents responsible for investigations of greater than average complexity—are competitive.

Introduction

Serves as a Criminal Investigator assigned to a field division (Law Enforcement) of the Bureau of Alcohol, Tobacco and Firearms (ATF). Independently conducts investigations that encompass the full range of violations under the laws enforced by ATF and conducts investigations related to specific cases, the organized crime investigation program, or for the purpose of gathering information on individuals or groups suspected of violating the above laws. Typically spends more than half his/her time on firearms and explosives control work and a relatively small amount of time on illicit liquor work that arises in the area to which he/she is assigned.

Major Duties

Gathers general information and intelligence. Obtains investigative leads and factual data through a variety of means. Develops informers and third-party contacts. Obtains assistance and cooperation of local, state and federal officers in his/her area, and, in turn, assists them in enforcing violations within the scope of ATF's enforcement activities. Maintains intelligence files and exchanges intelligence data with local, state, and federal agencies.

Conducts investigations related to specific cases. Observes suspect or suspects to determine habits and movements and to determine rendezvous and transfer points or the source of supply of weapons, liquor, explosives, bombs, or component parts. If necessary, submits requests for information (collaterals) to other ATF jurisdictions. When required, assumes undercover role to purchase contraband, to observe illegal activities, and to obtain additional intelligence. Attempts to develop reliable informers within the violation group for the above purposes, and periodically validates this intelligence information against intelligence gathered by other means.

Participates in raids, searches, seizures, and arrests. May coordinate additional investigators who assist in the above on cases for which he/she is responsible. May, in turn, assist other investigators in raids, searches, seizures, and arrests in cases for which they are responsible. Decides whether or not a search warrant is necessary, and, if necessary, obtains evidence sufficient to justify "probable cause" for issuance of the warrant.

Reviews all evidence at the conclusion of an investigation and prepares case report if evidence so justifies. Confers with U.S. Attorney regarding specific charges made in the indictment prior to the defendant's trial. Arranges for testimony of experts in such fields as ordinance, handwriting, explosives, and technical analysis that will support the government's case. Discusses with U.S. Attorney which of the prosecution's witnesses will testify and in what order the evidence against the defendants will be presented. As required, personally testifies for the government in court. Cases initiated by or assigned to the incumbent typically have several of the following characteristics:

The subject or subjects under investigation are either individuals or small groups that are loosely organized. Such individuals or groups are not usually affiliated with national organizations or related to groups in other locations. If affiliated, there is no connection which demonstrates a purpose to commit a coordinated criminal act. Subjects or activities under investigation are not likely to be of more than passing interest to the general public, even though they may be regarded as locally sensitive and may have a sensitive case number assigned by Bureau Headquarters.

Investigations are relatively wide in scope, i.e., occurring primarily in a geographic area that is fairly easy to cover, usually within a state or major metropolitan area or, occasionally, in portions of the bordering states. Collateral requests, if needed, are usually limited in number or are sent to two or three other states. The investigations conducted frequently produce one or two investigative leads to other possible violations of the law.

The number of third-party contacts is relatively limited and investigative leads are substantially accurate, if incomplete. Some basic element of the case was identified in the referral, informant's communication, or other origin of the case. Some of the potential witnesses are fairly cooperative, have substantive comments and facts, and indicate they will testify in court. The evidence gathered is primarily direct and substantive, although circumstantial evidence is gathered to prove the commission of overt criminal acts and usually does not involve proof of conspiracy.

If required, the undercover role is moderately difficult to establish and is maintained for a relatively short period of time. The investigator or his informant is accepted by the violator with some question and, if discovered, may be expelled and may be physically assaulted.

As assigned, participates in public relations activities, develops or modifies investigative techniques and procedures, assists in directing lower-grade investigators in on-the-job training, may serve in special study groups or task forces at Division Headquarters level, and, occasionally, may serve as Acting Group Supervisor or Acting Resident Agent in Charge. Performs other additional duties, as required. The performance of duties at this level requires the operation of government motor vehicles.

Supervision and Guidance Received

Works under the general administrative and technical supervision of a designated Group Supervisor or Resident Agent-in-Charge who provides advice and guidance on sensitive investigations or difficult technical matters. Conducts investigations with a minimum of direction and generally uses own judgement to determine which matters should be referred to supervisor. Case reports are reviewed for clarity, completeness, and sufficiency of evidence. May be assigned, for developmental purposes, full-time investigations typically performed at a higher level. In those instances, usually works under direct technical supervision of a higher graded investigator assigned to direct and coordinate the incumbent.

Other Significant Facts

May be called upon to move from one field office or division office to another depending upon the needs of the agency. Mobility is not limited to field offices within one division or one region. In addition, must be available to travel frequently during the course of assignments. This travel is not limited to locations in one division. Required to operate government-owned vehicles.

Must display required proficiency with firearms, as described in ATF Order 3000.8 "ATF Firearms Policy."

How to Apply

Persons who meet the educational and physical qualifications for the position of Special Agent with ATF, Customs, IRS or the Secret Service should submit a Standard Form 86 to the Office of Personnel Administration (OPA). The job title is "Treasury Enforcement Agent" (TEA). The written examination for these positions is administared by OPA. When an agency intends to interview applicants, it is given a register of those who passed the written examination—listed in the order of their exam scores (i.e., from 99 down to 70). Interviewers start at the top of the list and work their way down. Applicants who do not achieve a high score should not be discouraged. I once served on an interview panel that exhausted four entire registers to select four candidates for employment.

Appendix D

Sample Page:
ATF Explosive
Incident Report

This final page from the Bureau of Alcohol, Tobacco and Firearms "Explosives Incident Report—1993" [ATF P 3320.4 (7/94)(the most recent available as this book is written)], illustrates ATF's typical manner in public relations, ensuring that appropriate credit is given to every agency participating in an investigation.

. . . resulted in the explosion. The business partner was ultimately arrested on December 29 and held without bond pending a pre-trial detention hearing.

In April 1993, the FBI requested ATF assistance in an investigation involving two suspects who expressed an interest in killing a Wood County deputy sheriff by means of an explosive device. The suspects were members of a vehicle theft ring and were under investigation by the FBI and the Wood County Sheriff's Department at that time. The FBI agreed to locate and schedule a meeting with an individual who had access to explosive devices. It was subsequently learned that the intended target was a deputy sheriff who had arrested the principal suspect on breaking and entering charges, and who the principal suspect felt had been "harassing" the members of the theft ring. A meeting was arranged with an undercover ATF agent, during which the principal suspect stated that he wanted the agent to furnish him and his partner with explosive devices to be used in "blowing up" the Wood County Sheriff's Department: the Wood County Municipal Building, which housed the Parkersburg courtrooms and State probation department offices; and the deputy sheriff. A price of $5,000 was agreed upon for these tasks. Subsequent contact was made with the suspect that established his intent, and arrangements were made for the transfer of the device. He was shown the device, which consisted of four cases of dynamite and a remote control detonator, and directed the agents to place the device next to the vehicle of the targeted deputy sheriff. He was arrested when he attempted to detonate the device. He has since pled guilty to charges of attempted murder of a law enforcement officer by means of explosives. His sentencing is pending.

A 1989 investigation by ATF, the Marion County Sheriff's Department, the West Virginia State Fire Marshal's Office, and the West Virginia State Police resulted in the sentencing of a defendant in 1992 to 25 years' imprisonment on Federal conspiracy charges. The defendant had previously been found not guilty in State court of attempted murder charges. The investigation involved a bombing that resulted in serious injuries to a deputy sheriff. At the time of the explosion, the deputy sheriff was investigating an abandoned vehicle that had been reported stolen. The investigation, which involved an NRT activation, revealed that the defendant had rigged a door of the abandoned vehicle with the bomb in hopes of blowing up a police officer who had pursued him in a high-speed chase. The deputy sheriff survived his injuries, and is now the sheriff of Marion County.

On June 7, 1993, a defendant was sentenced to 15 months' imprisonment on charges of conspiracy to illegally manufacture and possess an explosive device, possession of an unregistered destructive device, and the manufacture of a destructive device. His codefendant was previously sentenced to 84 months' imprisonment. The sentencings stem from an investigation conducted by ATF and the West Virginia State Fire Marshal's Office. When testifying, the defendant had claimed he suffered from posttraumatic stress disorder as a result of the Gulf War, and was insane when he manufactured the two pipe bombs. His claims were ultimately refuted. It is believed that the devices were manufactured in retaliation for an altercation the defendant and codefendant had with another individual. Both defendants were injured while in the process of manufacturing the device.

Appendix E

Special Material re FBI

FBI "achievements" in the field of terrorism generally fall into two categories: cases they "adopt" without disclosing that the most critical aspects of the case were actually accomplished by other agencies; and instances where the "accomplishment" is described as "preventing a terrorist act." The latter, translated into what the FBI actually *did*, consists of having received a tip and interviewing the alleged would-be terrorists—informing them that "we know what you're planning" and warning of the consequences, should they choose to carry out the reported plot. Receiving tips is no accomplishment—considering the $3.5 million the FBI paid to informers in 1975 and their mandate, which makes it every police agency's duty to report such rumors to the FBI. "Resolving" the situation through aggressive questioning and dire warning is something any officer could do. Result: No one knows whether there really was a plot, so no one goes to jail.

Aside from G-man claims of credit—often false, [see Chapter 18]—there have been few objective assessments of FBI performance. The most thorough review was conducted by Congress' nonpolitical investigative arm, the General Accounting Office (GAO), following the mid-1970s heyday of domestic terrorists—

SDS Weathermen and Black Panthers [see Chapter 7]. GAO investigators were forbidden by the FBI to examine raw files and forced to rely on summaries of those files furnished by the FBI; even so, the results were dismal. GAO's "Report to the House Committee on the Judiciary," dated 2/24/76, showed 788 agents utilizing "less than 1,000 informants" assigned to "domestic intelligence" investigations; of the 797 investigations sampled by GAO, there were only twenty-four instances where a crime was alleged to have occurred and was reported to federal prosecutors or any other appropriate law-enforcement agencies; of these, eight persons were ultimately convicted: one for a federal offense (making false statements on a passport application) and seven for crimes under state law—i.e., bombing a theater, firearms offenses (both of which should have been reported to ATF), forgery, assault and robbery. The value (if any) of the FBI's contribution to these convictions could not be determined.

Hearings before the House Select Committee on Intelligence ("U.S. Intelligence Activities: Domestic Intelligence Programs," October 9 through December 10, 1975) included testimony by a retired FBI agent that his bureau's successes, such as they were, were achieved through illegal searches, bugs, wiretaps and an institutionalized procedure of official lying to conceal these crimes from their superiors in the Justice Department, and unofficial lying to hide their acts from the public. The evidence revealed that the FBI routinely violated the Civil Rights Act of 1968, which "makes it unlawful for two or more persons to conspire to injure, oppress, threaten, or intimidate any citizen in the free exercise or enjoyment of any right or privilege secured to him by the Constitution or laws of the United States." [Quote is from hearings text.] Without utilizing these illegal tactics, it's possible that those 797 FBI investigations would have produced nothing at all.

Myths exaggerating the FBI's accomplishments are propagated by their public relations section, which, in 1987, in addition to agents assigned this duty at posts across the country, had a headquarters public relations staff of 176 agent supervisors, writers, editors, analysts, clerks, secretaries, a four-person legal staff and assorted coordinators, chiefs, assistants and specialists, employed at an annual cost of $5,751,000. The FBI refused to disclose this information in response to my legal request under the Freedom of Information Act [#286,673] until they were urged to comply by Senator William S. Cohen of Maine—who also happened to be co-chairman of the Senate Intelligence Committee.

There's little hope that the FBI's attitude concerning legality or sharing information with the proper investigative agencies will change [see Chapter 9]. Unlike other federal bureaus, where laws give agents the right to a hearing before they can be penalized or fired, "accused FBI agents have no rights . . . no right to confront or even see the evidence against them, let alone know the identities of their accusers. They have no right to counsel. Not even a limited right to compel evidence on their behalf. No right to a hearing. And no appeals." [Quoted from a letter to *Federal Times*, 10/16/95, from Christopher Kerr, Southeast Regional Representative, FBI Agents Association.] That vulnerability has a dual effect: It keeps many potential candidates from considering an FBI career (ill-informed applicants, like I once was, don't discover this drawback until after they've passed the G-man's written test and oral interviews—an oversight that puts them in the embarrassing position of admitting their ignorance and withdrawing their application); but, more important to citizens, the FBI agents' knowledge that they serve at their supervisor's pleasure tells all of them, "Obey orders, *all* orders . . . or you're history."

Eliminating this handicap wouldn't alter that basic FBI philosophy that "whatever helps the FBI is right—even if it's wrong." Their practice of stealing credit—a habit that alienates thousands of law-enforcement officers and reduces the level of cooperation that ultimately solves many cases—began sixty years ago with the arrest of Bruno Richard Hauptman by New York City police detectives for the kidnap-murder of national hero Charles Lindbergh's infant son. This was an instance in which, despite prodigious efforts to solve a front-page case where they had no jurisdiction, the FBI's contribution was nil. Lindbergh himself gave *Treasury* agents a lion's share of the credit, but none of this slowed the FBI's claims for more than thirty years afterward as one of "the FBI's Most Famous Cases."

Executives trained by J. Edgar Hoover have, in turn, selected malleable agents and tutored them to share that pragmatic approach. It's a self-perpetuating process that produces generations of clones. Each new director promises change; none have altered their bureau's basic philosophy.

The following material was furnished by the FBI regarding their claims of success with "Terrorism" and published in the 1981 Annual Report of the Attorney General *to Congress and the Nation.*

TERRORISM

The Terrorism Section of the Criminal Investigative Division has the dual responsibilities of preventing terrorist acts through intelligence-type investigations and responding through criminal investigations when terrorist acts are committed.

In fiscal 1981, the Terrorism Section fulfilled its responsibilities by achieving significant accomplishments in its programs to combat the activities of the major terrorist groups. The most notable accomplishments are described below.

In December of 1980, seven Croatian National Resistance members were arrested for their involvement in a bombing and an assassination plot. Five of these individuals were convicted in March of 1981. Their plans had included the killing of a political foe and the bombing of a meeting attended by 100 people celebrating a Yugoslav holiday. This case was significant because it demonstrated how intelligence information gathered on a terrorist group can result in the prevention of terrorist activity.

In June of 1981, nine other members of the Croatian National Resistance were arrested and indicted on a variety of federal charges as the result of a RICO-Terrorism investigation. This investigation was in response to a murder, arson, bombing and extortion campaign waged by these individuals over the past several years.

The combination of these two cases constituted a severe blow to the operational capability of the Croation terrorist movement.

The Terrorism Program also made progress in curtailing the activities of the Irish Republican Army in the United States. In an operation directed at Irish Republican Army gun smuggling, FBI agents arrested three Irish Republican Army members and seized a large quantity of arms and ammunition destined for Northern Ireland. FBI assistance to the Immigration and Naturalization Service resulted in the identification, arrest and deportation of three other Irish Republican Army activists who were in the United States illegally.

The activity in the United States of the agents, representatives, and supporters of those Middle Eastern countries that advocate terrorism continued to be a major concern. The FBI closely monitored the activity of these groups and was able, through swift and effective reaction, to combat their use of terror and intimidation in the United States. The following examples are indicative of the FBI's response to Middle Eastern terrorism:

As a result of investigation of the assassination of Iranian dissident Ali Akbar Tabatabai, nine members of the Islamic Guerrillas in America have been indicted and convicted on a variety of federal charges; three Iranian students were arrested and convicted for attempting to purchase automatic weapons from an undercover FBI agent; an anti-Khomeini Iranian was convicted and sentenced to serve 50 years for bombing a convention of pro-Khomeini students; a former member of the U.S. Army Special Forces was arrested for the attempted assassination of an outspoken critic of Colonel Mu'Ammar Qadhafi of Libya and investigation into the nature and extent of the Libyan terrorist network is continuing; and information developed by the FBI that a Jordanian citizen was a Popular Front for the Liberation of Palestine operative resulted in the issuance of an arrest and deportation order for him by the Immigration and Naturalization Service. The type of effective response depicted by these examples reduces the attractiveness of the United States as a scene for violent or illegal activity by international terrorists.

Other pertinent *accomplishments by the FBI* in the field of terrorism include the prevention of a planned sabotage and assassination raid on the island of Cuba by the arrest of seven members of the anti-Castro Cuban terrorist group, Alpha-66; the conviction of a key member of the Cuban Nationalist Movement for perjury relative to his testimony before a grand jury in New York; the conviction of nine individuals on neutrality, gun control and munitions control statutes because of their involvement in a plot to attack the island of Dominica and overthrow the government; and the arrest of a prominent member of the Cuban Nationalist Movement on passport violations and local charges after a search warrant was executed at his residence, where an illegal passport, weapons, and drugs were found.

The following material is an analysis of that report:

Page 32, paragraph 3: The FBI claims sole and exclusive credit for convicting 5 Croatian National Resistance members. In fact, the case resulted from a joint investigation by ATF and the Cleveland Police Department in which ATF Special Agent Nicholaj Dikey penetrated the terrorist group, undercover, to secure the evidence which brought arrests for conspiracy to commit multiple murder. (See "Plot Foiled—3 Lives Saved" by Walter Johns, Jr., *The Cleveland Press,* 9/15/80.)

Page 32, last paragraph: the FBI claims credit for convicting 9 members of the Islamic Guerillas of America. In fact, these convictions resulted from ATF's investigation of IGA members buying guns under ficticious names to commit violent crimes; one defendant confessed to ATF and furnished information, which T-men corroborated through investigation in Maryland, Virginia, and New York, to solve the assassination of Ali Akbar Tabatabai. Since ATF had also uncovered crimes within FBI jurisdiction, the T-men turned this evidence over to the G-men and invited them to participate. (See *The Washington Post* 12/9/81; and see the *Portland Press Herald,* 1/11/82; and ATF Case #320403812009K.)

The same paragraph notes the conviction of 3 Iranian students. An undercover FBI agent sold machine guns to these Boston students; other G-men promptly arrested them. ATF not involved.

The same paragraph claims exclusive credit for an "anti-Khomeini Iranian," sentenced to 50 years for bombing. The FBI was investigating his first bombing, but the subject was identified, arrested and convicted on evidence acquired by ATF and the local sheriffs department (for firearms crimes and plotting to blow up a building at San Jose University). Aware of the FBI's interest, ATF brought them in to participate in the arrest. (See *The Mercury,* San Jose, CA, 2/3 & 4/81; *Tribune-TODAY,* California, 10/9/80; *The San Francisco Chronicle,* 10/11/80; and ATF Case # 481309802501K.)

Page 33, 2nd paragraph: Perjury conviction; no information known.

Same paragraph: the FBI claims sole credit for the convictions of 9 persons who plotted to attack the Island of Dominica and overthrow its government. This case was perfected by ATF agents via undercover penetration by an ATF Agent, surveillance, etc. Many of the crimes uncovered by ATF lay within the jurisdiction of other agencies; ATF invited Customs Agents, state and local police, and the FBI to participate in the arrests—this assistance was the FBI's sole contribution to this case. (See *Washington Star,* 7/13&15/81; *Baltimore Sun,* 6/23/81; *Phila. Inquirer,* 6/18, 19, 23/81; *New Orleans Times-Picyune,* 6/10/81; *Wash. Post,* 4/29/81.) The FBI claimed 28 convictions under "Terrorism"—24 of these (85%) resulted from ATF investigations where the FBI's actual contribution was ineffectual, negligible, or nonexistent.

Appendix F

Facts/History re Proposed Merger of Treasury Investigative Bureaus

Four of Treasury's five investigative agencies—ATF, Customs, IRS/CID and IRS Inspection—are units operating under revenue executives. It's not surprising that the chiefs of these agencies put a premium on collecting taxes, since that's their business. But ATF's expectation that venal gun dealers will respond to "voluntary compliance" rather than the risk of prison; the Customs Service's shift in emphasis from making arrests to "seeking informed compliance" by corrupt importers; and the IRS retreat from probing criminals to focus the world's best financial investigators on "legal sector taxpayers/nonfilers" (waitresses, cab drivers) seem a trifle weird—especially since revenue agents (rather than special agents) and their counterparts in ATF and Customs are more cost-effective in dealing with ordinary citizens who have the income to pay their tax debt without being jailed. This policy affects every IRS investigation because their special agents are supervised at the field level

a move to consolidate all Treasury's investigative
s . . . into one agency, an agency that might overshadow the
l rival it for newspaper space."

979 President Carter's reorganization team tried for a
arguing, "The lack of coordination and absence of policy
es cause wasted efforts and reduced effectiveness without
:ernible civil liberties benefit."

: are some who would still oppose this merger, despite its
table benefits in terms of economy, efficiency and effective-
:gardless of who might resist it, there are only two kinds of
following past failures to consolidate Treasury's investiga-
:s: bureaucrats and criminals.
osers are legion.

: is a list of crimes that fall within the jurisdiction of more
e Treasury agency. As we stand now, each offers opportuni-
confusion and inefficiency that cannot be addressed—as
ve in the past—by instructions to "improve communica-
mong the four agencies' offices in each city and nationwide.

Jurisdictional Interests

on: ATF investigates arsons, per se.
             IRS/CID investigates criminals who do
             not pay taxes on illegal profits.

assination: ATF investigates illegal weapon posses-
             sion by mental cases and felons.
             Secret Service has a primary interest in
             protecting certain officials.

bing: ATF investigates bombings, per se.
             IRS/CID investigates criminals who do
             not pay taxes on illegal profits.

b Making: ATF investigates illegal bombmaking.
             Secret Service has direct interest in po-
             tential assassins.

terfeiting: IRS/CID investigates criminals who do
             not pay taxes on illegal profits.
             Secret Service investigates counterfeit-
             ing of U.S. currency.

by sixty local district directors who have come up through the civil
examination or collections sections.

But the old IRS maxim—"We're not policemen, we're tax
collectors"—is shared by all revenue executives. GAO investigators have reported to Congress that non-law-enforcement officials
in Customs endanger undercover operations and informant identities by storing sensitive documents in an open filing cabinet in an
unlocked room. [See "Security Lax at Customs . . . " by Christy
Harris, *Federal Times*, 10/18/93.] David Burnham, author of *A Law
Unto Itself: Power, Politics, and the IRS*, says "The present structure, where a single organization is responsible for both criminal
and civil enforcement activities, creates serious conflict."

When it comes to interagency cooperation, the IRS attitude
sometimes makes the FBI look like real lawmen. Back when ATF
was part of the revenue service, IRS commissioner D. W. Bacon
wrote:

> Although this project has been in operation for only three or
> four weeks, the ATF undercover agents have been extremely
> successful in obtaining evidence on liquor violations and
> potential firearms violations. In addition, they have ob-
> tained valuable information on gambling, narcotics, white
> slavery and other criminal activities."

Bacon praised his ATF division's close working relationship with
his Intelligence division (now named Criminal Investigation
Division—IRS/CID) on gambling operations. Then he added:

> There is one danger in this situation, and I think you
> would want to watch it rather closely. If the undercover men
> are successful in further infiltration of the gangster element,
> there will undoubtedly be pressure or requests that their
> efforts be directed to investigation of violations not within
> our own jurisdiction. ATF agents should not be performing
> undercover work for . . . the Department of Justice (except
> in those situations where they are officially detailed and
> assigned for that specific purpose). . . . We should not, how-
> ever, continue our investigative efforts in non-revenue mat-
> ters without specific clearance from this office. [Memo to
> IRS Commissioner, Midwest Region, 5/31/67.]

Treasury supported its 1983 attempt to merge ATF agents into
the Secret Service with evidence of increased efficiency: savings of

$12 million during the transition year and savings of $29 million the next year. [See Hearings, Subcommittee of the Committee on Appropriations, House of Representatives (Treasury, Postal Service, and General Appropriations) for Fiscal Year 1983.] Savings would be even greater if all four Treasury investigative units were consolidated. In addition, the merger would end the need for costly transfers when one unit's workload diminishes in a particular area [see Chapter 4]; and there would be no need to fly agents in from an agency's distant offices—meals, hotels and transportation expenses—when a series of raids must be conducted simultaneously; or when the president briefly visits a city; or when a series of crimes requires greater manpower than a local office has [see Chapter 18].

Consolidation would enhance efficiency and economy by eliminating many high-paid executive positions at every level: one director (and staff); one SAC (and staff) in each district, etcetera. (Arguing against the 1983 ATF-Secret Service merger, ATF executives told congressional aides the plan would hurt morale by offering agents fewer promotion opportunities. Considering the survey by the National Association of Treasury Agents that found 84 percent favoring the move [The Agent, 3/84], it's more likely the chiefs were worried about their own jobs.)

Consolidation would let taxpayers support one (rather than four) offices in each city; one (rather than four) administrative staff for personnel and procurement; one vehicle fleet; one set of radio bands; and one coordinated filing system that would alert agents opening a new case on a suspect already under investigation by another agent. I can't count the number of times I drove to the far reaches of Maine or Missouri or Nebraska—sixteen hours round-trip driving to conduct an interview that took one hour—only to meet an agent from another Treasury bureau who'd wasted the same number of travel hours on a similar mission when either one of us could have done both jobs. Or the instances when I came across a lead to a crime I couldn't pursue because it was under a sister agency's jurisdiction; so I'd drive back to the federal building and refer the lead to the appropriate bureau so that one of their agents could retrace my steps to do his duty—if the witness or informant or suspect hadn't vanished and the lead hadn't gone cold.

Criminals are more flexible than agents. They engage in various crimes simultaneously, or move from one illegal enterprise to another—a shift that leaves their old adversaries sniffing a dead trail while the investigators they now challenge aren't even aware

that they exist. Any agent can point to . . . investigation worked well, but no one talks a . . . was compromised because—unknown to or . . . reaus were working the same gang and wires . . . Mahan, the great naval strategist, once said, " . . . aggregate of force, it is never as great in t . . . because it is not perfectly concentrated."

During my assignment to Interpol, I found . . . reception engaged in a friendly dispute with a . . . of the Royal Canadian Mounted Police (RCM . . . the RCMP, as Canada's only federal agency, . . . over the USA's fragmented law-enforcement . . . "But surely your detectives find themselves i . . . to time. What happens if an officer assigned . . . Montreal comes up with an informant with in . . . running? He doesn't want to share his inform . . . squad needs him. Isn't that the same thing w . . .

"Not quite," the RCMP man replied. "V . . . Montreal who's boss over both squads. He'd s . . . snapped his fingers—"like that."

One of Treasury's units—the IRS Inspectio . . . ble for suppressing internal corruption—shou . . . of the new Treasury bureau. Investigating . . . officials who may become one's boss (if he's f . . . is a job for an outside agency—in this case, . . . general.

Occasionally, someone suggests merging o . . . bureaus into the FBI. Aside from the morale . . . dix E], in most instances, agents who wanted . . . have done so. But a degree of mutual conte . . . both organizations have G-men believing the . . . and seeing themselves as superior; and Treasu . . . sentiment expressed by a Drug Enforcement . . . when a plan to merge DEA into the FBI was a . . . FBI guy's idea of going undercover is to l . . . important, the separation of investigative po . . . and Treasury has acted as a check-and-balan . . . served to avoid the specter of a national poli . . .

The consolidation idea isn't new. President . . . Treasury secretary wanted to merge his enfor . . . in the 1930s but, as Ralph Salerno and John . . . their book The Crime Confederation, the pla . . . then all-powerful FBI director J. Edgar Hoove . . .

Forgery Fraud: ATF investigates persons who use another person's identity to purchase firearms or explosives; many use checks or credit cards.

IRS/CID investigates criminals who do not pay taxes on illegal profits.

Secret Service investigates credit card fraud, financial institution fraud and the forgery of government checks and bonds.

Smuggling: ATF investigates the illegal importation of firearms or explosives.

Customs investigates illegal exports in violation of neutrality laws.

IRS/CID investigates criminals who do not pay taxes on illegal profits.

Terrorism: ATF investigates the illegal acquisition, manufacture, possession and trafficking in firearms and explosives.

Customs investigates offenses involving the export of weapons, including those to be used in foreign acts of terrorism.

IRS/CID has given vital assistance to other agencies in tracking terrorists' financial support.

Secret Service investigates acts that might threaten the president or other government officials and foreign dignitaries while in the United States.

Appendix G

History of ATF
Name Changes

March 3, 1863	Congress authorizes the Treasury Department to hire three detectives "to aid in the prevention, detection and punishment" of criminals.
1868	Congress passes the Act of July 20th; a reorganization.
1914	Another reorganization in the Bureau of Internal Revenue (BIR), prompted by congressional enactment of the income tax amendment.
1919	The Eighteenth Amendment results in creation of the Prohibition Service.
July 1, 1930	Responsibility for enforcing Prohibition is transferred from the BIR to the new Federal Bureau of Prohibition.
May 10, 1934	Prohibition is repealed. The BIR sets up the Alcohol Tax Unit to suppress the

production and distribution of nontax-paid liquor.

November 1951 Laws covering the tobacco tax are added to the division's jurisdiction. ATU becomes the Alcohol and Tobacco Tax Division of the IRS.

1968 New gun laws are enacted. Name changed to Alcohol, Tobacco and Firearms Division of the IRS.

July 1, 1972 ATF is removed from the IRS and given full bureau status under Treasury.

These major changes do not include innumerable internal ATF reorganizations.

Appendix H

Federal Firearms
Licensed Dealers

Considering how members of the gun fraternity claim to despise regulation, it's odd that thousands of them volunteer to be restricted and controlled far beyond the requirements imposed on other citizens by getting a gun dealer's license. Being licensed requires them to inventory their firearms, list their sources and record the identities of everyone to whom they sell a gun, not to mention actually opening their premises (and weapons) to inspection by ATF. And they pay for this "privilege." The license and its controls were intended for persons who made gun selling their business, not for ordinary citizens. These "hobby dealers" clog the wheels, make it virtually impossible for ATF to supervise real businesses (because from the records at ATF, inspectors can't tell whether a licensee sells a thousand guns a year or just two) and—often ignoring or defying the law by failing to keep proper records—they make it impossible for agents to trace crime guns.

Director Stephen Higgins and his revenue-oriented predecessors adopted a *laissez-faire* attitude toward licensees. In 1983 testimony before a congressional subcommittee, Director Higgins acknowledged that a gun dealer inspection program reduces the potential for criminal misuse of firearms and enhances ATF's ability to trace crime guns. He then acknowledged that each of his inspectors had checked only twenty dealers during all of 1982—i.e., one out of every fifty-eight gunshops. Well over 200,000 were never visited. Higgins admitted that 20 percent of those who were inspected were not keeping proper records. Asked how he dealt with violators, he said, "We may go back there in another year or two, and if we find the same kind of recordkeeping problems and the person hasn't made any effort to comply with the law, we would escalate our response to that. We might issue a letter [which carries no penalty] or tell the person they have so long to bring the records into compliance. If we go back and find they don't want to keep records, we might at some point move against them administratively to revoke their license."

These are dealers, licensed to dispense arsenals interstate. Wilfully failing to keep the required records is a felony. Ripping the Do Not Remove tag from a pillow would be more risky.

Director John Magaw is a lawman. He has opted for straightforward enforcement of the law regarding dealers. With fewer than 500 inspectors (who also conduct field inspections regarding ATF's alcohol, tobacco and explosives licensees), dealer violations of state and local laws are now being referred to appropriate authorities so that they may take action. The bureau began recommending against renewal of licenses for individuals who were not actually engaged in the gun business; many licensees withdrew applications and surrendered their licenses due to conflicts with state and local laws and ordinances. Pre-licensing contacts were initiated and, where warranted, full field investigations to verify qualifications and ensure that the applicant truly intended to engage in the business. During fiscal year 1994, 17,267 applicant investigations and 20,067 compliance inspections uncovered 10,625 violations of law by dealers. The number of licensed dealers dropped by about 80,000, dipping below 200,000 for the first time in decades.

Appendix I

Miscellaneous Studies and Statistics

From 1973 to 1993, American manufacturers produced 3.8 million handguns [NCJ-148201, 7/75]. Among state prison inmates who possessed a handgun, 9 percent acquired it by theft; 28 percent obtained it from an illegal market; 27% purchased it from a retail outlet [NCJ-136949, 3/93*]. During 1992, handguns were used to commit 930,700 crimes: 13,200 murders, 11.800 rapes, 339,000 robberies and 566,800 assaults [NCJ-147,003 4/94]. In 1993, Southern States accounted for 35% of the nation's population and 41% of the homicides [NCJ-151658 5/95]. Of the 40,002 federal officers performing duties related to criminal investigation and enforcement in December 1993, 1,959 (4.9%) were ATF agents [NCJ-151166 12/94].

Of all defendants sentenced in federal courts, 36.8% were given prison terms; among those sentenced for federal firearms/weapons offenses, 48.4% were given prison terms [NCJ-101043, 6/87]. As of

---

*NCJ numbers identify reports by: US Department of Justice, Bureau of Justice Statistics.

October 1993, there were 613,079 machine guns, silencers, short-barreled rifles, short-barreled shotguns, destructive devices and other weapons covered by Title II of the Gun Control Act (illegal unless registered with ATF) which were properly registered.

Federally Licensed Firearms Dealers, 1993. 246,984
Number Subjected to Qualification Inspection by ATF
Inspectors. 4,701
Number Subjected to Compliance Inspections by ATF
Inspectors. 22,330

At this rate, it will take ATF ten years to visit and inspect every licensed gun dealer.

Homicides by Firearms

Year	Count	Year	Count	Year	Count
1910	1,852	1935	6,506	1960	4,627
1911	2,347	1936	6,016	1961	4,753
1912	2,449	1937	5,701	1962	4,954
1913	2,821	1938	5,055	1963	5,126
1914	3,077	1939	4,799	1964	4,394
1915	2,885	1940	4,655	1965	5,000
1916	3,241	1941	4,525	1966	5,635
1917	3,793	1942	4,204	1967	7,711
1918	3,727	1943	3,444	1968	8,970
1919	4,567	1944	3,449	1969	9,542
1920	4,477	1945	4,029	1970	10,341
1921	5,509	1946	4,966	1971	11,492
1922	5,714	1947	4,922	1972	11,188
1923	5,648	1948	4,894	1973	11,249
1924	6,028	1949	4,235	1974	12,474
1925	6,216	1950	4,179	1975	12,061
1926	6,377	1951	3,898	1976	10,592
1927	6,310	1952	4,244	1977	11,274
1928	6,857	1953	4,013	1978	11,910
1929	6,540	1954	4,115	1979	13,040
1930	7,190	1955	3,807	1980	13,650
1931	7,532	1956	4,039	1981	12,523
1932	7,458	1957	4,010	1982	11,721
1933	7,863	1958	4,230	1983	10,895
1934	7,702	1959	4,457		

The United States suffered 437,667 battlefield deaths in all its wars, from the Revolution to Vietnam; more than 465,784 Americans have been murdered with firearms since 1910. Statistics for the years 1910 through 1963, obtained from the Division of Vital Statistics, U.S. Department of Health, Education and Welfare, were quoted by Carl Bakal in *The Right To Bear Arms,* New York: McGraw-Hill Book Co., 1966. Numbers for 1964–1971 are taken from analysis of the FBI's Uniform Crime Reports. The figures for the years 1972 through 1983 were furnished by Ms. Chris Waskiewicz, UCR Section, FBI, who advised that contributing police agencies only furnished a breakdown of wapons used for 59% of all homicides during this period; since we may assume that a number of the remaining 41% were committed with firearms, the actual total of gun murders is significantly higher. Bakal acknowledged that the data from the Division of Vital Statistics are understated also, because the death registration area did not include the entire country until 1933.

This computation is limited to gun *murders,* excluding more than a half-million firearms accidents and suicides, because ATF's agents combat the criminal element exclusively. Battlefield deaths are taken from *The World Almanac and Book of Facts, 1980,* published by the Newspaper Enterprise Association, Inc., New York.

Number of Cases Presented to U.S. Attorneys for Prosecution, 1990–1995

	ATF	DEA	FBI	Customs	USSS
Total	32,637	45,693	133,992	23,934	18,258
Per Agent	16.75	13.24	13.61	7.98	9.13
Cases Rejected by Federal Prosecutors	1,590	918	53,706	1,590	15,605
Percentage Rejected	5.0	2.0	40.0	6.6	85.5
Cases Prosecuted	31,047	44,775	80,286	22,344	2,653
Per Agent	15.94	12.97	8.15	7.45	1.33

Since 1988, ATF has conducted 9,748 investigations under its Achilles Program (which targets armed drug traffickers and career criminals); more than 16,421 of these criminals have been charged with possessing a firearm while trafficking in narcotics or while committing a violent crime.

ATF's Violent Offender Program has pre-identified 1,000 career criminals considered most likely to be a danger to society. The average offender "accepted" into this program has six prior felony convictions and has been sentenced to more than thirty-five years' imprisonment; 54 have previously received life sentences. Their identities are entered into the National Crime Information Center's computer and made available to law-enforcement officers nationwide. As of August 1995, police have reported encountering 372 of these subjects; of these, 87 were found to be in possession of guns or ammunition.

Appendix J

Value of the Gun Control Act of 1968

This is the result of a study I conducted to determine whether or not ATF's work in enforcing GCA-68 produced any practical and demonstrable benefit to Americans. My methodology is explained beneath the table that follows. Previous studies attempting to measure the efficacy of gun laws focused on comparing crime rates in states with tough gun laws versus crime in states with weak gun laws. This is absurd, since state laws differ in their provisions, data is maintained in varying forms and no researcher has been able to balance the demographics between New York and Nebraska. I didn't try to compare varying statutes in different areas; I compared one law's history for thirteen years, nationwide.

If ATF's work benefits the country, violent crime would drop when agents were most productive—a variable I measured in terms of how many criminals were actually brought to trial under federal weapons statutes. As verification, the opposite should also prove true—i.e., when agents were less productive and fewer career criminals were tried for offenses under GCA-68, violent crimes would rise. But it would not be possible to attribute these fluctuations to ATF's work against gunmen and traffickers if the same changes occurred with respect to violent crimes committed with other weapons. According to U.S. court statistics, the ratio of ATF defendants imprisoned exceeds the federal average.

As shown on the table, the inverse correlation (federal weapons prosecutions up and violent gun crimes down, or vice versa) was evident in twelve of the thirteen years studied, for a statistical significance of .003 ["0" is a perfect statistical significance] in the first year following the rise or fall in weapons prosecutions, and the same percentage for the year after that when most of the defendants convicted for these crimes were still incarcerated—that is, incapacitated from committing crimes.

But, with regard to violent crimes committed using all other weapons (knives, clubs), the inverse correlation appeared in only eight years for a statistical significance of .127 in the first year following the prosecutions, and .227 in the year after that.

Impact of GCA-68 Enactment upon Homicide

Year	Gun Murders	
1960	4,627	
1961	4,753 + 2.7%	
1962	4,954 + 4.2%	
1963	5,126 + 3.5%	
1964	5,148 + 0.4%	
1965	5,677 + 10.3%	
1966	6,414 + 13.0%	
1967	7,711 + 20.2%	
1968	8,970 + 16.3%	[GCA-68 became effective on 12/16/68]
1969	9,593 + 6.9%	
1970	10,560 + 10.1%	
1971	11,735 + 11.1%	
1972	12,322 + 5.0%	
1973	12,962 + 5.2%	
1974	13,876 + 7.1%	

In July 1972, ATF was detached from its parent IRS and reorganized as a separate bureau.

Gun homicides continued to rise, although the rate of increase slowed noticeably when GCA-68 went into effect and slowed even further when ATF was reorganized as a separate bureau.

SOURCES: Statistics for 1960–1963 are quoted by Carl Bakal in *The Right to Bear Arms,* New York: McGraw Hill, 1966, attributed by Bakal to U.S. Department of Health, Education and Welfare, Division of Vital Statistics. Statistics for the years 1964–1972 were furnished by Ms. Chris Waskeiwicz, Uniform

Year	Total Number of Defendants in Federal Firearms/Weapons Cases
1974	2,783 +429
1975	3,291 +508
1976	3,412 +121
1977	3,118 −294
1978	3,272 +154
1979	2,008 −1,264
1980	1,155 −853

Year	Violent Crimes w/Guns	Violent Crimes by Other Weapons
1975	346,902 +19,210 +5.7%	623,248 +36,220 +6.2%
1976	312,781 −34,121 −9.8%	617,059 −6,189 −1%
1977	307,565 −5,296 −1.7%	638,915 +21,856 +3.5%
1978	314,631 +7,066 +2.3%	680,064 +41,149 +6.4%
1979	349,200 +34,569 +11%	753,350 +73,286 +10.8%
1980	403,176 +53,976 +15.5%	823,634 +70,284 +9.3%
1981	408,487 +5,311 +1.3%	831,833 +8,249 +1%

1981	1,411	+256	1982	383,312	−25,175 −6.2%	824,630	−7,523 −0.9%
1982	1,873	+462	1983	335,665	−47,647 −12.4%	823,396	−1,234 −0.1%
1983	1,934	+61	1984	329,234	−6,431 −1.9%	859,818	+36,422 +4.4%
1984	1,857	−77	1985	340,939	+11,705 +3.5%	899,157	+39,339 +4.6%
1985	1,746	−111	1986	376,066	+35,127 +10.3%	1,021,647	+122,490 +13.6%
1986	1,957	+211	1987	365,687	−10,379 −2.7%	1,027,199	+5,557 +0.5%

[FIGURES IN LAST TWO COLUMNS
ARE FOR THE YEAR *FOLLOWING*
DATA SHOWN IN SECOND COLUMN]

Crime Report Section, Federal Bureau of Investigation. This table is confined to murder because, until 1974, the FBI did not report robberies committed with firearms.

Ms. Waskeiwicz advised that during this period, the police agencies contributing data to the FBI furnished a breakdown of weapons used for only 59% of all homicides. It is assumed that the ratio of murder by firearm was the same for the 41% of homicides where no weapon was specified as for the 59% where the weapon was reported. Consequently, the figures quoted above were computed by applying the same percentage to all homicides.

In six of the years, fluctuations in gun prosecutions preceeded substantially different changes between the numbers of crimes committed *with,* and those committed *without,* firearms. They are:

Prosecutions, Federal Gun Laws	Violent Crimes by Gun	Violent Crimes without Gun
1975 +18.2%	1976 −9.8%	−1%
1976 +3.7%	1977 −1.7%	+3.5%
1979 −38.6%	1980 +15.5%	+9.3%
1981 +22.2%	1982 −6.2%	−0.9%
1982 +32.7%	1983 −12.4%	−0.1%
1983 +3.3%	1984 −1.9%	+4.4%

SOURCES: Gun law prosecutions from Annual Reports issued by the Administrative Office of the U.S. courts.

Gun-crime statistics are from the Uniform Crime Reports (UCR) issued by the FBI on the basis of data submitted by police agencies. Some police agencies do not break down violent crimes committed with and without firearms.

There is no reason to assume that the ratio of gun crimes was higher or lower in localities furnishing complete data than in those localities that did not break down the number of offenses committed with guns.

Consequently, in order to determine a rational figure for all violent crimes nationwide, the percentage of gun crimes shown for each category of violent crimes reported by departments that *did* submit breakdowns—no more, no less—was applied to the total number of homicides, robberies and aggravated assaults reported by all departments.